"This is a story about the very heart and soul of an army: dedicated, courageous, competent, and candid leadership where the rubber meets the road. If you are interested in how a true warrior plies his trade, read this one . . . A powerful, unique slice of military history. You couldn't write this as fiction: nobody would believe it!"
                    —Lieutenant General Walter F. Ulmer, Jr., U.S. Army
                         (ret.), former Commanding General, III Corps,
                         and former CEO, Center for Creative Leadership

"A compelling roller-coaster ride read packed with heaps of heroism, courage, sacrifice, controversy—and a dash of humor—that defined 'Doc' Bahnsen as the warrior I knew him to be."
                    —Major General James L. Dozier, U.S. Army (ret.),
                         former S-3, 11th Armored Cavalry Regiment

"Written with rare candor, *American Warrior* is the no-holds-barred story of the most skillful combat leader and relentless fighter I knew in Vietnam."
                    —Lieutenant General Thomas M. Montgomery, U.S.
                         Army (ret.), former Commander, U.S. Forces, and
                         Deputy Commander U.N. Forces Commander, Somalia

"A most remarkable and true story of one of the greatest warriors of his generation."
                    —General Robert M. Shoemaker, U.S. Army (ret.),
                         former Commander, U.S. Army Forces Command

"A fast-paced story of one of the most intrepid warriors in the history of American arms. This book ensures that 'Doc' Bahnsen's astounding record of sustained battlefield heroics in Vietnam will not be lost to history."
                    —Lieutenant General Dave R. Palmer, U.S. Army (ret.),
                         former Superintendent, United States Military Academy,
                         and bestselling author of *Summons of the Trumpet*

"Bahnsen is bigger than life. More decisive and fearless than Patton. A better leader than Bradley. 'Doc' Bahnsen makes 'The Great Santini' look like a Sunday school teacher."
                    —Colonel Joe Sutton, U.S. Army (ret.),
                         former Commander, 12th Cavalry Regiment

"When I was a platoon leader for 'Doc' Bahnsen, it was the only time in 34 years in the U.S. Army that I knew exactly what I was expected to do every day—go out, find the enemy and kill him."
>—Major General William L. Nash, U.S. Army
>(ret.), former Commander, 1st Armored Division

"A personal and important account of 'Doc' Bahnsen's striking leadership and service in the Vietnam War, *American Warrior,* expletives and all, gives us the ability to flesh out the story of our nation's longest war. It also helps bring out the human dimension of that war and enables us to better understand a most confusing struggle."
>—Colonel James Scott Wheeler, Ph.D., U.S. Army (ret.), former White
>House Fellow, and professor of history, U.S. Military Academy

"Vietnam was a unique type of combat that required leaders to get personally involved. Some did it well, some not, and a very few like 'Doc'—one of the Army's greatest fighters in any war—had the feel, the smarts, and the guts to do it superbly."
>—General John W. Foss, U.S. Army (ret.), former Commanding
>General 82nd Airborne Division, XVIII Airborne Corps,
>and U.S. Army Training and Doctrine Command

" 'Doc' Bahnsen in Vietnam was a larger than life character who led and fought with flamboyant heroics reminiscent of George Armstrong Custer during the Civil War. His story and that of the men he served with is in large measure the story of the Vietnam War, without the political cant that has become so common. It is a story Americans can be proud of."
>—Lieutenant Colonel Lee Allen, U.S. Army (ret.),
>former Commander 2nd Squadron, and Executive
>Officer, 11th Armored Cavalry Regiment

" 'Doc' Bahnsen was absolutely aggressive, bold, courageous, and fearless in combat where his leadership skills and mastery of the art of war melded seamlessly and brought into being one of America's greatest warriors ever. His story is a marvelous read of heroism, camaraderie, sacrifice, and duty that turns the popular notion of what fighting in Vietnam was like on its head."
>—Lieutenant General Tom Griffin, U.S. Army (ret.),
>former Commanding General, Berlin Brigade, and
>Commanding General, 3rd Armored Division

"*American Warrior* is the real deal. General 'Doc' Bahnsen is a closet intellectual with stainless steel nuts; a character, a legend, and one of the most authentic tactical leaders our Army has ever produced. This is a no-holds-barred story of the ultimate warrior. It is powerful in its candor, energy, and love for American soldiers."

—Colonel Robert C. Stack, U.S. Army (ret.), former
Commander, 3rd Brigade, 2nd Infantry Division

"A fascinating and riveting story of an intrepid soldier. 'Doc' Bahnsen was a brave and audacious leader on the battlefield yet a brilliant and insightful master of the Art of War. A soldier for all seasons—an exemplar for future leaders and a treasure to our Army."

—Major General Leroy N. Suddath, Jr., U.S. Army (ret.),
former Commander, U.S. Army Special Operations Forces

"Quite simply, *American Warrior* is a story of the quintessential warrior reincarnated in modern times—very nearly too elemental for our day. One would like to freeze-dry 'Doc' Bahnsen in peacetime and add water in times of war."

—Colonel Douglas H. Starr, U.S. Army (ret.), former
Commander, 3rd Armored Cavalry Regiment

"Long gone is the flamboyant, charismatic leadership of yesteryear's George Pickett, U.S. Grant, 'Billy' Mitchell, Douglas MacArthur, George Patton . . . and 'Doc' Bahnsen—who'd never make major let alone brigadier general under the publicly and politically correct spotlight that shines on senior leaders today. But I remain convinced that every nation's army needs 'warriors' like Doc to win its wars. His story is a phenomenal and fascinating read."

—Lieutenant General Robert S. Coffey, U.S. Army (ret.), former
Commanding General, 2nd Armored Division, 4th Infantry (Mech)
Division, and Deputy Commanding General, U.S. Army Europe

"I'm one of the guys who got him promoted to general because we thought we might have to go to war. If I had to go to war tomorrow, I would want 'Doc' Bahnsen with me. There are very few guys I would fight so hard for off the battlefield and even fewer that I would trust with my life in combat."

—General Bill Livsey, U.S. Army (ret.), former Commander
in Chief, Combined Forces, Korea, Commander in
Chief, U.N. Command, Korea, Commander, U.S.
Forces, Korea; and Commander, 8th U.S. Army

" 'Doc' Bahnsen was a matchless combat leader with compelling charisma and a master at orchestrating combined arms with intuitive sense for the fight. His story is the best description of superb leadership in small-unit combat that I have read—ever. If *American Warrior* were a novel, it would be dismissed as unbelievable."

—Lieutenant General Frederic J. "Rick" Brown, U.S. Army (ret.), former Chief of Armor and Cavalry

"The true story of one of our Army's greatest combat soldiers and a must-read for anyone who loves our country and its warriors. A lucid, candid, and powerful story told with passion and wonderful insight."

—Major General Jim Ellis, U.S. Army (ret.), former Commanding General, U.S. Army Engineer School and Center

" 'Fight fiercely' has certainly been the mantra of 'Doc' Bahnsen since he was a cadet at West Point and, perhaps, long before that. Coming in second was never his idea of success. However, to experience being runner-up on occasion, such as for the Corps intramural championship his first class year, may have helped forge the steel that made him a superb combat leader. When challenged by a formidable opponent, such as 'Doc' and his Company C-1, victories on the fields of friendly strife are still cherished 50 years later."

—General John Shaud, U.S. Air Force (ret.), former athletic representative, Company I-2, and Chief of Staff, Supreme Headquarters, Allied Powers Europe

"From the time he joined my tank company as a platoon leader, I saw 'Doc' as an officer destined to lead soldiers in combat. *American Warrior* is a vivid portrayal of how that destiny was fulfilled fully and with memorable flair."

—Lieutenant General David K. Doyle, U.S. Army (ret.), former Commander, 3rd Armored Cavalry, and Deputy Commander, III Corps

"A great war story about brave and bold warriors and totally outstanding leaders. It also is the legacy of experience that has been translated into lessons learned for subsequent generations of warfighters."

—Colonel J. W. Thurman, U.S. Army (ret.), former Commander, 3rd Squadron, 12th Cavalry Regiment

Other books by Wess Roberts, Ph.D.

Leadership Secrets of Attila the Hun

Straight A's Never Made Anybody Rich

Victory Secrets of Attila the Hun

Make It So (with Bill Ross)

Protect Your Achilles' Heel

It Takes More Than a Carrot and a Stick

The Best Ever Advice for Leaders

AMERICAN WARRIOR

A COMBAT MEMOIR OF VIETNAM

BRIG. GEN.
JOHN C. "DOC" BAHNSEN, JR., U.S. ARMY (RET.)
with Wess Roberts

Foreword by
Gen. H. Norman Schwarzkopf, U.S. Army (ret.)
former Commander in Chief, U.S. Central Command, and
Commanding General, Operations Desert Shield and Desert Storm

CITADEL PRESS
Kensington Publishing Corp.
www.kensingtonbooks.com

CITADEL PRESS BOOKS are published by

Kensington Publishing Corp.
850 Third Avenue
New York, NY 10022

All Kensington titles, imprints, and distributed lines are available at special quantity discounts for bulk purchases for sales promotions, premiums, fund-raising, educational, or institutional use. For details, write or phone the office of the Kensington special sales manager: Kensington Publishing Corp., 850 Third Avenue, New York, NY 10022, attn: Special Sales Department; phone 1-800-221-2647.

CITADEL PRESS and the Citadel logo are Reg. U.S. Pat. & TM Off.

First Printing: March 2007

10 9 8 7 6 5 4 3 2

Printed in the United States of America

Library of Congress Control Number: 2006935118

ISBN-13: 978-0-8065-2806-9
ISBN-10: 0-8065-2806-0

Foreword

I have known John C. "Doc" Bahnsen since we were classmates at West Point, Class of 1956. We became friends there, and remain close friends to this day.

Doc was in Company C-1; my company was A-1. We were housed in separate barracks, though we attended many classes together. From our plebe days, we were both avid students of the profession of arms and military history. As young warriors in training, we also shared the professional view that war should be fought with stealth, maximum firepower, and rapid maneuver to defeat the enemy quickly and decisively and to minimize friendly casualties.

We got to know one another on a personal level shooting skeet, making weekend excursions to New York City, and going head to head in intramural competition.

One of my most lasting memories of our time together at West Point took place during a lacrosse game our first class year. Doc was a midfielder; I was a defender. Our teams were going at it tooth and nail when Doc came storming toward our goal with the ball in his net. No way was I going to allow him to score an unimpeded goal. His eyes were fully fixed on the goal as I rushed out and surprised him with a solid body check that landed him on his backside and dislodged the ball. Doc sprang back to his feet and we clashed over the ball. During our brief scrap, he smacked me with a dizzying blow to the side of my helmet with his stick. I suspect this wasn't inadvertent, but no foul was called.

When the first French trappers arrived in Canada during the 1600s, they found Native Americans using lacrosse as a training exercise for young warriors. I have always thought this might help explain why Doc played the game with unbridled passion. He played lacrosse like a warrior on a solitary mission—to win! And win he did. Doc led his team to victory in that most memorable match; he led it on to win the brigade championship that year.

Doc was a character at West Point. Everyone knew who he was. If he wasn't up to mischief of one kind or another, we all suspected he was cooking something up.

At West Point, we were not allowed to have automobiles until the very end of our first class year, and then we could drive them only from the end of afternoon classes until dinner formation. Those of us who purchased new automobiles during spring break had to park them in a large field well removed from the barracks area. As a result, when the bell sounded indicating the end of classes, there would be a mad dash as all of us ran to drive our cars for a short time.

I will never forget the first day we were allowed to drive.

I ran to get my car, and when I rounded the corner there was an unbelievable sight. Doc had somehow managed to beat us all to the parking area, and in his rush to get his car on the road, he hit a lamp post and sheared it from its base. The lamp post fell lengthwise and completely demolished Doc's brand-new black and white Ford coupe directly across the street from Colonel Mike Davison's quarters, our regimental tactical officer.

After waiting four years to drive our cars, Doc managed to total his car in five minutes. He never did anything halfway.

Doc would have been in hot water over that incident had Mrs. Davison not been home and come running out to see what all the commotion was about. When women were involved, Doc could charm his way out of most trouble, and Mrs. Davison handled the situation in such a way that the MPs didn't even write him a ticket.

After graduation from West Point, Doc and I, along with several others of our classmates, attended the Infantry Officer Basic Course at Fort Benning, Georgia. Our courses kept us busy weekdays. On weekends, Dave Horton, Jack Nicholson, Leroy Suddath, Doc Bahnsen, and I often hunted birds in the backwoods of Fort Benning.

One weekend, we all loaded up in Doc's new black and white Ford convertible he purchased to replace the coupe he totaled at West Point and drove to his hometown of Rochelle, about a two-hour drive due east of Fort Benning. His parents were very gracious and good people.

His mother fed us some of the best classic southern food I've ever eaten—deep fried quail.

The fields and woods around Rochelle were Doc's childhood stomping grounds. He hunted birds in them from the time he was able to carry and shoot a shotgun. Naturally, he became our hunting guide. As I reflect on that outing today, it revealed something about the way Doc guided soldiers in combat.

Doc had a bird dog named Tut that he was keeping at his parents place. Doc put Tut to work that weekend.

Along with the dog, we loaded up in Doc's convertible and headed to a spot where he remembered quail being plentiful. As Doc drove us through fields along the way, he prodded us into shooting at doves roosting on power lines. This was highly illegal and foolish. I'm happy to report we didn't do any damage. However, how he maneuvered his convertible to give us good shots that day was akin to how he later directed armored cavalry assault vehicles (ACAVs) to move around the edges of woods to give gunners good shots at enemy snipers roosting in trees fronting bunker complexes.

We soon arrived in Doc's favorite quail hunting area. He released Tut and started working him through the open fields as we walked behind ready to shoot. There was a virtually impenetrable mass of waist-high briars at the end of one field. Tut got within a few feet of the briars, stopped, and pointed without flushing any quail. I suspect Doc had sent Tut into briars before and his bird dog didn't want to go in them again. Doc became animated.

"Get in there, Tut! Find the birds. Find the birds. Let's go, Tut. Let's go, Tut. Get in there, Tut! Go get 'em."

Tut didn't budge.

"All right, Tut. I'm going in there. I'll get 'em. You guys get ready to shoot. Be ready to shoot. Be ready to shoot, guys."

Doc was wearing briar britches with leather fronts. He placed his shotgun in the port arms position and walked into the briars. Sure enough, he flushed quail, and we started banging away at them. I don't know how many we killed, but we had a good time doing it.

Doc came out of the briars no worse for the wear other than a few scratches on his arms. Before he said a word to us, he critiqued Tut's performance.

"Damn you, Tut! Hell of a bird dog you are, making me get in the briars. You're supposed to find the birds, not me. Next time, you do what I tell you. You get after 'em."

It was a comic opera, and the five of us got a good laugh out of it. It was also a demonstration of sorts, indicative of how Doc coached soldiers in combat. He never hesitated to land his helicopter and show unenthusiastic or confused soldiers what he wanted them to do.

After graduation from the Infantry Officer Basic Course, Doc and I received assignments to different units. Within three years, Doc transferred to armor branch. Largely due to this decision, we never served together again. Nevertheless, we remained good friends and saw each other socially whenever possible.

During our formative years at West Point, we were taught and mentored by an exceptional cadre of seasoned veterans who fought in World War II or Korea. Some of the most senior of them saw action in both wars. These great men molded our characters, shared their wisdom, and taught us the hard lessons of warfighting paid for by the blood of their fellow soldiers.

Our country was wholly engaged in the cold war during those days. With a cautious eye on the possibility of a nuclear war of mutual destruction, military planners fully expected the next war would pit our armed forces against those of the Soviet Union on a European battleground. Our training at West Point reflected this expectation.

If anyone in a prominent position anticipated more than a very small American involvement in the struggle between the communist North Vietnamese and the democratic South Vietnamese that sprouted up as World War II came to an end, he didn't let it be known in a loud enough voice.

Up until the mid-1960s, neither the curriculums at our service schools nor the protocols for combat arms unit training exercises focused on much of anything other than gearing our Army up for a conventional war with the Soviets. Classes on fighting insurgent warfare in a jungle environment were virtually nonexistent. Notwithstanding, Vietnam became the combat proving ground for our class.

I served two tours in Vietnam. My first tour coincided with Doc's, but our paths never crossed. I was a task force adviser to the Army of the Republic of Vietnam (ARVN) airborne division; he was busy commanding and training armed helicopter crews. I started my second tour when Doc had about six months left on his. He commanded an air cavalry troop and an armored cavalry squadron; I commanded an infantry battalion in a different area.

During both tours, I experienced the war up close and personal. I fought side-by-side and led battle-hardened veterans and brave young men who served valiantly, whose joie de vivre and dedication to duty underwrote victory in every battle we fought. I witnessed the individual heroism of soldiers who were neither afraid of the dirt and the dark nor the sight of their own blood. I also saw the fear on the faces of soldiers, young and old, when the going got tough, and was proud of them for having the courage to overcome moments of utter terror.

I saw the good our pacification efforts did in building schools, drilling wells, providing orphanages with food, medicines, and clothing, and so much more. I observed American doctors, dentists, nurses, and medics treating Vietnamese people suffering from acute illness and chronic disease. I could see the glimmer of hope the mere presence of American and allied forces put in the eyes of the native people. I also observed the aftermath of the extreme cruelty and savage carnage routinely unleashed on South Vietnamese noncombatants by the North Vietnamese Army (NVA) and its Vietcong operatives.

I was an eyewitness to the steady improvement U.S. advisory efforts, training, and equipment made in the ARVN's performance in combat. I led soldiers in routing out the enemy whenever and wherever we found him. The Vietcong was virtually wiped out during the Tet Offensive of 1968, and the NVA was my principal enemy during my second tour. They fought with greater military discipline than did the Vietcong. Nonetheless, we defeated them in every battle, and they never took and held one square inch of real estate while U.S. ground forces were present in South Vietnam.

Like Doc, I believed then and believe to this day that American intervention in the Vietnam War was just and right. It was a war we were winning militarily right up to the point when the Nixon administration ordered the withdrawal of U.S. ground forces. And despite the wake of turbulence and uncertainty our departure created, I am convinced the ARVN forces could have won the war had our government not terminated U.S. air and logistical support and cut off funds to the Republic of Vietnam government.

Before it ended, the Vietnam War claimed ten classmates and one ex-classmate. Many, many more of us were wounded in action. Our class produced a respectable number of rock-hard fighters whose decorations and awards for extraordinary heroism, gallantry in action, valor, and outstanding service were many. And then there was Doc Bahnsen. He returned from Vietnam with a chest covered by an impressive array of medals that spoke highly of his courage under fire and combat leadership. The nature and number of his decorations resulted in unanimous agreement that Doc Bahnsen was *the* fighter of our class. They also gave rise to enough apocryphal stories about him to fill a very thick volume, and the stories got better each time they were told.

For our twentieth reunion book, Dave Palmer, who later served as West Point's superintendent, wrote brief comments on what several classmates had done during the Vietnam War. He penned the following about Doc:

> Speaking of Doc, no account of the war would be complete if it did not mention his exploits. The story sounds incredible, but enough classmates witnessed and recorded—and later reported on—his deeds to indicate that the whole story is even more amazing than the established record. Altogether, he earned eighteen awards for valor. . . . On the first day of [squadron] command, Doc fought off an attack on his CP [command post], killing twenty enemy. The next day he was in a fight and his outfit accounted for eighty-five more. And so it went. He led by example, always in the thick of the fight. Among the weapons he personally used on enemy soldiers over a period of time were: armed helicopters, a mechanized flame thrower, a rifle, hand grenades, and his bare hands.

Over the years, I heard many of the stories going around about Doc's "Adventures in the Orient," as he calls them. A few really caught my attention.

During his time in Vietnam, Doc as a captain, later a major, successively commanded an armed helicopter platoon, an air cavalry troop, and an armored cavalry squadron. Yet, I heard stories told about several occasions when lieutenant colonels and colonels alike temporarily turned chaotic fights against a significantly larger enemy force over to Doc.

This kind of deference for a junior officer is something you don't find in the military. It's one thing to ask a subordinate's opinion; it's an entirely different matter to turn command over to a subordinate, even if just for the duration of an enemy contact. The way I heard it, these lieutenant colonels and colonels had observed Doc fighting on enough occasions that they had total confidence in his ability to orchestrate a messy battlefield into a harmonious operation in a matter of minutes.

I also heard tales about how Doc often fought outnumbered, but never outgunned. They told of his ability to simultaneously call in and adjust air strikes, artillery fire, and gunship firing passes on enemy positions. This skill is fairly unique in its own right. However, tales of Doc's "maestro of the battlefield" talents didn't end there. They went on to recount how Doc concurrently controlled the ground elements—positioning infantry, ACAVs, and tanks for the assault and providing them subsequent direction as the battle progressed. All things considered, this capacity is an extremely rare find in any one soldier, especially one in the thick of the fight while shooting at the enemy with his M-16 rifle out the door of his helicopter.

Hearing stories like these reminded me of something Field Marshal Erwin Rommel wrote: "In moments of panic, fatigue, or disorganization, or when something out of the ordinary has to be demanded from his troops, the personal example of the commander works wonders, especially if he has the wit to create some sort of legend round himself."

Without question, Doc created a legend around himself. No one I know ever doubted his undaunted valor and boundless energy for mixing it up with the enemy.

Long anticipated by his classmates and fellow soldiers, now comes *American Warrior*, a fascinating and informative book that clears up any and all questions I had stemming from apocryphal stories about Doc. I must say, I found the true stories about Doc much more amazing than any of the legendary tales about him. And I have no doubts about the veracity of these accounts.

Wess Roberts, Doc's good friend since their days together on the U.S. Army Combat Arms Training Board during the early '70s, spent the better part of four years tracking down and interviewing scores of Doc's former subordinates, peers, and superiors. From private to general, and in their own words, these eyewitnesses provide testimony and comments that verify and cross-verify every account in this book.

American Warrior is a vivid portrayal of Doc's experiences during the Vietnam War. Of course, it centers on Doc, but it also pays generous tribute to the hot-blooded fighters who fought with him and contains vivid descriptions of their heroism. It is also a tremendous salute to the forty-four soldiers who died under Doc's command. Contrasted against the astonishing number of enemy kills credited to units Doc led, this number is extremely low. Nevertheless, their loss was tragic for their families and friends, fellow soldiers, and to Doc personally. One loss was one loss too many for him. To that end, Doc memorializes every one of his soldiers killed in action. In addition, this book pays great respect to Doc's soldiers who returned from the war wounded—brave men whose sacrifice for country has too long gone unappreciated by the public-at-large. For some of his wounded, this book provides the definitive history of their lives. I also find *American Warrior* to be disarmingly candid. I respect a soldier who accepts accountability for his actions; I also respect how forthcoming Doc is in telling the true story of his legend.

I am personally familiar with many of the soldiers whose names appear in this book. George S. Patton, Hank Emerson, and Bob Haldane served as tactical officers during my days at West Point; Leroy Suddath was my roommate. Jim Dozier and Gus Johnson were my classmates. Bill Nash, Doug Starr, Jarrett Robertson, and others fought as lieutenants and captains under Doc Bahnsen and learned their lessons well. That paid huge dividends to the soldiers they led as colonels and generals under me during Operations Desert Shield and Desert Storm. I also know several others who contributed their thoughts and observations. Simply put, I can say that this book speaks about some of the very best soldiers and field commanders our Army has ever seen.

Doc retired on his own terms after a distinguished thirty-year career in our Army. Nevertheless, tales about him continue to be told and retold to generations of soldiers who never knew him in uniform. Some of these tales are entertaining, while others provide important lessons learned. In either case, I believe these stories have some degree of formative influence on budding warfighters today.

Now, with the publication of *American Warrior*, we have access to the true legend of Doc Bahnsen. Written in a unique, bold, and gripping style, this superb book is worthy of a prominent place among the best books on the Vietnam War.

—H. Norman Schwarzkopf
General, U.S. Army (ret.)

⋆ ⋆ ⋆

This book is dedicated to the forty-four soldiers of the 11th Armored Cavalry "Blackhorse" Regiment killed in action during the Vietnam War while serving under the command of Major John C. "Doc" Bahnsen, Jr. A list of their names appears in the appendix.

*Hast thou given the horse
strength? hast thou clothed his neck
with thunder?
Canst thou make him afraid as a
grasshopper? the glory of his nostrils
is terrible.
He paweth in the valley, and
rejoiceth in his strength: he goeth on
to meet the armed men.
He mocketh at fear, and is not
affrighted; neither turneth he back
from the sword.*

—JOB 39:19–22

✶ Prologue ✶

I was conducting aerial recon* with four pink teams, each team consisting of one OH-6A Cayuse light-observation helicopter, aka "Loaches," and one AH-1G Cobra gunship. We were looking for signs of the enemy and hoping to draw fire or otherwise stir up some action when I received a high-priority, time-sensitive message from regiment giving me the coordinates for a site on the edge of a small village near Chan Luu, where Vietcong (VC) messengers were supposed to be located.

Chan Luu was a hostile area. We had many fights in and around that location. Many of the young men from this village were members of the famous VC Dong Nai Regiment. This unit lost a lot of its soldiers during the Tet Offensive. There were very few young men left in the area to recruit as replacements. By 1968, about 50 percent of the VC Dong Nai Regiment was actually made up of NVA regulars brought down from the north as fillers.

I frequently received time-sensitive messages like this one and didn't need to be told their source to know where they came from. Officially, I didn't. I wasn't cleared for "special intelligence." I didn't need to be for that matter. I was cleared for everything I needed to know to get my job done but nothing more. That way, if captured, I couldn't tell my interrogators secrets I didn't know.

Nevertheless, I knew this information resulted from a radio intercept classified top secret by the Army Security Agency's 409th Radio Re-

*See Glossary, page 463.

search Platoon opconned to the 11th Armored Cavalry Regiment's S-2 intelligence officer. This platoon operated out of M-113 armored personnel carriers (APCs) that were surrounded by razor wire. What they did within those APCs was so hush-hush that the S-2, Major Andy O'Meara, wasn't allowed inside.

Shortly after assuming command of the regiment in July 1968, Colonel George S. Patton restructured the way the 541st Military Intelligence Detachment operated, changing it from a centralized operation to a decentralized organization that provided direct support to each squadron and the Air Cavalry Troop. The concept behind this change was called the Battlefield Intelligence Collection Center. In practice, this change put more intelligence assets at the front line, where their work had a much more immediate impact.

Regardless, Patton couldn't get the 409th to budge on how it operated. That was not good.

The secretive nature of their operation and the strict procedures the Army Security Agency used for passing radio intercept information up and down the chain of command typically created a time delay that made most intel the 409th produced turn up too late for us to act on it. Even then, the intel they passed on was normally couched in vague generalities, limiting its usefulness.

Given how the 409th operated, I was happier than a starving vulture on fresh roadkill to receive specific information on an enemy location.

The Loach pilots were our aero scouts. They led our formation toward the coordinates given in the message. Their paired Cobra gunships trailed behind and slightly above them. I was in my UH-1C Huey command and control helicopter, flying close behind and slightly below the gunships. En route, I radioed my Tactical Operations Center (TOC) and told my ops officer to send ARPs to the intercept point immediately.

The scouts flew to the area quickly and spotted three small Honda motorcycles parked outside an isolated hooch. They began circling at low level, keeping an eye out for armed enemy and suspicious activity. The gunships went into orbit at a higher level, ready to pounce on anyone who fired at the scout birds.

Four unarmed UH-1D Huey lift ships, aka "slicks," each loaded with six to seven crack infantrymen armed for bear, arrived in the area within fifteen minutes. These infantrymen were members of the Air Cavalry Troop's Aero Rifle Platoon (ARP) commanded by First Lieutenant Duke Doubleday. I directed the lift ships to land in a landing zone (LZ) that my crew chief marked with colored smoke. The ARPs dismounted and quickly dispersed, securing the area until the lift ships cleared. Doubleday then directed his ARPs to surround the house.

The ARPs had a sixteen-year-old interpreter named Huang. He carried an M-2 carbine, lived in the ARPs' hooch, and spoke passable English and French, along with his native Vietnamese.

Once in position, Huang called out and told those inside the hooch to come out and surrender. Not a minute later, they came out unarmed with their hands raised above their heads.

I told my pilot, Warrant Officer Mike Bates, to land as close to the hooch as possible. I got out and talked with Doubleday about his fresh catch of detainees: six VC suspects. Quick interrogation determined these suspects were a messenger team for the local VC, confirming the intel we'd acted on.

I told Doubleday to have his ARPs load the detainees on lift ships and take them to regiment for further interrogation.

Our next action was to conduct a security sweep of the village. Security sweeps were known as "skunk hunts."

During skunk hunts, we checked the identification (ID) of everyone in the village and looked for weapons, supplies, documents, and other signs of the enemy. Anyone old enough to have a proper ID who didn't was tagged as an enemy suspect. We detained suspects until a determination about whether to keep them or cut them loose could be made. When we picked up weapons and ammo, we torched the building where we found them. Weapons and ammo were prima facie evidence that whoever possessed them was VC. We also discovered armed paymasters carrying unit rosters and payrolls. These dumb shits usually resisted, which got them killed. We confiscated their piastres and used their rosters to check for VC by name during subsequent security sweeps. We also found rucksacks containing documents and maps that provided useful intelligence information.

Friendly villagers didn't like our skunk hunts but went along with them because they knew we meant them no harm. Unfriendly villagers hated our skunk hunts because they didn't like us and often collaborated with the Vietcong.

We spent a couple of hours in the village before wrapping things up. As we were preparing to leave, Doubleday and I decided to confiscate the three motorcycles. His ARPs loaded them on a lift ship and took them back to Alpha Pad.

Former specialist four Mike Gorman, crew chief on Doc's aircraft at the time, speaks about action subsequent to the capture of the VC messengers.

"Major Bahnsen came back to our helicopter and told Mister Bates to take it up and hover between one to two hundred feet. He wanted a bird's-eye view of the ground because the people in this village were visibly upset over our being there and seemed to be especially pissed about us detaining the VC suspects.

"After we got off the ground, Major Bahnsen radioed Lieutenant Doubleday and told him to get his people ready for extraction.

"Extraction is a very dangerous maneuver for everyone involved. The troops are bunching up instead of dispersing like they do on insertion, and the helicopters are sitting still on the ground instead of moving slowly just off the ground like they usually are during insertion. This makes both the troops and the helicopters tempting targets and places them in a position where they are extremely vulnerable to enemy fire.

"Always last off the ground, the ARPs moved to the LZ and waited until they had visuals on the lift ships before popping smoke.

"The extraction went without a hitch, but Major Bahnsen was concerned that some of the villagers might get a wild hair up their ass and start shooting at us as we took off.

"He radioed the Loach pilots and said, 'I want you to line up and come in low and slow over the village. Let these people get a good look at your miniguns.'

"In the war of hearts and minds, this place had already been lost to the other side. No telling what the war history of this village was, but these people didn't like us before we got there and we didn't make them our friends that day.

"The four Loaches maneuvered in one at a time and slow danced at rooftop level before pulling up. Everything that wasn't nailed down went flying in a cloud of dust and rice grains. I'm certain that pissed off anyone in the village who didn't already hate our guts. But no shots were fired.

"After a few minutes, Major Bahnsen got back on the radio and said, 'That's enough. They get the point. Clear the area.'

"As we were clearing the area, I spotted this kid dressed in a white shirt and khaki shorts. He had run out of the village, headed down the edge of a dirt road between a rice paddy and a small field, crossed over, and ran into a clump of thick, thick trees.

"I told Major Bahnsen what I'd seen. He had Mister Bates land immediately.

"As soon as we touched down, Major Bahnsen told my door gunner, Specialist Four Tuffy Tufanchian, and me to 'Go get 'em,' as if we were bird dogs being sent to retrieve downed game.

"We were accustomed to being Major Bahnsen's bird dogs. We didn't mind at all when he sent us to retrieve this suspect. It was exciting. Helicopter crews rarely had the opportunity to see action on the ground.

"Tufanchian had a .45-caliber pistol. I grabbed my M-16. We ran down the edge of the field just in front of the trees where I'd last seen the suspect. He must have been watching the helicopter because he didn't notice us when we ran past him and I caught a glimpse of him in my peripheral vision. I stopped and pointed him out to Tufanchian. The kid was squatting down in some thick undergrowth behind some trees. He was well hidden. I was lucky to have spotted him.

"We ran over to the suspect and poked the muzzles of our weapons right at his nose, taking him by total surprise. He was absolutely terrified, didn't resist, and remained calm.

"We took him back to our ship and loaded him in. Mister Bates lifted off and flew to an ARVN base camp, an armor unit about ten minutes away.

"When we dropped him off, Major Bahnsen told the American adviser to the ARVN unit that we suspected this kid, in his late teens, to be a VC. The adviser said the ARVN interrogators would find out either way. Major Bahnsen also told him that there may be more VC hiding in the village. The adviser said he would send a platoon to check it out. It would take the ARVN platoon at least thirty minutes to make it to the village, plenty of time for any VC stragglers to leave. Major Bahnsen told the adviser that we'd keep an eye on the village until they arrived.

"We flew back to the village and flew in a low orbit looking for suspicious activity until the ARVN arrived with an M-41 Walker light tank on point, followed by a deuce-and-a-half truck load of soldiers.

"It was midafternoon when we headed back to Alpha Pad. I didn't realize the ARPs had taken the motorcycles as a war prize until we landed and I saw Specialist Five Sammy Dublin, a Loach crew chief, working on one of them. Major Bahnsen told me that was his bike.

Lieutenant Doubleday kept one, and the other one was given to Major Peters, our ops officer."

Doc resumes.

Despite hot and heavy fighting right through December, as New Year's Day approached, my staff recommended that we arrange a combined Christmas–New Year's party for the troop—the Air Cavalry Troop, 11th Armored Cavalry Regiment. They didn't have to twist my arm to get my approval.

An Australian rock band (complete with go-go dancers) touring South Vietnam military bases was hired to play at the party. To accommodate the band, Sergeant Gary Nelson orchestrated an unauthorized appropriation of a rather large bandstand. It was dismantled where Nelson found it—on the fringe of another unit's area—and moved by manpower alone across the field to Alpha Pad. A custom-built reverberation wall featuring a large peace symbol was joined to the rear of the bandstand after its reassembly.

On the day of the party, a very large trailer filled with beer and soda was parked near the bandstand. The beer and soda were unloaded, iced down in large wash tubs, and readied for self-service before supper.

This was never intended to be a stag party. American Red Cross "Donut Dollies" started arriving in the troop area just after noon and kept arriving right up to party time. And a dozen or so bar girls from Bien Hoa, secreted onto base inside an empty POL (petroleum, oil, and lubricant) tanker, appeared before the music started.

I might have been tempted to spend New Year's Eve partying with my troopers if not for another affair at the Rex Hotel in Saigon that evening.

The regiment's staff and senior line unit officers were having an informal dining out at the Rex. I invited a dozen or so of my pilots to join us. Some of us flew to Saigon; others rode down in a three-quarter-ton truck driven by Warrant Officer Ray Lanclos in what was a bona fide late afternoon "thunder run"—an unarmed and unescorted mad dash down a road subject to ambushes.

Retired Colonel, then Major, Glenn Finkbiner, the 11th Armored Cavalry Regiment's S-4, talks about the party in Saigon.

"Colonel Patton was on leave in Hawaii, but several of us on his staff went to Saigon for what was a dining out of sorts. I flew down with Major Jim Dozier, the S-3, and Major Andy O'Meara, the S-2. We landed at the Free World Heliport and took a Lambretta cab to the Rex Hotel.

"A popular hangout for military brass during the war, the Rex Hotel was a five-story building located in the heart of Saigon. Our dining out was being held on its rooftop in the Garden Café, an open-air café that seated four hundred.

"We took the elevator to the top floor. When we walked out on the rooftop, we were greeted by the sight of all these beautiful people: men dressed in tuxedos and beautiful women dressed in long evening gowns slit to their waist and smelling of expensive perfume. There were a few Americans and Europeans among them, but most were Vietnamese. The women far outnumbered the men.

"We looked out of place among these fancy folks. We had just come out of the field. We'd cleaned up some but were wearing our fatigues, web gear, and steel pots and carrying M-16s.

"The café's menu included a variety of Vietnamese, French, and American dishes—all of it quality fare. Music was playing in the background. The bar was famous for its mixed cocktails, but also served everything from cheap local beer to expensive French wine. The view of downtown Saigon from the café was simply spectacular.

"I was much impressed but somewhat disturbed by it all. Here we were at a fine affair after having left a combat zone less than an hour before. It was like we were inside a bubble of tranquility safely separated from the war. I think we all had difficulty rationalizing that but we just stacked our steel pots and rifles in the corner by our table, ordered a drink, and started looking at the menu.

"I don't remember exactly when Doc and his crew showed up, but there was no mistaking their arrival. One of his pilots popped a hand-held flare just as they walked in the hotel's front door. The damn thing illuminated just as it cleared the rooftop, causing a momentary panic among some of the guests. I would have taken cover myself if Dozier hadn't calmly said, 'The Air Cav Troop has arrived.' So much for the bubble of tranquility we'd been enjoying.

"Doc's pilots were well-disciplined, first-rate fighters who feared nothing and bored easily. When they weren't on a mission or otherwise engaged in some meaningful activity, they were usually up to mischief. Nothing terrible, but when they landed in trouble, Doc always got them out.

"It was a stable evening and everyone was on his best behavior for the most part.

"Sometime around twenty-two hundred hours one of Doc's pilots went to the elevator, pulled the pin on a smoke grenade, pressed the lobby button, and tossed the grenade inside just as its doors closed. When smoke started billowing up the elevator shaft, Dozier decided it was time for us to go."

Doc resumes.

Some of my pilots returned to Alpha Pad, others got hotel rooms. I spent the night in Saigon with my friend Phyllis "Fif" Shaughnessy, a contract U.S. State Department employee involved with the pacification program.

1 January 1969—Saigon

I woke up midmorning. That was very unusual for me. I was normally out of bed, dressed, and ready to go before sun up.

Fif and I caught a Lambretta cab to the Free World Heliport, where we met up with my pilots.

My primary command and control helicopter (tail number 528) and two lift ships were on the ground waiting to fly us back to Bien Hoa Air Base. When I walked over to my helicopter, I was greeted by a backup crew consisting of First Lieutenant Bill Maestretti, Staff Sergeant Rodney Yano, and Specialist Four Carmine Conti.

Maestretti was sitting in the *left* seat. That was a bit odd to me because the pilot always sat in the *right* seat. The helicopter had its cockpit doors in place. Another oddity. I mostly flew with them off to hear gunshots when we were being shot at. Flying without cockpit doors also provided me with an unobstructed view of the ground and an open space through which I could fire the M-16 rifle that I always carried on my lap.

As I boarded the helicopter, I looked for my steel helmet, M-16, load-bearing equipment (LBE—pistol belt and harness), and sack of grenades. None of it was in the aircraft. This was *very* unusual. This gear *always* rode with me. Normally, I would have someone's ass over that, but it was a short fifteen-minute ride back to Bien Hoa and I didn't want to make a fuss.

Former specialist four Carmine Conti talks about the mission to retrieve his commanding officer from Saigon.

"Mid-morning, I was alerted for a mission to pick up Major Bahnsen in Saigon and bring him back to Bien Hoa. I flew as Major Bahnsen's crew chief early in his command but had since been reassigned. Crew chiefs didn't like to fly with Major Bahnsen. Oh, he was an incredible combat leader but he did numerous things that scared the hell out of us. On top of that, Major Bahnsen was routinely in the air at first light and didn't shutdown until well after dark. Flying with him could be frightening and unusually exhausting. I coped with any fears I had about flying with Major Bahnsen by resolving that whatever bad that was going to happen would happen so why worry about it. And I learned to get by on less than my regular amount of sack time.

"As given, this mission was nothing more than a quick flight down to the Free World Heliport and back to Alpha Pad. It was New Year's Day and both sides in the war were supposed to be observing a cease fire. No matter, I prepped Major Bahnsen's helicopter as if we were going on a combat mission. Standard procedure for all troop helicopters. I don't remember why I didn't remove the cockpit doors. Probably just wanted to make the ride more comfortable—less wind and ambient noise. Rounding up his personal gear never crossed my mind. He handled that on his own when I flew as his crew chief and I was unaware of any change to that routine.

"Staff Sergeant Rodney Yano was hanging out on the flight line and picked up on the fact that my door gunner was nowhere to be found. He ran over to me and asked if he could come along. Yano loved to fly but, as a technical inspector, wasn't getting much time in the air. He was on his third tour in Vietnam and had lots of experience flying on combat missions. And like everyone else in the troop, I liked the guy . . . a lot. He didn't have to ask twice.

"Yano ranked me, so I had him fly in the crew chief's position and I rode in the door gunner's seat."

Doc resumes.

We had pink teams on routine aerial reconnaissance that day, but I gave no thought to one of them rousing up enemy contact. I had anticipated a quiet day in the regiment's area of operations (AO).

Confident that nothing was going to happen en route to Bien Hoa, I strapped into the right seat without bothering to put on my Nomex gloves.

I'd invited Fif to Bien Hoa for the day, possibly the night. I had her sit in the jump seat, centered immediately behind the pilot and copilot seats. She was out of the crew's way and had a good view out the bubble.

Within five minutes after liftoff, I was flying lead with the lift ships close behind when I received a radio call from my operations officer, Major Don Peters.

"Thunderhorse Six, this is Thunderhorse Three, over."

"Three, this is Six, go ahead."

"Six, Red Two-One reports enemy contact. Coordinates follow."

I continued talking with Peters while Maestretti wrote down the coordinates of an area approximately sixteen kilometers north of Bien Hoa.

"Do you think they need me out there?"

"I think they do."

"Roger that, I'm on the way."

"Roger, I'll inform regiment you're en route."

Ferrying U.S. government civilians from base to base was a common practice in Vietnam. That's how they got around. Having Fif along for the flight to Bien Hoa was perfectly legit. I had full authority to grant her permission to fly in mine or any other troop helicopter, as long as it wasn't on a tactical mission. But taking a civilian into combat action without prior approval from higher headquarters was strictly forbidden, something that could get your ass in a sling. I didn't have that approval and wasn't about to take time to get it, which meant Fif had just become an unauthorized passenger. I should have landed the helicopter and let her out before proceeding to the contact area, but I didn't.

I broke my call with Peters and radioed the pink team leader.

"Red Two-One, this is Six, over."

"Six, this is Two-One, over."

"Two-One. Understand you've made contact. I'm en route to your area. Give me a sitrep, over."

"Six, this is Two-One. My scout bird took fire from these bastards and I rolled in with rockets and miniguns. I sent my scout bird back to check the area and the bastards shot at him again! Estimate company sized, over."

"Roger Two-One. Hold on. I'm on the way. Stay clear of AA fire. Get a FAC on station."

"Roger that."

Andy O'Meara comments on Doc coming out to the contact area.

"I was flying as an observer with the scout pilot that morning. Doc's dialogue with the pink team leader caused me to picture the cavalry coming to save the day in a Western movie. But that was Doc. He was indestructible. When his troops ran into trouble, he always seemed to arrive in time to save their day."

Doc resumes.

We arrived over the contact area within minutes. The pink team leader had already called in artillery fire, which was on the way. He advised me that an Air Force forward air controller (FAC) was in the area with fighter-bombers available.

We couldn't spot enemy soldiers, but the muzzle flashes from their rifles divulged their well-concealed location.

I was unaccustomed to flying in the right seat and that made it awkward for me to adjust the artillery fire as we made counterclockwise orbits at fifteen hundred feet. Yano and Conti opened up with machine gun fire on each pass, which caused the enemy to duck and contained him in position.

After a few passes, I radioed the FAC and asked him to call in some air strikes. I told him that we were going in lower to mark the enemy's position. I told Yano to get ready to drop a white phosphorous grenade. I maneuvered my helicopter over the spot where I wanted the air strikes concentrated and told Yano to mark.

Everything was progressing perfectly when, without warning, all hell broke loose!

I heard a loud bang at the same time a thick fog of white smoke filled the entire cabin. I thought we'd been hit by a friendly artillery round, but the telltale white smoke and an intense burning-match odor told me something else had happened: the white phosphorous grenade detonated before it cleared our helicopter.

Carmine Conti resumes.

"I was placing suppressive fire on the enemy's position when the helicopter pitched and rolled the instant the marking grenade exploded. I tumbled to the cabin floor, unable to hear or see anything but white smoke. I thought I was dead. Then something brushed against my knee and I realized I was still alive."

Doc resumes.

Specks of burning phosphorous were flying all over the place, hitting all of us and setting fire to the helicopter's insulation!

I looked back over my left shoulder. The smoke was thick but I could clearly see that Yano was badly wounded. It was a horrible sight. The explosion blew his left hand almost completely off and he took most of its impact in his chest and face. His arms and face were covered with burning phosphorous. He was bleeding profusely and appeared to be having difficulty seeing. I couldn't imagine how much pain he must have been feeling.

Carmine Conti continues.

"I saw Yano hunched over. He appeared to be on the verge of falling out of the helicopter. I was dazed so it must have been instinct that prompted me to crawl over and get hold of him. I pulled Yano into the middle of the cabin. His left forearm was bleeding badly; his left hand was dangling by a few strands of sinew. The rest of him didn't look much better but he was in total control of his mental faculties.

"Yano got hold of a first-aid kit, picked out a tourniquet, and handed it to me. I was confused as to what he wanted me to do with it until he yelled loud enough that I could hear him tell me to tie it above his left elbow. I did, and that slowed but did not completely stop all of the bleeding.

"By all rights, Yano should have sat down and remained still to avoid aggravating his ghastly wounds. He didn't.

"I'd no sooner tied the tourniquet around his arm than did rounds of ammo start cooking off inside the cabin. My personal M-16 was on the floor and burning. Our M-60 ammo was afire and fire was spreading to our stockpile of grenades.

"Acting with unwavering self-control and unbelievable courage, Yano stood up and started kicking burning ammo out of the helicopter while using his right hand to throw grenades out the door. Fire was burning all around him and the cabin was still full of white smoke. It was a surreal sight but the most selfless and courageous act of heroism that I saw during the war, and I saw a lot of heroic actions."

Doc resumes.

I was still looking at Yano, wondering what to do when, by his own initiative and with total disregard for his own life, he immediately started using his right hand and mangled left hand to pick up and hurl all remaining smoke grenades, ammo, and burning debris out the side door. Streams of blood went flying through the air and splattered all over the cabin every time he slung his left hand, incurring additional wounds in the process.

I turned back to see where the helicopter was headed but couldn't see through the smoke. It had to be evacuated from the cabin immediately. I pulled my door's safety latch and kicked it off. Just as the door cleared, a rush of incoming air flamed the fire, setting the whole cabin ablaze.

Carmine Conti continues.

"My ears were ringing and I was disoriented but wasn't so far out of it not to understand that Yano needed my help. I picked up my M-16, threw it out the door, and started helping him. His actions had already prevented a terrible situation from turning into a total disaster, and his example inspired me beyond words."

Doc resumes.

Amid all the confusion, I temporarily lost directional control of the helicopter and it started going down. I keyed my mike, "Mayday! Mayday! This is Thunderhorse Six. I'm on fire. We're going in."

Just as the nose of the helicopter was about to hit some trees, I regained control, pulled up, and keyed my mike, "I think we can make it."

I then radioed my pink team leader.

"Red Two-One, a Willie Peter just detonated inside our cabin. I've got a fuckin' mess on my hands. I'm heading for Twenty Ducks. You've got the fight, over."

"Roger, Six. I'll re-mark and call for backup."

There were several hospitals in the vicinity, with Twenty Ducks (the 93rd Evacuation Hospital at Long Binh) being the nearest, about ten minutes in a Huey. Peters radioed the 93rd's helipad to get us clearance to land and gave the hospital staff a heads-up that we all had white phosphorous wounds.

Despite the brief flying time, fire was still smoldering in the cabin, and I didn't know if we could make it to the hospital before our aircraft stopped flying. It was a tense predicament, one of those situations that cause your pucker factor to go off the scale.

Carmine Conti continues.

"In my dazed state of mind, it seemed like getting all of the ammo and large chunks of burning debris out of the helicopter took forever. In reality, it only took a few minutes of controlled but frantic effort.

"Although some insulation was still burning, Yano and I had unburdened the helicopter of all ammo and grenades—explosive stuff that could have blown us out of the sky.

"I helped Yano sit down and stood behind him with my hands on his shoulders to keep him from rolling out of the helicopter during what was a wild ride to Long Binh—a ride during which Major Bahnsen never appeared to be rattled by the uncertainty of whether or not we would go down in flames or land safely."

Doc resumes.

I glanced back over my shoulder. Conti was standing behind Yano and holding him by his shoulders. Yano was sitting in a pool of blood on the cabin floor. The sight of his horrific wounds and the stench of burning flesh made me sick. I had to look forward quickly before I spewed my breakfast on Fif, who was energetically brushing burning phosphorous off her face, arms, and legs.

My hands felt like a cluster of hot pokers was being pressed into them. They really hurt, but I couldn't allow myself to think about my pain. I had to concentrate my thoughts on flying. I flew full power to the 93rd, headed straight for the hospital's landing pad, and hard-landed my smoking helicopter.

Then Major and Blackhorse S-1 Dale Hruby recalls this incident.

"I was in the TOC and heard Doc's mayday and that he was on his way to the Ninety-third, only a few minutes' driving time from regimental headquarters. I quickly summoned my driver and headed to the hospital.

"We arrived just in time to see Doc's aircraft making its approach to the helipad. Smoke was bellowing out its doors: we could see flames inside the aircraft. Firefighters, a doctor, and several medics were gathered round the helipad, waiting for Doc to land.

"The moment the helicopter's skids touched ground, the firefighters got to work putting out the fire before it consumed the aircraft. Simultaneously, the medics started pulling bodies out. The smell was horrible but the sight was worse. These folks were literally being burned alive.

"It wasn't until this moment that anyone besides Doc's people knew Fif was onboard. That was a real shocker, but the medics just went about placing the wounded on stretchers.

"I picked up one end of the stretcher Doc was laid on. It wasn't funny at the time, but Doc would later introduce me as the guy who pulled him out of a burning helicopter."

Carmine Conti resumes.

"I was able to walk into the hospital on my own. Before dismounting the helicopter, I grabbed hold of my door gun, then slowly walked into the emergency area carrying an M-60 trailing a partial belt of ammunition.

"I'm positive that I was in shock and must have been a scary sight to behold. Everyone started backing away from me. I couldn't comprehend the situation and sat down on a chair. The next thing I remember was Sergeant First Class John Ryan, our forward area non-commissioned officer in charge, kneeling in front of me with his arms outstretched and asking me to give him my weapon. I did, and the medics went to work on me right away."

Retired Major General, then Major, James Dozier, one of Doc's West Point classmates, reveals more about this incident.

"Lieutenant Colonel Merritte Ireland commanded the 1st Squadron. Being the senior lieutenant colonel in the regiment, he assumed command while Colonel Patton was on R&R [rest and recuperation]. Ireland took Captain Jerry Rutherford, one of my assistants, with him in Patton's command and control helicopter and followed Doc to the contact area to coordinate any reinforcements he may need.

"We were monitoring Doc's frequency so we knew right when the trouble started. Rutherford provided a steady stream of commentary back to us over another frequency. When it appeared Doc would make it to Long Binh, Ireland and Rutherford headed back to regiment.

"Not thirty minutes after Doc landed at the Ninety-third, we received an urgent call from them telling us that their CO, Colonel John Kovaric, wanted whoever was in charge of the regiment to get over there. Doc was raising hell!

"I couldn't find Ireland. The Blackhorse XO, Lieutenant Colonel Bill Haponski, was in Di An attending a triple combination New Year's Day dinner, farewell party for Lieutenant Colonel Jack Faith, and a welcoming party for Haponski (Haponski was set to replace Faith as commander of the First Squadron, Fourth Cavalry Regiment).

"In Ireland and Haponski's absence, I decided to go myself. Major

Glenn Finkbiner was in the TOC and wanted to come along. We took a jeep to the hospital.

"Finkbiner waited in the hallway when I reported to Colonel Kovaric in his office. The doctor was fuming and went off on me. He didn't even return my salute and left me standing at attention.

"Instead of telling me about the condition of our wounded, Kovaric started ranting about the incident in Sicily during World War II when General George S. Patton Jr., our commander's famed father, was visiting his wounded at the Ninety-third Evacuation Hospital and slapped a patient who didn't have any physical wounds. That infamous incident made headline news around the world.

"Kovaric told me he knew Colonel Patton was the Eleventh Cavalry's commanding officer, and he didn't want another 'Patton incident' on his watch. He also told me he knew Patton was on leave and needed someone who could get Doc under control.

"I told him, 'I'm the guy you want. I'm here. Tell me what the problem is.'

"Fif had been treated and taken to a female ward. Doc had been treated and taken to a male ward. Despite hospital rules separating female and male patients, Doc was insisting on being in the same ward with Fif.

"Kovaric said he wasn't going to put up with Doc's hardheadedness and wanted to medevac him to another hospital, but Doc wouldn't agree.

"Adding fuel to the fire of an already hot situation, Kovaric told me that he was going to send a formal report up his chain of command recommending Doc be relieved of command for taking an unauthorized passenger into combat.

"Kovaric ended his tirade by stating, 'We've done our best to fix your man. Now you've got to get him out of here.'

"I told Kovaric I would go talk to Major Bahnsen.

"Fif's being on Doc's helicopter was not good news, but her condition was more important than a policy violation at the moment. I sent Finkbiner to look in on her while I went to talk with Doc."

Glenn Finkbiner describes Fif's appearance.

"I'd never seen Fif when she didn't look good. Her clothes were always clean, her hair done just so, and her makeup on.

"She looked a mess when I saw her in the hospital that afternoon. Her clothes were speckled with burn holes. She had some ugly burns the left-side of her face. Most of the exposed parts of her body were covered with a blue colored copper sulphate solution that halts combustion of white phosphorus particles.

"Fif was a tough woman with a lot of experience in Vietnam, but her first brush with combat left her pretty shaken up.

"I should make something very clear about this tragic event: taking Fif into combat was a bad decision on Doc's part, but it had absolutely nothing—zero—to do with what happened during the mission. What happened would have happened had Fif been sitting in her Saigon apartment at the time."

Jim Dozier resumes.

"I told Doc what Kovaric said.

" 'Bullshit! I'm not going anywhere.'

" 'Doc, you've got to settle down. Let's go look in on your wounded.'

"Maestretti and Conti were covered with nasty phosphorous burns. They were in serious condition but would live. Yano's condition was critical. He had awful wounds to his face. Bandages covered his left hand and forearm. He was badly charred in places and pitted with phosphorous burns in others. He had inhaled some of the white phosphorous and could barely talk. I didn't think he would make it. But the doctors were still working on him, so I had my fingers crossed.

"After we visited his wounded, Doc seemed calm and I thought it safe for me to leave.

"When Finkbiner and I arrived at the hospital, one of Doc's aircrews was cleaning the debris out of his helicopter and inspecting it for damage. By the time we left, the helicopter was gone.

"Later that evening, we got a call from the hospital telling us that Yano was dying. Major O'Meara had returned to regiment by then. I asked him if he wanted to come along. He said 'yes.'

"When we got to the hospital, we were told that Kovaric had Fif medevaced to the Third Field Hospital at Tan Son Nhut Air Base in Saigon just after dark. Doc was pissed, but there wasn't a thing he could do to stop it.

Doc resumes.

Major Don Peters, Warrant Officer Mike Bates, and a couple more of my troopers stopped by the hospital to check on us. I took them to see Maestretti and Conti, then Yano.

They didn't stay long with Maestretti or Conti because Yano's condition was going from bad to worse and they wanted to see him while they still could.

Yano was virtually covered with blue paste. He was conscious and talked to us in a raspy voice—like he had a bad chest cold. Even though the prognosis for his recovery was very grim, we were all hoping he would somehow pull through.

Dozier returned with O'Meara shortly after my troopers left the hospital. Yano's condition had taken a turn for the worse. I'd like to think that he knew we were by his side, but he was heavily sedated and could no longer talk. I held his good hand for a long time, offering a silent prayer as I did. There really wasn't much I could say, so I just told him to "hang tough."

The doctors did everything they possibly could to save him, but that wasn't in the cards: Staff Sergeant Rodney Yano died from phosphorous poisoning before sunrise.

Carmine Conti concludes.

"By all that is Holy, I should have taken that grenade. Fate alone put Yano, not me, in the crew chief's seat. Our survival that day was assured only by Yano's extraordinary courage and calm amid crisis while he personally teetered on death's door."

4 January 1969—93rd Evacuation Hospital, Long Binh

Ireland came to visit me the morning Yano died. He told me that I was confined to quarters until Patton returned. That was fine with me. I wasn't going anywhere, anyway.

Lying in bed while my burns crusted over with scabs, I thought about the New Year's Day mission.

Everybody in the troop liked Yano. He was just starting his third back-to-back tour. His courageous actions saved the life of everyone else onboard my helicopter. A better soldier there never was.

When someone in my unit needed help, I didn't hesitate in going to their assistance. That's just the way I was; it was part of my nature as a soldier and how I commanded. I shouldn't have taken Fif into the fight without prior authorization. I was fully expecting to be relieved of command, sent home, and have my name stricken from the promotion list to lieutenant colonel. Nevertheless, I had no regrets over my actions and was prepared to accept the consequences of them.

I was going over all of this in my mind when a nurse gave me some pain medicine. I'd started to doze off when the sound of metal striking metal woke me up. It took a few seconds for the blur to clear before I could see what was making that irritating noise.

Colonel George S. Patton was standing at the foot of my bed tapping the barrel of his .357 Magnum pistol against the rail. The sight of that big ugly pistol startled me. I expected Patton to be pissed, but not pissed enough to shoot me. For a split second, I thought he might.

At the time, I didn't appreciate the extent of the dramatic irony of that moment. The 93rd Evacuation Hospital was the *same* unit in which Colonel Patton's father brandished one of his famous "white pistols" during his notorious World War II slapping incident in Sicily. And now that I know Colonel Kovaric was worried about another "Patton incident," I think he would have gone into cardiac arrest had he been present.

Patton made eye contact with me just as he started in.

"Goddamn it, Doc! You dumb sonofabitch! I'd shoot you myself if you weren't *my* sonofabitch! Get your shit together! I'm taking you back to regiment!"

Patton didn't say another word. He just turned and headed toward the door.

I was struggling to put on a hospital robe when the nurse on duty in the ward screamed after him.

"Colonel Patton, you can't just come in here and take a patient without proper clearance! I don't care who you are. You're not taking Major Bahnsen out of this hospital until you do. I won't allow it!"

A nurse trying to tell Patton what he was going to do was as fruitless as telling a lioness trying to feed her cubs to wait until the prey dies from natural causes. Patton didn't even turn around. He just kept walking straight ahead and out the door.

The nurse turned and looked at me. She ordered me to get back in bed, as if I'd follow her orders instead of Patton's. Not a chance in hell of that happening. I put on some hospital slippers and shuffled after Patton without taking time to gather up my personal belongings.

I made it outside and found Patton sitting in his jeep's front passenger seat. I wasn't about to ask him to step out and let me in. So, in a rather awkward move, I carefully slid over the side of the jeep and was just about to sit down on the rear bench seat when Patton told his driver to get moving. The jeep lurched forward, throwing me for a loop. Fortunately, the seat cushioned my fall.

Patton used every second of the short ride back to Bien Hoa to give me an old-fashioned ass chewing. And like his father, Colonel Patton had a dramatic way of lacing his words with colorful profanity when he wanted to emphasize a point. This was one of those occasions.

"Doc, you dumb sonofabitch! I hope you realize just how far *I'm* sticking *my* neck out to save *your* damned career! I'm not taking any action! I don't want you to ever say a word about Fif being in your helicopter! Ever! Do you understand?"

"Yes, sir, I do."

"And you make damn sure none of your people ever mention it."

"Yes, sir!"

"Well you better. I go on R&R and come back to find out that you've screwed up royally. That won't happen again! I don't give a shit where I am—you will *never* do something *that* damn stupid again!"

"No, sir, I won't."

"Fuckin' right you won't! Another thing you better understand, I don't want her flying in *any* regimental helicopter again! And she's not allowed in your troop area again! Never! Can you get that through your thick head?"

"Yes, sir!"

As we pulled up to regimental headquarters, Patton placed his hand on the handle of his holstered pistol, turned and looked me square in the eye, then said, "If you ever do something that stupid again, you won't have the luxury of a court-martial. I'll deal with your sorry ass myself."

I got the point.

Patton got out of the jeep and stood in the way of my climbing out the front. I gently slid over the side and stood up as straight as I could. Patton looked me up and down and shook his head in disgust.

"Doc, get your ass out of that hospital outfit and put on your uniform. I don't give a shit about how bad you're hurt. I need you back in action. Now! If I didn't need you so bad . . . I'd have left you to rot in that fuckin' hospital."

I didn't say a word. His message was clear. There was nothing more for me to say. I just saluted him and headed for my troop area in the jeep sent to pick me up.

Andy O'Meara provides some details about what happened when Patton returned from leave.

"The day Patton returned from Hawaii, we held our usual evening briefing. At its conclusion, Merritte Ireland cleared the room except for the primary staff, the S-1, 2, 3, and 4.

"Ireland told Patton what had happened; Dozier filled in the holes. There was a gut-wrenching tone to what they said. They told Patton they hadn't made an official report, but Colonel Kovaric was raising hell over the whole affair and wanted Doc's head on a pike.

"Ireland was senior to Doc. Dozier and Finkbiner were in his same year group. Hruby and I were his juniors. Before they started discussing what should be done, I spoke up.

" 'I need to excuse myself. It's not up to me to pass judgment on superiors, but there is just one thing I want to say before I leave. This man is a fighter. He's priceless. When I go to fight in World War III, I want Doc on my flank.'

"Doc had vices, but what he'd done was an innocent mistake. It wasn't like he lied, cheated, or stole in the line of duty.

"I've always believed the Army needs to protect guys who will close with the enemy because they're few and far between. You'd think in the profession of arms that everyone would be a warrior at heart. Not so, there are very few warriors. In my mind, Doc was one of the greatest to fight in Vietnam."

Jim Dozier reveals some previously untold elements of this incident.

"I was scared to death to tell Patton about Fif being in Doc's helicopter. Patton was forever trying to keep them apart. He'd gone so far as to order Doc to stop going to see her in Saigon. I really didn't want to be the bearer of bad news, but I was the one who'd handled the situation in his absence.

"Patton was very, very upset over Doc's taking Fif into a hostile action. His first instinct was to relieve Doc. What other choice was there? Doctor Kovaric was already making waves that could muddy the water for taking less drastic action.

"Colonel Patton never told his staff to keep quiet about Fif being on the helicopter. He didn't have to. The entire Air Cavalry Troop knew about it. Patton wasn't worried about that; this was the kind of thing they kept to themselves.

"He asked me if this had been reported to the First Infantry Division, our opcon headquarters. I told him, 'No, sir.' He said, 'Good, I'll go tell them myself.'

"Patton had already had a long day, flying in from Hawaii and all, and it was getting late. He waited until the next morning before going to Lai Khe."

Retired Major General, then Lieutenant Colonel, Leroy Suddath, one of Doc's West Point classmates, had just assumed command of the 2nd Battalion, 28th Infantry Regiment when this incident occurred. He talks about Patton's going to the 1st Infantry Division.

"The morning after he returned from leave, Patton went to the First Infantry Division's headquarters at Lai Khe, where he talked to his fellow West Pointers and old friends Brigadier General George Cantlay and Colonel Bill Patch.

"Cantlay and Patch knew Doc well. They knew how valuable he was to the troop, the regiment, and the division. So what if his personal conduct was controversial at times? He was too good a leader and fighter to lose over taking an unauthorized civilian passenger into a hostile engagement.

"It was Patton's decision to make, not theirs. But if it were, screw policy! They wouldn't take action against Doc. If Patton could handle it quietly, they would keep the incident to themselves."

Retired Lieutenant General Orwin C. Talbott, then Commanding General, 1st Infantry Division, tells what he knew about this incident.

"My memory draws a blank about Bahnsen flying into combat with his girlfriend on board. I've never heard about it until now [2005]. Patton never talked about it with me; neither did anyone on my staff.

"I can't tell at this point in time what I would have done about something like that. I always tried to follow the line in combat, and I had a lot of combat time starting with Patton's Third Army in World War II.

"My experience in combat taught me to be judicious in following the line, especially when dealing with someone like Bahnsen. He was a little rough around the edges, but he was a great fighter, a really great fighter. He was very aggressive, but not illegally so. At least not to my knowledge."

Retired Lieutenant Colonel Lee Allen, who later served with Doc on the U.S. Army Combat Arms Training Board, made the following observation about Patton and policy.

"Patton was a battle-hardened warrior. He didn't fear the enemy at all, and he feared policy even less. He'd been looking for a way to keep Doc in command of the Air Cav Troop and his old friends in the First Infantry gave him that way.

"In doing what he did, Patton placed his own career on the line, as did several other senior officers. Something like that was highly unusual at the time. Anytime for that matter. But it goes to show what those highly unusual officers were willing to do to save the career of a young officer they respected."

Leroy Suddath continues.

"Colonel Patton was no stranger to Colonel Kovaric or his staff. He visited his wounded at the Ninety-third Evac regularly.

"Before going to see Kovaric, Patton stopped by the Air Cav Troop, where he picked up a mint-condition Czech Model 58 assault rifle from the ARPs. The ARPs had a conex, aka "The Fort Knox of weapons," that was stocked with some of every weapon used on both sides in the war, plus spare parts.

"Czech 58s resembled Russian AK-47s and ChiCom 56s but had machined rather than the stamped steel receivers found in their counterparts. The Czech 58s even used a better grade of wood for their stocks and hand guard. You could tell a Czech 58 was a superior weapon just by looking at one alongside an AK-47 or Type 56. This made Czech 58s highly prized, and you couldn't get your hands on one easily.

"When Patton arrived at the hospital, the first thing he did was visit its commander, hand him the Czech 58, and say, 'I'd like you to have this.' Kovaric acted a bit confused and asked, 'Why?' Patton told him, 'Because it's a goddamn bribe.'

"I suspect Patton's 'bribe' took Kovaric by total surprise and left him with little to say. I'm sure Kovaric was still anxious over the possibility that Doc might start raising hell again or something else might come down that would cause the Ninety-third to make infamous headlines once again.

"Kovaric told Patton he wanted Doc transferred to another hospital. Patton said he was taking Doc with him. Kovaric could handle the paperwork in his own time.

"Patton never said anything about Kovaric recommending Doc be brought up on charges. Who knows? Patton's naturally intimidating presence along with the 'bribe' may have been enough to get him to back off.

"But the 'bribe' story doesn't end there. After all the fuss the nurse made when he went to get Doc, Patton must have had second thoughts about one Czech 58 being enough to keep Kovaric quiet. This explains why Patton had the ARPs take Kovaric a jeep trailer filled to the brim with an assortment of captured weapons for the hospital's museum."

Doc resumes.

It was years later before Patton mentioned any of this to me. He just sniggered over doing a lot of ass kissing to save my career.

This was typical Patton. He never hesitated in going to bat for someone in his unit. He never expected favors in return. He never talked about things better left unsaid.

Maestretti, Conti, and I separately recommended Yano for our nation's highest medal for gallantry. I also recommended Yano be posthumously promoted. Patton endorsed these recommendations.

Rodney J. T. Yano received a posthumous Medal of Honor and a promotion to the rank of sergeant first class.

A range at Fort Knox, Kentucky, was subsequently named in Yano's honor, as was a hangar at Fort Rucker, Alabama. All fields on the Patton family farm in Massachusetts are named after fallen heroes of the Blackhorse, including one named "Yano." In January 1997, T-AKR 297, a U.S. Navy container ship refitted into a cargo ship large enough to transport an entire armor battalion task force, was formally named the USNS Yano.

In the history of war, many soldiers have become heroes as the result of their gallantry in one battle. Doc Bahnsen's reputation as a warrior became legend as the result of two tours in one of the United States' most difficult wars during which his nonstop heroism was recognized by eighteen medals for gallantry. The amazing story of his combat leadership and undaunted valor begins in October 1965.

★ PART 1 ★

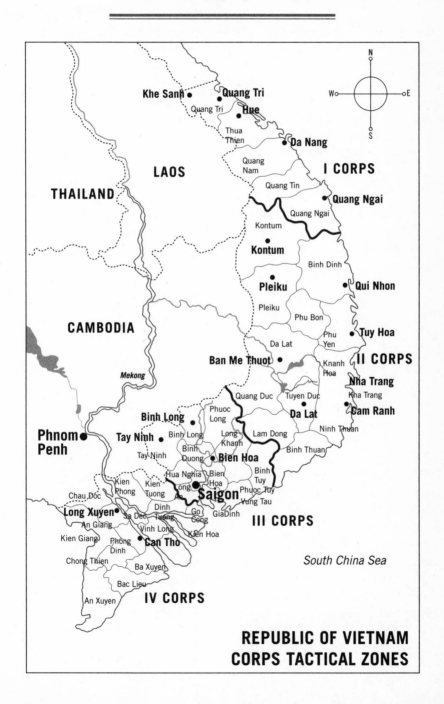

N
W   E
S

Khe Sanh ●   ● **Quang Tri**
Quang Tri   **Hue**

Thua
Thien   ● **Da Nang**

LAOS

Quang
Nam

I CORPS

THAILAND

Quang Tin

● **Quang Ngai**
Quang Ngai

Kontum

Kontum
●

Binh Dinh

● **Qui Nhon**

CAMBODIA

Pleiku
●

Pleiku

Phu Bon

Phu
Yen   ● **Tuy Hoa**

Da Lat

Ban Me Thuot ●

Knanh
Hoa

II CORPS

Mekong

Nha Trang
●
Kha Trang

Quang Duc   Tuyen Duc

Da Lat
●

● **Cam Ranh**

Binh Long ●

Phuoc
Long

Long
Khanh   Lam Dong

Ninh Thuan

**Phnom
Penh** ●

Tay Ninh ●

Binh Long

Binh
Duong   ● **Bien Hoa**

Binh Thuan

Tay Ninh

Hua Nghia

Bien
Hoa

Binh
Tuy

Chau Doc

Kien
Phong   Kien
Tuong

Long
An   ● **Saigon**

Phuoc Tuy
Vung Tau

Long Xuyen ●

Dinh

Sa Dec   Dinh
Tuong

Go
Cong   GiaDinh

III CORPS

An Giang

Vinh Long

Kien Hoa

Kien Giang

Phong
Dinh   ● **Can Tho**

Chong Thien

Ba Xuyen

South China Sea

Bac Lieu

An Xuyen   **IV CORPS**

REPUBLIC OF VIETNAM
CORPS TACTICAL ZONES

✶ Chapter 1 ✶

4 October 1965—en route to Tan Son Nhut Air Base, Republic of Vietnam

The flight stateside to Vietnam is a long one. It gave me time to reflect on my past and present life.

The Bahnsen family lived in what was Flensburg, Denmark, before the Schlesweig-Holstein loss to Prussia after the Franco-Prussian War. They were proud Danes who didn't adapt well to German rule. Accordingly, they immigrated to the United States during the late 1880s.

In 1890, my great-grandfather and great-grandmother were murdered in southern Alabama. My grandfather chased their murderer all the way to Texas, but never caught him. Neither did the law.

My grandfather, Dr. Peter F. Bahnsen, after whom I picked up the nickname "Doc," came to the United States with his parents. A self-taught veterinarian, Grandpa was appointed Georgia's first state veterinarian. He later retired to his "model" dairy farm in Americus.

My father and mother, John C. Bahnsen and Evelyn Williams, were married in Waycross, Georgia, in early 1934. I was born in November of that year. My brother Peter was born two years later.

In 1924, Dad graduated as the senior ranking cadet from Riverside Military Academy in Gainesville, Georgia. He wanted to continue his education, but Grandpa Bahnsen didn't believe my dad needed further formal schooling and called him home.

After Dad returned home, Grandpa Bahnsen put up the money for him to try his hand in several business ventures, including farming, but they all went belly-up during the early years of the Great Depression.

During this period, Dad joined the Army Reserve. He was a first lieutenant when he received a one-year call up to command the Civilian Conservation Corps (CCC) camp in Waycross.

Dad loved the Army and would have made it his career, but, as a reserve officer, he was discharged during the drawdowns of the 1930s. When he left active duty, Dad vowed that should he have sons, they would become Regular Army officers, a status granting immunity from reductions-in-force.

After separating from the Army, Dad became the civilian commander of various CCC camps throughout Georgia until the buildup for World War II began in 1940. His last job in the CCC was to close camps as the men working in them reported for military duty.

In 1941, my dad was hired on as the Wilcox County soil conservationist, and he moved our family to Rochelle, an agricultural community noted for the production of broilers, cantaloupe, cotton, peanuts, timber, and watermelon.

I grew up hunting and fishing in the south Georgia fields, woods, and swamps. My best friends were mostly country boys who lived on farms. We took off our shoes as soon as we could in the spring and went barefoot until the frost came in late fall.

Dad was an avid horseman. He made sure Peter and I had a pony or a horse to ride from the time we were able to hold on to a saddle horn. We also owned bird dogs, and Dad taught Peter and me to hunt with dogs from a young age. I also made and flew model airplanes. I suppose this childhood hobby was the beginning of my lifelong love of flying.

I attended Rochelle schools until my freshman year in high school, then went to live with my grandpa Bahnsen and aunt Bee in Americus because its high school offered more math and science courses than I could get at home.

A year later, I returned to Rochelle for eighteen months before heading to Marion Military Institute in Marion, Alabama, for some much needed prep schooling.

I played B-squad basketball and A-squad football on the junior college teams at Marion and became well prepared academically for what I hoped would be the next phase of my education: West Point.

Over the years, my dad made several key political connections. One of them, Senator Walter F. George, gave me a principal appointment to the U.S. Military Academy at West Point, New York.

I graduated from Marion Military in January 1952 but remained there to study for the West Point admission exams I took two months later at Fort Benning, Georgia. When the exams were over, I went home to earn some pocket money measuring land for the U.S. Department of Agriculture.

I reported to West Point in early July. It was the answer to my childhood dreams. A military career was the only career I ever wanted, and there's no better place to start a military career than West Point.

Incongruous with my career ambitions, I had a lackadaisical attitude toward most academic studies at West Point. Only military subjects and physical education interested me enough to really apply myself.

I won my numerals pole vaulting on the plebe track team, and I became an avid intramural athlete for Company C-1 throughout my cadet days. Besides being an intramural wrestler and swimmer, I played intramural football, lacrosse, and soccer.

I met Captain Hank "The Gunfighter" Emerson while serving as the captain and coach of my company's lacrosse team. Emerson was a tactical officer in another regiment, but he and his good friend Captain George S. Patton had me assigned to them as cadet training officer during my first class summer field training at Camp Buckner—the field training site at West Point.

In this capacity, I helped Patton plan and execute the air mobile exercise for the yearling class. Neither of us realized that the summer of 1955 would be replayed many times over in combat thirteen years later in Vietnam.

This beginning of a lifelong association with these two distinguished officers (Emerson made lieutenant general; Patton retired as a major general) was a molding one for me. They liked my "spirit" in particular and took great pride in my performance during tactical training that summer.

When first class summer was over, Patton and Emerson tried to have me made a cadet company commander, but that was not in the cards with my company tactical officer. When that door slammed shut, they asked me if I wanted to serve on a cadet staff. I told them, "Hell no! I want to lead!"

Based on their strong recommendation, I was appointed a cadet lieutenant and platoon leader and given additional duty as my company's athletic representative, putting me in charge of all our intramural teams.

I truly enjoyed my first class year for several reasons, one of the most memorable being the exhilaration I felt over my company's team run on the brigade intramural championship, the Banker's Trophy. We came in second out of twenty-four companies. That still frustrates me. I wish I could round up my teammates, turn back time, and have another go at first place.

During my time at West Point and before, I had dreamed of becoming an Air Force fighter pilot. When I failed the eye exam for Air Force flight training during my first class year, that dream went by the wayside.

I stood 406 out of 480 when my class graduated from West Point on 5 June 1956. Because of my low class standing, infantry and artillery were my choices for a combat arms branch assignment. I chose infantry.

Shortly after graduation, I reported for duty as a student in the Infantry Officer Basic Course, followed by Airborne School, at Fort Benning.

Two major turning points in my life took place while I was attending the Basic Course. In December 1956, I married my childhood sweetheart: Patricia "Pat" Fitzgerald. I also passed the physical exam for Army flight training and was selected to attend Fixed Wing Flight School immediately following the completion of airborne training.

Flight school took place at Camp Gary, Texas, and Fort Rucker, Alabama. I was one of the first in my class to solo, after seven hours and fifteen minutes' flying time with an instructor pilot, but finished in the middle at graduation. The school was a lot of fun and Pat and I enjoyed Texas in particular. I became a master mason in my home lodge during this time and remain a member of Rochelle Lodge #190 to this day.

After flight school, I returned to Fort Benning as an aviator in Artillery Flight, 3rd Aviation Company, 3rd Infantry Division. During this assignment, I attended the 3rd Army's sixty-day Fixed Wing Instrument Qualification Course in Augusta, Georgia, and finished first in my class. My motivation for taking this training so seriously was a series of severe accidents by aviators in our unit who lacked instrument tickets (that is, weren't qualified to fly by instruments).

In November 1957, Pat gave birth to our first son, Jon Christian, at Columbus, the quintessential sleepy southern town abutting Fort Benning's main gate.

In 1958, the 3rd Division was deployed to Germany, where I was soon made director of instruction in the 3rd Aviation Company's Aerial Observer School. In this capacity, I spent hours upon hours flying an L-19 Bird Dog in circles over the Grafenwöhr firing range teaching forward observers the aerial adjustment of artillery fire, becoming an expert at adjusting artillery fire from the air in the process. This well-honed skill would prove *very* useful in later years during combat operations in Vietnam.

During my time in Germany, I attended a six-week Intelligence Officer Course at Oberammergau, finishing first in my class because I found it interesting. This training qualified me to be an S-2, a job I would never hold, but what I learned about the Soviet order of battle came in handy in future years because the NVA often employed Soviet tactics.

Later that year, I asked First Lieutenant David K. Doyle to get me assigned as a platoon leader in his company, and he did. Soon after, in early 1959, I requested a transfer to the 1st Tank Battalion, 68th Armor. The 3rd Aviation Company's leaders were astounded by my request, but approved it.

Serving under Doyle was a godsend for me. He was a competent soldier, a superb trainer, and a caring commander. I stayed under Doyle's mentorship until he was transferred to E Company to square it away.

Doyle and I later served together as instructors at Fort Knox and went on to simultaneously command squadrons in the 11th Armored Cavalry Regiment in Vietnam. He had a tremendous career, retiring as a lieutenant general.

Doyle's replacement was a nice enough fellow but he didn't have a clue about commanding a tank company. He lasted about six months before being relieved from command during the company's Annual Training Test at Hohenfels. Despite his shortcomings, my loyalty to him put me in good stead within the battalion. And although he left under a cloud, the spectacular Officer Efficiency Report (OER) he wrote on me was enthusiastically endorsed by my battalion commander. That OER got me off to a good start as an armor officer.

Like my budding armor career, my family grew during this assignment. In June 1959, Pat gave birth to our second son, Bradley Duncan, in the Würzberg Army Hospital.

In June 1960, I assumed command of B Company. I held that position for a year as a first lieutenant. It was a great unit with many fine officers and noncommissioned officers (NCOs). The highlight of this command came when we qualified seventeen of seventeen tanks on the Tank Crew Qualification Course at Grafenwöhr on the first run, an unheard of achievement at the time. This feat resulted from training, training, and more training fueled by the esprit de corps that comes from true teamwork. It also resulted in my first Army Commendation Medal. I later wrote about this achievement in my first published article for *Armor* magazine.

Upon completion of our three years in Germany, Pat and the kids returned to Rochelle while I was assigned temporary duty (TDY) at Fort Wolters, Texas, to attend the Rotary Wing Aviator Course. Following this training in the OH-23 Raven light-observation helicopter, I received orders to attend the Armor Officer Advance Course at Fort Knox, Kentucky.

As a student at Fort Knox, I didn't receive formal instruction about Vietnam or fighting in the jungle. It was too early in the war for "lessons learned" to be integrated into the curriculum. However, I did have the informal opportunity to learn a great deal about the war and fighting in the jungle from two foreign officers.

My tablemate for part of the advanced course was Captain "Pierre" Tran Van Thoan, a South Vietnamese Army officer. He was half French and very well educated and polished. His wife came from a wealthy family, so they socialized with the elite in their country. We became very good friends and, over the course of many conversations, Pierre provided me with a superb background and rundown on the fight against the Ho Chi Minh–led communist North Vietnamese.

Another tablemate was Lieutenant Colonel Nobuji Oda, a Japanese Defense Force officer, who impressed me as a superb soldier.

Oda commanded a tank platoon in Burma during World War II. Notwithstanding the fact that all of his tanks not lost to mechanical failure were destroyed over a short period of fighting with British forces, the experiences Oda shared with me about fighting with tanks in jungle terrain came in handy when I commanded an armor squadron during my second tour in Vietnam.

I graduated in the middle of my advanced course class but was selected to stay on at the Armor School as an instructor in armored cavalry and air cavalry tactics in the command and staff department.

This assignment gave me the opportunity to get to know officers I would serve with in future years. It also helped me become well schooled in armor tactics and gave me the opportunity to influence the early development of air cavalry tactics.

Important changes in my family life occurred during my three years at Fort Knox. Pat gave birth to our daughter, Leeanne, on my birthday in November 1962. Her birth was followed by my father's death in August 1963 at the young age of fifty-nine. Dad lived long enough to see my brother and me make Regular Army captain, but too short a time to get to know his grandchildren. His death was followed by Pat giving birth to our third son, James Fitzgerald, in February 1964.

In 1964, I left the Armor School to attend the U.S. Army Command and General Staff College at Fort Leavenworth, Kansas. I was one of the first in my West Point class to be selected for this schooling.

Attending the Command and General Staff College brought me together with a lot of old friends, former students, and West Point classmates who had just returned from the war. I had plenty of off-duty time to hunt birds, improve my golf game, read widely, and become a thirty-second-degree Scottish Rite mason.

The core curriculum was not a great challenge for me. On every test where my own solution could be one of the options, I always selected *that* tactical solution. I also enjoyed sharpshooting instructors who were weak in their subject areas. Unsurprisingly, I did not endear myself to my instructors, but I did win the "Tiger of the Year" award from my section mates.

The mounting war in Vietnam first hit my thoughts in 1961 when the call went out for volunteers to be advisers in the counterinsurgency effort there. My brother, Peter, a Special Forces officer, and several of my close friends responded to that call. I had no desire for going to war in an advisory position. I could have volunteered to fly helicopters in Vietnam. But at that point in the war, helicopter units were transportation branch aviation companies, not my area of interest.

As my time at Leavenworth drew to a close, U.S. forces were becoming more and more engaged in the fighting. As the pace of the fighting picked up, going to Vietnam started to become more appealing to me. Moreover, combat arms aviators were starting to take charge of our aviation assets and transportation branch aviators were moving back into their support role as maintenance officers.

I finished in the lower third of my Command and General Staff College class in June 1965 with a diploma in one hand and orders to Vietnam in the other. I was thirty-one years old, cocky and self-confident, fit and ready, teeming with testosterone, and eager to experience my first battle. However, the bubble of my enthusiasm burst when I read my orders: they had me going to Vietnam as a CV-2 Caribou pilot—I would be flying a fucking transport aircraft in a combat-support role.

I was an armor officer and an aviator. The armor side of my career had been extremely well handled by armor branch, but the aviation desk at the Department of the Army (DA) had responsibility for my orders to Vietnam. The Military Personnel Center requisitioned the aviation desk for a CV-2–qualified staff college graduate. I was a staff college graduate and only needed to attend a transition course at Fort Benning to become CV-2 qualified.

I was damn unhappy about this turn of events.

I called the aviation desk officer, a lieutenant colonel, and asked him to have my orders amended. I wanted to attend UH-1 transition training and be assigned to a gunship unit. He told me I was going to fill the CV-2 pilot requisition no matter what I said or did. Besides, flying a fixed wing transport in Vietnam was plum duty. He thought I ought to thank him for keeping me out of harm's way.

As my CV-2 training wouldn't begin until early August, I had about forty-five days of forced leave, so I took my family home to Rochelle.

After arranging for Pat and the kids to live in East Point, an Atlanta suburb, while I was in Vietnam, I had a lot of time on my hands and needed something to do to stay out of trouble.

As a kid, I was fascinated with the crop dusters flying in our area. As an adult, dusting crops appeared to be exciting flying and risky enough to be interesting. I went looking for a crop duster and met D. F. "Dee" Idol, who had two Piper J-3 Cubs equipped with five-hundred-pound hoppers for dust.

I persuaded Dee to take me on as his second pilot for a month or so. My training commenced that same afternoon, beginning with how to hand prop the hundred-horsepower engine. The rest of my training was also hands-on.

Dee told me to follow his lead. We took off from a section of paved country road and flew low level all the way to the local airport at Fitzgerald. Dee proceeded to circle the field at about fifteen hundred feet, then again at less than one hundred feet—a high recon followed by a low recon. He then lined up on the grass strip and flew down the runway at grass-top level with me right on his tail. At the end of the runway he did a steep climb, went into a 180-degree turn, then headed back in the other direction. I followed him, being careful to keep my airspeed up in the turn.

We continued this for about six or seven runs, working our way across the field. After we finished, we landed next to the field. Dee critiqued my performance, and then we flew back to his roadside parking area. There was still an hour or more of daylight; plenty of time for my first crop dusting mission: fifty acres of cotton with tall trees at one end and a power line running alongside a road at the other end.

My time spent crop dusting was not without excitement. I once flew through some telephone lines, my plane's metal prop cutting all eight strands cleanly. Another time, I flew so low that I came back with peanut vines in my wheels. On two occasions, I took out the tops of trees after pulling up too late from a dusting pass over a field bordered on one end by a pecan orchard. Once, on takeoff from a very narrow road, I took out a piece of my plane's wing covering on a fence post that I didn't see until it was too late. Dee took all of this in stride and only deducted from my pay what the telephone company charged him to repair the damaged lines.

Everywhere we went, I met farmers who knew my dad and had good things to say about him. I renewed old acquaintances and saw a lot of buddies I'd grown up with. They all knew I was headed for Vietnam and got a real hoot over me killing bugs to get ready to kill Vietcong.

I wasn't excited about reporting for CV-2 training and my demeanor reflected that sentiment. The major who ran the course did not like my attitude from the get-go. I caught crap from him daily, but nothing he said bothered me. In fact, I was hoping to be flunked out of the course. I passed my flight checks but purposely failed the written exam twice. Much to my disappointment, I left Fort Benning certified to fly the Caribou.

As I packed my gear for Vietnam, I didn't give much thought to the politics of the American effort. Going to war seemed like the right thing to do at the time: killing communists to save democracy, and Vietnam was as good a place as any to do just that. The thought of being shot at, getting killed, or killing the enemy didn't bother me then, and never would.

Leaving Pat and the children behind was hard. Pat was a marvelous mother and devoted wife. She would keep the home fires burning, but saying good-bye when you're going off to war is gut-wrenching.

War is serious business, and going to war places great strain on even the best of marriages, makes your kids start thinking they'll never see you again, and has other consequences on a soldier's life that should *never* be taken lightly.

☆ Chapter 2 ☆

I arrived in Vietnam just over halfway through the March-December Defense Campaign of 1965. The U.S. mission was to contain the enemy while building base camps and logistical facilities to support our expanding role.

Militarily, South Vietnam was divided into four Corps Tactical Zones (CTZs) from north to south. The I CTZ was primarily the responsibility of the U.S. Marine Corps. It abutted North Vietnam along the Demilitarized Zone (DMZ) and extended over the five northernmost provinces in the foothills and narrow coastal regions east of the Annamite Mountains.

The U.S. Army had responsibility for the II and III CTZs. The II CTZ was the least-populated region. It encompassed the rugged central highlands, central plateau, and adjacent coastal regions. The III CTZ consisted of the densely populated silty clay plain and swamps surrounding Saigon, but not Saigon itself. Saigon was its own military district. The Army of the Republic of Vietnam (ARVN) had a III Corps, so to avoid confusion between ARVN and U.S. Army commands, the U.S. Army headquarters in the III CTZ was designated II Field Force, Vietnam.

ARVN units had primary responsibility for the IV CTZ, which took in the heavily populated Mekong Delta; a fertile farming region sometimes known as the rice basket.

I was on orders as an aviator to the 145th Combat Aviation Battalion "Warriors." The 145th's lineage distinguished itself as the first combat aviation battalion in Vietnam. This outfit was equipped with fixed and rotary wing aircraft, and I was slotted to fly its CV-2 Caribou airplanes. I reported to my new battalion commander, Lieutenant Colonel Charles M. Honour Jr., determined to get another assignment.

After some small talk about my past assignments, I let Honour know outright that I did not want to fly Caribous for him and that the only reason I'd been slotted to fly a *transport* was because the dumb shit aviation desk assignments officer refused to send me to UH-1 transition training. I told him that I wanted to get into the fight, and the best way to do that in an aviation unit was to fly *gunships* (the armed UH-1 Bell Iroquois series helicopter commonly called a "Huey").

Honour was a warrior and discerned me as a kindred spirit. He assigned me to command the gunship platoon in the 118th Aviation Company (Air Mobil Light) "Thunderbirds." He assured me I could get UH-1 certified in my unit. He also told me, since I was on the promotion list to major, that platoon command would only last until I was promoted. I told him that wasn't a problem.

I remained at battalion headquarters until 10 October doing odd jobs for the S-3, who was a bit behind on his work. This was easy duty and a good orientation period because I got to know people from all the units in the battalion before I reported for duty with the 118th.

✶ Chapter 3 ✶

10 October 1965—118th Aviation Company (AML), Bien Hoa Air Base

The 118th Aviation Company (AML) was redesignated the 118th Assault Helicopter Company three months after I reported in, making it the first assault helicopter company in Vietnam. When I reported for duty, Major Jack Seliskar commanded the 118th. He was a Leavenworth classmate, but I did not know him well. He was a senior major and a good guy who personified the Thunderbird's motto: "It Shall Be Done."

Seliskar had recently assigned another officer as the gunship platoon leader and told him he could keep it for thirty days, long enough for an OER in combat. For the time being, he assigned me to work with the company operations officer, who was to see that I received my UH-1 transition training.

The 118th was located on the southern end of Bien Hoa Air Base, where each of its three aviation platoons had a parking area on Thunderbird Pad—the company helipad area, aka "Birdcage," next to the runway.

Bien Hoa Air Base came under an intense rocket and mortar attack in the early morning hours on 1 November 1964. The U.S. Air Force lost a squadron of B-57 bombers during this attack. Four of 118th's soldiers were killed and several of its buildings were destroyed, but all of its helicopters weathered the attacked without damage.

Before this attack, the 118th parked its aircraft in close proximity alongside the runway with their rotor blades tied down and secured to the tail hook, leaving them totally unprotected and highly vulnerable to rocket and mortar fire. This attack turned the obvious need for revetments into a top priority.

Building revetments required a lot of hard labor. The 118th's troops spent most of their off-duty time filling and placing sandbags in five foot high L-, E-, and sometimes U-shaped barricades with just enough open space to park a helicopter. When I arrived, the Birdcage still didn't have enough revetments for all the 118th's helicopters.

The runway was short and wide. It was oiled but topped with patches of old perforated steel planking (PSP) until it could be paved. Meanwhile, potholes were a problem that had to be dealt with daily.

Wet or dry, the weather was a big factor in Vietnam. When it rained, the area's silty clay turned into mud that stuck fast to your boots or anything else it touched. When it was dry, ground traffic, along with earth-pounding rotor blade wash generated during helicopter takeoffs and landings, created fine red dust that permeated your clothes, affected your breathing, triggered sanitation problems, and made constant maintenance a necessity

All missions were planned, briefed, and conducted out of the operations building. A radio was always on, telephones were used to maintain contact with battalion headquarters, and hard copy messages were delivered regularly, if time allowed, for big missions.

Each platoon had a building for storing door guns and other gear. There was an area where fuel trucks parked until everyone settled into their revetment for refueling and rearming. An ammunition bunker stored 2.75-inch rockets, 40mm grenades, and 7.62mm ammo.

The South Vietnamese government acquired several French villas along Cong Ly Street in Bien Hoa and leased them to the United States as housing for officers in the earlier arrived helicopter companies.

We trucked back and forth from the company area to Cong Ly Street in deuce-and-a-half- or three-quarter-ton trucks driven by whichever officer's turn it was to drive.

Thunderbird Villa had lush gardens, a large dining room (room service was available for a very small charge), and a lounge that served cheap drinks. We were housed two, in some cases three or four, to a well-furnished two-bedroom apartment separated by a shared bathroom.

Young Vietnamese girls worked at the villa as hooch maids. Each one cared for several officers' rooms and took care of their laundry. Officers vied for the best-looking hooch maids, most of whom provided *personal* services to pick up a little extra money and a few PX goods. There was no open debauchery. For the most part, what went on inside the villa remained there. Goings on of these sorts came under the unofficial "Don't ask, Don't tell" policy at the time.

Our NCOs and enlisted men lived in Quonset huts on Bien Hoa Air Base and ate their meals at the company mess hall. They quickly learned how to enjoy themselves off base, when time allowed, and the local merchants and business owners competed for their patronage. The American Club, a spacious restaurant, bar, and massage parlor next door to the Thunderbird Villa, was one of their favorite haunts.

I had two instructor pilots for my UH-1 transition training: Chief Warrant Officers Ron Madsen and Vann Sherrill. Both were outstanding pilots who really knew their business.

Madsen served an enlisted tour in the Navy before signing on to fly helicopters in the Army. He was the more demanding of the two and a competent trainer, despite his impatience and outspokenness with me.

Sherrill was my primary instructor pilot. He was a tremendous soldier and a good man who I found especially easy to work with and fly beside.

My formal training began on 12 October and took about a week. I then started logging hours with various pilots in the unit flying lift ships on routine "pigs-and-rice" and "ash-and-trash" support missions.

Regretfully, Sherrill was killed in action on 23 October. Because U.S. casualties in the war were not large in number at that time, his death came as a shock.

Ron Madsen recounts the loss of his good friend.

"Vann and I were out on a standardization ride. It was really a pretty day, not too hot.

"We had been doing autorotations, having fun, taking turns to see who could get closest to the touchdown point when we got a call from our operations saying they needed a medevac at a certain area. They asked if we had the fuel to do it. We did, so we immediately headed in the direction given. We got the ground force's frequency from the code book and made contact as we got close to its position. We asked if they were in a secure area; they said all was quiet.

"We asked them to pop a smoke grenade. We identified color and proceeded to land.

"The usual landing procedure was to come in pretty high, then bottom the collective and make a fast descending spiral, with a steep flare on the bottom to decelerate before touchdown. Sometimes we held a little pedal to be out of trim, which would throw off the aim of enemy soldiers leading you with a weapon.

"We landed and picked up a wounded American soldier accompanied by a medic. Once they were secure, we flew to the hot spot at Saigon. An ambulance with a doctor met us and put the wounded soldier under good care right away. The medic stayed on board with us for a lift back to his unit.

"We were running low on fuel, necessitating a refueling stop before flying to the medic's unit.

"When we landed to refuel, I asked Vann if he wanted to fly in the right seat for a while. He said after we dropped the medic off, we could go for lunch, and he would change seats with me then.

"Before we could get the medic home, we received another medevac call. Having plenty of fuel and the medic on board, we headed for the location given.

"Once again, same routine: area seemed secure, the soldiers on the ground popped smoke, and we called color before making our final approach toward the LZ.

"Vann was flying from the left seat, doing an overhead spiral to land. As he flared our helicopter for landing, I had the impression of two men standing up to our left.

"It all happened so fast, the familiar crack as a bullet hit the helicopter. The helicopter pitched when Vann let loose of the cyclic and grabbed his neck. I grabbed the controls.

"Everything seemed to be moving in slow motion.

"Vann cocked his head toward me. He had a surprised look on his face. Blood was squirting through his fingers, spraying the instrument panel and me. It's a picture that will forever be etched in my memory.

"I was hollering for the medic as I dove to the right, trying to accelerate. Vann started to slump. The medic stood behind him, applying a compress bandage in an attempt to stop the bleeding.

"I started talking to Vann. 'Hang on!' I told him. 'I'll have you at the hot spot in just a few minutes. Don't give up! Hang on!'

"It was already too late! His legs started to clamp on the cyclic. I had to lean across him to pull them off the controls. The medic saw what I was trying to do and used his left hand to help me. I still kept talking to Vann, encouraging him to hang on.

"I couldn't see the radio frequency to get Saigon because Vann's blood was splattered all over the console, but there's a switch you can throw to get an emergency channel, and I threw it.

"It seemed like ages before we got to the hot spot, but it wasn't. I pulled one-hundred-percent power all the way in. An ambulance, medics, and a doctor were waiting for us at the landing pad.

"I had just touched down when a medic opened the door and the doctor stepped up and leaned into the cabin to check Vann for life signs. The doctor shook his head at me, it was too late. I shut down and got out, walked around to the other side . . . it was like a bad dream but you couldn't wake up.

"The bullet entered through the left doorpost and hit Vann in the right jugular vein. Standing there, the impact hit me . . . I started crying and wanted vengeance. The crew chief was wet-eyed, too. Everyone thought a lot of Vann. I had the crew chief get in the front seat and we returned to base.

"When someone in the company was killed, the first day everyone would talk about it until they knew what had happened. After that, it was never mentioned again, except weeks or maybe months later."

Doc picks up the story as Madsen landed at Thunderbird Pad.

I remember vividly seeing Ron Madsen land at Thunderbird Pad and climb out of his aircraft. He was traumatized.

I looked inside the cockpit. Blood was splattered all over the place and there was a big pool of it on the floor and beneath the seat where Sherrill had been sitting. It was hard for me to believe how much blood there is in a human body.

This was a very sobering experience for me. I knew Sherrill and liked him a lot. He was the first soldier I served with to get killed.

I would soon find out that good soldiers get killed along with poor ones. There's no way to sort that kind of thing out. More often than not, inches and seconds make the difference between who lives and who dies in combat. Of course, getting killed can also be nothing more than bad luck.

Escorted by a company honor guard, Sherrill's body was flown to Tan Son Nhut Air Base, where it was shipped home. Honor guards for the dead were routine at the time. They ceased as American losses started to increase.

Former captain Jack Waters, commander of the 1st Platoon "Scorpions," recalls flying with Doc during this period.

"I was just leaving First Platoon to become the company operations officer when Doc arrived at the One-Eighteenth. We flew together frequently. I helped him sharpen his UH-1 skills and taught him what I knew about navigating the countryside.

"Doc was a year ahead of me at West Point. I didn't know him as a cadet, but our experiences at the academy gave us lots to talk about as we flew. Doc was personable and I really enjoyed our time together.

"Before I left the Scorpions, Doc often led the Bandits as they flew gunship support for my slicks. Knowing he was there to protect me and my aircraft was always a special comfort. I trusted him completely and knew he would stop at nothing to keep us as safe as possible.

"Doc was aggressive and ambitious in a positive way. He was driven to do his best in everything he did and had a charismatic personality to go along with his high-energy level. The Army needs leaders with these characteristics, especially in combat. The fact that he went on to become an outstanding combat leader and general officer came as no surprise to me."

Doc resumes talking about his early days in the 118th.

In preparation to take command of the Bandits, I spent the next two weeks flying routine slick missions, rotating between the Scorpions and 2nd Platoon "Choppers" to gain experience flying with different pilots.

⋆ Chapter 4 ⋆

I commanded a tank platoon and a tank company in Germany during some of the hottest days of the cold war. The close proximity of Soviet Union and Warsaw Pact forces, particularly their forty or so mechanized infantry and tank divisions prepositioned for a westward onslaught through the Fulda Gap, kept everyone on edge and gave us good reason to train hard and be ready for anything.

Vietnam was different. We were at war, not lying in wait for war.

I was untested in battle but eager to lead soldiers in combat. Accordingly, assuming command of the Bandits became one of the highlights of my military career. I took a liking to all the Bandits right away and they didn't seem to have any problem with me becoming their leader. I was the new kid on the block and was an eager learner; everyone saw that and was most helpful.

The Bandits were the first armed helicopter platoon in Vietnam. When I assumed command, it consisted of sixteen pilots and thirty-two enlisted crewmen. Equipment-wise, the platoon had six UH-1B armed helicopters. Four of these helicopters were armed with quad M-60C 7.62mm flexible machine guns (flex-guns) externally mounted in pairs—one on each side of the aircraft. Controlled from the copilot's left front seat position by a gun grip and reflex-type sight, they could be maneuvered through an eighty-degree horizontal arc and a ninety-five-degree vertical arc. The basic load for each flex-gun was fifteen hundred rounds, for a total of six thousand rounds. Controlled from the pilot's right front seat, the two side-mounted rocket pods housed seven 2.75-inch folding fin rockets.

Two Bandit gunships were a configuration of grenade-and-rocket-bearing aircraft nicknamed "heavy hogs." The chin-turret-mounted 40mm grenade launcher on these aircraft gave them a protruding snoutlike appearance. Their rocket pods could hold thirty-four more rockets than "hogs" outfitted with two side-mounted rocket pods housing seven 2.75-inch folding fin rockets. The technicalities of jargon aside, we called our grenade-and-rocket-armed helicopters "hogs."

The M-75 automatic grenade launcher was aimed vertically and horizontally using a reflex-type flexible hand control sight mounted above the copilot's seat. Both the pilot and copilot could access its master armament control. Its ammunition was fed through a chute from a rotary drum that could be loaded with up to 302 rounds.

The pilot operated the hog's two side-mounted rocket pods, which were capable of housing twenty-four 2.75-inch folding fin rockets.

The heavier the load, the more difficult a hog was to fly, especially on takeoff. Individual 40mm rounds aren't all that heavy, but a hundred or so add a lot of weight. And as the 40mm grenade ammo went up, the number of 2.75-inch rockets had to come down, or you couldn't get airborne.

Our hogs were not equipped with quad flex-guns. However, both the crew chief and door gunner manned a door-mounted M-60 machine gun. Bandit pilots and copilots were individually armed with a .38-caliber pistol carried in a shoulder holster.

Gunships were designed to kill people, destroy equipment, blow up bunkers, and protect slicks carrying infantry into and out of hostile LZs. We generally flew alongside and to the rear of the slick formation. If a slick took fire, its crew chief or door gunner immediately dropped a red smoke grenade to mark the enemy location. Gunships would then try to spot the enemy and kill him, or at least suppress his fire until the slicks flew out of the contact area.

The Bandits also did LZ recon and preparation, looking for the enemy on the edges of the area. Occasionally, we surprised enemy forces as they tried to run out of the area, and that's when we got some shooting in—firing away at fleeing targets. If it was a battalion-sized lift operation, the 197th/334th Aviation Company, an all-gun company, usually did the recon and preparation for the 145th Battalion.

When no air assaults were scheduled, the Bandits were missioned out in two-ship teams to either hunt or protect.

Hunting missions were in support of a particular ARVN unit. These were normally day-long missions operationally controlled by an American adviser. Many hunting missions turned out to be dry runs. However, in some cases they turned into hot and heavy action that resulted in our killing a lot of the enemy, destroying bunkers and matériel, and getting our aircraft shot up by enemy small-arms and automatic weapons fire.

Protect missions were very popular. It was a rare day when there was no request for gunship support of ground operations.

There was always a waiting list to get into the Bandit platoon. The pilots on this list knew how to fly helicopters but lacked experience flying gunships. The general approach to training new gunship pilots was to put them in the copilot's seat, give them a practice firing run, and send them out on missions to gain experience. I got checked out on all the weapons systems by flying missions with each pilot on a rotating basis. This allowed me to accelerate the development of my gunship and flying skills and helped me get to know the men in my platoon quickly. Chief Warrant Officer Howard Bennett and Warrant Officers Warren George and Larry Mobley were the pilots I remember flying with on most missions. Captain Glenn Weber and First Lieutenants John Bearrie and Fred Miller were my team leaders during this period.

Although many warrant officers were capable leaders, flying was what they'd trained for and flying was their job. I didn't allow them to command a section. That position was occupied by a commissioned officer, a lieutenant or captain, whose duty it was to lead first and fly second. To my way of thinking, this combination made for a solid team that paired proficient and aggressive pilots with officers whose job it was to take the fight to the enemy.

Some warrant officers who displayed exceptional leadership skills were granted direct commissions during the war, but most didn't want anything to do with being a commissioned officer.

Then First Lieutenant John Bearrie recalls his first impressions of Doc as the Bandit platoon leader.

"I arrived in Vietnam in October of '65 and was assigned to the Bandits right away. I'd been flying guns for a month when Captain Bahnsen took over the platoon. From day one, I noticed a certain Patton wanna-be flamboyant flair in Doc. Some of us found this resemblance amusing.

"Doc wore tanker boots that have long leather straps that wrap and buckle around their uppers. Every now and then you'd see an armor officer walking around in a pair of these nonstandard issue boots, but Doc was the only person I ever saw wearing a pair of them in an aviation unit. Those boots really made him stand out, so much so that my good friend and fellow pilot, Lieutenant Fred Miller, came up with 'Big Boots' as a nickname for Doc. We later shortened it to just 'Boots,' but never called him by either handle to his face. He knew about our nicknames for him. I suspect he didn't mind the attention.

"As with Patton, Doc's flamboyancy was not pretense but personality. Doc was a hard-charger who knew how to get things done when no one else could. You can't really fault someone for being true to self, and it's hard to criticize exceptional achievers.

"Doc was as courageous a fighter as I ever knew in Vietnam. He initially flew helicopters like he was driving a tank, too abrupt for a helicopter's controls. I could forgive him for that, because every pilot flies that way until he learns better. He also violated enough of the cardinal rules for gunships to make us nervous about getting killed or shot up needlessly when flying with him. But I never second-guessed Doc and always followed his lead.

"I didn't know how Doc would make out as our platoon leader. The Bandits were a tight bunch of terrific gunship crews before he took over. It's hard to improve something like that. But I have to say that he accomplished what I thought was improbable, because under his leadership we became a tighter, tougher, more aggressive, and more effective fighting unit."

Then Captain Ted Jambon recounts his arrival at the 118th and Doc's passion to remain leading the Bandits in battle.

"I arrived in November of 1965. The unit was on a mission somewhere to the north and would return in a few days. Waiting its return, I set up my room in Thunderbird Villa, and then spent most of my time hanging out in the bar.

"When the unit returned, Major Seliskar informed me that since I had operations experience, I was to be the next operations officer. I would take over in two weeks when the present ops officer was rotated. I was also informed that the Bandit platoon leader, Captain John "Doc"

Bahnsen, was senior to me. He was in line to become the ops officer, but he preferred to remain the Bandit platoon leader. Doc and I met and agreed that rank was not going to be a factor between us; he would follow my orders when we were on missions. I soon learned that rank was of less importance than ability in the One-Eighteenth."

Doc resumes.

Although we were at war and doing a fair amount of killing, the 118th was very involved in civic action that did tremendous good for the Vietnamese people. In fact, all U.S. battalion and higher commands had a civil affairs staff officer responsible for overseeing and coordinating civic action. Some projects were a one-time affair, others were carried on throughout the war.

Ted Jambon remembers his first encounter with civic action.

"When I arrived in the unit, one of Major Seliskar's first questions was, 'Do you speak French?'

"When I said I did, he had me get into his jeep and we drove directly to Bien Hoa's Catholic orphanage. En route, he told me that no one at the orphanage spoke English, only French and Vietnamese.

"The orphanage was run by Sister Louise, a Frenchwoman. When I introduced myself to her in French, she broke out in tears, repeating several times, 'God, you've answered my prayers; you finally sent me someone who speaks French.'

"Major Seliskar wanted to know what it was Sister Louise had been trying to ask for but no one could understand because of the language barrier. What she wanted was penicillin for babies born with syphilis who'd been left at the orphanage door by their prostitute mothers.

"So informed, we left and soon returned with Captain Joe Altamonte, our flight surgeon, who brought along penicillin and other medical supplies that he used to treat the children."

Doc resumes speaking about civic action.

The men and women of the U.S. armed forces are some of the most caring, giving, and compassionate people who can be found anywhere. Wherever our armed forces have fought, they have also freely and openly shown their compassion to the native people.

Civic action projects in Vietnam numbered in the thousands, from the beginning to the bitter end of the war. I don't know how or when these projects began, and I don't care. All that matters to me is that we were there to do some good for the Vietnamese people—some of that good was carried out on the battlefield and some of it was accomplished by civic action. I might add that a considerable amount of the money and goods that went into these various projects was donated by members of our armed forces and their families back home.

Whenever we captured food or material that could be put to good use through civic action, we did just that: we took from Charlie and gave to the poor and needy in our AO. One day, twenty-two bags of rice captured during a search and destroy mission north of Phu Loi were donated to the Bien Hoa Orphanage. There were many more days like that one.

We always pitched in whatever we could spare from our own stores to help the local people, especially orphans.

Donations made by the Thunderbirds to the Bien Hoa Orphanage for one week alone included two cases of jam, twelve pounds of sugar, a hundred pounds of peanuts, six hundred pounds of white rice, two hundred pounds of powdered milk, a case of bath soap, a dozen wash cloths, fifteen tooth brushes and tooth paste packs, six dozen diapers, assorted children's clothes, ten pounds of salt, and two cases of candies. Medical supplies and cleaning products donated that same week included a case of chlorine bleach, a case of insect spray, a case of antibiotic eye ointment, and two boxes of assorted vitamins.

Another week's donations included brown sugar, powdered soup, assorted jams, canned vanilla pudding, raisins, corn beef, canned beef, peanut butter, egg noodles, white rice, powdered milk, boxes of clothing, and assorted toys.

When we had solid intelligence that the Vietcong was about to assail a village, we used our lift ships to evacuate civilians to a safe place. When lift ships weren't available, we used our gunships to evacuate civilians in need of immediate medical attention. We undertook these missions regardless of the fact that some of them required us to fly into hostile areas where our helicopters came under enemy ground fire.

Doctor Altamonte treated children at several area orphanages and made a weekly visit to the leper colony at Tan Uyen, where he treated patients for leprosy as well as other ailments. Another solider in our company heavily involved with civic action was Specialist Amisano, who held conversational English classes for the residents of Cong Ly Street as well as for members of the Bien Hoa National Police.

Besides these civic action projects, the Thunderbirds were involved with numerous others. I can't remember any soldier who hesitated to participate.

✳ Chapter 5 ✳

Late November 1965—Thunderbird Lounge

I had four small kids and a faithful wife waiting for me in Georgia. Before leaving the states, I swore to myself that I'd never become involved with a native woman.

I broke that vow shortly after arriving in Vietnam.

Thach Thi Hung, aka "The Dragon Lady of Bien Hoa," stood about five feet, eight or nine inches, tall for a Vietnamese woman. She was striking in appearance, especially in the traditional Vietnamese *ao dai*— a long slit tunic worn over loose-fitting pants.

I met Hung in the Thunderbird Lounge one Saturday night shortly after taking command of the Bandits. We were having a company party that night; there was lots to eat and drink and juke box music for dancing. I was introduced to her and asked her to dance. She liked the way I slow danced and told me so after a few minutes on the floor. Hung was a bona fide charmer and I liked the way *she* slow danced, too much for my own good.

Although she'd arrived with Warrant Officer Larry Mobley, Hung asked me to take her home that evening. As the party was winding down, she hailed a Lambretta cab and away we went through the back streets of Bien Hoa to her home.

Hung had a very nice place. She had done well in the bar business of Bien Hoa, owning or partially owning several of them.

A maid and cook were waiting for her when we arrived. Hung offered me an omelet, fresh fruit, good French wine, and some freshly baked French bread served up by her maid and cook.

After we ate, she changed into a long flowing silk robe and let her hair down. I got to know this enchanting woman extremely well over the next few months.

Hung was only twenty-five years old, but wise beyond her years. I told her up front that I was married and had four kids and that I wouldn't give up my family for her or any other woman—a fact incongruous with my behavior at the time, but no less the truth. Hung didn't mind. She thought I was cute, a lot of fun, and a good dancer, and she had a *thing* for pilots.

✳ Chapter 6 ✳

Major Orlie J. "Jim" Underwood, a senior major and longtime fixed and rotary wing pilot, assumed command of the Thunderbirds during a change of command ceremony that also duly recognized Major Jack Seliskar for his leadership and selfless service while commanding the 118th.

From the moment I met him, Underwood impressed me as someone who I was going to like working for. I liked Seliskar and got along with him very well, even when he had to become involved with a run-in I had with another one of his officers.

The company maintenance officer, a captain, was a self-important transportation corps officer. He controlled the maintenance of our helicopters and we had to deal with him, like it or not.

He made the mistake of coming over to my room one evening to chastise me for my lack of interest in the upkeep of my helicopters. I lost my temper and beat the crap out of him. Like an elementary school kid tattling to the school principal, he reported me to the company commander.

After hearing my side of the story, Seliskar gave me a good ass chewing, and that was the last I ever heard about the incident.

Our maintenance officer gave me wide distance from then on and never said a damn thing to me except in the line of duty. He did let it be known around the company that he thought I was a little crazy, which neither bothered me nor gave anyone reason for concern.

This particular captain was not the first support puke to cause my back to get up and he would not be the last in my career. I really did not care if certain people wanted to be combat service or combat service support careerists in our Army, but they should never take the killers of our trade lightly or chastise them for their priorities.

✶ Chapter 7 ✶

Christmas 1965—Bien Hoa Air Base

Spending Christmas away from your family makes for feelings of long-
ing and loneliness that are hard to imagine. The holidays are especially
lonesome when you're a soldier fighting a war halfway around the
world. To me, "Joy to the World" would have been a communist defeat
in Vietnam and a safe return home for all Americans involved in the
fight. But that was not to be. I wrote a special Christmas letter to Pat
and the kids that I hoped would be an uplifting message for them.

Between ongoing missions, I attended Bob Hope's USO show at Bien
Hoa Air Base. Hope was a great American and a lifelong friend to the
men and women of our armed forces. Along with a talented troupe of
entertainers, Hope made us feel good about what we were doing despite
the mounting antiwar protests back home.

✶ Chapter 8 ✶

Flying gunships brought me close to the ground action. I could see people aiming and shooting at me. That made the hackles on my neck stand up and generally pissed me off. But the *thunk, thunk, thunk* of bullets hitting my helicopter never caused me to lose sleep or sweat being killed.

My first enemy kills were black pajama–clad VC running down a rice paddy dike. Initially, I really felt sorry for them as we cut them down, but I got over this feeling quickly and had no problems with the killing part of my profession. Even when I saw bloody and torn up enemy bodies close at hand, my feelings for them remained cold and distant. I had great sympathy for enemy wounded and made every effort to treat them with compassion. But my remorse was then, and always will be, for U.S. casualties.

Early in the morning, Jack Waters and I met Ted Jambon in the operations shack, where he assigned us a scheduled extraction of long-range reconnaissance patrol (LRRP) teams operating in the jungle north of Chon Thanh. Jambon briefed us on the situation as he knew it and gave us the ground control frequency.

For command and control purposes, Waters was the flight leader. I was the gunship team leader in support of his flight of three lift ships. An officer from the LRRP unit was the mission commander. He was to fly in Waters's helicopter. Waters gave me the start helicopter time, the various radio frequencies for the mission, and other needed information. I returned to the Bandit platoon area, designated the crews to fly, and briefed them on the mission. All routine.

We started on time and followed the lift ships, trailing about five hundred meters to their rear, and flew toward Chon Thanh at an altitude of twelve to fifteen hundred feet—all standard operating procedure (SOP).

The extraction site was typical jungle interspersed with small fields of tall elephant grass. Elephant grass grows in dense clumps up to ten feet tall. Its yellowish or purple stems are coarse and hairy and about an inch thick close to their base. Its two to three foot long leaves have razor-sharp edges and pointed ends that are about an inch wide. Vietnamese farmers use elephant grass as fodder for their cattle. Patches of it are home to all kinds of birds and critters, including snakes. Fields of elephant grass are all but impenetrable to foot traffic, which makes them tough trodding for infantrymen.

As we approached the extraction site, Waters radioed the LRRPs on the control frequency but got no response. He repeated his call until a radio telephone operator (RTO) returned it. Whispering, the RTO said the LRRPs were in imminent contact with a sizeable Vietcong force. As he was talking, my team started our descent to cover Waters's helicopter, one gunship on either side of his aircraft, about six hundred feet to the rear. We were looking for the LRRPs, but couldn't spot them.

There wasn't a LZ in the pickup area with enough room for more than one helicopter at a time. That meant we weren't going to be able to get the LRRPs out in a hurry. The enemy presence made the extraction dangerous. Regardless of time and danger factors, it was decided to make the pickup one helicopter at a time.

Waters called the LRRPs and told them to pop smoke to mark their location. The first LRRP team popped smoke. Waters spotted it and called the color. The LRRPs rogered color and Waters started his approach toward the LZ.

I thought at the time that Waters's approach was too long and slow, making his aircraft an attractive target to any .51 caliber in the area.

Sure enough, just as Waters started his descent, all hell broke loose! I could see green tracers from a .51 caliber racing up at him and heard the clearly identifiable "popping corn" sound of intense AK-47 fire directed his way. I saw his door gunner kick out a red smoke grenade and begin firing in the direction of the green tracers, just as Waters aborted his approach, turned away from the enemy fire, and started a hasty climb back to a safer altitude—twelve hundred feet or so.

My gunship team went to work without delay.

The Vietcong positions were well concealed. We couldn't see enemy soldiers, but their highly visible green tracer rounds divulged their position. We worked that position over with rockets, grenades, and machine guns on the first pass. The green tracers shifted toward my gunship before we banked for a second firing pass.

The LRRPs saw VC moving to get into a better position to shoot. They radioed and told us where to adjust our fire.

Making a second firing pass at treetop level, we spotted the LRRPs, radioed their location to Waters, and continued to hose down the entrenched enemy positions while taking fire and dropping more red smoke on their position. By the time we made a third firing pass, the .51-caliber green tracer rounds ceased and the AK-47 fire eased up. No doubt, we took out the .51 caliber and killed several enemy armed with AKs.

Orbiting high over the extraction site, Waters conferred with the mission commander onboard his aircraft and the LRRP ground team leader. They assessed the situation safe enough to make another attempt at a pickup.

Waters lined up again and started his approach on the LZ from a different direction. The LRRP team popped smoke. Waters called color and then made a much steeper, faster approach to the LZ. My gunship team tracked his helicopter and placed more flex-gun fire on enemy positions. We could hear the pop of enemy rounds being fired in our direction. We took a few AK-47 hits; none caused serious damage to our aircraft.

Waters completed the first pickup and made a hasty low-level take-off. As soon as he cleared, a second lift ship flew in to pick up the second LRRP team, making a steep and fast approach to the LZ. A third lift ship came in the same way for the third extraction, and, after dropping off his first load, Waters returned to make the fourth pickup.

We extracted four LRRP teams that day. Only the first pickup involved enemy fire. We may have killed the entire enemy force. There's no way to know because we didn't conduct a ground sweep after the contact.

I soon learned that extractions like this one were routine duty for the Thunderbirds and that most of their heroism in flight went unrecognized. That didn't bother anybody, especially Bandit aircrews. The

Thunderbirds were warriors and warriors aren't inspired by the prospect of awards and decorations. Warriors are inspired by the opportunity to inflict maximum harm on the enemy with the intent to live to fight another day.

All the same, based on the LRRP commander's recommendation, my gunship team was awarded the Air Medal with Valor device for heroism during aerial flight. This was my first medal for valor.

✳ Chapter 9 ✳

17 January 1966—Thunderbird Villa, Cong Ly Street, Bien Hoa

When I arrived in-country, there was little true antiaircraft fire in the III CTZ, largely because the Vietcong didn't know how to properly aim at moving targets. As such, they shot at our helicopters with AK-47s that fired 7.62x 39mm ammo, which had a relatively small ball. And, because the Vietcong usually hit our aircraft in nonvital areas of the tail section, if at all, our helicopters could take a lot of AK-47 hits and still keep going. However, a single AK-47 round to a fuel pump, hydraulic line, or another vital part could quickly disable a helicopter. As the war progressed, the enemy became much more effective at bringing down our helicopters with AK-47 fire.

The enemy was also equipped with ChiCom .51-caliber heavy machine guns. Its projectile weight is a bit heavier, its case length is over one inch longer, and its case diameter is a fraction of an inch wider, but this weapon's ballistic performance is virtually identical to that of a .50 caliber. Besides standard 12.7 × 108mm ball ammo, the .51 caliber shot armor-piercing and incendiary rounds. Armor-piercing rounds can shred a helicopter's vital parts, and incendiary rounds set fire to anything that is flammable. The .51 caliber also used a 4:1 ratio of ball-to-green tracer rounds. Its tracers looked like blazing baseballs when they came streaming up at you. Charlie was pretty good at using tracer trajectory to adjust heavy machine gun fire at slow-moving, low-flying aircraft. All things considered, being shot at by one of these weapons placed you in harm's way and raised your fear factor immediately.

Whether the enemy was shooting at you with AK-47s or .51 calibers, flying helicopters *was* dangerous duty and *every* little lesson learned contained information that could prove vital to your survival even on routine missions.

The early leaders of the 118th understood the value of such information and started putting together a mimeographed field guide based on mission debriefings that articulated most of the do's and don'ts for gunship operations. Normally called "Banditisms" or "The Cardinal Rules," this guide was required reading for all pilots new to the 118th. I'd seen a copy of this work in progress during my teaching stint at Fort Knox, and it all made sense.

After the LRRP extraction mission, Jack Waters and I met our pilots and copilots at Thunderbird Lounge to discuss what could be learned from it.

We talked about the need for direct low-level flights to pickup points. There would be no milling around in the sky above a designated pickup area trying to spot the ground teams, because doing so was asking for trouble.

We also talked about the use of colored smoke during extractions. The enemy often monitored our radio frequencies and would pop the same color of smoke he heard us call when trying to identify friendly ground forces or LZs. This deceptive tactic created both confusion and misdirection that lured some of our helicopters into traps, many of them getting badly shot up in the process.

Word spread quickly to be very cautious anytime you spotted multiples of the same colored smoke pluming skyward from well-concealed positions bordering a LZ. Calling for a second color of smoke was one way to deal with this VC trick. Ground teams later used homing radio signals to guide us to their location. This was a much improved technique, but even then, extractions were dangerous.

Having a few drinks while talking about what we learned from our missions was also a good way for helicopter crews to get to know one another personally.

✴ Chapter 10 ✴

Major Underwood called me to his office to inform me that my platoon was being attached to the Marine Corps in support of their lift ship operations. I wasn't ever told exactly why we were chosen for this mission. Underwood just put it to me in a way that made it sound like we were selected based on our superb reputation as a solid gunship platoon in the 145th Combat Aviation Battalion. After getting this mission, I went to the battalion TOC for a more thorough briefing.

I reported to the battalion S-3, Major Larry Baughman, an old friend from our days in the 3rd Infantry Division. This mission came down on such short notice that he gave me verbal TDY orders for it.

Baughman told me I was to take all my crews with as much equipment as we could load onto our helicopters for at least thirty days with the Marine Aircraft Group 36, 1st Marine Aircraft Wing (MAG 36). This outfit was working out of Ky Ha just south of Da Nang. MAG 36's aviation units had been conducting almost continuous missions in recent weeks and all twelve UH-LEs in its gunship squadron, VMO-6, had been shot down or disabled. The Bandits were to fill in until VMO-6 could get its aircraft repaired or replaced. On arrival at Ky Ha, I was to report to Colonel William G. Johnson of the U.S. Marine Corps. Our primary maintenance support was to be provided by an Army unit at Chu Lai. Our backup maintenance support was to be provided by the Marines.

Operating out of Bien Hoa, we supported ARVN and U.S. Army operations, and our gunship tactics dovetailed with tactics used by other friendly aircraft units in our area. Flying with the Marines, whose tactics varied with ours, would take some adjustment.

The Vietcong was the main enemy in the III CTZ at the time. Operation Double Eagle would be our first experience fighting the People's Army of Vietnam (PAVN; the regular military forces of the Democratic Republic of Vietnam, more commonly called the NVA).

The VC usually wore black pajamas and used guerilla tactics. The NVA wore distinctive green or tan uniforms and pith helmets and employed tactics taught to them by their Soviet advisers.

We knew supporting the Marines in their fight against the NVA would be different from what we were used to, but the short prep time didn't afford us time to talk about it.

A total of eleven officers and fifteen enlisted men would make the trip. One of our helicopters was down and couldn't be repaired quickly enough to fly in this operation.

✶ Chapter 11 ✶

28 January 1966—near Thach Tru, I CTZ

I would have liked to have witnessed the largest amphibious assault of the Vietnam War, but I was at Bien Hoa helping my platoon make its final preparations for TDY with MAG 36.

Here's what I missed seeing:

The Navy and Marines rehearsed the amphibious landing phase of Operation Double Eagle in the Philippines during daylight hours, under clear skies, and on calm seas. Far less favorable weather greeted the U.S. Navy 7th Fleet's Task Group 76.6 when the real deal initiated off the coast of Vietnam during predawn hours, under poor visibility, and on rough seas.

After one cruiser and a destroyer prepped the beach with naval gunfire, four battalion landing teams consisting of some five thousand Marines and their supplies were put ashore. Despite the bad weather and operating under blackout conditions, both the Navy and the Marines performed this incredibly large amphibious assault exceptionally well and with striking efficiency, signaling the first day of Operation Double Eagle, a large-scale maneuver designed to thwart increasing NVA activity that was making its way southward across the DMZ.

✶ Chapter 12 ✶

Former Bandit pilot Larry Mobley recounts his thoughts about supporting MAG 36.

"I flew to Ky Ha with Captain Bahnsen in Bandit Three, the aircraft with the number three painted on its tail boom. It was one of our two hogs. We didn't talk much, took turns flying, and got a bird's-eye tour of the coastline

"Before joining the Army to fly helicopters in Vietnam, I served an enlisted tour in the Marines pulling guard duty at the U.S. embassy in Burma. I was excited to have the opportunity to fly gun support for the Corps. It was going to be a homecoming of sorts for me. I knew how the Marines functioned and understood their pride in and loyalty to the Corps. I was pleased to have the opportunity to fight alongside them, if only for a brief time."

Doc begins.

Day was just breaking when we lifted off from Thunderbird Pad and began the long, almost seven-hour flight up South Vietnam's coastline. The trip was uneventful. We flew over vast stretches of sand spotted by irrigated rice paddies, made two fuel stops, and landed at Ky Ha—a coastal salt farming area covered by drifting sand dunes set on a long narrow beach.

Colonel Johnson was relieved we'd arrived. He quickly briefed me on the general situation, then turned me over to Major Bob Purcell,

VMO-6's operations officer, who would serve as our primary point of contact.

From the moment we landed, the Marines treated us faultlessly. They fed us well, put us up in GP-medium tents, and extended the use of their field showers and all other facilities.

We'd just started to settle in when Purcell sent word that he needed us ASAP. However, as we'd already flown for a long time that morning, neither we nor our gunships were ready for immediate duty. We spent the rest of the afternoon stowing our gear and readying our aircraft and weapons systems for combat operations, which began the next day.

On 30 January, it was still dark when we ate a hot breakfast of powdered eggs, bacon, toast, and home-fried potatoes with our Marine hosts. After breakfast, I split my helicopters into two fire teams: a light team consisting of two aircraft and a heavy team with three aircraft.

For the most part, I tasked one gunship team to protect UH-34 Sea Horse lift ships inserting Marines and supplies into LZs near heavy enemy concentrations, and tasked the other with combat assault fire support for Marine ground operations.

My crews flew 4.3 hours the day after we arrived at Ky Ha. That may not seem like much flying time, but it makes for a long day when you factor in refueling, rearming, maintenance, and mission briefing time.

On 31 January, our missions were much the same as the day before. However, we logged over twice the flying time—9.6 hours, making for an incredibly long flying day.

We spent 1 February, our third day at Ky Ha, pulling maintenance on our aircraft and weapons. Operating off the sandy beach was playing hell with our turbine engines and eating up our rotor blades, especially tail rotors.

The barrels on our flex-guns and grenade launchers were not in great shape when we left Bien Hoa, but we couldn't find replacements for them before heading north. Now, after a few more days of shooting, they were just about smooth, with not much rifling left in them. However, the sorry condition of our barrels didn't keep us from shooting. Rounds shot out of a worn barrel disperse more than you want for precision fire, and wobble instead of spiral toward the target. Neither of these conditions ever placed any Marine in danger of taking our gunship fire, and a wobbling round can kill the enemy just as easily as a spiraling one. Regardless, I would have been as happy as a farm boy on a plate of cheese grits if someone found us new M-60C and M-129 barrels.

Joining the Bandits the day before we departed Bien Hoa, Warrant Officer Warren George was an experienced UH-1 pilot but had never flown gunships. The latter reality limited his flying time but neither limited his usefulness nor the important role he played during Double Eagle.

George worked in supply as an enlisted man and impressed me right away as a very resourceful fellow. For these reasons, I had him pull additional duty as our supply officer.

I wish I could have had more latitude with giving George more flying time instead of having him spend so much time scrounging spare parts for our helicopters. From the day he flew his first gunship mission, he was the kind of fighter who'd rather go without supper than turn down a chance to kill the enemy. And, I might add, he liked eating.

✯ Chapter 13 ✯

One of the first problems we had to square away when we arrived at Ky Ha was where to refuel.

The USS *Valley Forge*, aka "*Happy Valley*," was an aircraft carrier officially classified as a Landing Platform Helicopter. This ship steamed up and down the coast about three miles offshore. The Marines often flew out to this carrier for refueling. I asked Colonel Johnson if we could do the same. He told me he would get instructor pilots (IPs) to fly with us for the required takeoff and landings to become carrier qualified. After certification, we could use the *Valley Forge* to refuel. He also provided me with the carrier's tower radio frequency, just in case we needed to medevac casualties to its hospital facilities.

The Marines put us to work too soon for me to take Johnson up on his offer. We initially refueled at the Marine facility on the beach or at the Army facility at Chu Lai. During operations, this arrangement quickly proved too time consuming, and I took the initiative to investigate an alternative.

Within the first few days at Ky Ha, I took a flight of two helicopters out to the *Happy Valley* to watch the landing procedures. We circled the carrier watching Marine helicopters landing and taking off. I was not impressed by the difficulty of it all, especially on the calm seas that day.

I radioed the carrier's tower and told them I had a flight of two for refueling. They cleared me to Spots 7 and 8—big-numbered circles on the deck. We got our spacing and started our approach. As we touched down, we bottomed our collectives and got out for the refueling process. Our blades were still turning when a couple of Navy deck hands came rushing over to our helicopters with a stencil and spray painted a red USN and anchor on top of the white Thunderbird emblazoned on the side of our ships. It was the Navy's way of assimilating us into their flight operations. We all got a kick out of it.

The deck crew told us they would hot refuel—we wouldn't have to shut down our engines—if we were ever in a hurry. Refueled, we mounted up for our first carrier takeoff and did so without incident. As soon as we got back to the platoon, I informed the rest of the crews of our experience and told them to start using the carrier for refueling. From that time on, we routinely refueled on the *Happy Valley* during operations to avoid the congestion we normally encountered at the Marine beach facilities and at Chu Lai.

We found out that the Marine pilots generally stopped long enough to go down to the officer's wardroom for a hot meal. A hot meal was a real treat in this area of the war, so we started partaking of the offerings made available by our Navy friends. My crews really liked eating on the carrier. Meals were served on fine china complete with silverware set on white linen tablecloths, and fresh milk and fruit were always available.

We'd all become very proficient in carrier operations before Colonel Johnson saw me late one afternoon and asked how it was going. I told him, "Fine." We got to talking when he remembered he was going to get us carrier qualified. I told him we had already made over a dozen landings on the *Valley*. He asked if we'd used an IP.

"No, sir. We just did it on our own."

Johnson shook his head in amazement.

"Well, Captain Bahnsen, if you and your pilots want to become completely carrier qualified, you'll need to make some night landings."

"How many?"

"Five."

"Yes, sir. I'll see that we do."

After putting in an already long day, we all flew out to the *Valley* and did five nighttime "touch and goes" without the supervision of an IP.

Carrier qualified, we flew back to the beach and got some much needed sleep.

Our primary assignment on 2 February was fire-team support for a Marine company that was part of a battalion-sized search and destroy operation. Warrant Officer Larry Mobley and I took off in Bandit 3 with Lieutenants John Bearrie and Fred Miller flying their gunship in close trail. Mobley was to teach me some fire team leader tactics while we provided this support; Bearrie was doing the same for Miller, which was the only reason they were flying together. I rarely teamed commissioned officers unless training was involved.

I had a radio frequency, a call sign, and a set of coordinates, which was about all I needed for working with Marine ground units. They were accustomed to having air support and were always easy to work with in combat.

As our two-ship team approached the Marines, I made radio contact with their commander. He wanted to talk and asked me to land on the road alongside his company, which was deployed in tactical formation and moving to its first objective. He halted his company as Mobley sat our helicopter down. Because I didn't anticipate being on the ground long, I told Mobley to keep our rotor blades turning.

With map in hand, I walked over to get a quick briefing from the Marine captain. We had barely introduced ourselves when a radio call reported that his point squad had been ambushed. I asked him where the squad was located. He pointed up the road and said they were maybe a hundred meters from our position. I could hear the small-arms fire as I ran back to my helicopter. Mobley pulled pitch, took us up to a couple hundred feet, leveled off, and flew over the road toward the ambush site. Bearrie made a steep descent and brought his aircraft into formation behind us.

The Marines marked their front with smoke. I could see small-arms fire coming out of nearby trees. Mobley and Bearrie flew our two gunships on a low-level run over the trees, and we riddled the NVA position with flex-gun fire, rockets, and grenades. The Marines were in very close contact. Some of our ordnance hit as close as fifty meters to their front. The Marines kept putting out smoke as we made repeated firing passes over the tree line, taking intense fire on each pass.

It was a hot and heavy, but brief, action. The few NVA who survived our onslaught scurried into the trees, their ambush having been turned against them.

Both helicopters were almost out of ammo and were running low on fuel. I radioed the Marine company commander and asked what else we could do for him before we left to rearm and refuel. He had wounded that needed to be evacuated and asked if we could get them out before the enemy got to them. I told him no problem.

Three wounded Marines were down in a grassy area about a hundred meters from a stream that ran in front of a thicket of trees near a cemetery on the bottom edge of a foothill. NVA taking cover in the thicket of trees were shooting a huge volume of AK-47 and SKS rounds at the half-dozen or so Marines providing cover fire for their wounded.

After a high-level recon, Mobley took our ship in for the pickup, landing just beyond the cemetery, between the wounded and the stream. As we landed, the NVA turned their fire on our ship. Orbiting above us, Bearrie and Miller peppered the thicket of trees with flex-gun fire.

Sitting on the ground in Bandit 3 without flex-guns, Mobley and I had just a few rockets and grenades remaining, but we felt invincible as we sent our crew chief and door gunner to retrieve the wounded Marines. The NVA would have liked to have done us in. Our helicopter took a few AK-47 rounds, but no one got hit.

Our crewmen had the wounded Marines onboard within two minutes. Mobley pulled pitch and headed toward the aid station fifteen kilometers east on the beach at Ky Ha.

John Bearrie picks up the story at this point.

"About two kilometers west of the Marine beach facilities, Doc's helicopter took sniper fire as it flew over a small hamlet. His crew chief and door gunner shot back as Mobley continued flying toward the beach. Miller and I could do no better. We were out of flex-gun ammo, so our crew chief and door gunner laid down as much door-gun fire as they could as we flew over the hamlet.

"We landed, dropped off the wounded, and proceeded to the refueling area where we would also rearm. We didn't lollygag, but we did take a few minutes to wolf down C-rations for lunch. While we were eating, Doc mentioned something about the sniper fire. He didn't see it as any big deal after what we'd been through earlier that morning and was eager to get back to the real action.

"Doc was flying when he and Mobley lifted off. I was just finishing up a tin of apricots, so Fred took the controls and followed after them. Curiously, instead of climbing to the usual fifteen hundred plus feet, Doc took his ship up to about eight hundred feet and set a course for the hamlet.

"As he approached the hamlet, the sniper fire started anew. Doc's crew chief and door gunner blasted back. He cleared the hamlet, made a one-eighty turn, and flew back over the target—a big no-no in the book of Banditisms.

"Of course, Fred followed suit. I took a last bite of apricot, placed the empty tin on the floor beneath me, and put some flex-gun fire on the snipers' location. I remember there being three or four of them, and they stopped shooting before we cleared the hamlet.

"That wasn't good enough for Doc. He wanted to make sure we got 'em.

"Still flying at eight hundred feet, Doc made another one-eighty and overflew the target for a second time—blasphemy according to the book of Banditisms. He should have gone up to at least fifteen hundred feet and called for a firing pass from a different direction, but he didn't. This time, Doc overflew the target without taking fire.

"Once again, Fred followed suit but as we flew over the hamlet, the snipers opened up on us with a heavy volume of AK-47 fire. Most of it missed our helicopter, but a few rounds came up through the floorboard and chin bubble. One round hit the empty apricot tin and sent it whizzing through the cabin. Several more rounds came up through the sheet metal floorboard, sending small bits of shrapnel into both of my calves. The last round blew out the heel of my left boot.

"My whole foot went numb immediately. I looked down. I couldn't see much blood but my heel felt like it had been belted by a baseball bat.

"Just then, a gray smoky mist, created by the floorboard oxidizing from the heat of the penetrating bullets, came rising up from the floor and caused some momentary confusion in the cockpit. Hurting like hell, I fanned the mist with my hands and quickly made out that our instruments were reading okay.

"Miller radioed Doc and told him that we'd taken rounds but our aircraft was okay, that I'd been hit in the foot, and that he was flying me back to the aid station.

"Given that our aircraft was still flying and that I was going to live, Doc radioed our heavy team and had one of its helicopters join up with him en route back to the Marine company we'd been supporting that morning.

"Meanwhile, Fred landed on the aid station's pad. Some Navy corpsmen ran out and carried me into the aid station—a big tent with four or five examination tables. A Navy nurse cut the laces off my boot and pulled it off. The nurse then made a vertical cut in both of my pant legs before raising them up over my knees. A Navy doctor took a look at me. He said my wounds didn't appear to be serious on the surface, but they needed to be X-rayed just to make sure. He told the nurse to apply a compress bandage over my heel, then have me medevaced to the *Valley Forge*.

"While all this was going on, a couple of Navy corpsmen carried in a litter laden with a Marine who'd just stepped on a land mine. I looked over at him. His legs were a mangled mess of bloody tissue and bone fragments. Suddenly, he started screaming, 'Oh, my balls! Oh, my balls!'

"It was a ghastly sight and an agonizing cry of what must have been horrible pain. I really felt ashamed that my piddling wounds might distract medical attention away from him. Fortunately, they didn't.

"Along with the critically wounded Marine and one less seriously wounded, I was loaded on a Marine UH-34 Sea Horse and medevaced to the USS *Valley Forge*. It wasn't far out at sea. We touched down on its deck within five minutes.

My left foot and both calves were X-rayed. After the film was developed, a doctor went over the X-rays with me. The shrapnel hadn't penetrated far and could be picked out easily, no stitches would be required. The AK-47 round grazed my heel without hitting any bones, nothing more than a blood blister about the size of an Eisenhower dollar. If it had struck a fraction closer to my instep, I'd have been in serious trouble. The doctor wrapped up his reading of my X-rays by telling me, 'You're one lucky sonofabitch.'"

"I spent the night on the *Valley Forge*, sleeping between freshly laundered sheets and eating a really good dinner.

"I doubt the seriously wounded Marine lived. The other Marine made it okay."

Doc talks about events taking place while Lieutenant Bearrie was being treated.

I radioed the Marine company commander to let him know I was returning to his AO and was ready to provide whatever support he needed. He told me he'd like us to make a reconnaissance flight over the forward edge of the battle area (FEBA) to see if I could make out the size of the NVA force immediately in front of him. I rogered his request and flew ahead of his position.

We made a high-level recon on our first pass. It looked pretty quiet, but the trees were abundant and their foliage was dense. I decided to make a low-level recon to get a better look—a maneuver reminiscent of my crop dusting days, but far more dangerous: cotton and peanut plants don't shoot at crop dusters.

As we made our low recon, the NVA began shooting at us with everything they had. My crew chief returned fire while my door gunner tossed out a can of red smoke to mark the enemy's position just as we broke left to set up for a firing pass. I was pumped and primed. We supersized an order of grenades and rockets and delivered it to the NVA shooting at us. My wingman came right in behind us, topping off our assault with a full-size serving of flex-gun fire.

I'm sure we killed a bunch of NVA, but we were still taking fire. Now I was really pissed.

I radioed my wingman, "Bandit Three-Four, this is Six. Move up close."

"Roger, Six. I'm right behind you, over."

"Roger, Three-Four. The dumb bastards still want to fight, let's put them down for the count. Follow my lead, out."

This was our third firing pass. We fired all of our remaining ordance, no doubt killing a bunch, but not all, of the NVA concealed in the dense forest below.

I'd been keeping the Marine captain up to speed over my FM radio. I let him know we'd exhausted our ammo and were leaving to rearm and refuel. The enemy force in front of him was at least two companies, maybe a battalion. I told him to call in artillery fire. He rogered my transmission and my fire team headed back to the beach.

Rearmed, refueled, and ready for further action, we returned within the hour. By the time we got back, the Marines had brought in heavy artillery and tactical air strikes that killed most of the remaining NVA force. There were a few stragglers in the immediate vicinity. My fire team got rid of them in no time.

Before heading back to base, we spent another hour circling the area looking for signs of enemy activity and covering the marines while they swept the area.

It'd been a good day for us. We'd taken hits but hadn't lost a ship. Bearrie had been wounded but he was going to be just fine. All totaled, we logged 6.8 hours' flying time during what for the marines was a relentless ten-hour contact with the enemy.

I was glad to hear that Bearrie's wounds wouldn't keep him down long. Violating Banditisms? Well, rules were one thing. Breaking them to get into a position to shoot an enemy shooting at me was another. I had my own rule of engagement for these situations: "Don't turn your cheek in a gunfight." Some dink bastard shot at me, I shot back. It's that simple.

✶ Chapter 14 ✶

3 February 1966—Ky Ha and Quang Tin Province

We were up and at it early. By day's end, we'd logged just over seven hours' flying time in support of Marine lift ship operations and combat assault missions.

Marine lift ships randomly alternated the compass direction for approaching a LZ. One time they would go in from the west, the next from the north, and so forth. You couldn't anticipate the direction, so you had to be alert when their pilots didn't let you know the direction of their approach ahead of time. Although we had to adapt our tactics, support of Marine lift ship operations was generally uneventful.

Fire-support missions were much more eventful. Marines fight up close and personal. We had to make low-level firing passes to keep an eye on them while placing our fire on hostile positions. We also had to maintain tight discipline during firing passes. Getting sloppy could get you killed for the wrong reason.

Former warrant officer Warren George describes one action where too many easy targets resulted in a near disaster.

"I'd never flown a gunship before joining the Bandits, but I was good at flying slicks—a different sort of challenge. Flying slicks was a matter of getting to and from LZs without getting shot up or killed. Flying gunships was a matter of protecting slicks and going after enemy forces threatening or doing harm to our side. This meant you had to be able to fly, shoot, and maneuver through antiaircraft and small-arms fire, avoid other aircraft in the area, stay out of treetops, and remain calm when your bird took hits.

"We hadn't been on Double Eagle long before I got my second gun mission.

"The NVA had been giving the Marines hell all morning, but the Marines couldn't shoot at them because the NVA were holed up in a canal that protected them from direct ground fire.

"A Bandit fire team flew to the contact area to assist the Marines.

"I was flying with MacAffee, another warrant officer. He wouldn't let me touch the controls because I was too new with guns. I understood his thinking and was happy that I'd be able to get some time shooting the flex-guns.

"We started flying back and forth along the canal, shooting NVA on every pass. Our crew chief and door gunner leaned out the sides of our aircraft as far as they could to get in as much shooting as possible on every pass. They were having a great time killing the enemy.

"I don't remember how many firing passes we'd made, but MacAffee was breaking for another when our door gunner fixated on the enemy below, leaned way out, and fired forward, hitting the hydraulic line leading to the flex-gun on the right side of our aircraft.

"Well, now we were in a hell of a mess. Helicopters don't fly too well without hydraulic fluid and ours was pouring out the hole in the line. Fortunately, MacAffee kept his cool. He called the fire team leader and told him our hydraulic line had been hit and we were going back to Ky Ha. If it had been a larger hole, we would have gone down right there, but it wasn't and we didn't, and everything worked out fine. MacAffee wrestled the controls all the way to Ky Ha, where he did a running landing that could have killed us, and probably would have, if he hadn't been such a skilled pilot.

"We had a good maintenance crew. They repaired our bird quickly and we rejoined the fight before the fighting was done for the day."

✷ Chapter 15 ✷

Bearrie spent a night recuperating on the *Valley* before we flew out to pick him up. His foot was too swollen for him to put a boot on, so I gave him a couple of days off. He got a lot of ribbing over his slight wound, but he took it all in good stride and was back flying in no time.

By our fourth or fifth day at Ky Ha, we'd pretty much settled into a ritual of long days filled with a combination of routine lift ship escort duty and thrill ride–style combat assault missions. The enemy put a few holes in our helicopters, but we killed a lot of them in return. For the most part, the NVA were easy targets during this operation. They fought out in the open way too much. That unsound tactic gave our gunships a lopsided advantage.

Warren George talks about providing gunship support for Marine forces on the ground.

"I think we scared the Marines more than we did the enemy at times. We flew lower and faster than Marine UH-1E gunships and placed gunfire much closer than the Marines on the ground were used to getting. The reason behind this, other than tactical differences, was that our aircraft had flexible machine guns and Marine gunships had fixed machine guns. Our gun system allowed the pilot and copilot to manipulate the direction of our machine guns during firing passes; the Marines couldn't do that. They had to line their gunships up with the target before engaging it."

Doc resumes.

The flying conditions during Double Eagle made it necessary for us to spend a lot of time looking after our helicopters and equipment. Warren George found a steady supply of spare rotor blades at the Army's facilities at Da Nang, and that really helped us keep flying.

I didn't spend much time on the flight line during maintenance sessions. Helicopter maintenance is handled by the crew chief and maintenance personnel, who prefer that officers stay out of their hair while they're working. Pilots do pre- and postflight checks on the aircraft, noting anything that requires attention, and pass that information along to the crew chief.

Larry Mobley tells of an incident where Doc grounded him because he refused to fly a helicopter that needed a new tail rotor.

"Helicopters can absorb a lot of damage and still fly home. We often found bullet holes in noncritical places on the airframe and just covered them up with green tape as a temporary measure until maintenance personnel could repair them properly. The same technique was used to cover up bullet holes in rotor blades until they could be replaced. However, based on their size, dents in a rotor blade's leading edge, especially the tail rotor, can take a helicopter off the flight line.

"One evening, after a very long day of fighting, Doc and I inspected our aircraft after shutting down on the beach for the night. I spotted a dent in the leading edge of our tail rotor and pointed it out to Doc, but he didn't pay much attention to it. The next morning he was assigning crews for the day and said he and I would fly Bandit Three.

"I told him, 'No, sir. I'm not going to fly in that aircraft until its tail rotor is replaced.'

"Doc didn't take my refusal kindly.

" 'Okay, Mobley, you're grounded. Miller, you're flying with me in Bandit Three.' "

"Being grounded suited me just fine. That aircraft wasn't safe to fly and I knew it. Forty-five minutes later, the damaged tail rotor created such a severe vibration in the rudder pedals that Doc and Miller had to return.

"I felt vindicated, but I didn't expect Doc to apologize. That wasn't in his makeup. He didn't speak to me for three days, which was his way of letting me know he was pissed. I just hung around the area, caught up on my sleep, and did some reading. It was like a mini-R&R with no place to go.

"On the morning of the fourth day, Doc assigned me to a crew and that was that. I went back to flying and never heard another word about being grounded."

Doc resumes.

VMO-6 got back on its feet sometime around 15 February, a little sooner than anticipated. We were honored to have filled in for them, made some good friends among the Marines and Navy, and did some fierce fighting almost daily.

✭ Chapter 16 ✭

John Bearrie recounts the Bandits' last night at Ky Ha.

"We spent most of the afternoon loading up our gear and pulling maintenance on our aircraft. That evening, the Marines threw a party for us to express their appreciation and say good-bye. There was plenty of food and lots of beer.

"Entertainment for the evening pitted the Army against the Marine Corps in arm wrestling and beer-can-bending contests. Arm wrestling was first up.

"Fred Miller, a former offensive lineman at Oregon State, was a strong guy and our best arm wrestler. I'd seen him arm wrestle numerous times and he'd never lost.

"The Marines set up a table for the event. Fred took a chair facing a muscle-bound Marine officer. Bets were placed and the action ended within seconds after it had started. Fred slammed the Marine's arm to the table in quick order. The Marines weren't going to let us have their money that easily. So they pitted another then another of their toughest against Fred. I remember him winning eight matches in a row.

"Fred was getting tired when the Marines brought in a ringer: an enlisted man who had to duck to get through the door. This guy was huge. His hands hung down to his knees. It took two big books under Fred's elbow for him to elevate to this guy's right hand. Well, as you might expect, Fred lost, which made the Marines very happy.

"The next event was bending beer cans by striking them across the bridge of your nose. Now mind you, in those days beer cans were made of sturdy metal, not out of flexible aluminum like they are today.

"A Marine with a large, protruding snoot sat down at the table, raised a beer can, and brought it down hard across his nose, bending the damn thing virtually in half. We were all amazed by this feat and asked him to do it again, which he did several times. Now it was our turn. I was elected to represent the Army.

"Sitting down at the table, I picked up an empty can and mimicked the Marine. My vision blurred instantly. All I could see was a black void filled with shooting stars. When my vision cleared, I looked at the can. Except for a very small dent, it looked new. So, like a fool, I tried it again. This time I hit my nose so hard that I almost knocked myself cold, but the result was the same as before. The Marines collected their bets and then told us that their guy had been in an aircraft crash that left his nose in bad shape and a doctor implanted a steel plate to fix it. It was all good fun. No fortunes lost or made."

✳ Chapter 17 ✳

17 February 1966—Ky Ha, I CTZ, and Bien Hoa, III CTZ

We got an early start, finished loading up, said our so-longs, and flew back down the coastline to Bien Hoa.

We left Thunderbird Pad with five gunships and returned with five. All of them had bullet holes. Bearrie was wounded, but would fully recover. We got to see another part of Vietnam, became carrier qualified, and experienced another part of the war. The Bandits were good soldiers made better by the experience.

Based on the recommendation of Marine Air Group 36, Headquarters, U.S. Army Vietnam (USARV) awarded medals to all Bandit pilots and air crewmen for gallantry in action on 2 February 1966. Doc Bahnsen received his first Silver Star. Several pilots received the Distinguished Flying Cross. Other crew members received an Air Medal with Valor device. A second recommendation by Marine Air Group 36 resulted in the Bandit platoon receiving a Navy Unit Commendation Medal for heroism during Operation Double Eagle.

✳ Chapter 18 ✳

I had two priorities on returning to Bien Hoa: aircraft and weapons maintenance, and writing home. Our crew chiefs, gunners, and maintenance personnel attended to my first priority; I took immediate responsibility for the second.

I wrote Pat and the kids to let them know I'd made it back to Bien Hoa safely. Being involved with Hung didn't interfere with my writing home on a routine basis, nor did it lessen my love and concern for my family. I never rationalized my affair with Hung then, and I wouldn't now. It happened, and it happened in the face of the fact that all was well with my marriage at the time.

I remember asking Pat about how the kids were doing in school and in general. I didn't tell her often enough, but I tried to thank Pat for being such a great wife and mother, and I always thanked her for the care packages. Besides cookies, gum, and other treats for me, Pat routinely sent something for the children at the Bien Hoa Orphanage—clothes, diapers, what have you. It all went to good use. Pat's letters reported what was going on at home and often contained a note or a drawing from one or more of our children.

The day after we returned from Operation Double Eagle was also met with tragic news. We got word from battalion that Lieutenant Colonel Chuck Honour, the 145th's commanding officer, was killed in a helicopter crash. He had lifted off from Tan Son Nhut Air Base with three medical personnel on board and headed toward Bien Hoa. About ten miles northeast of Saigon, Honour's low-flying aircraft was thought to have come under Vietcong automatic weapons fire just before it hit a high-voltage power line and crashed. All aboard were killed instantly.

I knew Honour but didn't know much about the others flying with him. Captain Albert Merriman Smith Jr., the son of Pulitzer Prize–winning White House correspondent Merriman Smith, was flying as Honour's pilot. Specialists Christopher Lantz and Gary R. Artman were serving as the enlisted crew that day. His three passengers were Captain Thomas William Stasko, a doctor serving in the 51st Field Hospital at Tan Son Nhut Air Base; and nurse Second Lieutenants Carol Ann Drazba and Elizabeth Ann Jones from the 3rd Field Hospital also at Tan Son Nhut. Drazba and Jones were the only nurses killed in action during the war, which also claimed the lives of six other women in uniform.

After all the combat action we'd seen with the Marines without incurring a serious casualty, hearing about fellow soldiers being killed on a routine flight was a shock.

The Bandits started getting requests for missions as soon as we returned to Bien Hoa, but we couldn't respond to them right away. Our helicopters were in dire need of maintenance, and the rifling inside our machine gun and grenade launcher barrels had worn smooth. They needed to be replaced ASAP, but ASAP was a slow process through normal supply channels.

Shortly after we returned to Bien Hoa, Warren George asked my permission to go to Saigon in search of new M-60C and M-129 barrels. Based on what I'd seen him do supply-wise during Double Eagle, I was convinced that if anybody could find replacement barrels, George could.

Warren George tells of his fabulous find.

"I knew from my enlisted days working in supply that the only way to get blood out of a supply turnip was to talk face to face with supply sergeants. There were a lot of supply rooms on Tan Son Nhut Air Base. I was determined to visit all of them, if that's what it took to get some replacement barrels.

"After dropping by several supply rooms without any luck, a supply sergeant told me the same thing I'd been hearing all day, 'Sorry, sir. I can't find a single flex-gun or grenade launcher barrel on my books.'

"I was about to give up hope. I thanked the sergeant for checking and started walking out the door when he said, 'Sir, hold on a sec. Just 'cause I don't have 'em on my books doesn't mean there ain't any.'

"I asked him what he meant by that. He said, 'Come on.' I followed him outside, where he pointed to a stockpile of conex containers.

" 'See that conex . . . the one closest to us? Well, if I remember right, there's some of those barrels you're lookin' fer in it.'

"We walked over to the conex and he opened it. Looking inside, I saw the mother lode! The damn thing was filled to the brim with M-60C and M-129 barrels.

" 'How many can I have?'

" 'All of 'em. Ain't on my property books.'

" 'Sergeant, I'm going back to Bien Hoa to get a deuce and a half. I'll be back tomorrow.'

" 'See you in the mornin', sir. I'll help you load 'em.'

"I got up before dawn the next morning, drove to Saigon, and returned before dark with a deuce-and-a-half full of M-60C and M-129 barrels—enough barrels to resupply our platoon and every other gunship outfit in the battalion with some to spare."

Doc resumes.

Those new barrels improved our shooting accuracy substantially. Good for us, bad for the enemy. Just the way I liked it.

We spent the next two weeks flying routine missions. Several involved shooting and taking fire, but I can't recall any single significant contact during this period.

✶ Chapter 19 ✶

20 February 1966—Thunderbird Pad, Bien Hoa Air Base

Lieutenant Colonel Horst K. Joost replaced Chuck Honour as the 145th's commander. Joost joined the Army in 1937 at the very young age of fifteen and served in every enlisted grade before being commissioned. He knew what soldiering was all about and what soldiers expected of their officers. Joost was also a fixed and rotary wing–qualified pilot involved in the early development of airmobile doctrine and tactics.

Before assuming command of the 145th, Joost was the executive officer of the 173rd Airborne Brigade. The 173rd participated in the first major joint American-ARVN combat operation of the war, introduced long-range reconnaissance patrolling as a warfighting technique, and conducted the first search and destroy missions in War Zone D, a hotbed of Vietcong activity and a stronghold of its support facilities. The 145th Combat Aviation Battalion had been providing the 173rd lift ship and combat assault support since it first arrived in-country. As a result, Joost was well aware of the battalion's capabilities and knew many of its officers.

✫ Chapter 20 ✫

I first met Captain Gerald "Gerry" Cubine in early 1966, when he reported to the 118th Assault Helicopter Company. He was from Savannah, and we knew a lot of the same people from Georgia. Cubine was a fun-loving, aggressive soldier who had a great zest for life.

After a few days of flying slicks, Cubine let it be known that he wanted to fly gunships. He wanted to fight. He wanted to "pull the trigger." And, he had "combat leader" written all over him.

Although Cubine was a junior captain, Underwood quickly discerned him as having the leadership aptitude to replace me as the Bandit platoon commander. To that end, Underwood tasked me to train Cubine on gunship tactics, techniques, and procedures (TTPs) and to get him qualified on all weapons systems.

Cubine had just started flying with me when we were given a mission to escort a flight of lift ships on a routine Special Forces extraction. The pickup point was a hot LZ located in an unsecured area adjacent to suspected enemy locations. The extraction procedure was fast in and out, with my gunship fire team providing overhead cover.

As our formation approached the pickup point, I added collective and pushed forward on the cyclic, gaining enough airspeed to move ahead of the lift ship formation. I then made a high then a low recon over the right flank of the LZ while my wingman did the same over the left flank. The Special Forces teams popped smoke to mark their position, which also provided us a very good visual indication of wind direction and speed. I called color. The Special Forces team leader rogered color and reported enemy forces were definitely in the area.

I assessed the situation as one calling for a gun run before the slicks moved in for the pickup. Taking a read on the wind's direction and velocity based on the marking grenade's smoke trail, I decided to make a downwind approach and radioed my wingman.

"Bandit Three-Five, fire mission. Four pair, break right. I'll take the right side of the smoke, you take the left."

Flying with the wind would give us added ground speed during the attack and increase the range of our rockets. We would have to decrease our speed as we broke in front of the LZ so as not to overfly the enemy positions and to avoid redlining rotor blade RPM during the diving right turn.

As we approached the LZ, my wingman and I cut loose with four pairs of rockets, while our copilots blasted away with flex-guns and our door gunners sprayed the suspected enemy positions with their M-60s.

I broke to the right well away from the target area and was starting to turn and circle when my helicopter came under a fusillade of enemy small-arms and automatic weapons fire. Several rounds hit the door frame and Plexiglas window right beside me. Pieces of Plexiglas tore into my upper right arm and shoulder. I didn't feel any real pain, just enough to know that I'd been hit. More than anything else, getting hit made me mad as hell. I looked back over my shoulder and saw that some of the Plexiglas hit my crew chief, but he was too focused on firing his machine gun to notice.

Cubine was really absorbed in firing the flex-guns. He didn't realize we'd been hit until he stopped shooting and noticed the damage to the door when I leveled the helicopter and started a climb to line up for another firing pass. I told him that I'd been hit—a minor cut in my arm. Trying to pooh-pooh the hits to project a macho image, I said, "It's no big deal. Our crew chief is hit, too. We'll get patched up later. Right now, we've got dinks to kill, and soldiers to extract."

My fire team made a second heavy assault on the enemy position that silenced their fire altogether. This allowed the lift ships to make the pickup without any problem.

When we landed at Thunderbird Pad, I told Cubine to get someone to look after our helicopter. The damaged door needed to be replaced and the holes in the fuselage required some patching. I took our crew chief with me to the dispensary to have our wounds looked after.

Captain Joe Altamonte, our flight surgeon, was on duty. He used forceps to extricate Plexiglas and metal fragments from my upper arm and shoulder. The entry wounds were small enough to close on their own; sutures weren't required. A medic swabbed my lesions with iodine and put a bandage over them. My crew chief's wounds were treated the same way. We both got a tetanus booster on the way out the door. The entire process took less than fifteen minutes.

I hold great admiration for the men and women of our armed forces who have died in combat—whose loved ones received a posthumous Purple Heart in their honor. However, my crew chief and I, and many, many others wounded in war, received the same medal of valor and returned to duty the same day. The extent of the wound has nothing to do with receiving a Purple Heart.

✭ Chapter 21 ✭

5 March 1966—Michelin Rubber Plantation, near Phouc Vinh

I was about to be promoted to major, and majors didn't command aviation platoons at that time in the war. That meant my time as Bandit platoon commander was winding down.

A couple of weeks out, I would become the 118th's operations officer. Until then, Cubine and I flew together routinely. I enjoyed having him fly with me. He was a damn good pilot and not afraid when the bullets flew. He was cool in a crisis. He could laugh and joke under fire, something I always admired in soldiers.

A couple of days after I'd been wounded, Cubine was flying with me as part of a fire team in support of an ARVN infantry unit on a search and destroy mission near Phouc Vinh, an area suspected to be infested by a large Vietcong force. Approximately fifteen kilometers north of Bien Hoa, the terrain in this area was dense jungle bordering the western edge of the foothills that eventually rise eastward into the Central Highlands. Rubber plantations surrounded the small hamlets that were home to farmers and plantation workers.

As we approached the ARVN's position, I radioed its American advisor for a situation report (sitrep). He told me the ARVN were on the move but hadn't made initial enemy contact. I told him we would remain in the area and to call me when he needed us. In the meantime, I decided my fire team should do something useful.

We started making orbits over the edge of the rubber, looking for targets of opportunity. We hadn't been at it long before the American ground adviser to the ARVN unit radioed to warn us that he had called in an air strike on a suspected heavy machine gun emplacement. He advised me that my fire team should orbit farther south to clear a path for the fast movers.

I looked overhead and saw a flight of two Air Force F-100s circling the area to set up for their bombing runs. I radioed my wingman and told him to follow my lead and started to orbit southward.

The first jet went in okay, dropping two five-hundred-pound high-drag bombs on the edge of some very dense jungle. It was just pulling up from its bombing run when the second jet followed the same trajectory and dropped two more. The first jet circled back and followed the same flight path to drop a second load. As it was pulling up, we saw a thick stream of .51-caliber green tracer rounds chasing after it. The second jet was making its final turn to line up for another strike on the target. Its pilot didn't see the tracers following the lead jet, and the enemy stopped firing before he could take notice. Just as the pilot released a second load of five-hundred-pounders and pulled straight up—almost directly over the enemy gun position—a flurry of .51-caliber rounds slammed into his aircraft's fuselage.

Before his aircraft went flying off to a fiery death, the pilot punched out, made about three oscillations in his chute, and hit ground less than a hundred meters from the gun that shot him out of the sky.

I knew what we needed to do.

"Bandit Three-Five, this is Six. Cover me. I'm going to roll in on that gun and fire four pair. Then I'm going to pick up that pilot. Stay low and keep clear of the gun position."

I made a quick descent to treetop level, fired four pairs of rockets, broke right, and circled back. The rockets silenced the .51 cal. I then made a quick landing almost on top of the Air Force pilot, who had landed on a narrow dirt road about fifty meters in front of the jungle.

As our helicopter's skids touched ground, Cubine jumped out and ran to the pilot. I could see at least a couple dozen dinks making their way out of the jungle and coming toward him. Just a few meters after clearing the jungle, they suddenly came to a halt. They just stood there looking at us without firing a single round in our direction. I can only assume that they were totally stunned by our action. That was fine with me, because even with my wingman circling above, we were sorely outmatched at the moment.

Cubine grabbed the pilot by the arm and led him back to our helicopter. I pulled pitch before Cubine could strap himself into the seat, did a one-eighty, and quickly departed the area. We were on the ground less than two minutes. We flew the pilot back to Thunderbird Pad and dropped him off at operations, where arrangements were made to ferry him back to his unit at Tan Son Nhut Air Base.

We returned to the contact area and resumed our combat assault support for the ARVN infantry. They were engaged in a substantial firefight by the time we got back. It didn't take long for us to end it. We pounded Charlie with all we had; it was more than he could take.

Within the week, my crew got an invitation to be the guests of honor at Captain P.V. McCallum's glad-to-be-alive party at the 416th Tactical Fighter Squadron's headquarters at Tan Son Nhut Air Base. Such affairs are an Air Force tradition for pilots who survive a bailout over enemy territory. We got permission from Underwood to attend, but only with the understanding that we would return home the same night. A bad mistake on our part.

We flew down in one of our gunships. McCallum was happy to see us, and the fighter jocks really treated us well. There was lots of good wine to drink, enough steaks for seconds—the best steak I ate in Vietnam—along with backslapping, talk about how it happened, and so forth. We had a ball and got shit-faced drunk.

Neither of us was willing to admit how drunk we were, so Cubine and I mutually agreed that we could fly home. The Air Force guys were surprised as all hell that we were actually going to fly home in our condition. I think they may have had doubts that we would until after they drove us out to our helicopter and watched our takeoff.

I remember it being a clear night with twenty miles or more visibility. After strapping in, I called the tower to get clearance for takeoff. I pulled pitch and went straight up in as steep a climb as I could to about five thousand feet. I was too screwed up to level off any lower. Using the directional compass heading as my guide, I made a dead reckoning approach toward Bien Hoa.

Cubine was no help to me. Our crew chief and door gunner immediately passed out in the rear of the helicopter. I was struggling to stay awake, so I chewed on Cubine, giving him hell for being so drunk.

It's a short flight from Saigon to Bien Hoa when you're sober, but a long, frightening one when you're drunk. I managed to stay on course and got serious as we neared Bien Hoa. After a lot of screwing around with the radio, I was able to tune in on the frequency for Bien Hoa tower and got clearance to land just as we were about dead center of the company's runway. We were way too high for a low-level approach and, given my condition, I was basically afraid to circle around for a second approach.

I dropped collective and began a circle-to-land approach—making tight corkscrew-like turns. The circle-to-land technique is one of the most difficult approaches. It has a lot to do with paying simultaneous attention to the physics of flying and the elements that Mother Nature plays with aircraft. About two hundred feet from touchdown, I added collective to increase the pitch of the rotor blades and pulled back the cyclic to bleed off airspeed, which brought up the helicopter's nose and gave it a cushion of air to land on. Slowly, but surely, and almost straight to the ground, we landed in the biggest space in our company area.

I was in no shape to hover to our revetment and did not try—the smartest decision I made that night. I'd been lucky so far, and I didn't want to take further risks. I shut the engines down as soon as we landed. I don't think the rotor blades had stopped turning before we unassed ourselves from the helicopter and went directly to operations and caught a ride to Thunderbird Villa. I don't know how it got there, but our helicopter was parked in its revetment the next morning.

Air Force pilots were always quick to thank helicopter crews who came to their rescue. The glad-to-be-alive party was world class. Flying drunk was scary and damn stupid on my part. Pure luck saved us.

Retired Lieutenant Colonel Orlie J. "Jim" Underwood recalls his reaction to this incident.

"I heard about Doc and Gerry's dicey trip back from Saigon the next morning. Drinking didn't bother me. Drinking and flying did. However, helicopter pilots risked their lives everyday, so I was willing to cut them some slack when I could, and when no real harm was done.

"I saw the two of them the next morning. Doc acted like nothing happened; Gerry avoided direct eye contact with me. I asked them how they liked the party. Doc raved about it. When he finished telling me his story, I told them they were dumb shits for flying drunk.

"Doc and Gerry were live wires but good men who you could trust to do a tough job. You didn't have to tell them something twice. I saw no need to take further action over this incident."

Doc resumes.

The last ten days of my Bandit command were pretty much like the first ten and all the days in between: routine lift ship escort missions, hot and heavy combat assaults, daily heroism on someone's part, and the best of camaraderie. I went to Vietnam wanting to go to the fight and to fly gunships. Commanding the Bandits enabled me to accomplish both goals.

Doc Bahnsen and Gerry Cubine were later awarded the Air Medal with Valor device for heroism in aerial flight during the rescue of the downed U.S. Air Force pilot.

✷ Chapter 22 ✷

15 March 1966—Thunderbird Pad, Bien Hoa Air Base

Change of command at the platoon level doesn't involve a formal ceremony, so no military rites or rituals took place the morning Gerry Cubine assumed command of the Bandits and I replaced Ted Jambon as the
118th's operations officer.

I was happy to turn my platoon over to Cubine. The Bandits loved
him from day one, and their morale stayed high under his leadership.
Jambon assumed command of the Scorpion platoon from Jack Waters,
whose tour of duty was up. Jambon left things in good shape, so there
were no big problems waiting for me.

Ten days of transition time were built into the schedule for these
leadership changes to become fully operational. I spent some of my time
with the Bandits, and some of it overseeing operations. Jambon flip-
flopped between easing out of operations and acclimating to the Scorpions.

Jim Underwood had commanded the company about four months.
He was a tremendous leader who raised morale with his joie de vivre,
and he genuinely cared about his people. Notwithstanding his marvelous sense of humor, he was no clown or softie. His excellent leadership instincts were complemented by a commanding presence, and he
was tough-minded and emotionally detached when he had to be.

Underwood loved to fly the helicopter. He let me run company formations on air assaults and rarely got on the radio. I was the Thunderbird liaison with all supported units during assault missions, unless
higher headquarters specifically called for Underwood.

Being in the lead helicopter was a big deal for most aviation company commanders, but their formations looked like crap. Underwood flew in the rear of the formation to increase his responsiveness to emerging situations and to keep his formations tight.

To facilitate pilot morale, one of Underwood's first actions as commander of the 118th was to order Thunderbird Lounge to remain open all the time. This order took balls in the environment of the day.

Jim Underwood talks about this controversial order.

"Our company operated twenty-four hours a day, so our pilots and crews worked odd hours. Flying was dangerous and often stressful duty. Our helicopters got shot at much more than they were hit, but every time they flew, our crews risked their lives.

"I felt it was important for our pilots to be able to unwind when they returned from missions. If they wanted a beer or a shot of whiskey, I didn't want them to go into town for it. The same went for food. I didn't want my pilots going to bed hungry. Food was always available to them at the villa.

"I didn't care if my pilots had female company in their rooms. Unless they did something really stupid that I had to do something about, what they did on their own time was their business. All I asked in return was that they be ready and able when it was their turn to fly. God help them if they weren't.

"Neither Chuck Honour nor Horst Joost, who successively commanded the battalion, had a problem with me keeping the Thunderbird Lounge open all the time. If fact, they thought it was a good idea. I implemented that idea, but caught hell over it from a couple of general officers. I couldn't have cared less what those generals thought about how I ran my company. Their asses weren't getting shot at every damn day. Once they had their say, they never mentioned it again."

✴ Chapter 23 ✴

18 March 1966—Long An Province

Ted Jambon recalls the events of this day.

"Although I had officially replaced Jack Waters as the Scorpion platoon leader, he was flying pigs-and-rice missions with me as part of my orientation. At sixteen twenty hours, while flying in the vicinity of Duc Hoa, I received a rapid reaction request to help evacuate ARVN wounded out of the field.

"I rogered the request and was joined en route by two additional Thunderbird lift ships, along with Jim Underwood and Doc Bahnsen in a command and control helicopter. An escort of four Bandit aircraft joined us en route.

"The extraction site was in the boonies near Long An, about thirty kilometers south of Duc Hoa. The action was taking place in a treeless, flat plain covered with tall elephant grass.

"We were a few minutes out when I contacted the American adviser to let him know we were approaching the area and asked him for a sitrep. He said the ARVN troops were dug in and engaged in a fierce firefight with Vietcong. ARVN wounded were being moved to the rear of the contact area.

"While we were talking, I noticed several ARVN H-34 helicopters circling to the west, just out of small-arms range. I asked the adviser why these aircraft hadn't extracted the wounded. He said the ARVN pilots were refusing to land before the fighting was over. Unfortunately, a ceasefire wasn't forthcoming, and the wounded needed immediate evacuation.

"As our flight of four lined up to land in a diamond formation, the Bandits made a gun run to suppress enemy small-arms fire near the LZ, which was very close to the front line of the battle."

Doc begins.

Soldiers of the ARVN's 25th Infantry Division and the Vietcong were dug in and exchanging a huge volume of bullets. The ARVN had suffered numerous casualties and had moved several of their wounded back to the edge of the LZ. Other ARVN wounded remained on the ground where they'd been hit. None of us wanted to wait around for these wounded to be eventually carried to the LZ.

When our flight landed, Underwood stayed with our helicopter. I took our crew chief and door gunner and ran to where the ARVN wounded were scattered in a field of elephant grass. They'd all taken several rounds and were bleeding from head to toe. The combination of their loss of blood and pain had them all bordering on shock.

Our gunships were doing a good job of suppressing the VC's ability to fight, but there was a steady volume of small-arms fire coming toward us. We made several trips back and forth, picking up a wounded soldier and carrying him to one of our helicopters, then going back for another, until we had them all loaded up. It didn't take long because we'd landed close to the action. All totaled, we extracted thirty-one wounded ARVN soldiers.

Ted Jambon continues.

"Wounded onboard, we did a one-eighty and headed toward Cong Hoa Military Hospital, a South Vietnamese facility on the outskirts of Saigon. It was against SOP to take ARVN wounded to American medical facilities, if one of their hospitals was nearby.

"I'd just leveled off when an ARVN officer lying on the floor just behind me started shouting, 'No Cong Hoa! No Cong Hoa! Long Binh! Long Binh!'

"None of us spoke more than a few words of Vietnamese, but I clearly understood what he was saying. I turned to tell him that we were indeed going to Cong Hoa and saw him pointing a revolver at me. 'No Cong Hoa! No Cong Hoa! Long Binh! Long Binh!' he repeated over and over.

"I don't know if he would have actually shot me on approach to Cong Hoa's helipad, but he was convincing enough that I wasn't about to argue. We set course for the U.S. Army's Ninety-third Evacuation Hospital at Long Binh, bypassing Cong Hoa Military Hospital on the way.

"Our arrival pissed off some of the Ninety-third's medicos. A lieutenant colonel came rushing, yelling at me that we'd have to take these wounded ARVN soldiers to one of their own hospitals. The ARVN officer still had his revolver pointing at me. I told the doctor that maybe he ought to tell him. The doctor got the message. The ARVN wounded were taken in and treated immediately.

"It was a little unnerving at the time, but I didn't really blame the ARVN officer for not wanting to be taken to Cong Hoa. It had a reputation for being a butcher shop. Wounds to the limbs were often treated by avoidable amputation."

Doc resumes.

I don't question Jambon's recollection, but I can't recall a single incident when an American doctor, nurse, or medic refused to treat ARVN wounded, or wounded enemy for that matter. Nor do I recall any SOP prohibiting the evacuation of ARVN wounded to our hospitals.

Notwithstanding, Jambon being forced at pistol-point to lead our evacuation flight to Long Binh was anything but an everyday occurrence. Aside from that oddity, the mission itself was a routine extraction. And despite returning to the Birdcage with a few hits in our helicopters, it was no more hazardous than many others.

By the time we dropped these wounded off at the 93rd Evac, their blood was caked all over my uniform and boots. When I got back to the villa, I just took them off and had them burned.

The ARVN regularly honored the leadership of the American aviation units that supported them. For this mission, they awarded the Republic of Vietnam's Cross of Gallantry with Silver Star to Jim Underwood, Jack Waters, Ted Jambon, Jerry Free, Kent Valentino, and me. I hadn't kept track, but I was credited for carrying ten ARVN wounded off the battleground.

⋆ Chapter 24 ⋆

31 March 1966—Thunderbird Pad, Bien Hoa Air Base

I'd been looking forward to this day for a long time. It was the day that I would be promoted from captain to major, passing from company-grade to field-grade rank.

My promotion ceremony took place at the 145th Combat Aviation Battalion's headquarters, where Lieutenant Colonel Horst K. Joost pinned a major's gold oak leaf insignia on my collar. As custom dictated, I bought for the bar later that evening at Thunderbird Lounge. The tab was sizeable, which came as no surprise. When someone else is buying, soldiers drink long and hard.

✴ Chapter 25 ✴

April 1966—Thunderbird Pad, Bien Hoa Air Base

April was my first full month as the 118th's operations officer. It was good duty, and I really enjoyed flying with Jim Underwood. He was absolutely fearless and never flinched under fire. We flew twenty-one days and logged over five hours of air assault time on several of them.

Underwood instilled good all-around discipline. Flying in tight formations soon became a habit. We didn't think about it. We just did it. Taking enemy fire en route to or from a mission didn't deter us. Our door gunners usually just returned fire as we pressed on.

Risk was involved anytime we got in our helicopters. The company went on air assault after air assault involving a continuous string of thrill-filled days that turned daring-do adventure into the ordinary. We were just doing our duty, day in and day out, either inserting or extracting American and ARVN soldiers. Missions that involved action for which you later received a medal were highlights, but you didn't know these were medal-worthy events at the time. Heroic acts often went without official notice.

✶ Chapter 26 ✶

10 May 1966—Thunderbird Pad, Bien Hoa Air Base

Even before I went to the sound of the guns, I liked to write about combat tactics. It was a good way to share what I knew with other soldiers. When I arrived in the 118th, I was handed loose pages containing the do's and don'ts of gunship tactics. These rules were called "Banditisms" in recognition of the early Bandit platoon pilots who wrote them based on what actually worked and didn't work in combat.

After I became the 118th's operations officer, I had the opportunity to publish these rules in one coherent publication. I gathered up the previously printed pieces and parts, got some old gunship hands together to add to them, and put the rules in chapter form. I then had *Tactics and Techniques of the Armed Platoon of the Air Mobile Company* published in booklet form.

None of it was original, but it was all good thinking that made sense—the kind of stuff that could save your ass and other people's lives.

Our mimeograph machine couldn't spit out copies like a newspaper press, but we managed to produce about a hundred copies. It was an instant hit, read by pilots in virtually every gunship outfit in Vietnam.

I was surprised to learn that Apache pilots operating in Afghanistan and Iraq were using it as a guide for their gunship missions nearly forty years later. The Apache is unquestionably a much more capable aircraft than the Huey we flew in the Bandits, but this anecdote goes to prove the durability of fundamentals that can get you through complex situations.

✳ Chapter 27 ✳

22 May 1966—north of Cu Chi

We conducted a series of early morning air assaults for ARVN units in various locations in the north and northwest sectors of the III CTZ. Following these assaults, Underwood and I flew up to the Tay Ninh area, where we met with a brigade commander in the U.S. Army's 25th Infantry Division to coordinate an upcoming air assault in his AO. We didn't stay long, just long enough to get the information we needed, have something to eat, and refuel our aircraft.

A scud layer of low clouds and haze, limiting our visibility to a mile or so, encircled us on liftoff for the ride back to Bien Hoa.

Several miles north of the village of Cu Chi, while flying underneath less than a thousand foot ceiling, we passed over an area of dense forest and thick vegetation. Just before we overflew an open space, we spotted a squad of Vietcong standing around what looked like a tunnel entrance near some bomb craters. Although we were only a couple of miles outside the perimeter to the U.S. Army 25th Infantry Division's headquarters, there hadn't been any other aircraft flying over this area during the past couple of hours. This explains why they were surprised by our sudden appearance. We didn't know what these dinks were up to, but they were too close to the 25th's perimeter for us to do nothing.

Underwood and I always flew in a UH-1D command and control ship armed only with M-60 door guns, but that didn't stop us from going after the enemy on every opportunity, and this was an opportunity.

We started circling the area and told our crew chief and door gunner to cut loose on the enemy with their door-mounted M-60s. Before we completed our first orbit, the VC opened up with their AK-47s and .30-caliber machine guns. Underwood continued our circle, flying through a hailstorm of bullets, while our crew returned fire. Our ship was riddled with bullet holes, but our crew killed one VC soldier and wounded several others.

Because the bad weather forced us to maintain a low altitude, making a second pass was a dumb move on our part. Nevertheless, we had just made the turn for a second run when we came under a heavy volume of fire from scattered positions—there was a lot more than one squad of VC down below. Heartened by the thrill of battle, Underwood continued making a second firing pass, and our crew's M-60 fire reduced the VC's numbers.

We were unaware of it at the time, but this was the location of an entrance to the now-famous Cu Chi tunnels, which housed a small enemy village underground. The extent of this underground complex wasn't known until after the war. Located about thirty kilometers northwest of Saigon, these tunnels provided a major support base from which the Vietcong mounted all kinds of activities throughout the war.

We now know that the Cu Chi tunnels were part of a two-hundred-kilometer underground network of caves that included areas for command and control functions, hospitals, kitchens, briefing rooms, billets, storage, gathering places, and hideouts. Passageways were cramped spaces with just enough room for one person at a time to walk in a crouched position. The upper-soil layer for these tunnels varied in thickness, but most of it was three to four meters thick, sturdy enough to support the weight of tanks and self-propelled howitzers and withstand direct hits from artillery rounds and small bombs. The United States routinely bombed the hell out of this area, but the Vietcong quickly repaired any damage done or dug replacement tunnels.

Despite the heavy volume of fire coming at us from all directions, Underwood continued to circle the area in a dodge-and-weave fashion and bounced in and out of the low-hanging clouds when the bullets got close. Alternating their fire out of both sides of the cabin, our crew was having a hell of a good time, but we were still flying too low for any comfort.

Underwood pulled our helicopter up and flew to the side of the action while I pinpointed the map coordinates of the contact area. I then radioed Cu Chi control with a sitrep and got a frequency for the near-

est artillery unit. Cu Chi control immediately launched a standby gunship team to our area.

I contacted the artillery unit's fire direction center (FDC) and asked
for the howitzer battery's location so I could determine the gun-target
line—essential information when adjusting artillery fire from the air.
Once I determined the gun-target line, Underwood moved our aircraft
parallel to it so I could better observe and adjust incoming artillery
rounds.

I initially called for a white phosphorous round with a time fuse set
for a two-hundred-meter height of burst. I liked this technique for adjusting artillery fire because you can clearly see a white phosphorous
airburst at that height, which allows you to make bold adjustments for
successive rounds.

I adjusted a couple of white phosphorous rounds before I called the
FDC and requested fire for effect, using variable time fuses—an excellent way to kill enemy troops in the open. The artillery battery's six
howitzers fired six successive 105mm high-explosive rounds that detonated at a height of twenty feet over the VC position and the surrounding area.

Before I could assess the damage from the artillery strike, the standby
gunship team leader radioed me for instructions for their aerial assault.
I directed him to make a firing pass at the tunnel entrance and lifted the
artillery fire for the time being. Although we'd just showered the area
with shrapnel and killed a good number of the enemy, a sizable enemy
force met the incoming gunships with a torrential volume of small-arms
fire. Both aircraft took numerous rounds that resulted in critical damage, forcing them to return to Cu Chi for repairs.

Now I was really pissed! I called for a second artillery fire for effect then radioed an Air Force FAC, who'd just arrived on the scene.
The ceiling over the target was marginal for an air strike, but the
depth of the overcast was not that thick. I asked him if it was possible
to bring in a tactical air strike. He rogered "yes" and told me he was
going to bring fast movers down through the scud. Although we were
getting seriously low on fuel, we remained on station to watch the air
strike.

Within a couple of minutes, two fighters came roaring down through
the haze, dropping high-explosive bombs on their first pass and napalm
on their second.

The 25th Infantry's operations officer had been monitoring our little battle and sent an infantry company in APCs to assist. They were still en route when I radioed its commander and turned the fight over to him, letting him know we'd return after refueling.

We hot refueled at Ch Chi and arrived back over the contact area within fifteen minutes.

The infantry had dismounted their APCs and were advancing toward the tunnel entrance on foot. Because of the adverse weather conditions, they were having some difficulty locating it. I radioed the infantry commander and told him we would mark it. Underwood took us in at a very low level, flying just a few feet above the tunnel entrance to ensure accurate placement of our smoke grenade.

By this time in the battle, the Vietcong had figured out that Underwood and I were the ones who'd called in artillery and air strikes on their position, so they were eager to knock our bird out of the sky. They sent a withering hail of light machine gun and small-arms fire at us as we made our approach. Hitting and doing some minor damage to our aircraft, the gunfire forced Underwood to break right before we could drop smoke. We checked the instrument panel, determined our aircraft was in good enough shape to continue the mission, and circled back around for a second go at marking.

Although our door gunners placed a heavy volume of suppressive fire on the tunnel entrance, another withering hail of enemy machine gun and small-arms fire drove us away. A third and a fourth pass yielded the same result. Undaunted, Underwood flew us back a *fifth* time, and this time our crew chief tossed out a can of red smoke that landed within a few feet of the tunnel entrance.

Once they knew where to go, the infantry quickly moved in and killed all the VC trapped outside the tunnel.

We were involved in this enemy contact for an hour and fifteen minutes. It was a chance encounter that really got our adrenaline pumping. Before we stopped our rotor blades for the day, we logged 8.4 hours and made fourteen landings. That's a hell of a lot of combat operations flying time for one day.

We did a lot of drinking and storytelling that evening. Underwood and I both enjoyed a good fight and this was a good one to talk about.

We were credited with fifteen enemy kills. I'm sure the artillery and air strikes killed a hell of a lot more, but they were taken off the battlefield before the infantry swept the area and counted dead enemy bodies. We were also credited with the discovery of the large force massing outside the 25th's perimeter in preparation for a surprise attack on the American base camp at Cu Chi.

Our crew chief and door gunner were both awarded the Air Medal with Valor device for heroism during this engagement. Underwood and I were both awarded the Distinguished Flying Cross.

∗ Chapter 28 ∗

This was my last day of flying in the 118th. I logged four hours of flying time and made fourteen landings during air assault operations—troop insertions and extractions at various locations in the III CTZ.

As a career Army officer, I felt I needed to refine what I knew about leadership by commanding in combat. I wanted to test my mettle under fire. My eight months in the 118th gave me the opportunity to do just that.

I logged over one hundred fifty hours of flight time as the company ops officer. Most of this time was during air assault operations, making as many as sixteen landings on some days. That was a lot of flying, and it gave the enemy plenty of opportunity to shoot one or more of us down. But that didn't happen. No Thunderbird pilot or crewmember was killed during my time as the Bandit platoon leader or as the company ops officer. We knew what we were doing and we were good at it. We were also lucky; very lucky at times.

During the Vietnam War, the Army changed officer assignments frequently. The one-year tour policy for Vietnam caused most of this instability. Nobody stayed anywhere very long. A lot of careers were made or ruined on short duty assignments. As a Command and General Staff College graduate and as a field-grade officer, I was fated to spend some of my time in Vietnam serving in a staff assignment, and I received orders to report to the 12th Combat Aviation Group headquarters at Long Binh. My assignment was as an assistant S-3, one of five in the group. I didn't relish the thought of pulling staff duty in a war zone, but I was fully committed to do my best whenever and wherever duty called. Fortunately for me, because of the close proximity between Bien Hoa and Long Binh, my new assignment didn't require me to give up my room at the Thunderbird Villa.

✶ Chapter 29 ✶

The 1st Cavalry Division was the only division deployed to Vietnam with sufficient organic aircraft to support its missions. All other U.S. Army divisions, separate brigades, and regiments depended on nonorganic aviation assets for their air assault operations. U.S. Army aviation units also supported ARVN and Free World Military Assistance Forces. It wasn't long before there were a lot of U.S. aviation units in-country and these assets required both command and control.

The 1st Aviation Brigade was organized in March 1966 as the senior command headquarters for all nonorganic Army aviation elements in Vietnam. Initially, the brigade consisted of two combat aviation groups: the 12th Group in the III CTZ, and the 17th Group in the II CTZ, along with nine combat aviation battalions and forty-five aviation companies. Later on, the 11th, 160th, 164th, and the 165th Aviation Groups were brought in to command the Army's nonorganic aviation units.

A dual reporting arrangement, in which operational control of the brigade's aviation assets came under the ground commanders they supported, proved to be workable and efficient despite the occasional mishaps and growing pains amid the sweeping change in warfare brought on by airmobility.

The 12th Aviation Group arrived in-country from Fort Benning in August 1965. It was located at Tan Son Nhut Air Base until June 1966, then moved to Long Binh, three miles west of Bien Hoa, and was renamed the 12th Combat Aviation Group. Colonel Raymond P. "Potter" Campbell, a fellow West Pointer, was its commanding officer. He wore two hats in this assignment. He commanded all II Field Force nonorganic Army aviation assets and was the II Field Force aviation officer. The group was made up of six combat aviation battalions with thirteen assault helicopter companies and sixteen additional aviation and support elements. It had about eleven thousand total personnel at its peak staffing level. The operations section had just set up shop at Long Binh when I reported for duty.

My boss was Lieutenant Colonel Bill Heisel, the S-3. His brother, Major Clarence Heisel, one of my bosses at the Armor School, recommended me to him.

Army aviation was bulging with majors in those days. Senior majors, even an occasional junior lieutenant colonel, commanded aviation companies ordinarily commanded by a senior captain or a junior major at most. It was common for majors to report to majors, especially in aviation units. For a number of reasons, reporting to someone of peer rank isn't something you'd choose to do no matter how capable or likable the person. I was a junior major and damn lucky to be reporting to a lieutenant colonel.

Campbell and Heisel were great soldiers who happened to be armor officers; another lucky break for me. We were all experienced tankers and cavalrymen who'd spent time in Germany in the cold war environment that kept you on your toes. We'd all cross-trained as aviators and were serving in an aviation unit. We spoke the same language. We thought alike.

Campbell qualified in helicopters as a lieutenant colonel. Heisel had been an aviator for a while and gained a lot of air cavalry experience patrolling the border between West and East Germany. They both gave mission-type orders and let you do the job, which made it a pleasure for me to work for them.

Campbell spent a lot of time questioning me about my experiences on air assault and gunship missions. He took particular interest in Jim Underwood's technique for leading company air assaults from the rear of the formation. He wanted to know what I thought about it.

I told him that leading from the rear was contrary to my instincts, as some soldiers might take it as cowardice. However, that was not the case with Jim Underwood.

Campbell asked me if I thought he should issue a directive making it mandatory for commanders to fly in the trail ship on company assaults. I told him that was something company commanders should decide for themselves. He took my advice.

Standardized air assault and gunship tactics, techniques, and training were still emerging in those days. Campbell knew how important standardization gunnery training was in tank units and saw the potential benefit standardized gunnery training in aviation units would be.

Campbell thought a gunnery shootout featuring the best gunship crew from each of the group's nine armed helicopter platoons would raise the overall standards of marksmanship in the group. This idea did not sit well with many of his subordinate commanders. They felt it would distract from their primary missions. It wasn't popular with most gunship pilots, either. They felt gunnery training was not needed in a combat area However, Campbell was a jagged-jaw leader with sufficient self-confidence to make unpopular decisions. He asked me to draft a plan for a gunnery competition.

Although many gun crews were proficient, gunship procedures varied widely. Poor fire control appeared to be one of the major problems. Continual problems with malfunctioning guns and nonstandard zeroing of weapons contributed to this predicament.

In armed helicopter combat, hitting and killing the target in the shortest amount of time is critical. The question I had was how to measure these dynamics in a competitive training exercise. Counting holes in ground targets would be too people intensive. Time could be hard to measure. I was thinking about these considerations when a thought occurred to me. An object the size a fifty-five-gallon drum is a very small target for helicopter weapons. Any gun crew trained to hit one consistently would gain much better control of its combat fire; a good thing for friendly troops and a bad predicament for the enemy. It's what I call a win-win situation. I came up with the idea of dropping a fifty-five-gallon drum into water then shooting it until it sunk, eliminating the need to count holes. Barrel sink time could be measured by a stopwatch. And I could run the entire competition with the help of a single flight crew.

I paid a visit to Bandits and talked to them about my plan. They were warm to the idea but had a lot of questions that couldn't be addressed without some trial runs. Gerry Cubine assigned one of his gun crews to me for the day and committed to assigning a crew the next day and for as many days as it took for me to work out the kinks.

I procured a deuce-and-a-half truckload of sealable fifty-five-gallon barrels from the POL supply center and had them delivered to a spot near the Birdcage. This made it convenient for them to be picked up and flown to the test site as needed. For the test site, I decided on a half mile wide point in the Dong Nai River about ten miles north of Bien Hoa. This site was in a free-fire zone where gunships routinely tested their weapons and shot at targets of opportunity when returning to Bien Hoa. There weren't any farms or buildings in that area. The only people you saw out there were playing for the wrong side in the war.

I loaded four barrels in the back of a UH-1B and, with the Bandit gunship in trail, flew out to test my plan for the competition. En route, I radioed the Bandit aircraft commander to discuss the procedure for the first trial run.

His gunship would fly behind my aircraft in normal air assault support distance—fifty meters to my right and two hundred meters to the rear—at an altitude of one thousand feet. My crew chief would push a barrel out the rear cabin door as we approached the middle of the river. I would break left and circle back to observe and time his attack on the target. The gunship could break when the barrel left the door, but was prohibited from overflying the target, going below an absolute altitude of two hundred feet, or flying at less than sixty knots airspeed. He could use all of his aircraft's weapons but was limited to a max of six 2.75-inch rockets. The choice of weapon was left to him and his gun crew. He had a time limit of fifteen minutes to sink the barrel. Time would start when the barrel hit the water and end when it sank.

It took several days of rehearsals to determine how best to conduct the competition. We learned some interesting things in the first three or four trial runs. Rockets and grenades are area fire weapons that can't consistently hit a target as small as a fifty-five-gallon barrel under the conditions specified for this competition. It would be damn near impossible to judge either rocket or grenade gunnery, but we would not rule out the use of those weapons. The flex-quad 7.62mm machine gun was accurate enough for a target of such small size. Closer was better. You had to be within nine hundred meters—tracer burnout range—to get on the target quickly.

After the Bandits helped me work out the competition's bugs, I presented my plan for a Top Gun competition to Heisel, who approved it before we took it to Campbell.

Scoring would be based on time. Each gunship would have four preliminary firing runs. The eight gunships with the lowest combined average would qualify for the finals. The finals would consist of two firing runs. The gun crew with the lowest average barrel sink time would be named the "Top Gun."

Colonel Campbell liked my plan and took Lieutenant Colonel Heisel and me with him to brief Brigadier General George "Phip" Seneff, the 1st Aviation Brigade commander, and Lieutenant General Jonathan O. Seaman, the II Field Force commander, on the whys and wherefores of the competition. They both enthusiastically endorsed the Top Gun competition and gave their approval for a small number of helicopters to train for it each day.

I drafted a message for Colonel Campbell's signature, announcing the date of competition along with the rules and other need-to-know information. The competition was announced in June. The gun crews had until 14 September to practice. I offered to assist any platoon that wanted to practice for the competition. The Bandits were the only platoon that took me up on my offer, which left me with too much time on my hands.

Being slotted in a staff was tough on me. I had to find something to keep myself busy or I'd go nuts. I had to find some way to make myself useful or I'd drive other people nuts. I spent most of my time over the next several months visiting aviation units, talking with commanders and crews about their successes and needs, giving pointers on how to improve combat effectiveness, and reporting back to my boss. My reports were honest and positive. If I saw or heard something that needed to be addressed, I talked it over with the responsible commander and let him handle it from there.

I started the Top Gun competition on 15 September. It took seven days to complete.

A Bandit crew consisting of Chief Warrant Officer Wyburn H. Burroughs, Warrant Officer Marvin W. Schmidt, Specialist Richard Wehr, and Private First Class Payton Crawford took first place, distinguishing themselves as the Top Gun in the group. They sank one of their barrels in two minutes twenty seconds. They also sank one in two minutes forty-four seconds. These were the fastest times in the competition.

Former Bandit pilot Marvin W. Schmidt recounts some of his Top Gun experiences.

"Doc Bahnsen in an unforgettable character who made Top Gun an unforgettable event for me and I suppose everyone else who participated.

"My crew won because we understood the rules of engagement, practiced, adapted our tactics to the competition's parameters, and hoodwinked Doc.

"We had just replaced our UH-1Bs with C-models. The UH-1C was a faster, more powerful helicopter. It had a new rotor hub and wider main rotor blades. It also had dual hydraulic systems to increase survivability. If one system failed, the other would take over, and you could keep flying rather than be forced to land. These and a few other improvements over the B-model made Cs a much improved gun platform, a smoother ride, and snappy to fly.

"The C-model's hydraulic systems put out three thousand psi, about twice that of the B-model. This posed a perplexing problem with flex-gun hydraulic fittings that were engineered for the B-model's psi load. We found this out right after mounting the first flex-gun system on a C-model. The pressure on these fittings caused them to break seal and leak hydraulic fluid. Even with the dual hydraulic system, it made maneuvering the flex-guns unreliable and could have jeopardized our ability to fly.

"I succeeded Warren George as the Bandit armaments officer, so finding a way to stop these fittings from leaking was my responsibility. At least that's how I saw it. I discussed the problem with Specialists Attebury and Kozlowski, a couple of very capable armorers who worked in the Bandit gun shop. They told me not to worry about it; they knew how to prevent the leaks.

"They used clear epoxy to seal the outside of every flex-gun hydraulic fitting—fifteen to twenty of them, maybe more, on each pair—on the four Bandit helicopters armed with quad M-60s. Sure enough, that stopped them from leaking.

"I imagine whoever disconnected those fittings had a hell of a time. But I was long gone before that happened. Knowing we could rely on our flex-gun hydraulic controls gave us confidence during combat operations. It also gave my gun crew a mental edge in the Top Gun competition. We knew the hydraulic arms on our guns would work properly.

"We also came up with a few strategies for the competition. During combat assaults, our gunships flew in fire teams. If you were flying lead, you always had a wingman to protect you. The rules of engagement for Top Gun didn't call for you to fly with a wingman. This meant we could fly in a short teardrop pattern rather than the longer racetracks flown in combat operations. Flying in a teardrop pattern allowed us an advantage: we could make more passes at the target within the time allowed.

"During our practice runs, we figured out that Doc would be observing from a height of one thousand feet and wouldn't be able to estimate the height of our helicopter accurately. Flying a bit lower than the two-hundred-foot minimum specified for the competition would allow us to spot the target easier. We also found out that by making a high-banking turn just before we overflew the barrel, Crawford, our door gunner, could see and shoot at the barrel most of the way through our entire turn.

"Firing rockets at something as small as a fifty-five-gallon barrel with any kind of precision is futile. That being the case, we decided to fire three pairs of rockets at the barrel just as soon as it hit the river. If Burroughs—he fired the rockets—was lucky enough to hit the barrel, terrific! If not, the geyser created by rockets exploding on contact with the river would die down before we were within tracer burnout range of the target.

"Practice taught us that there was very little chance of hitting that small a target at long range. So, just for the competition, we boresighted our flex-guns to converge at about one hundred fifty meters—about half the beaten zone range for combat operations.

"Sinking one of those barrels quickly was a function of how fast and how many holes you could put in it. We decided to shoot a higher number of rounds per minute than normal, and that meant we would expend our basic load of machine gun ammo quickly. Fortunately for us, Crawford was a real pro. He figured out how to link multiple 7.62mm ammo belts together, which extended our firing time and, thereby, increased our odds of sinking the barrel faster than the competition.

"Every trick of the gunship trade was put to test in Top Gun. Some were pretty good. One proved dangerous.

"A door gunner on a competing crew attached his M-60 to a bungee cord. That allowed him to lean out the cabin door, traverse his weapon under his ship, and keep firing as the gunship broke from the target. During one firing pass, this guy's gun had a stoppage—a hangfire. Without realizing what the problem was, he quickly hauled his gun into the cabin to clear it and the hangfire round cooked off, hitting the pilot in one of his big toes. This turned into a hilarious incident only because no one got killed or seriously wounded, and the aircraft was only slightly damaged.

"Doc ran Top Gun in heats, like a track meet. Each gunship flew a sortie then returned to Bien Hoa to reload and wait for its next call out. That is, if your time was good enough to get you into the next heat. We sunk the first barrel on our second pass. I think it was the fastest sink time in the whole competition.

"Our slowest sink time was on our final barrel. On this run, three of our flex-guns shut down. The cumulative vibration of our helicopter during the previous ten to twelve hours loosened some rivets in these guns' receiver group assembly, causing them to become inoperable. This was a common problem with flex-guns because they were mounted on their side, which was not the way they were engineered to operate. But what the hell, we still had one flex-gun and both door guns—more than enough firepower for us to sink the barrel in a respectable time."

Doc resumes.

Watching a demonstration—before trying to do—has long been recognized as key to effective training. In that regard, one of the most valuable aspects of the Top Gun competition was that it afforded participating crews the opportunity to observe other crews' tactics and techniques at close range. The competition also resulted in several important lessons learned, especially ones based on the tactics and techniques used by the winning crew.

The Top Gun crew flew short teardrop courses rather than the long racetrack patterns, and their door gunners fired longer and better. The Top Gun pilots held altitude and airspeed steady during their firing runs to give the gunners the best chance to find and hit the target. Preflight zeroing, boresighting, and weapons checks by the ground crews contributed materially to keeping the Top Gun's weapons firing smoothly. I didn't know about it then, but don't know now how much flying below the two-hundred-foot minimum set for the competition contributed to Schmidt's crew success. But I must say that I admire their initiative in going for nothing less than top honors. My kind of people.

The competition gave Colonel Campbell what he wanted: evidence that aerial gunnery standards in some units were low and needed command emphasis. The competition also convinced him that all nine gun platoons needed routine refresher gunnery training to maintain a high degree of proficiency and to train replacement personnel that were arriving daily. He had me write up the lessons learned from the competition and used them to coach his subordinate commanders.

★ Chapter 30 ★

28 September 1966—Long Binh

I'd just wrapped up Top Gun when it came time for me to have my own flying skills tested. I was heading home soon and needed to take an instrument check ride if I wanted to fly fixed wing aircraft once I arrived back in the states. There was some irony to it. I'd been slotted to fly fixed wing aircraft in Vietnam. And I would, one time, for this reason only.

Major Bob Pulmondium, a good friend from Leavenworth, served in the group standardization section and was my fixed wing instrument flight examiner. He took me up in a U-6 Beaver for an hour and a half. I passed with flying colors and took him to Thunderbird Lounge for a celebratory toast.

★ Chapter 31 ★

1 October 1966—Long Binh

I checked out a UH-1B and flew from unit to unit to visit the superb pilots I had served with during the past year. They'd become my friends; our friendships forged in the heat of battle. Saying good-bye to these brave men wasn't easy. However, leaving Vietnam was not difficult.

I was glad to have had my mettle tested and for the opportunity to lead an armed helicopter platoon in combat. This experience taught me that there is only one way to lead in combat: by personal example. You need to set the proper example day to day. You need to show courage and be calm in the face of fire.

General George S. Patton Jr. taught that self-confidence is the greatest military virtue. If you don't have confidence in yourself, you can't expect soldiers to place their confidence in you. If you don't believe in yourself, you can't lead effectively. Soldiers have to believe in you or they won't follow your lead. Simply put, self-confidence is the keystone for effective leadership in combat. When it's removed, effective leadership collapses faster than a mud hut in a major earthquake.

As a combat leader, you have to instill and maintain discipline and avoid pettiness or worry over things that don't matter. Warfare involves decisions that can save or take lives. There isn't time to tarry when making decisions in the heat of battle. You study the problem the best you can, in the time you've got, and get on with it. Soldiers want to be told what to do and will do it, if they have confidence in you. You've got to give them positive and timely direction, especially when the bullets start flying.

How you treat soldiers in combat is very important. Their lives have value. They have hopes for the future. They have families and friends waiting for them to return home. If you understand this, you'll treat soldiers with respect. When treated with respect, soldiers respond in kind. Mutual respect builds trust. You have to trust other soldiers with your life and be trusted by soldiers who need you to help them survive.

The war was picking up pace as I left. More and more U.S. military units were arriving and our casualties were increasing.

Doc Bahnsen was awarded the highest point rating possible on all three OERs he received during this tour of duty, with the sole exception of being dinged two-tenths of a point for occasional lack of tact while serving in the 12th Combat Aviation Group.

Major Orlie J. Underwood, the 118th's commanding officer, wrote the following about Doc's leadership of the Bandits.

As a combat leader he was called upon daily to lead attacks upon known and suspected enemy bunkers, emplacements and automatic weapons positions. His cool, calm leadership ability was demonstrated on numerous occasions as he led these strikes in the face of fire. He was quick to size up the ground tactical situation, analyze conditions and react with support or recommendations which were truly outstanding. He continually trained his platoon and molded them into one of the finest fighting units in Vietnam. He is responsible for developing armed helicopter tactics which have proven to be the most successful among the armed helicopter platoons in combat.

Orlie J. Underwood wrote these comments about Doc's performance as the 118th's operations officer.

His work was characterized by his thoroughness, dependability, foresight and outstanding effectiveness.... His ability to remain calm and cool when the situation was critical and when the unit was under heavy fire had a stabilizing effect on all air crewmembers.

And Colonel Raymond P. Campbell Jr., the 12th Combat Aviation Group commander, penned these praises.

As an Assistant S-3, Major Bahnsen was, in particular, my project officer for the improvement of armed helicopter gunnery....

Taken in all, this program [Top Gun] has changed the 12th Group helicopter gunnery capability from a marginal into a very positive combat asset. It has significantly reduced the likelihood of our firing into friendly troops as well as increasing our effectiveness in daily battle. And much of this gain is directly due to the imagination, tenacity, and professional understanding of Major Bahnsen. I will fight to have him work for me in future assignments.

Doc resumes talking about leaving Vietnam for the first time.

I received orders assigning me to the Pentagon. This came as no surprise. A tour or two of Pentagon duty is in the cards for most career officers. I was looking forward to it. I was also looking forward to seeing Pat and the kids. It had been a year since we had seen one another.

How you say good-bye in a war zone varies individually. Some guys like to have big parties, others prefer leaving quietly. In Vietnam, virtually everyone got some sort of sendoff, often a party for several people leaving about the same time.

I had mixed emotions in regards to Hung. She found out in June that she was pregnant. I was straight up with her from day one. I did not want a baby with her, and she knew it. I did everything possible to encourage her to have an abortion, all to no avail. She insisted on having our baby.

I never figured out what she was gaining by having our child without me around to help. If this bothered her, she never showed it. She seemed to take my going home to my family well. She even helped me shop for gifts and clothes for them.

I dealt with this messy situation as best I could. I had guilty feelings as I packed. Those feelings stayed with me for a long, long time, even though I did all I could to block them out of my mind.

★ PART 2 ★

✷ Chapter 32 ✷

8 October 1966—Atlanta and East Point, Georgia

Pat picked me up at the Atlanta airport. It was a good homecoming. I was happy to see my kids, and they were excited to see me. Pat had done a good job of raising them during my absence. I knew she would.

I spent all of October and most of November on leave at East Point, spending time with my family and just taking it easy.

In spite of my infidelity, my relationship with Pat was on solid ground when I returned from Vietnam. But the strains of my new assignment, along with my decision to volunteer for a second tour in Vietnam, would shake our marriage apart.

✶ Chapter 33 ✶

Early November 1966—Washington, D.C.

I took a trip to Washington, D.C., to find a place for my family to live.

Leroy Suddath and Charlie Sarkiss, two of my West Point classmates, were stationed at the Pentagon and living in townhouse apartments in Camp Springs, Maryland. I knew living near these close friends would help my family adapt to our new environs quickly, so I rented an apartment in the same complex. I also made plans to carpool with Leroy and Charlie.

✶ Chapter 34 ✶

1 December 1966—The Pentagon, Washington, D.C.

I reported for duty with the Office of the Assistant Chief of Staff for Force Development (ACSFOR). Major General Mike Davison, my regimental commander at West Point, was the deputy ACSFOR at the time. That created a fortunate situation for me. I corresponded with General Davison several times before and during my tour in Vietnam. He was well aware of my assignments and schooling since leaving the academy and knew I wanted to contribute to the war effort. I went to see him the morning I reported for duty.

Davison informed me that I was being detailed as a staff officer in the Operations Branch, Plans and Programs Division, Army Aviation Directorate. My primary responsibility would be to verify the readiness of aviation and air cavalry units deploying to Vietnam. My initial assessments would come from written reports and telephone contact. I would expand these assessments with firsthand information during visits to the units and with Army agencies and major commands outside the Washington area. I was to look at people, equipment, and training to ensure that deploying units were fully staffed with personnel qualified in the right military occupational specialties and that they had their full table of organization and equipment (TO&E) and mission-essential equipment on hand.

My immediate boss would be Lieutenant Colonel Julian D. Farrar, a ground officer and a great guy who depended on the branch's aviators to provide him with aviation expertise. The division chief was Lieutenant Colonel Robert M. Shoemaker, one of the leading movers and shakers in Army aviation.

After helping my family get settled into our new apartment, I got busy with my new assignment.

Duty in the Pentagon was interesting. As a junior major, I carried a lot of important actions—briefings, recommendations, approvals, etc.—around the building and got to know some superb soldiers and most of the key players in our Army at that time. Some were generals, some were senior field grades who later became generals, and some were my peers and juniors. Among others, I met regularly with Lieutenant Colonel Vern Lewis, the deployment readiness officer in the Deputy Chief of Staff for Operations (DCSOPS), to update him on aviation and air cavalry unit progress.

Making connections with the right people gives you a leg up on future opportunities no matter what you do for a living. However, the bonds you form during a military career are particularly strong because they are constantly reinforced by long-term association, by mutual dedication to a common purpose, and by sharing hardships and celebrating successes together. Beyond that, close bonds formed in the military often become relationships that last a lifetime because you come to count on one another like family.

This assignment coincided with the major buildup for the war. I worked ridiculously long hours doing everything possible to get our aviation and air cavalry assets ready to deploy. I normally left home at 0600 and didn't return until 1900 or later. This was six days a week, sometimes seven. There were many days when my schedule didn't mesh with the guys in my carpool. That sometimes left Pat without a car when she really needed it.

I ate breakfast at home but rarely had anything substantial for lunch. I usually ate a cold supper when I got home. Pat always had a plate of whatever she had fixed for her and the kids waiting for me in the fridge.

George Washington University offered evening graduate classes at the Pentagon. I planned on getting a master's degree at some point in my career. I saw this as a good opportunity to start and decided to take classes a couple of nights a week. My veteran's benefits paid 90 percent of the cost of this schooling. I justified taking night classes based on traffic congestion. The traffic going out my way was slow and backed up in the early evening. By the time the classes were over, I could get home in thirty minutes instead of the sixty to ninety it took during normal commute time.

My schedule didn't allow me to see much of Pat or our children. When I did see them, I was usually worn out and couldn't give them the attention they deserved. I never felt good about that situation. I was simply caught up in my career and put it ahead of all else, creating a serious strain on my marriage and family life.

Working at the Pentagon stretched the pocketbooks of uniformed personnel. There wasn't enough military housing in the vicinity to accommodate even a good portion of those of us assigned to the Pentagon, and the cost of living in the area was high. My quarters allowance only covered about one-half of my housing and utilities, and we lived in a small apartment. That meant the walking-around money I would have reaped by living on post in a less expensive part of the country was spent on rent. Fortunately, I was a pilot and my flight pay added approximately another 30 percent to my base pay.

To maintain eligibility for flight pay, you had to fly a minimum of four hours a month, but you had a three-month window. For example, you could fly twelve hours in one month and be good for three months. The annual requirement was eighty total hours with ten hours of night and twelve hours of instrument flying. You also had to pass a written exam and flight physical.

All the pilots in the Aviation Directorate flew out of Davidson Army Airfield at Fort Belvoir, Virginia. I usually flew a T-41 Mescalero, the military version of a Cessna 172. I flew to places like Harrisburg, Pennsylvania, Richmond, Virginia, and other small airports in the area. I would land, have supper at the airport coffee shop, and fly home. Instrument and night flying time were easy to accumulate as I routinely flew cross-county at night.

I occasionally flew a U-6 Beaver on official business, including a couple of trips to Fort Rucker, Alabama. I flew an H-13G Sioux helicopter once. This two-seat general-purpose helicopter saw its first combat action in the Korean War and was being phased out of service. I would have spent more time in helicopters, but they were not available. I also became qualified in the U-8F Seminole (a twin-engine Beech aircraft mostly used for VIP transport) during off-duty hours.

After leaving Vietnam, I maintained contact with Hung through a friend in the 118th. She would take letters to him, and he would put them in an envelope addressed to me at my Pentagon office. My letters to her were sent via that same friend.

About three months after I returned home, I received a copy of my son Minh's birth certificate and several photos of him. There was no father's name on his birth certificate, but I knew he was my son. This created a very difficult dilemma for me. I wanted to do right by Minh, but I did not want to mess up my family life any more than I already had. Plus, fathering a child outside of marriage was not good for your military career, especially if you were married to someone else.

I retained Minh's birth certificate and photos in a sealed envelope to be opened only by my brother, Peter, in the event of my death. I told no one about Minh until many years later. I sent money to Hung for several months—enough to clothe and feed our son—but stopped when she quit writing me. My friend in 118th wrote and told me Hung had a new boyfriend. I never heard from her again.

I met Phyllis "Fif" Shaughnessy when she came diddy bopping through the Pentagon one day to visit pilot friends she'd met while working for the American Red Cross in Vietnam. She was then employed by the International Recreation Association under contract with the State Department and was on her way back to Vietnam to teach recreation in the pacification program. Fif was adventuresome, spirited, happy-go-lucky, and easy for me to like right away. I was looking forward to seeing her when I returned to Vietnam.

✶ Chapter 35 ✶

21 January 1968—Washington, D.C.

The spring and early summer of 1968 were particularly interesting periods during which events occurred that turned the course of the Vietnam War, heavily influenced the civil rights movement, and decided the election of the next president of the United States. These events started with the Tet Offensive that began on the eve of the lunar New Year celebration and lasted until late February.

The NVA's longtime commander, General Vo Nguyen Giap, made plans to time a brutal and bloody major offensive with Tet, hoping to undermine the United States' determination to win the war on the battlefield and hand our country a demoralizing political defeat back home. Tet had always signaled a holiday truce in the war. Hanoi and Saigon both indicated that this year would be no different, which explains why the Tet Offensive came as a major surprise.

The fighting was widespread, photographed at length, and televised ad nauseam. Giap's estimated eighty thousand troops, mainly VC, conducted brutal and bloody attacks in province capitals throughout South Vietnam. Vietcong soldiers broke through the outer wall of the U.S. embassy in Saigon as well, but all ended up getting killed in the process. American bases throughout South Vietnam came under heavy attack. Barbaric attacks were carried out against thousands of innocent civilians, especially in Hue. Giap knew upfront that he would take heavy losses and never counted on winning a military victory. However, he got what he wanted.

News reports gave the impression that the enemy prevailed on the battlefield, but that simply wasn't true. American forces had taken the lead in the war by that time, and they kicked a lot of Vietcong and NVA butt during Tet. In fact, Vietcong loses during Tet seriously diminished what then remained of it as a viable military force.

Tet turned the hearts of many Americans against the war, aligning their sympathies with thousands of students caught up in the antiwar sentiment spreading like wildfire across college campuses. It also served as the opportunity for Giap to move large NVA units farther south than they'd ever been in the war.

Tet took a personal toll on President Lyndon B. Johnson, causing him to give up any hope of winning a military victory. In a televised speech to the nation on 31 March, he announced a partial bombing halt over North Vietnam, a capitulatory course designed to entice the North Vietnamese into going to Paris in May for a peace powwow. He dropped a second shoe by ending his remarks with an unexpected announcement that he would not seek another term in office.

The Civil Rights Act passed in 1964, but it didn't end racism. The Reverend Dr. Martin Luther King Jr. took on the Moses role in leading the way for the United States to become a land of promise for all people. Especially so for African Americans, who had never achieved equal rights in the over one hundred years following Abraham Lincoln's signing of the Emancipation Proclamation that put an end to their forebears' slavery.

King, who was the United States' most respected civil rights leader, was awarded a Nobel Peace Prize in recognition of his efforts to end abject poverty and racial discrimination. He was also a passionate and powerful speaker who stirred up deep emotions in people committed to his cause as well as in people digging in their heels to slow its progress. No doubt, some idiots thought taking King out would put an end to the civil rights movement, and one such idiot shot and killed him while he was standing outside his motel room in Memphis on 4 April.

Martin Luther King's assassination created despair and turmoil that spilled over into rioting, looting, and destruction in several major cities, including Washington, D.C.

More akin to a limited rebellion, the Washington, D.C., riots started shortly after the news of King's death aired over the radio. Law enforcement agencies were woefully unprepared to do much about what took place. The National Guard was even less prepared for riot control duty. Miraculously, only twelve people died while a thousand buildings burned during three days of rioting.

On the second day of all-out chaos, I became one of many officers stationed in the Pentagon to be *volunteered* for riot duty. Somebody came up with the idea that Army officers donned in dress greens bedecked with medals and riding around in jeeps would help restore calm to the city.

I didn't like the idea from the start. But nobody asked my opinion. I went home, changed into my green uniform, and returned to the Pentagon. I spent the rest of the day riding around Washington unarmed with my driver. What a shitty mission that was! All we did was watch looters running up and down the streets pilfering anything they could carry. I did stop and talk to a young man who asked about my medals. I ended up giving him a recruiting pitch.

Restoring calm wasn't much fun and it sure as hell had nothing to do with ending the riots. Being unarmed amid rioters who were packing pissed me off more than anything else. That situation was stupid and irresponsible on the part of whoever came up with the idea for this fool's errand. Mercifully, this was my one and only *combat* day while stationed at the Pentagon.

Johnson's decision not to run for a second elected term opened the door for Democratic Party presidential hopefuls to toss their hat in the ring. Promising to end the war if elected, Robert F. Kennedy, the younger brother to President John F. Kennedy, soon had a lock on being the Democratic Party's candidate but fell to an assassin's bullet shortly after midnight on 5 June in Los Angeles.

RFK's murder was exceptionally unnerving because our country was still recovering from JFK's assassination in Dallas about four-and-a-half years earlier. His death opened the way for Hubert Humphrey to garner the Democratic Party's spot on the ballot. However, Richard M. Nixon defeated Humphrey that November, an unlikely turn of events had RFK not been assassinated.

Ironically, as defining as these turning-point events were in our country's history, not one of them changed what I was doing to help aviation and air cavalry units prepare for deployment to Vietnam.

My mentor from West Point, Lieutenant Colonel George S. Patton, was serving as a division chief in DCSOPS when I arrived at the Pentagon. I routinely corresponded with him after leaving West Point. He was well aware of my assignments, my accomplishments, and my desire to command an armor unit in combat.

I frequently saw and spoke to Patton. He invited me to his home for dinner a number of times. Our dinner conversation was kept to small talk and pleasantries that involved all present. Our private conversations focused on armor and air cavalry warfighting tactics and combat leadership.

I truly enjoyed my friendship with Patton and became a better soldier for it. However, our time together at the Pentagon was cut short when he received orders for Vietnam—his second tour. Patton was on the promotion list to full colonel and had been selected for brigade command, which meant he was going back to Vietnam in a significant assignment.

Retired Colonel John Collins, who became chief, Campaign Planning Group, Commander U.S. Military Assistance Command Vietnam (COMUSMACV) in September 1967 and later served as a senior analyst in the Congressional Research Service, recalls arriving in Vietnam with Patton.

"Lieutenant Colonels George Patton and John Collins arrived aboard the same aircraft at Bien Hoa International Airport in June 1967. When George's left foot hit the tarmac, Deputy COMUSMACV General Creighton Abrams promised him command of the Eleventh Armored Cavalry Regiment [ACR] after six months on USARV's staff. That warped many colonels who hoped to be the Eleventh ACR's top dog, because it was the only armor command in Vietnam.

"Lieutenant General Bruce Palmer, USARV's Deputy Commander (William Westmoreland in absentia retained command of that component), soon pinned daddy's solid silver eagles on George with great fanfare. I pinned mine on by myself in a broom closet in the dead of night."

Doc resumes.

Colonel Leonard D. Holder assumed command of the Blackhorse on 15 March 1968. He died in a tragic helicopter accident six days later. His untimely death upset the command slate when some unknown senior personnel officer in theater assigned Colonel Charles R. Gorder to command the Blackhorse the next day. This action was at odds with General Abrams's plan, and Patton replaced Gorder by Abrams's direction on 7 July 1968. Gorder was a good officer, but he was not an Abrams protégé.

When Patton learned he was to assume command of the Blackhorse, he got hold of me at the Pentagon and asked if I would like to command his Air Cavalry Troop. It wasn't like he'd said, "Hey, Doc, I've got a great staff job for you." He was dangling a combat command right in front of my nose. I could smell it. It made me drool like a hungry hound dog staring at a hunk of prime beef. Combat command is a warrior's ultimate aspiration and is deeply rooted in his ethos. I agreed to his offer on the spot. However, as DA Armor Branch controlled my assignments, I told Patton I would have to check with the people there.

The people in Armor Branch didn't think I needed to command another troop. I had already commanded a tank company successfully, and they didn't view my commanding an air cavalry troop as a step up. They recommended that I complete my three-year assignment in the Pentagon, get promoted, and then return to Vietnam as a lieutenant colonel in command of an armor squadron.

I got hold of Patton and told him what they said. He said, "Bullshit! You've accepted the job. I'll see that you get it."

Patton called me in late June and told me to pack my bags, orders were en route. He insisted that I go to AH-1 Cobra Transition School before I left the states. This involved a three-week course at Hunter Army Airfield in Savannah, Georgia. The earliest I could go was in August with a report date to Vietnam of early September. Meanwhile, I wrapped up my open actions before leaving the Pentagon.

My decision to join Patton in Vietnam was devastating to Pat, and she let me know it. Leeanne had been diagnosed with juvenile diabetes at age five and needed close monitoring daily. Bradley was born with Down syndrome and required a lot of care. Along with raising our two other boys, these circumstances really pushed Pat to the limit. But she never failed to give them any less than the best care a mother could provide.

Pat felt I didn't care enough about our children to make any effort to help her. She felt I cared more about my Army career than my marriage to her. She'd had enough. I couldn't fault her feelings, but that didn't make the situation easier.

My marriage was in a tailspin, but I was not going to walk away from my responsibility to provide for my family. For the time being, Pat and I set aside our differences and made plans for her and the children to return to Georgia.

Retired General Robert M. Shoemaker, then Lieutenant Colonel and
Chief, Plans and Programs Division in the Aviation Directorate,
relates his impressions of Doc during his tour of duty in the
Pentagon.

"Doc was a junior major when he arrived at the Pentagon, but he didn't let that get in his way. He was a tremendous staff officer determined to succeed no matter the task or obstacles involved. He thrived on work and complex assignments; the more you piled on his desk, the better he performed. He used force rather than polish to get the job done at times, but I always considered any complaints I caught as a result a small price to pay for prompt and positive solutions to the problems he was given.

"Doc wasn't perfect; he had flaws. He was a mission-oriented, nonstandard soldier who stood apart from the prevailing stereotype officer who doesn't ruffle feathers just to get ahead. I gladly tolerated his flaws because I knew that's what I had to do in order for the Army to get the most out of one hell of a fighter."

✶ Chapter 36 ✶

I was eager to fly the Cobra. I'd flown Hueys modified into gunships, but this helicopter was a gunship by design. Although they could be used for reconnaissance, Cobras had one mission and one mission only: to shoot.

The AH-1G Cobra was a tandem-seat aircraft that carried a pilot and copilot only. The pilot flew from the rear seat. If he had to, the copilot could fly the aircraft using a fly-by-wire system, but the "stick" and main flight controls were mounted in the pilot's position. The pilot controlled the 2.75-inch folding fin rockets housed in twin side-mounted M-158 seven-tube or M-200 nineteen-tube pods. The copilot operated the flexible chin-turret that housed an M-134 7.62mm minigun and an M-129 40mm automatic grenade launcher. This armament array was more or less standard, but as with Huey gunships, Cobras could be armed with variant weapons systems.

The Cobra's enclosed cockpit lacked air conditioning. Air vents provided fresh air. When it was hot and muggy outside, it was hot and muggy inside. The Cobra's wide-blade rotor gave it a lot of power. It was much faster than a UH-1B Huey and had no problems staying up with UH-1D lift ships on air assault missions. Its slim thirty-eight-inch-wide fuselage presented a much smaller target than a Huey. No Cobra pilot ever complained about that.

The course was from 12 August until 3 September. Ground classes were involved, but the heart of the course was twenty-five hours of flight time and gunnery training. Except for one moment of sheer terror, my training went smoothly.

On my night "qual" ride, I was hovering from the parking ramp out to the takeoff pad right at dusk. You normally hover at three to four feet of altitude. During our training, the IP would intermittently cut engine power to test our emergency skills in performing an auto rotation. The recovery procedure was not difficult, but you had to react quickly. The IP even did this as you were hovering out for takeoff. The engine suddenly quit as we were hovering. I thought my IP had cut power. He'd said nothing to me otherwise. I went through the standard procedures for an engine failure and landed. As soon as the skids touched ground, my IP ripped off his helmet, unassed, and ran away from the helicopter as fast as he could.

I looked to my right front and saw Major Bob Molinelli, my good friend and fellow student, running toward my helicopter pulling a fire extinguisher on wheels behind him. I glanced over my shoulder and saw red fuel flames blazing and realized that we'd had a catastrophic engine failure with a resultant fire.

Time wasn't on my side. The fire was quickly making its way toward the cockpit. I had to get out or I'd soon be a crispy critter. I unbuckled and attempted to open the pilot's hatch. Acting in haste, I moved the handle to the first notch, instead of the second, which would have allowed me to open the canopy fully. It was only with Molinelli's help that I managed to get my fat ass through the partially open canopy and escape.

My IP suddenly reappeared after the fire was extinguished and the area safe. He sheepishly asked me why I didn't see the fire. I didn't answer his stupid question but demanded to know why he didn't tell me about the fire over the intercom. I was too pissed to pay much attention to the sorry-ass excuse he mumbled. I lost all confidence in him over this affair.

We went back to operations and got another helicopter assigned to us. The remainder of my night qual flight was uneventful.

✴ Chapter 37 ✴

After Cobra transition training, I spent about a week at home. I stayed with my mother. She was not happy about my decision to go back to Vietnam and was particularly unhappy with me over my deteriorating relationship with Pat. I understood her feelings on both accounts but her displeasure with me couldn't change either situation.

Pat had taken the kids to Rochelle, where they were living temporarily with her parents. She didn't give me a very warm reception when I showed up at their door. She thought I was going off to get myself killed, a thought that never crossed my mind.

I spent almost no time with Pat and used what little time I had to be with my children. Jimmy and Leeanne were still young, so I mostly played in the yard with them. Chris and Brad were a bit older, so I spent time with them hunting doves and fishing.

When the week was up, I said my good-byes to my family. A childhood friend drove me to the airport in Atlanta from where I made my way back to Vietnam.

★ PART 3 ★

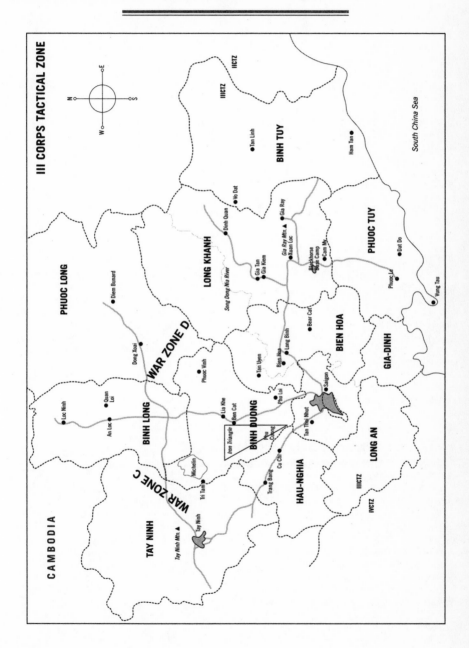

✷ Chapter 38 ✷

14 September 1968—en route to Tan Son Nhut Air Base, Republic of Vietnam

The big picture in Vietnam changed both politically and militarily while I was working in the Pentagon.

South Vietnam became a boiling cauldron of chaotic politics shortly after World War II, when the Japanese left and the French tried to reestablish colonial rule. This turmoil didn't change once the French pulled out. It didn't matter who was appointed prime minister or to any other high political post; the person didn't remain in office long. President Ngo Dinh Diem was an exception: he stayed in office for about nine years, before being assassinated in the aftermath of a military-led coup that ousted him in November 1963.

The next couple of years were rife with coups and countercoups that saw another two presidents and three prime ministers come and go.

When I joined the war in 1965, General Nguyen Cao Ky was prime minister. In 1967, General Nguyen Van Thieu was elected president, and Ky vice president, in the first free election in South Vietnam. They were still in office when I returned to the war.

Ironically, free elections did nothing to change South Vietnam's repressive, opportunistic, and exclusive politics. Making matters worse, the provisional civilian government was falling apart because of fractious geographic rivalry. This prolonged political instability caused the United States to send more and more military aid, advisers, and units to do the fighting ARVN forces were reluctant to do.

I gave this latter condition some thought at the time and have thought about it since. Most of the senior members of the ARVN had been fighting this war for twenty years. Some longer. They had done a lot of killing and had seen a lot of family and friends killed. War was the day-in-and-day-out life they knew, and they were growing weary. The only chance most of them had to get away from it was when they came stateside to attend one of our military service schools. I couldn't blame them for standing back at times. All they were doing was trying to stay alive.

It did not matter to me who ran the South Vietnamese show. I was interested in the people who led the units that fought with us. If they were willing to fight, they became my fast friend. There were ARVN units that fought valiantly, particularly those that weren't led by political hacks who became senior officers for all the wrong reasons. The ARVN's 1st Infantry Division and its Airborne Division exemplified the best of the best of South Vietnam's fighting forces.

As the fighting intensified, our troop strength multiplied. There were about 385,000 U.S. military personnel in Vietnam when I left in 1966. Ground combat engagements were then being mostly fought by ARVN soldiers supported by American advisers, airpower, artillery, and intelligence operations. By early 1968, U.S. troop strength grew to over five hundred thousand, and American units were doing most of the fighting. Consequently, we were killing significantly more of the enemy, but our casualties were on the rise.

There were about five thousand Americans killed in action (KIA) and another thirty thousand wounded in action (WIA) during 1966. This was a sharp and substantial increase over the approximately fifteen hundred KIAs and over seventy-seven hundred WIAs for the five previous years. In 1967, there were over ninety-three hundred U.S. forces KIA and over fifty-six thousand WIA.

The Tet Offensive in early 1968 resulted in over fifteen hundred Americans killed and seventy-seven hundred wounded. These casualty numbers got much more attention back home than did the estimated forty-five thousand NVA and VC battlefield deaths during that same period. The number of enemy wounded during Tet was never revealed, although it has been put at three to five times this death total. North Vietnam's General Vo Nguyen Giap never made his casualty numbers public, if for no other reason than they were so disproportionately high that they would have demoralized *his* army and heartened the spirits of *his* enemy, particularly the ARVN.

By the end of 1968, over fourteen thousand KIAs and some thirty thousand WIAs would be added to the casualty totals for U.S. forces in

Vietnam. Despite these numbers being far, far less than those of the enemy, they were high enough to accelerate our government's waning interest to prosecute the war. The media didn't help this situation. Almost every newscast began with casualty numbers reported over television footage of American dead and wounded. This sensationalized reporting outweighed stories about the progress we were making and put unnecessary fear in the hearts of soldiers' families back home. It also provided banner fodder for antiwar protests and marches all across the United States.

Phase five of the counteroffensive campaign was underway when I returned to the war. From early 1966 to late 1967, our battlefield success wiped out a large part of the Vietcong, and our intelligence operations had virtually dismantled its organization. The counteroffensive was a follow-up, countrywide effort aimed at hunting down Vietcong stragglers and restoring the South Vietnam government's control of territory lost to the North Vietnamese after the Tet Offensive. As far as I could tell, we were winning the war despite decisions being made to end the war diplomatically instead of by outright military victory. These decisions hobbled our fighting forces from taking the fight north and across the Cambodian and Laotian borders, where we could have destroyed enemy soldiers, sanctuaries, and supplies and crippled the NVA beyond recovery.

The only time I engaged any sizeable NVA force during my first tour was in Operation Double Eagle. Fighting the NVA would be the rule, not the exception, during my second tour. Where the Vietcong liked to strike and run, the NVA often struck and stuck around. These opposing tactics didn't worry me in the least. I was prepared to destroy the enemy no matter how he chose to fight.

✶ Chapter 39 ✶

I was picked up at Tan Son Nhut Air Base and flown by helicopter to the 11th Armored Cavalry Regiment's headquarters, which were located in a field just outside the northern perimeter of Bien Hoa Air Base.

Organized in 1901, the 11th Cavalry Regiment gained fame by making the last horse-mounted cavalry charge in U.S. history during General John "Black Jack" Pershing's expedition into Mexico against Pancho Villa and his bandits. It was the last combat horse cavalry unit in the U.S. Army, transitioning from horses to armor before World War II, and was redesignated as the 11th Armored Cavalry Regiment in 1948.

The Blackhorse arrived in-country on 7 November 1966 as part of the major buildup in U.S. forces that took place during my absence. It saw a lot of action right from the start and was involved in heavy fighting during the Tet Offensive.

In Vietnam, the 11th Armored Cavalry was a separate regiment in II Field Force. It conducted operations throughout the III CTZ, a territory in which hostile engagements occurred daily. At various times, part or all of the regiment was placed under operational control of different American divisions in II Field Force: the 1st Infantry, the 1st Cavalry, and the 25th Infantry. Conversely, American ARVN, and Free World infantry units were opconned to the Blackhorse routinely.

The regiment had three armored squadrons: 1st Squadron "First of the Blackhorse," 2nd Squadron "Eagle Squadron," and the 3rd Squadron "Workhorse." It also had an Air Cavalry Troop "Thunderhorse," a Headquarters and Headquarters Troop, and several attached and op-conned units, including the 919th Engineer Company "Red Devils," the 409th Radio Research Platoon, the 541st Military Intelligence Detachment, and the 37th Medical Company.

Colonel George S. Patton was the thirty-ninth colonel of the Blackhorse and its sixth commanding officer in Vietnam. He was a protégé of General Creighton Abrams, who was a protégé of Patton's famed father during World War II.

Soldiers loved Patton. He was an influential and outstanding officer. He had worked for a good group of commanders and knew how to work for top guys. His experience taught him how to get approvals, which usually take a long time, done in a hurry.

He also knew the importance of a good staff. Patton believed that a staff's only purpose in life was to support their commander in their areas of responsibility. It would have been difficult to find a better staff than Patton had when I arrived in the regiment. They were mature soldiers, they produced, they got things done, and they supported Patton and his subordinate commanders in a totally positive manner.

When Patton assumed command of the Blackhorse, it had been ridden hard and put up wet. It needed some serious attention to get back in shape. Patton saw his mission as taking the fight to the enemy and killing as many of them as possible. I shared his point of view. One of his first actions was coining a new battle cry for the regiment: "Find the bastards, then pile on!"

Patton saw battles developing very rapidly once the enemy was found. And the combined firepower of the regiment's organic aircraft, infantry, artillery, and armor gave it unique ability to respond to battle developments with flexibility and speed.

Although the regiment's armor elements often initiated pile-on operations, Patton's big-picture view was that a pile-on generally proceeded with the Air Cavalry Troop's pink teams conducting aerial reconnaissance, looking for enemy soldiers and bunker complexes. Once the enemy or enemy locations were sighted, the pink teams maintained visual contact while the troop's lift ships inserted ARPs to fix the enemy in place. While the ARPs were en route, the pink teams often worked the contact area over with miniguns, rockets, and grenades.

Artillery fire and tactical air strikes were normally called in before ground elements entered a bunker complex, but could be called in at anytime and for as long as necessary. As these leading elements held on to the enemy, one or more of the armored squadrons' ACAVs brought in infantry reinforcements opconned to the regiment from the closest infantry division. The Air Cavalry Troop's lift ships also brought in reinforcing infantry.

Once the enemy location had been overrun, the ground forces swept the area, looking for stragglers, documents, weapons, supplies, and so on.

The keystone principle to Patton's absolutely brilliant pile-on strategy was: The Blackhorse never breaks contact. In other words, once a fight started, the regiment piled on the until the enemy force was defeated.

When I arrived at the Blackhorse, the pile-on strategy was untested. However, it made sense to me and had the full support of Patton's staff and squadron commanders.

As I would discover very quickly, the single flaw in Patton's pile-on strategy was that it was a frontal assault, leaving the enemy escape routes to the flanks and rear of the contact area. I saw this happen several times before coming up with the idea to use tracks to bust jungle completely around the contact area before launching the ground assault. Any enemy attempting to escape across the resultant swath became an easy target for the troop's pink teams.

Patton was excited to see me, as I was him. As we greeted each other, I remember thinking that I was one of the luckiest officers in the Army: I'd been selected to command the Air Cavalry Troop of the 11th Armored Cavalry Regiment, a prize assignment in a first-rate outfit under the command of Colonel George S. Patton, a first-rate leader and fighter I respected highly. I thought the Blackhorse would make a difference in the war and was looking forward to going after the enemy. I was fully taken in by the regiment's battle cry and knew it would be my job to "find the bastards."

Before I assumed command of his Air Cavalry Troop, Patton wanted me to visit the 1st Squadron, 9th Cavalry, 1st Cavalry Division to get an orientation on the latest air cavalry tactics.

The 1st of the 9th arrived in Vietnam in the fall of 1965 and was the premier air cavalry unit in Vietnam three years later. Based on actual body counts and best-guess estimates, this famed squadron accounted for 50 percent of the 1st Cavalry's enemy kills during the war.

Although the I CTZ was primarily a U.S. Marine Corps responsibility, the 1st Cavalry deployed there just before Tet, and the 1st of the 9th was still operating in this area.

✴ Chapter 40 ✴

I spent the night at Bien Hoa and caught a Caribou shuttle the next morning to Phu Bai, a few miles southwest of Hue. It was a long flight that took up most of the day. I spent the rest of the day and night in Hue with Fif, who was working in the area.

I'd never been to Hue. Fif and I took a quick tour of this ancient imperial city. Many of its beautiful historical buildings were severely damaged and thousands of its innocent civilians viciously murdered by the NVA during Tet. This needless killing and destruction was a damn shame by any standards, except by Ho Chi Minh's. He had no qualms about killing innocent civilians or destroying cultural landmarks in his quest to conquer South Vietnam, and his army fought by his standards.

We ate dinner that night at a beautiful outdoor French restaurant overlooking the Perfume River. The food was excellent, and the view of the city was gorgeous. It was hard to believe I was in a war zone again.

∗ Chapter 41 ∗

16 September 1968—C Troop, 1st Squadron, 9th Cavalry, 1 CTZ

I was picked up the following morning and flown by helicopter to C Troop, commanded by Major John M. Toolson. I'd known Toolson since he came through the Armor Officer Advance Course in 1964.

I spent a day and night with Toolson, flying in the left seat of his UH-1C helicopter. He flew me all over his AO, giving me a bird's-eye view of U.S. base camps and the destruction and debris the Tet Offensive left in its wake.

Toolson was an excellent host, and he provided me with solid information on the tactics the 1st of the 9th had found useful since arrival in Vietnam. It was a good orientation for the days ahead and got me pumped up for action.

✶ Chapter 42 ✶

My assumption of command wouldn't take place for a few days. In the meantime, Patton and other officers in the regiment gave me background and tactical briefings to prepare me for my new assignment.

Patton's plans to energize the Blackhorse included realigning the Air Cavalry Troop to its TO&E, which had been operationally altered by previous commanders to complement their warfighting strategies.

Accordingly, the Air Cavalry Troop was transformed into a gunship company soon after the regiment arrived in Vietnam, with one gunship platoon in support of each squadron. This was misaligned with the TO&E that teamed gunships with aero scout helicopters (pink teams) for aerial recon under the command of the Air Cavalry Troop commander. Once contact was made, pink teams took up a combat assault role in support of the ground forces. As needed, the troop's pink teams could be placed in support of the squadrons. Realigning the gunship and aero scouts began before I arrived. Based on my earlier experience as an air cavalry tactics instructor, I was fully confident that I could quickly right any utilization wrongs I might find with the troop's aviation assets.

The troop's infantry had been made into a LRRP platoon. LRRPs had a place in the war. However, Patton didn't see a place for them in his regiment. I agreed. Patton wanted to realign the troop's infantrymen from LRRPs to ARPs (the Aero Rifle Platoon) as called for in the TO&E. Instead of being intelligence gatherers under the LRRP concept, the ARPs' mission would be that of hunters—to make contact intentionally, not avoid it. I was to be his change-agent charged with making this realignment. I had no problem with that role.

Patton informed me that the ARPs were not up to snuff and that I might need a new platoon leader. He assured me that decision would be mine alone, but that I could have any lieutenant in the regiment should I want a new one.

First Lieutenant Dennis Reardon was the ARP platoon leader. Reardon was an Infantry Officer Candidate School (OCS) graduate who had gone to jump school before joining the Special Forces. He completed a Vietnamese-language course at the Defense Language Institute before deploying to Vietnam. I considered him to be a highly qualified, physically fit officer with a lot of spirit and want to. He was a LRRP through and through, and he worried about putting any of his soldiers into situations where they might be shot or hurt, which was not a bad attitude.

Despite Patton's misgivings, I decided to give Reardon the opportunity to be part of my leadership team. If he could get on board with our new mission, I would be glad to have him.

Concurrent with finding the enemy, Patton gave me the mission to take the lead in developing intelligence that he could use to plan B-52 strikes on large enemy complexes and other high-value targets.

A third mission for the troop was to conduct bomb damage assessments (BDAs) after B-52 strikes. Most strikes took place at night, and we would conduct the BDA at first light. If a hasty BDA was called for, our aero scouts would fly low and slow over the area and report back. Our normal procedure for BDAs would be to secure a LZ nearby, insert ARPs, and make our assessment with our boots on the ground.

Realigning the troop to its TO&E began soon after Colonel Patton assumed command of the regiment. Major Bob Wagg, my predecessor, briefed me on what he'd done to date and informed me that operations under the troop's TO&E had yet to be battle tested. He also gave me a very candid assessment of the leaders in the troop. I later found his observations to be exactly right.

After my precommand briefings wrapped, I still had a little time on my hands, so I decided to get checked out in the OH-6, as I might have occasion to fly one in my new assignment. Major Jack Powell, the regiment's aviation officer, assigned an IP to me. I logged four or five hours with him, but did not get fully checked out before assuming command of the troop.

✶ Chapter 43 ✶

24 September 1968—Air Cavalry Troop, Alpha Pad, Bien Hoa Air Base

Major improvements in the troop's aviation assets preceded my arrival. These improvements are worth noting, as they affected the TO&E I inherited and significantly improved the troop's ability to fulfill its mission.

The first of these improvements involved the Aero Scout Platoon: its Korean War–era OH-23 Raven helicopters were replaced by OH-6A Cayuse light-observation helicopters (aka "LOH," "Loach," or "Little Bird")—a much faster, more maneuverable, and more robust aircraft. The second improvement involved the Aero Gun Platoon: its nineteen UH-1C Huey gunships were replaced by nine AH-1G Cobras—a faster and more maneuverable aircraft that had twice the firepower of a Huey gunship.

With a total personnel strength over three hundred officers, NCOs, and enlisted men, the troop's TO&E consisted of Headquarters and Operations sections that had two UH-1D Huey command and control helicopters; an Aero Gun Platoon consisting of nine AH-1G Cobras; an Aero Scout Platoon with ten OH-6 Cayuses; and an Aero Rifle Platoon consisting of five UH-1D Huey lift ships and a platoon of infantrymen. The troop also had a Transportation Direct Support Maintenance Detachment and a Signal Corps Avionics Maintenance Detachment.

Although the TO&E called for the five UH-1D Huey lift ships and a platoon of infantrymen to all be under one captain in the Aero Rifle Platoon, I didn't operate that way. I had a captain who ran the helicopters in what I called the Lift Ship Platoon, and a lieutenant who commanded four squads of crack infantrymen that made up the Aero Rifle Platoon and reported to me directly.

The morning I assumed command, Major Wagg assembled the troop at Alpha Pad; its base camp was located in a large field about a mile north of regimental headquarters. Colonel Patton, his command sergeant major, and several staff officers were present.

The first order of business was to present awards to several soldiers. The second order of business was the change of command ceremony. Per military tradition, First Sergeant A. C. Cotton passed the guidon to Major Wagg, who passed it to Colonel Patton, who passed it to me. I returned the guidon to Sergeant Cotton and he took up his place in front of the troop formation.

Wagg then made some short remarks, thanking everyone for their service and Colonel Patton for allowing him to command, then he welcomed me to the troop, cueing my turn to say something.

My remarks were short and to the point. I thanked Colonel Patton for the opportunity to lead the troop, telling him publicly that I was honored to be selected for the job. I thanked Bob Wagg for his service. I told the superb group of officers, NCOs, and enlisted men assembled for the formation they could expect me to lead by personal example. I would only ask of them what I was personally willing to do. I told them straight up that our mission was to find, fix, and kill or capture as many enemy soldiers as we could. I asked for their loyalty and that they not mince words with me. I would keep them up to date and level the bubbles on any issue.

I've always believed that a new leader's first order of business is to get to know his troops quickly and well enough to understand what puts fire in their bellies and what makes their stomachs turn. Getting to know his troops also gives a leader some idea of their capabilities. It provides him insight on how to develop their abilities, bolster their self-confidence, and avoid alienating them unintentionally. With all this in mind, I told my troopers that I wanted to meet each one of them as soon as possible.

After my remarks, Colonel Patton gave a stirring talk encouraging my troopers to follow their leaders and to kill the goddamned sonsofbitches—the enemy. He assured them that I was a bona fide killer and would set the example for them. The troops loved his colorful, profane talk. Father had nothing over son when it came to pep talks.

After Patton's remarks, I turned the formation over to Sergeant Cotton, and he dismissed the troops.

Patton hung around to have cake and Kool-Aid with us before heading back to regimental headquarters. After he left the area, I assembled my executive officer (XO) operations officer, and the platoon leaders to give them a better, more detailed orientation on what I expected of them.

Major Norman Cunningham, the Aero Scout Platoon leader, asked to be excused early to rendezvous with his Air Force FAC friend for a recon flight. I had no problem with his request. We could catch up later. However, later never came.

The FAC's L-19 aircraft went down in dense jungle and wasn't found until months later. Cunningham was the first soldier under my command to be killed in the war. He was a fellow West Pointer from Van Nuys, California. I never got to know him, but he was well respected within the troop.

Within hours of assuming command, I took Captain Don Peters, the Aero Gun Platoon leader, up with me in an AH-1G Cobra for a refamiliarization flight over the general vicinity around Bien Hoa.

On the way to the revetments, I got into a very short discussion with my new operations officer. He insisted I get checked out by one of the troop's IPs before flying. I let him know that I was qualified to fly AH-1s and reminded him that I was the troop commander and didn't require either his permission or approval to do anything.

This very short discussion was the first of three candid conversations with my ops officer over the next couple of days. He quickly convinced me that he was the wrong guy for the job. I replaced him with Don Peters, who was promoted to major soon after. But letting my ops officer know I was in charge was enough said for day one.

Peters and I were soon airborne. South of Bien Hoa, along the highway to Vung Tau, I noticed a plume of smoke rising from a wheel-mounted armor vehicle. I took the helicopter down for a closer look and saw a firefight in progress between a company-sized unit and an undeterminable-sized enemy force. I came up on the guard frequency and called, "Anyone on guard, this is Thunderhorse Six. I'm in a fully loaded AH-1 and would like to help out with the action south of Bien Hoa. Give me a frequency."

An unknown pilot returned my call and gave me a tactical frequency to contact the ground unit involved. I was circling above the action when I called the unit and asked how I could help. Someone on the ground gave me some directions and popped smoke to indicate the forward edge of their position. Nothing more was necessary. Peters and I made a couple of firing passes during which we expended all of our ammo. I called the unit and told them that we could go back to Alpha Pad, reload, and then return to provide further assistance with the fight. Whoever I was talking to thanked us, but said other gunships were en route, so he wouldn't need further assistance from us.

I later found out that a Thai convoy had been ambushed and they had called in gunships from other units to help. Because we were on the scene before those gunships arrived, we just joined the fracas. Although highly probable, I don't know if we killed any enemy.

Refamiliarization flight and first enemy contact in a Cobra accomplished, we returned to Alpha pad. A good first day, as I saw it.

⋆ Chapter 44 ⋆

25 September 1968—Alpha Pad, Bien Hoa Air Base

I used part of the second day of my command to familiarize myself with the troop's facilities and layout.

The troop area at Alpha Pad included an operations shack, troop billets, a combined EM-NCO-officers' club, several other buildings used for various purposes, and a few vacant buildings. Most buildings were one level with clapboard siding, an unpainted tin roof, and an open area covered with meshed wire running along all four sides near the roof that provided ventilation.

All toilets were small outhouses, two to four holers, with cut-in-half fifty-five-gallon metal drums to collect waste. These drums were pulled out and burned regularly by hired local Vietnamese "shit burners," who used diesel fuel to set fire to the waste—a sanitary way to get rid of it quickly, but not a pleasant scent when the wind blew your way.

Our showers were outdoor affairs without much privacy. Our water storage tanks were metal. The sun beating down on them during the daytime gave us naturally heated water for evening showers.

There was an outdoor movie screen, with wooden benches for viewing, located in the center of the troop's buildings. When we could get them, we regularly showed movies in the evenings.

I initially had a small shack with an indoor shower and sink that the XO and I shared as our quarters. Shop vans were the living quarters of choice for most of the senior field-grade officers in the regiment. I later procured one for my personal use. The inside was outfitted with a bunk, clothes closet, small desk, and a sink. A shower was attached to the outside.

Running north to south was a very short one thousand foot PSP runway. Off to its side there were two rows of six-foot high sandbag revetments where we parked all twenty-six of our helicopters.

The northern perimeter of the runway ran into a mound of dirt topped with chain-link fencing and coiled concertina wire, and was manned and patrolled by Air Force security or some reinforcing Army unit. As an additional security measure, the troop's scout ships performed "rocket runs" over the perimeter at first light and again at dusk, looking for enemy forces preparing to launch rocket and mortar attacks on the base.

The main inspections and most repair work for the troop's helicopters were performed by my Transportation Direct Support Maintenance and Signal Corps Avionics Maintenance detachments at Blackhorse base camp—a large bowl area carved out of the jungle and surrounded by tree-covered hills. Located approximately twenty miles due east of Bien Hoa and twenty miles south of Xuan Loc, Blackhorse base camp was routinely referred to as "Xuan Loc." When I arrived, one of the regiment's squadrons was always posted at base camp for security.

✶ Chapter 45 ✶

26 September 1968—Alpha Pad, Bien Hoa Air Base

Five former Air Cavalry troopers recall their first impressions of Doc's first few days and weeks as their new commander. Two former Blackhorse staff officers tell what they recall about Doc's early actions, and Peter Bahnsen relates his only visit to the Air Cavalry Troop.

Then Captain Peter Noyes, who became the Troop's XO, begins these accounts.

"I was a fixed wing aviator prior to my second tour. My thoughts were to leave the Army before being ordered to Vietnam again. However, I was selected for promotion to major and a friend told me I needed to go to the rotary wing transition course and back to Vietnam.

"I arrived at the Air Cav Troop just a few days before Major Bahnsen. He asked me if I would like to be his executive officer and laid his cards on the table. He told me what he wanted and expected and asked if I could work for him as a major, as I was soon to be promoted.

"That afternoon, he took me to the regimental staff briefing. Afterward, he and Colonel Patton told me that I was to be the best administrator and logistician in the land. I tried to explain that I had no experience in those areas. That didn't matter to them; they just expected me to do my very best.

"I was given a new first sergeant, Sergeant First Class A. C. Cotton, to assist and train me in my new job. Cotton was a soft-spoken southern gentleman who had to be at the front of the line when God passed out common sense. His loyalty, professionalism, and devotion to duty were unparalleled. He had the utmost respect of his subordinates and superiors.

"There were a lot of areas requiring improvement. It seemed that the more you got into fixing them, the more you found wrong. No reflection on Bob Wagg. He took the troop as far as he could in his short command time.

"Our first challenge was to constitute an accurate personnel roster. Every military unit was required to submit a morning report, which was a means of accurately accounting for assigned personnel. This had been neglected for some time.

"Accountability of unit property, such as helicopters, was nonexistent. We worked around the clock to straighten out the mess, mostly at the Xuan Loc base camp. I would say it took us about six weeks to build a foundation to know where we were and how to get to where we wanted to be.

"I was also responsible for writing up awards and decorations as well as closely monitoring the welfare of our troops. Along these lines, one of my duties was to write letters, for Major Bahnsen's signature, to the families of our soldiers who were killed in action. I didn't write many because we didn't have many troopers killed, but words can't express how much writing those letters bothered me. I looked at those young men as members of my family.

"We had some real problems with our assigned mess personnel, and we didn't have a mess hall. All cooking and eating was being done outside an empty building. When Major Bahnsen saw this setup, he shook his head and said, 'Pete, we don't have to live this way. I don't care if we're here for another day or the rest of the war, I want that building made into a mess hall.'

"Major Bahnsen believed leaders have three opportunities a day to raise morale: breakfast, lunch, and supper. He wasn't about to have his troops eat sitting in the dirt unless they were in the field, and certainly not next to a vacant building that could easily be converted into a mess hall.

"Food quality was another matter of immediate concern for Major Bahnsen. The food served at Alpha Pad was dreadful. This situation needed to be corrected immediately. We gave the mess sergeant every chance. However, after a few days, slight, if any, improvement was noted. So we replaced him.

"Our new mess sergeant was younger, positively motivated, and innovative. He turned the vacant building into a first-rate dining facility that served up quality chow. Coffee, hot chocolate, soup, desserts, and pastries were available twenty-four hours a day. Anyone returning from the field after supper time could get something decent to eat instead of eating C-rations or opting to go to bed hungry.

"Major Bahnsen also told me he wanted the officers to have their own club. I made that happen. The building wasn't big, but adequate. All the officers pitched in during their off-duty time to fix it up as well as we could.

"My job was to see to it that our troops had what they needed. And I did just that, especially if it was a matter of survival.

"We had a document register and requisitioned our equipment and supplies per Army regulations. I can assure you that we did everything above board to make the supply system work, but when the system failed to deliver, we procured a lot of items to include major end items, such as jeeps, by other means.

"Major Bahnsen personally organized a 'midnight requisition' for salt and pepper shakers, flatware, and napkin holders at the One-hundred-first Airborne's officers' club. Most of the One-hundred-first was up north and he didn't see any reason to have these items go unused when they could be put to use in our mess hall. It seems silly now, but you couldn't get stuff like this by requisitioning it through legitimate channels.

"We did the very best we could to take care of our troops. Life was a lot different in Vietnam. This was the first time most of these young men had been away from home and they went through some very trying experiences.

"It wasn't long before the foresight, combat instinct, and leadership ability of Major Bahnsen, coupled with his no-nonsense approach, made the Air Cav Troop the best combat unit in the theater of operation."

Retired Command Sergeant Major, then Sergeant First Class, A. C. Cotton comments on Doc's taking over the troop.

"Until Colonel Patton arrived in the regiment, my time in the troop had been spent mostly in the field with the ARPs and working in operations. The troop commander at the time was a good man but too laid back for Patton's taste. Our first sergeant didn't meet Patton's standards, either. Patton relieved both of them.

"Colonel Patton knew Major Bahnsen would be arriving shortly, and he put Major Wagg in command in the interim. I'd worked with Major Wagg and he asked me to be his first sergeant.

"When Major Bahnsen arrived, he talked to me briefly about staying on as his first sergeant. The troop's condition was not good. It had been going through a tough time for a while, and I was not looking forward to being first sergeant. I was a cavalryman, not an administrator. I had limited knowledge of administrative matters and wanted to be in the field. I was a relatively young sergeant first class. There were several more experienced E-7s senior to me in the regiment. Colonel Patton would have given Major Bahnsen any one of them he wanted for the job, but he wanted me.

"Major Bahnsen had a close relationship with Colonel Patton. Both of them were extremely aggressive guys. Soldiers really liked them because they didn't allow buck-passing and held their subordinate leaders accountable. Their philosophy was to get the person responsible to do his job so the person above or below him didn't have to do it. This really earned them the respect of their enlisted men.

"Major Bahnsen was a people person who knew how to take care of his soldiers. He was a quality guy, extremely loyal to his troops, and would do out of the ordinary things to help them in any way he could. But he was not soft. He was headstrong and would relieve you in the middle of an operation if you weren't doing what you were supposed to.

"I enjoyed working with him right from the start. As soon as we got our records straightened out and took care of other problem areas, I went to the field with him every chance I could.

"I heard stories about Major Bahnsen taking extreme risks in battle. That was really different from most officers I knew—most soldiers for that matter. I'd done a lot of fighting and thought I was up to fighting alongside anyone. But I have to tell you, fighting alongside Major Bahnsen made me nervous at times. He fought in the thick of the battle and didn't worry about getting killed."

Former sergeant Bob Roeder talks about the LRRP platoon before Doc arrived and the challenges Doc faced in converting it to the ARP platoon.

"I was a nineteen-year-old kid who'd volunteered for both the draft and LRRP duty. Volunteering for the Army was easy. So was volunteering for LRRPs. Qualifying as a LRRP was hard.

"When I joined the troop, it had LRRPs, not ARPs. Its new LRRP volunteers went to MACV's Recondo course run by the Fifth Special Forces Group at Nha Trang. This very tough three-week course had a washout rate of about fifty percent. The final test was an actual mission. If you came back alive, you passed.

"Our platoon leader, Lieutenant Reardon, didn't send just anybody who wanted to go. You had to go on four or five missions beforehand. If you did well enough, he would send you to the Recondo course. If he thought you weren't up to the job, he'd transfer you out of the platoon.

"A typical LRRP mission lasted several days, most of them with sleepless nights. Our missions involved intelligence gathering, watching villages to see who was coming and going, sitting along trails to monitor enemy troop movements, calling in air strikes on any large enemy forces we observed, and capturing an enemy soldier, or two, once in a while.

"We didn't fire our weapons unless absolutely necessary because there weren't many of us out there, usually about five to seven. If the enemy engaged us, we weren't doing our job the way it was supposed to be done. We were cautious about not being discovered even during insertion, which is why we tried to avoid being inserted by pilots who popped their rotors when they dropped us off. Anytime there was a high probability that we'd be discovered, we didn't go on the mission.

"Within a few days after Colonel Patton took command of the regiment, things began to change. We stopped sending replacements to the Recondo course. Instead of going on every mission that came down, we started training newbies.

"There were rumors about someone coming to take over. Big changes were in the wind but we didn't believe anything would change about how we operated. LRRPs were an elite group. We liked how we did things. We were against change. We were in for a real shock.

"The day Major Bahnsen took command, he let us know LRRPs were out, ARPs were in. We would no longer avoid enemy contact. Major Bahnsen was going to use us like birddogs. Except the birds we would be trying to flush out carried weapons.

"Several of the more experienced LRRPs wanted to debate him. They got their asses chewed. Major Bahnsen didn't cotton debate over his directives.

"Major Bahnsen was tough, bullheaded, and determined to have the troop fight Colonel Patton's and his way. This really made the LRRPs mad and bitter. Most people don't like sweeping change when they are comfortable with how things are.

"Several people were up for rotations and left the platoon. About eleven of us stayed over as ARPs, joining the new guys we'd been training for an altogether different mission.

"I didn't like this change myself, but I stayed on and soon got used to it. Being an ARP became the job I was supposed to do. I think that's how the other guys felt, and we soon changed how we felt about Major Bahnsen.

"Major Bahnsen led by personal example from day one. When he was leading a battle from the air, it was not unusual for him to land and lead us straight into the thick of things. I didn't like that. I wanted him to stay up there—above us. When he was on the ground with us, I always worried that he'd get wounded or killed. He was the troop commander. No one expected him to take point on an ARP mission."

Former first lieutenant and Thunderhorse pilot Mike Bates, a warrant officer when Doc arrived at the troop, talks about his first impressions of his new commander.

"When Doc spoke at the change of command ceremony, I thought of him as a broom brought in to sweep out old ways. I knew right away that he'd encounter resistance, especially from the LRRPs.

"Doc didn't come across as someone who thought he knew it all, but he was very good at reading people and could see right through any bullshit anyone tried to feed him. He had a disarming quality that gave us the sense that he was the real deal: a leader we could be comfortable with and have full confidence in no matter the situation. Men in combat want to be led, especially by someone like Doc.

"My first few days of flying with Doc involved a lot of mutual sizing up, and it didn't take long for him to win my confidence and admiration.

"Soon after he arrived, we flew over an infantry platoon that had an M-132 Flamethrower (a Zippo) out front. They had taken fire from an enemy bunker complex and were having difficulty moving the Zippo into position for a counterattack.

"Although it was a hot area, Doc had me land so he could talk face to face with the platoon commander.

"I dropped him off then went back up to circle overhead. Before I had time to complete my first orbit, I saw Doc climb aboard the Zippo and begin directing the damn thing toward the bunker complex—straight toward a bunker from which he was taking heavy enemy fire.

"Before I could move our helicopter into position for our door gunners to put suppressive fire to his front, Doc sent a stream of blazing napalm at the bunker, sending it up in flames. It was really quite spectacular.

"The fight was over almost as soon as it started. Our guys had taken fire from some camp-watchers, who must have all been in that one bunker because, once it went up in flames, the shooting stopped.

"Action over, Doc dismounted the Zippo and radioed me to pick him up. I sat down in the same LZ where I dropped him off. He climbed in and we took off as if nothing had happened.

"This was the first time I witnessed Doc in real action. He was focused, fearless, and fierce. I remember thinking to myself, wow! How long has it been, if ever, since he's operated a Zippo? That's when I made up my mind to learn everything I could from him.

"From my perspective, Doc's greatest initial challenge in taking command was winning the respect, confidence, and loyalty of the troop. All good combat commanders know this, few do it well. At least that was my experience.

"What made this challenge particularly difficult for Doc was the major overhaul the troop was undergoing. Not everyone was for it. Several murmured about it. A few resisted it.

"Still, he was converting one or two soldiers at a time, sometimes more, as they witnessed his combat leadership firsthand. Soldiers have to see to believe. Improbable as it was, a mass seeing-is-believing event took place one evening in the troop area.

"The ARPs were a rugged bunch who liked to mix it up whenever and wherever they could. When we couldn't get hold of a movie for evening entertainment, the ARPs sometimes held unrefereed wrestling matches that took place on an NCAA regulation mat they pilfered from a Navy special services unit."

Former ARP specialist four Rex Saul picks up this story.

"Several of us were hanging around one evening, having a go at some friendly, but competitive wrestling. We'd been drinking for a while when someone noticed Major Bahnsen walking toward us. We assumed he would put an end to our fun.

"He walked up and asked what was going on. Jim Weller, the biggest

ARP and our best wrestler, was standing with his shirt off. He'd just pinned three guys in a row and was a bit drunk. Well, Weller challenged Major Bahnsen. Much to our astonishment, he said, 'Sure, I'll wrestle you, and any and all comers.'

"That really surprised us. Not only was our new commander letting us grab-ass, he was joining in."

Former specialist four Jim Weller talks about this incident.

"There's some background to this story. Soon after Major Bahnsen took command, I took his jeep into Bien Hoa for the day and didn't return until well after dark. I was good and drunk by the time I got back. I didn't ask permission to use the jeep and that pissed a lot of people off. Besides, the bars in Bien Hoa were off-limits at the time.

"Major Bahnsen told me he could have my ass over what I'd done. I knew that and was expecting, maybe wanting, to get punished hard. He ended my Article Fifteen hearing by fining me fifteen or thirty-five dollars and telling me to get my ass back to duty. I was too good a soldier to lock up in the Long Bien jail. He needed me out fighting.

"At the time, I thought Major Bahnsen was too chickenshit to give me the punishment I deserved because he was making a lot of changes and needed all of us to like him. I was wrong."

Rex Saul continues.

"Major Bahnsen took off his fatigue jacket and stepped center mat. No one, I mean no one, anticipated what would happen next.

"Weller stepped onto the mat and the two of them engaged, briefly. In a flurry of impressive moves, Major Bahnsen grabbed Weller and flipped and tossed him every which way with the ease of a rottweiler toying with a rag doll, landed him on his back, and pinned him. Match over. Matches ended for the evening. We were all surprised, none more than Weller."

Jim Weller wraps up his thoughts on this famous wrestling match.

"Major Bahnsen pinned me pretty quick. Maybe if I had been fresh and sober things would have turned out different. But I wasn't, and they didn't. I had a lot of respect for Major Bahnsen after that. We all did."

Mike Bates continues.

"Doc was an intramural wrestler at West Point and used what he'd learned from that experience to defeat the biggest and toughest ARP.

"Up to this point, a lot of troopers had doubts and reservations about Doc, especially those who hadn't seen him in combat. Those qualms and uncertainties went by the wayside as the result of this wrestling match. I have always believed that more than any other thing Doc did before or after, this was his defining moment as the troop commander. It was a regular mass conversion."

Then Major Jim Dozier, who became the Blackhorse S-3 after Doc took over the Air Cavalry Troop, remembers witnessing a gutsy move on Doc's part.

"I witnessed Doc in a lot of actions during our time in the Blackhorse. He was a warrior's warrior. I particularly remember one day when I was trailing Doc over an area where two friendly ground units were mistakenly engaged in a firefight.

"Doc keyed his mike and called, 'Cease-fire! Cease-fire!'

"Without waiting for the bullets to stop flying, he proceeded to land his helicopter between the two units, got out, walked to its front, and held his arms out with his palms at a ninety-degree angle, à la a traffic cop, and the shooting stopped. It was very gutsy on his part. I have no doubts that his boldness saved lives."

Then Captain and Blackhorse S-5 Lee Fulmer recalls coming back from a pacification mission with Doc.

"You wouldn't think Doc Bahnsen would ever support pacification efforts, but he did. His troop had lots of helicopters and he made them available to me. I used them to get my team and supplies in and out of remote areas quickly and safely.

"I remember coming back from one mission in particular. I was riding in the back of Doc's helicopter. We were flying low, looking for anything out of the ordinary, when we caught a single VC out in an open area. Mike Bates banked the helicopter and came back around over the area while the rest of us watched the VC scurry into a spider hole.

"Doc told Bates to land. As soon as we touched ground, Doc told me to go get the VC. Armed only with a .45-caliber pistol, I jumped out of the helicopter and ran over to the spider hole. I found the handle and pulled the top up just high enough to toss in a smoke grenade.

"The VC came crawling out AK-47 first. I knocked it out of his hands, grabbed him by the throat, and stuck the barrel of my pistol right in his face. He offered no resistance. Doc's crew chief and door gunner ran over with some rope, bound his hands, and loaded him in the helicopter.

"When I climbed back in, Doc looked at me with a big grin on his face and said, 'Goddamn, Fulmer. That took balls. I was just bullshitting. I really didn't think you'd do it.'

"We weren't on the ground more than a few minutes and were soon on our way to regiment with a fresh POW for the S-2 section to interrogate.

"I was feeling good about myself and what I had done. Everyone in the TOC seemed to be impressed as well. After about fifteen minutes of glowing in the limelight, Doc comes into the TOC and informs me in front of everybody, 'Hell of a hero you are, Fulmer. You captured an old woman.'

"Of course, everyone got a big laugh out of that, and it pretty much ruined my day. Up to that point, I was thinking I was a hero.

"Doc was having too much fun at the time to tell me what he was going to do. To Doc, a VC was a VC, man or woman. And he believed my capturing a VC the way I did was worthy of recognition. What he did was go back to his troop and write me up for an Air Medal with 'V' device."

Doc talks about his brother Peter.

My brother, Pete, served two tours in Vietnam, in 1965 and 1968. During his first tour, Pete commanded an A Team in the 5th Special Forces Group. That kept him busy, but he found time to visit me during my first tour when I was flying out of Bien Hoa Air Base with the Bandits.

After Vietnam, he came home, went to Spanish-language school, and was assigned to the U.S. military advisory group that assisted the Bolivians in chasing down Ernesto "Che" Guevara.

On completion of his adventures in South America, Pete returned to Vietnam and served at the battalion and brigade level in the 101st Airmobile Division.

Then Major Peter Bahnsen, S-3, 2nd Battalion, 501st Infantry,
101st Airborne Division, talks about an in-country R&R he took
to visit Doc.

"I took an in-country R&R to go visit my brother at Bien Hoa Air Base shortly after he assumed command of the Air Cavalry Troop. I had expected some downtime and a few drinks together. As soon as I arrived at Saigon, he picked me up in his command chopper and hauled me to his base camp.

"We hadn't been at his base camp long enough to have a cold one before his ARPs radioed his TOC to report they'd made enemy contact. Not one to miss the fun, Doc decided he'd better lend them a hand. He insisted that I go with him and had me ride in the jump seat to watch and offer suggestions on his infantry's tactics. The next thing I know, we're in the field getting shot at by VC and my brother is living it up in his element.

"This was not my first experience getting shot at in a helicopter. When the Marines were still new at flying helicopters in Vietnam, they liked to fly low over rice paddies and villages. I thought that made them easy targets.

"While commanding Kham Duc, I got a lift in the back of a Marine helicopter to go pick up the latest SOI [Signal Operating Instructions]. On the way back to my base camp, we were flying low over a rice paddy when we came under fire and got hit by twenty-seven AK-47 rounds.

"One round came up through the cabin floor and struck the package I was carrying, sending floating bits of paper whirling around the cockpit. It made me think how useless and unprotected an unarmed person is in a helicopter when it starts taking hits. Getting shot in the rectum while riding in the back of a helicopter on R&R is undignified and was not my idea of how a soldier should go down.

"As soon as we returned to his base camp, I insisted that he take me back to Saigon. He could fight his wars on his own time. I had enough shooting going on at my location without getting shot at during R&R.

"I told my brother, probably in less than diplomatic terms, that this was the last visit he would receive from me on any R&R.

"Doc liked to fight any time, any place. I believed in choosing the time and ground for a fight."

✷ Chapter 46 ✷

Retired Colonel, then First Lieutenant, Jerry W. "J. W." Thurman,
an aircraft commander in the 2nd Squadron's flight section,
recalls an incident that would require assistance from the
Air Cavalry Troop three days later.

"We had recently moved to Blackhorse base camp to refit, rearm, and pull maintenance on equipment that had been through prolonged and heavy fighting in the Lia Khe vicinity. Our squadron was also taking its turn at base camp security, so we had a lot of activities going on at the same time.

"On this Sunday morning, Lieutenant Colonel Lee Duke was assuming command of the Second Squadron from Lieutenant Colonel John Prillaman. While preparations for the ceremony got underway, a flight crew that included Warrant Officers Bill Rollins and Jerry Harris, Specialist Five Blaine Shepherd, and Specialist Four John Matuska took off in a UH-1 for the routine morning recon of the road going east out of base camp. A ground soldier in the Australian squadron working with the Blackhorse had made friends with Shepherd and Matuska at the EM club and asked if he could go tag along, as he rarely rode in a helicopter. Rollins, the aircraft commander and pilot, approved the Aussie's request.

"This road was heavily used by convoys going in and out of base camp. The enemy was well aware of this and frequently mined the road and sometimes set up ambushes at vulnerable spots along it. Low-level aerial recon was necessary to spot mines and superfluous movement before trucks started rolling down this road each morning. A second aerial recon was made just as twilight was setting in. The purpose of this recon was countermortar. The VC liked to set up for nighttime mortar attacks while there was still some light.

"After the change of command ceremony, we noticed that Rollins and his crew had not returned. They hadn't made radio contact since takeoff and didn't respond to our attempts to contact them. We suspected something was amiss but didn't know what, so we went out in three birds to search for them. We'd all flown this road many times. A big part of it passed through dense jungle, and there always seemed to be a Vietcong presence in that area.

"We flew back and forth for a couple of hours, to no avail, before giving up our search on account of darkness. We resumed searching the following morning. Once again, we came up empty handed.

"Meanwhile, regimental operations asked the Air Cav Troop to assist us in locating the missing helicopter."

✳ Chapter 47 ✳

1 October 1968—between Bien Hoa and Xuan Loc, Long Khanh Province

One of my scouts spotted the missing helicopter on the third day after it went down. I flew to the crash site immediately.

The helicopter had crashed in the bottom of a ravine in very heavy jungle. We could make out the Blackhorse markings on the aircraft, but not much more. I quickly scrambled a squad of ARPs and had them inserted about a half-mile from the crash site in the only LZ I could find. After the lift ship cleared the LZ, Bates landed our helicopter and I joined my ARPs on the ground.

Former ARP sergeant Bob Roeder recalls what happened next.

"This was a hot area. I'm sure there were dinks around, but for one reason or another they kept out of sight. The trees and undergrowth were so thick that the only way we could get to the crash site was by wading in a stream that was chest deep in places. I took point. If Doc wasn't right behind me, he wasn't more than three back. His pilot was hovering overhead and guided us toward the crash site over the radio.

"We'd been wading for a while when I went around a bend in the stream and saw the helicopter about twenty-five meters ahead. It had slammed nose first into the side of the ravine, and was sitting in water; deeper in the front than in the rear.

"I stopped to scan the area for dinks. You never knew when they would use a situation like this to ambush you or set out booby traps. I could see one of the crew in the rear compartment. His head and shoulders were leaning slightly out of the aircraft. A lizardlike critter was sitting on top of his head, gnawing away at his face. I had a pocket camera with me and took a quick photo of this grisly sight right before the critter heard us and jumped into the stream. (The regiment's S-2 confiscated my film during the mission debrief. I guess he thought the photo was too horrible to risk it showing up in a newspaper or magazine.)

"Sensing our immediate area to be secure, I gave the hand signal for other ARPs to take up defensive positions in front and both sides of the downed aircraft, then proceeded forward."

Doc resumes.

The first thing I noted was the left door gunner was wearing Australian jungle boots and fatigues. He was still strapped in, but he wasn't wearing a CVC helmet. All four of the helicopter's crew were still strapped in with their CVC helmets. The impact folded the helicopter forward. It appeared they'd died from broken necks on impact. They'd been dead for three days. Their eyeballs had popped out of their sockets, and their bodies were bloated. They were really gruesome to behold.

I radioed regiment, reported what we had found, and suggested they get a CH-47 Chinook to airlift the entire wreckage from the stream before we attempted to get the bodies out.

Waiting for the Chinook to arrive, one of my troopers discovered leeches on his legs. The rest of us dropped our pants very quickly to see if we had any. Sure enough, we were all covered in leeches from the waist down. I must have had fifteen to twenty of them sucking the blood out of me. We all lit up cigarettes to burn the damn things off.

Bob Roeder resumes.

"Before the Chinook arrived, troops from Second Squadron made it to the crash site. They'd brought body bags with them. Rather than wait longer, a few of us climbed into the helicopter and got the crew out. It was a struggle. Once we had them bagged up, Doc took point as we more or less floated them downstream to the LZ."

Doc resumes.

We loaded the dead on a lift ship and sent it to base camp. Before lifting off for Xuan Loc to standby if needed, we had a second leech check and painted all the bruised spots with an antiseptic.

J. W. Thurman wraps up this incident.

"I went to the regiment's mortuary to identify the bodies. They were all great soldiers—good men who served their country with distinction and honor. Except the Aussie, I knew them all and felt a special closeness to them. It was terrible to see soldiers I knew in such a ghoulish condition.

"The only wound found on any of them was a bullet hole through Rollin's temple. From what I could tell, he was flying very low when a golden BB [a lucky small-arms shot] hit and killed him instantly. Everyone else died on impact. A hell of a day! One I'll never forget."

✳ Chapter 48 ✳

From day one, I began to build the teamwork needed to engage the enemy in our AO. Within a few days, I noticed that my scout pilots were beginning to become skilled hunters, as they were becoming more and more able to find well-camouflaged VC in the woods, around the rice paddies, and in the stretches of jungle habitat. I also noticed that my gunship pilots were becoming more proficient at covering their pink team partners (scout ships) during aerial reconnaissance.

The ARPs were on unit alert every day. They could be scrambled with a signal from operations within five minutes, ten minutes max, and be inserted most anywhere in our AO within twenty minutes. Our lift ships could carry six to seven fully loaded ARPs, depending on density altitude. Max load weight also varied according to the time of day, as helicopters are able to lift more on cool mornings and less as the temperature rises in the middle of the day.

Transforming the LRRPs into ARPs was a slow process. They were not comfortable with the new requirement to close with and kill the enemy. Nor did they fully understand how to gain and maintain enemy contact. The major problem, as I quickly realized, was Lieutenant Reardon. He was rightly worried about taking casualties and would not put his soldiers in a position where they might take enemy fire. Casualties are not wanted by anyone, but incurring casualties is inherent to the nature of war. You try to minimize it but you can't let thoughts about taking casualties hamper your ability to lead.

On routine days, we went hunting for the enemy. I would normally liftoff early and follow my pink teams, like a hunter following his bird dogs. Our AO for the day was usually designated by the regimental S-3, and he generally assigned us an area close to where one of the squadrons was conducting ground reconnaissance.

Former first lieutenant Gary Worthy, who became the Aero Scout Platoon leader after Major Cunningham came up missing in action, begins.

"Major Bahnsen sent a white team [two scout ships] out to recon the area around Chan Luu. This was a proverbial hotbed of VC activity. I'd been out there many times and rarely came back without some sort of enemy contact.

"I was the team leader. We hadn't been poking around long before I spotted VC running down a dirt path and into a ten- to fifteen-foot-thick hedgerow running between some rice paddies. I was flying low and slow, making myself an irresistible target, and got what I was begging for within seconds: VC started shooting at my ship.

"I pulled up, came back around, and flew down to make a gun run. My observer fired his M-79 out the door just as we were overhead. My wingman also made a gun run. We were having a hell of a time shooting up the hedgerow.

"We had just taken a second volley of ground fire when I saw two dinks running out of a stream bed and toward the hedgerow. One of them stopped briefly and laid something down next to a tall tree, but I couldn't make out what it was.

"The dinks were in the middle of the hedgerow. I couldn't see them, but they shot back. I pulled pitch and started climbing to a higher altitude to get out of ground-fire range.

"I radioed the TOC and told Major Peters what I'd found. He told me to stay in high orbit; Major Bahnsen would be at my location soon. Major Bahnsen arrived shortly after I rogered Major Peters's instructions. I gave him a sitrep."

Doc resumes.

En route to the contact site, I alerted operations to launch two squads of ARPs and have others standing by. Worthy told me he'd seen a squad-sized VC force moving down a dirt path next to a thick hedgerow between rice fields. A stream ran alongside the dirt path; its banks were covered with thick underbrush. I made a quick decision to insert the ARPs on the stream bank opposite the dirt path. The thick underbrush would afford them substantial cover.

My door gunners prepped the LZ with a heavy concentration of M-60 fire. The lift ships were in and out without touching down. The ARPs made quick contact and shot a couple of VC, but they were not pursuing the enemy as aggressively as I wanted. I told Bates to land, grabbed my rifle and LBE, and headed toward the ARPs, who were standing in the stream bed.

Lieutenant Colonel Bill Haponski, a West Point classmate and the regiment's S-3, was flying with me as an observer.

I took point and led the ARPs sloshing quickly downstream until we reached the point where we had last seen the enemy. I literally stepped on a wounded VC hunkered down in the stream with wet grass over his head. I grabbed the bastard and, with the help of a couple of ARPs, dragged him out of the water.

Retired Colonel Bill Haponski, a newly minted lieutenant colonel at the time, begins with commentary about Doc, and then recounts this enemy contact as he recorded it in his journal and on an audiotape to his wife the following day.

"The only problem I ever remember between Doc and me, and I told him, was that he and Patton had the idea they had to play war as a game, and that pissed me off. War was no game. I told Doc this attitude was going to get both of them in trouble. The plus side of that, I know, was that he could get through some tough moments a lot easier than some others. The minus side was that he could unnecessarily endanger his men as well as himself. As I recall, when I talked with Doc that way, he would say, 'I know, I know, you're right.' And then Doc would go off and be Doc. I love him but I still get pissed at that attitude. You have to assess it, however, in the larger context of his courage and leadership, and in the context of my very different personality.

"I recorded the 6 October 1968 action in my journal and in an audiotape letter to my wife as follows:

"Yesterday, I lived many years in one day. It began with an operation in the vicinity of Chan Luu. I accompanied Doc Bahnsen in his C&C [command and control] ship, and soon his scouts had a sighting. We circled, and then I saw him, a VC running along a stream, trying to evade. I asked Doc to put me down and I would police the man up, so down we went and Doc led the small element he had already inserted.

"The brush was thick and we moved slowly. It's a strange sensation, knowing that men a few feet away are waiting to kill you, and knowing that they have the advantage.

"Down to the stream we went and floundered in the water, making our way to the spot. I then began taking pictures. We slipped and some of us fell, and the few of us helped one another along. Then we saw him a few feet away, and he surrendered, having jammed his weapon in attempting to fire.

"This led to an embarrassing incident for me. The prisoner spoke some English, enough to say a few words, but not enough to give us any information, and we wanted to know the names of the other VC in the vicinity. We quickly found, though, that he did speak French. Doc turned to me and said, 'You can speak French can't you?' And I scratched my head. He wanted me to ask the prisoner for the names of the other VC we hadn't yet taken. And do you think that I could even come up with a basic sentence in French like, 'What is your name?' It was just beyond me, yet it was only what, a few weeks ago or a few months ago, that I could have at least stammered out something like that? So you see how I have regressed intellectually in this environment.

"We treated this prisoner well because he told us what we wanted to know anyway. Lower-ranking VC sang like canaries when captured. Higher-ranking VC generally gave us mixed information that was hard to sort out.

"The leaches attacked, and I beat them off my leg. We were in the open, a bad spot. Then we started into the bank, covered with dense growth. In a moment we came upon another VC, badly wounded in the leg from the fire we had delivered from the air. The poor creature was dragged out, his horrible thigh wound gurgling. I stripped off my belt and used it as a tourniquet around his leg, struggling waist deep in the mire. The leeches had attacked him, and I picked them off. We called our C&C ship which hovered as we struggled to load the wounded man. Soon the aircraft had him. We were still in the open, exposing ourselves to help save enemy wounded.

"Then the prisoner indicated more VC with weapons in the thicket, and wanting to take them prisoner rather than kill them, back we went. The leeches were eating into my legs. Another dozen were swimming toward me. I plucked them off, snakelike creatures, and they left bloody welts.

"Doc and his ARPs had just resumed the search when the ARP next to me shot. I was still filming and didn't see that a VC had come out of the thicket a few feet ahead of me with his weapon pointing directly at me. The ARP dropped him with one shot in the stomach. At this point my camera had stopped running, but I did not know it because of the noise of the firing. The brush was so thick I had not even seen the ARP next to me.

"Another helicopter hovered and we loaded the wounded VC for evacuation. Still there were more, armed we knew, and still we searched. Fear has a way of leaving a man when he is busy. Now we were too busy, too exhausted, and too leach-ridden to fear. We could not find the others, could not get them to surrender. There was only one course left: call in the gunships.

"The Cobras came, firing into the thicket we had just exited. The combined fury of their miniguns and rockets, only a hundred yards away, was frightening.

"I had another engagement to meet, so I left by helicopter, finding out later that three more VC were taken captive, two horribly wounded, one a woman."

Doc resumes.

This aggressive action, secured by scouts and guns overhead, was seen by a lot of people and set the tone for future actions by the troop. I was so absorbed in the action that I did not realize Bill was with me on the ground until we started loading the wounded POWs on the helicopters. He got out of the helicopter unarmed and used a home movie camera to film part of the action. Bill Haponski was, and is today, a great friend, but we could not have been more different in our approach to the war.

Gary Worthy resumes.

"After the action was over, I flew back to the spot where I'd seen the VC soldier lay something down by a tree. I landed and had my observer pick it up. Turns out it was a Russian-made semiautomatic pistol wrapped in cloth. I presented it to Major Bahnsen that evening as a souvenir."

Mike Bates comments on this enemy contact.

"This contact took place in a known Vietcong sanctuary. It was the same area where, in early September just before Doc arrived in-country,

Colonel Patton landed his helicopter in the middle of a large enemy force and led a squad from the Big Red One [the 1st Infantry Division] in attacking a three-man antitank team, killing two and capturing the third. Patton was awarded the Distinguished Service Cross for his extraordinary courage and valor on that day.

"We made contact with the enemy every time we flew near Chan Luu. Doc led assaults on this area at least five or six times. Every one of them resulted in enemy dead and captured."

Lieutenant Colonel Bill Haponski recommended Doc for a Bronze Star with Valor device for gallantry above the call of duty during this hostile engagement. Colonel Patton endorsed Haponski's recommendation. The medal was awarded at a ceremony several weeks later.

✷ Chapter 49 ✷

An enemy sanctuary throughout the war, War Zone D was a large area north and northeast of Bien Hoa Air Base. One of the southern forks of the Ho Chi Minh trail extended deep into this hostile territory, which was scarred by smaller trails, many of them hidden from aerial view by the one, two, and sometimes three layers of jungle or forest canopy. Underbrush thrived in this area and was especially thick along stream banks.

The provincial town of Tan Uyen was a five-minute flight north and a bit east of Bien Hoa. A fifteen-minute flight to its northwest would take you to the provincial town of Phouc Vinh. An improved road surfaced with red laterite known as 1 Alpha ran between these two towns. Hamlets surrounded by cultivated fields lay to the west of 1 Alpha. To its east was an area where rubber plantations once thrived. Farther east was virgin jungle that ran east into the heart of War Zone D.

At about 1600 hours, Warrant Officer Tom Davis, one of my scout pilots, flew into an area midway between Tan Uyen and Phouc Vinh to make an aerial BDA of a B-52 strike that went in the previous night. This area was a hotbed of enemy activity and, like a feisty cockroach undeterred by a visit from an exterminator, the enemy was resilient and often survived B-52 strikes.

Well, Davis was out there in the air doing his job and Charlie was in the jungle below doing his. During the course of his assessment, Davis came in low and slow and his ship was hit by a fusillade of automatic weapons fire. Davis's OH-6 went through some treetops and tumbled to the jungle floor not far from a burned out, crater-filled area left in the wake of the B-52 strike. Their bird was totaled beyond repair, but neither Davis nor his observer incurred serious wounds.

I was already in the air and proceeded directly to the crash site.

Retired Colonel Andy O'Meara talks about how he became involved with this mission.

"I was en route to Lai Khe with Colonel Patton for a briefing at the First Infantry Division's headquarters.

"We could hear Doc talking on the radio and heard him say, 'I've got a bird down.' We were near the area where the helicopter had been shot down and soon spotted the wreckage.

"Doc already had ARPs securing the crash site when he landed in a nearby LZ just before we sat down. Patton talked with Doc briefly, then told me, 'Andy, stay here and see what you can do. I'm going to Lai Khe.'

"The pilot and observer were both bloody but were going to make it. After being patched up by an ARP medic, they were medevaced for further treatment. Doc decided that salvaging the mangled helicopter was a waste of time, but to save as much of it as possible. Some of his ARPs went about dismantling the miniguns, radios, and other undamaged parts of the helicopter. You didn't want to leave anything behind that the enemy could pick up and use against you later."

Doc resumes.

A huge storm front began to move in while we were on the ground. I wasn't too concerned because I thought we could get out before it hit us. We'd been at the crash site for nearly two hours. Everything worth salvaging had been taken out. I was just about to have lift ships sent out to pick us up when I noticed the storm had moved in quicker than anticipated. It was led by a big black thunderhead several thousands of feet thick. Heavy lightning started to strike all around us. Then a monsoon rain came pouring down.

I waited a bit for the storm to pass, but it settled over us and wasn't going anywhere soon. I radioed my TOC and told Major Peters that a storm over our location presented conditions too hazardous for flying. He was to keep all helicopters at Alpha Pad and send lift ships out to pick us up in the morning.

It was getting dark and we had nothing to do. O'Meara was a solid leader and a damn good fighter. I asked him for suggestions. He told me that recent recon reports indicated heavy nighttime enemy troop movements in this area. He recommended we each take an ARP team and set ambushes on opposite sides of the road.

I agreed. It was a good idea. Being stuck out in the boonies overnight gave me, with O'Meara's help, a perfect opportunity to give my ARPs some on-the-job training in night ambush techniques. I led a squad in setting up an ambush on the west side of 1 Alpha; O'Meara led the other squad and set up his ambush to the east of 1 Alpha.

As it turned out, we had a miserable night out in the jungle. It rained and rained. Lightning bolts danced all around us, giving off occasional strobe light effects that caused us to see imaginary ghostlike movements. Very eerie. The storm must have been too much for Charlie because he stayed put for the night.

When the rain let up, mosquitoes came out in mass. The ARPs always carried mosquito netting and insect repellant, but those damn things nearly ate O'Meara and me up. We were ill prepared to spend a night in the jungle and totally unprepared to battle swarms of mosquitoes. I was bitten so many times that I had red welts all over my face and neck and hands. O'Meara didn't fair any better.

We were picked up at first light. It had been an uneventful night but one that helped me relearn an important Boy Scout lesson—be prepared—the hard way.

✶ Chapter 50 ✶

This area was laced with trails the enemy used to move supplies in from Cambodia for redistribution to units further south. No one had worked this area before, but I suspected it would be infested with Vietcong.

It was early in the morning when I sent two scout birds ahead of my helicopter. We were on a hunt. The 1st Squadron was on its way to a nearby area for ground reconnaissance and to reinforce my troop if necessary. The ARPs were on strip alert at Alpha Pad.

Former first lieutenant Gary Worthy talks about this hunt.

"Warrant Officer Guy Ballou and I were looking for signs of enemy activity, hunting in tandem, flying low and slow.

"We'd been out nearly two hours when we flew over a small village, across a huge field covered with elephant grass, and started orbiting at treetop level over the edge of a jungle fronted by tall bamboo. It looked like a good place for Charlie to hide.

"As I went into my turn, I got a glimpse of something that looked out of place. I radioed Ballou to tell him I was going in for a closer look. He pulled up to about a hundred feet and went into a tight orbit to the side of my bird, ready to engage the enemy with miniguns should I take fire.

"I went down lower. My skids were touching the top of the bamboo as I used my prop wash to blow it back in order to see the ground. I looked down and saw several pieces of bamboo furniture, tables, and chairs. Cooking and eating utensils were on the tables. I couldn't make out much else.

"I pulled up and reported what I'd seen to Ballou. I asked him to take a second look while I provided cover for him.

"Ballou went in exactly like I had and saw the same thing. He'd just pulled up when we started taking ground fire. Ballou's crew chief, Sergeant Robert Hepler, dropped red smoke. We both pulled off to the side and hovered at about ten feet. I wanted to see where the fire was coming from before making a firing pass. I also called Major Bahnsen to give him a sitrep."

Doc resumes.

I told Worthy and Ballou to stay put. I wanted to assess the situation. I moved immediately to their location and took a quick look from a safe altitude. Based on what Worthy told me and what I could make out, it looked like an enemy base camp.

A typical Vietcong base camp had a bunker complex with overhead camouflage. They were stockpiled with food, ammunition, and supplies. Most of them had underground tunnels with sleeping areas, medical aid stations, and command centers.

Once sighted, destroying an enemy base camp became top priority. Sweeping the area around base camps after they had been destroyed often resulted in our discovering maps and documents that provided timely intelligence on enemy plans and activities.

Because Worthy and Ballou had taken fire, I decided to start a pile-on operation. Artillery was available. I used it to soften the target before inserting ARPs to fix any remaining enemy in place.

Retired Colonel and former Blackhorse S-3 Bill Haponski picks up the story.

"I was in the regimental C&C helicopter. I don't remember why Patton wasn't using it at the time. I arrived at the contact area almost simultaneously with Doc. I well remember observing the artillery fire and gunship strikes on the bunker complex. Any VC that survived had to have been well dug in.

"Doc radioed me almost as soon as I arrived in the area and requested I bring in the First Squadron to reinforce a final assault on the base camp. I radioed the First Squadron's commander, gave him the grid coordinates, and told him to move to the contact area as fast as possible."

Doc resumes.

I quickly pinpointed the map coordinates for the base camp. I then radioed my TOC and told whoever I talked to that I wanted him to launch two ARP teams to the contact area. Next, I called in an artillery fire mission.

I got my signature white phosphorus two-hundred-meter height of burst within a hundred meters of the bunker complex on the first round, made one adjustment, and called the artillery FDC.

"Repeat range, battery six rounds, fire for effect."

A thirty-six-round volley of 155mm high-explosive projectiles came raining in. The artillery battery had its howitzers laid out in a lazy W pattern. Rounds from the two center pieces hit dead center of the bunker complex; rounds from the other four pieces battered its flanks. I liked what I saw. I called the FDC and told them to repeat fire for effect. The following thirty-six rounds looked so good that I called for another fire for effect.

The Vietcong in the bunker complex shot at my scouts. That pissed me off. I wanted to pound the bunker complex hard to kill anyone in it. The artillery battery put a total of 108 rounds on the bunker complex, blowing it to pieces.

Gary Worthy continues.

"Major Bahnsen called a cease-fire. He then told me to take my white team in over the bunker complex to make an aerial assessment of the damage. With Ballou in trail, I went in low and slow, not expecting to see any live VC. All of a sudden, three VC crawled out of a smoldering bunker and started shooting at my bird with AK-47s set on full automatic.

"In the twinkling of an eye, my bird was riddled with holes from end to end. One round came up through the chin bubble and ricocheted off my chicken plate—body armor—which slowed it down before it penetrated up through my left jaw, twisted and lodged in the right side of my neck. Blood filled my mouth instantly! I had to spit it out to keep from choking.

"My observer started grabbing at the controls, but he didn't have a clue about flying or making an emergency landing. I had to keep knocking his hands away. I was conscious and able to fly. I keyed my mike.

" 'This is White Six. I'm taking fire. I've been hit. I'm going in.'

"I knew I had to get on the ground in a hurry and headed back to the large grassy field we'd flown over earlier. It was a short distance away, maybe two hundred yards."

Bill Haponski continues.

"About that time I heard Lieutenant Worthy's mayday. Doc radioed me and asked me to provide cover fire if things got hot; he had to go in to get his men out. I watched him land in a large clearing near Worthy's helicopter."

Former specialist five George Zubaty was a combat medic who made the transition from LRRP to ARP.

"My team had just inserted on the edge of a huge LZ when we saw two Loaches coming in to land. The first one landed; the second landed close behind it. Neither one was on fire. Still, I could tell something was amiss because they landed so quickly and close together, and because Major Bahnsen's Huey came in right behind them and landed right in front of the first Loach.

"The pilot in the second Loach unassed his bird in a New York minute and ran up to the first Loach. Major Bahnsen did the same.

"All of a sudden, I heard someone call, 'Medic!' That was my signal.

"I beat feet to where Major Bahnsen and the others were gathered. I recognized Lieutenant Worthy right away, he was badly wounded. He was breathing fine but his uniform was soaked with blood. Blood was gurgling out of his mouth. He kept spitting it out to keep from choking, splattering blood on all of us. I could see the entry wound but couldn't find where the bullet exited. Placing a pressure bandage under his chin would have dammed up the flow of blood and strangled him to death.

"I told Major Bahnsen, 'There's nothing I can do. We need to get him to a hospital before he bleeds to death.'

"Mister Ballou told me, 'Help me get him into my helicopter. I can have him at Lai Khe in two minutes.'

"As I was strapping Lieutenant Worthy in the observer's seat, Mister Ballou was on the radio telling the First Division's MASH that he had a badly wounded man on board. He would have him there in two minutes. He needed medics waiting at the landing pad."

Guy Ballou picks up this story.

"I kept my TOT [turbine outlet temperature] gauge redlined all the way to the First Division, where air traffic control told me to take a position in the traffic pattern. I ignored their instructions and flew straight to the MASH's pad.

"I dragged Worthy inside, he was bleeding like a stuck pig. I didn't think he was going to make it, and all the medics were just standing around. Nobody would treat him! I was pissed.

"I pulled out my .38 and walked over to a doctor and told him to treat Worthy right away, or I was going to kill him. Suddenly, people were all over Worthy. I left and went back to the fight."

Doc resumes.

First Lieutenant James Crowley, a pilot relatively new to the Aero Scout Platoon, was monitoring our radio frequency and heard Worthy's report that he'd been hit and was going down. He instinctively knew we needed help over the contact area and flew in to assist.

Before getting back in my helicopter, I examined Worthy's scout ship. It was full of holes but I couldn't see any major damage to it. Nevertheless, I wasn't going to chance having it flown out. I called my TOC and told them to have maintenance come and lift it back to Xuan Loc, where it could be properly repaired.

Bill Haponski continues.

"Within a minute or two, I heard the report of a second Loach going down. It had crashed into the bunker complex. I radioed Doc to tell him I would give him cover from my ship, but got no response. I looked down and saw Doc's helicopter take off and move the short distance to a LZ not far from the crash site."

Former Thunderhorse pilot Mike Bates picks up the story.

"The bunker complex was very close. You could see it from where we'd landed to assist Worthy. I figured that if Crowley and his crew chief were still alive, they needed help right away. I tried to get Doc's attention but he was talking to some people and didn't notice me. I made a decision to go help Crowley, knowing Doc would find a way to get there as soon as he could.

"I was in the air less than a minute when I spotted a LZ about seventy-five to a hundred meters from Crowley's smoldering Loach. I landed, shut my helicopter down, and headed toward the crash site. Specialist Five Jim Gray, my crew chief, removed the pintle from his door gun mount, picked up his M-60, and came with me. He was an experienced fighter, and I trusted him to get me in and out of the area. I left the door gunner on the ground to protect our helicopter."

Bill Haponski continues.

"I knew the people moving toward the downed Loach could use some help, so we descended. We flew close to the treetops. My door gunner laid down a steady fire with his machine gun, and I fired my carbine into the underbrush near someone, whom I took as Doc, whenever we could get a glimpse of him progressing toward the mangled scout ship. Only later did I learn that it was actually Mister Bates, who was making his way toward the wreckage."

Mike Bates continues.

"Crowley's ship was right in the middle of the bunker complex. It was resting nose first and leaning on its right skid that had, along with the left skid, collapsed on impact. The whole aircraft was smoking. The rear section was ablaze.

"Crowley's crew chief was alive and climbed out of the aircraft on his own. Crowley was alive but still strapped in his seat and not doing well. He couldn't talk, and I couldn't see where he'd been hit. I could see that his right leg was broken and his foot was stuck under a floor pedal.

"The smoke was increasing and I was worried that flames were about to consume the entire wreckage. Ratcheting up my pucker factor that was already close to going off the scale, we started taking intermittent small-arms fire from dinks hiding in spider holes arranged in a semicircle in front of the bunker complex. Every time one of them shot at us, Gray fired back. However, the dinks were being careful not to engage us to the point that our gunships would roll in on their position. All they wanted to do at this point was harass us.

"I realized I needed to hurry before a bad situation got worse.

"Taking a second look, I tried to find where Crowley was hit, but couldn't. I attempted to get his leg out from underneath the foot pedal, but couldn't. I struggled to pull Crowley out of the cockpit, but couldn't. His foot that was stuck under the foot pedal was holding him in place. Then I thought to myself, Crowley's foot is the least of his problems, and then I wrenched it free.

"I put Crowley over my shoulder and headed back to our helicopter. I was sweating heavily in the jungle heat, and Crowley seemed to be getting heavier with every step I took."

Bill Haponski continues.

"I will never forget the sight of Bates down there. Even with all the suppressive fire my door gunners were placing on the enemy position, Bates was taking fire as he carried the half-naked corpse over his shoulder, and struggled back to his helicopter. The enemy also shot at my helicopter, but to no avail."

Mike Bates resumes.

"I was almost to our helicopter when Doc came running up. He stayed beside me the rest of the way and asked where Crowley had been hit. I told him, 'I don't know.'

"Doc said, 'Let's get him in the helicopter, then we can check him out.'"

Doc resumes.

We laid Crowley on the cabin floor and pulled his uniform down around his ankles. He was obviously hurt very badly. He was having trouble breathing and had started to turn gray. On closer inspection, we saw an entry wound in the left cheek of his derriere but couldn't find an exit wound.

We had already called in a medevac and it was setting down about this time. Gray and the door gunner were still laying down suppressive fire, as was Bill Haponski's aircraft as it orbited overhead. Just a few days earlier, my troopers saved Haponski's life, and he returned that favor by helping save ours while we recovered Crowley and his crew chief.

The medevac ship sped Crowley and his crew chief to the MASH at Lia Khe, about five to seven minutes away. The crew chief survived, but unfortunately Crowley bled to death from internal injuries before he could be treated.

I waited near the base camp for the 1st Squadron to arrive, but it didn't show up in time to do me any good. Lieutenant Colonel Briggs Jones, the squadron commander, got lost en route—twice—before getting to my location well after the enemy had cleared the area. He was no help at all. His uselessness spoiled what would have been a textbook pile-on operation.

Jones was suspected of being unable to perform in a fight, and this action put one more black mark on his record. Not long after this episode, a VC sapper squad penetrated his CP area and killed three of his soldiers. That was the final straw. Colonel Patton relieved him for cause. His relief was more than justified in my view and I told Patton so when he asked me.

Gary Worthy resumes.

"Ballou got me to the Big Red One's MASH in no time. Medics weren't waiting at the landing pad. Ballou chewed a doctor's ass for that. Once they got started, the MASH's doctors and medics saved my life.

"As soon as I was stable enough, I was medevaced to the Twenty-fourth Evac Hospital at Long Binh. My crew chief came to visit me there. He'd counted sixty-seven holes in our helicopter and presented me with a slug he dug out of it. The armor plating under his seat had saved him. I was glad about that. We were both lucky to have survived."

Doc resumes.

Worthy was in need of further medical treatment that required him to be evacuated stateside. I hated to lose him. He was a damn good pilot and a solid platoon leader who trained his pilots well. Crowley's death hit me hard. He was on the way to becoming a top scout pilot. Driven by his fearless enthusiasm, Crowley fought full throttle.

A few days after this action, Patton told me it'd come down through channels that Ballou pulled a pistol on a doctor at the 1st Division's MASH.

I told Patton, "That's news to me."

Patton replied, "He probably deserved it."

I agreed with Patton's assessment and that was that. It was never mentioned again.

My experience in this action convinced me that the most effective way to bring in a reinforcing armor unit was to fly to its location and guide it to the contact area from the air. Reinforcement by air was much easier, as I personally led the lift ships into a LZ.

Bill Haponski wraps up.

"I admire Doc for his and his crew's actions of that day, well above and beyond the call of duty. That evening Doc thanked me for staying on station and providing cover fire during the rescue. Small potatoes to what he and his crew had been doing below me in the jungle."

For heroism during this hostile engagement, First Lieutenant Gary Worthy received the Distinguished Flying Cross and Purple Heart, and First Lieutenant James Crowley was posthumously awarded the Distinguished Flying Cross and Purple Heart. Doc, Warrant Officer Mike Bates, Specialist Five Jim Gray, and their door gunner received the Bronze Star Medal with Valor device.

✶ Chapter 51 ✶

Retired Colonel, then Major and Blackhorse S-2, Andy O'Meara provides background information on this mission.

"The Ba Da Secret Zone was located east of First Infantry Division headquarters at Lai Khe and west of War Zone D in a free-fire zone that contained no friendly indigenous people. Any and all people found in it were the enemy and could be shot on sight.

"Rubber plantations dating back to the time of French colonization once spread across this part of South Vietnam, but they had been abandoned for several years and their neglect produced secondary jungle growth. A few roads built by the French remained serviceable. We used them when operating on the ground in this region. It also had lots of trails dating back to who knows when, as well as abundant rivers and streams.

"The Ba Da Secret Zone was the refitting and training area for the K-Four Battalion of the VC Dong Nai Regiment that operated in this area extensively. Early in the war, the K-Four Battalion consisted of locally recruited men and teenage boys. After Tet of '68, it had difficulty recruiting; most young boys were either dead or had fled to Saigon. To keep the battalion going, NVA regulars were being brought down from the north as fillers.

"The Blackhorse encountered the K-Four Battalion often. It was a pretty high-spirited unit and always fought hard.

"The Air Cav Troop had conducted aerial recon of this area but it was difficult for its scout pilots to see through the jungle canopy that was multiple layers thick in places. Several B-52 strikes had targeted likely centers of enemy activity but we hadn't made ground BDAs to assess what, if any, good they'd done. We did have sketchy intel reports based on limited ground recon conducted by light infantry units. I wanted a more thorough and extensive ground recon of it to get a better feel for enemy activity.

"Based on our limited intelligence on the Ba Da Secret Zone, we thought the enemy was using its trails and waterways as routes of supply; particularly to bring in 122mm rockets from the north.

"The PRU [Provincial Reconnaissance Unit] out of Long Khanh Province worked for the regiment from time to time. I contacted them to see if they would be willing to conduct a LRRP mission for us; one so deep into the Ba Da Secret Zone we wouldn't be able to provide them with artillery support if they ran into trouble. They agreed and opconned a platoon to me.

"The Air Cav Troop's lift ships inserted the PRU platoon late in the afternoon. It was a perfect LRRP insertion: get 'em in quick without making contact or drawing attention.

"Around noon the next day, the PRUs' interpreter radioed the regiment's TOC and reported that the platoon leader popped an ambush on a company-sized or possibly larger NVA unit. The platoon leader was killed during the subsequent exchange of fire. They were in serious trouble and needed help right away.

"As the S-2, this mission was my operation up to this point. Now that elements from the regiment were being deployed, it became the S-3's, Major Jim Dozier's, operation."

Doc picks up from O'Meara.

We received a call from regiment to scramble pink teams, ARPs, and lift ships to assist in the rescue of the PRU platoon. We were also told that an infantry platoon from the 2nd Battalion (Mech), 2nd Infantry Regiment, 1st Infantry Division was mounting up in four ACAVs and would soon be on its way to reinforce.

I assembled two pink teams, two squads of ARPs, and four lift ships. We were airborne within ten minutes. On arrival over the contact area, I located a LZ two hundred meters east of site where the PRUs ambushed what was suspected to be a company-sized or larger NVA unit.

The ARPs were to move out to the PRUs' position and lead them back to the LZ for extraction.

The ARPs were hustling beside a trail bordered by jungle on one side and a bomb crater–filled area on the other, when they came under an intense concentration of automatic weapons fire from the edge of the tree line. The ARPs popped smoke and two Cobras rolled in with minigun and rocket fire that killed several NVA soldiers and forced about fifty more of them further back into the jungle.

Bates had our ship in a counterclockwise orbit, allowing me to observe the ground below. I spotted an NVA soldier, a straggler who hadn't moved out with the others. He was lying next to a bomb crater, presenting me with an easy target. I immediately shot him with my M-16, which signaled my crew chief and door gunner to follow my red tracer fire with their M-60s. He was perforated by bullets. As Bates brought our helicopter back around, I saw the NVA soldier roll into the bomb crater.

I did not see any other NVA at the time, so I radioed my ARP platoon sergeant and told him to get up and get moving toward the PRU's position.

As they approached the position where we'd just killed the NVA soldier, Bates landed on the trail and I dismounted. I wanted to search the dead NVA and talk to the ARP platoon sergeant about his exfiltration route, once he reached the PRUs. I was in a hurry and didn't think to take my M-16, my LBE, or my sack of grenades with me, nor was I wearing my pistol.

As I approached the bomb crater, a second NVA assault opened up, and I dove into the crater. Bates pulled pitch and quickly gained altitude. The ARPs were within twenty meters of me and they hit the ground.

Andy O'Meara begins his account of this mission.

"Jim Dozier and I were in a command and control ship following behind Doc all the way out to the Ba Da Secret Zone. Jim was running the show over the regiment's net and talking to Doc on the First Infantry's frequency. We were not listening to the Air Cav's net, so we couldn't hear what Doc was saying to his people.

"We were within two hundred meters of Doc's ship when his ARPs inserted, then went into a high orbit over the contact area. We had a bird's-eye view of the ARPs coming under fire and the Cobras repelling the NVA assault. We were orbiting above Doc's helicopter when he landed and got out. Then Doc's helicopter took flight suddenly, leaving him on the ground. There was a lot going on in a very tight area, but we saw Doc come under fire just before he jumped into the bomb crater with a dead NVA soldier. We could see the ARPs. They were about twenty to thirty meters away. They had taken cover and were returning fire. Doc was all by himself.

"Jim Dozier was a brave guy, bullets didn't scare him. He told our pilot to land. Our pilot put us in on the same spot from where Doc's helicopter had taken off just moments before.

"There was gunfire all around us. Dozier grabbed his M-16 and jumped out. I grabbed my Car-15 and followed after him. It didn't take us five seconds to get into the bomb crater with Doc. He was really pissed at his pilot for leaving him on the ground and was yelling at Bates, as if he could hear."

Doc resumes.

I hollered at my ARPs and told them to crawl over to my position and to bring a radio. Several of them, including an RTO, quickly low crawled into the bomb crater with us. I got my hands on the radio and chewed Bates's ass and then gave my gunships orders to fire on the NVA ambushers:

"Red Two-One, Red Two-Two, this is Six. I want you to line up, come in low over my position, and give these bastards everything you've got. Blow the hell out of everything from my immediate front to the tree line."

"Two-One, roger."

"Two-Two, roger."

"Popping smoke, call color."

"Roger, this is Two-One. I've got yellow."

"Two-Two, yellow."

"Confirm, yellow. Get 'em!"

The Cobras rolled in and came over us extremely low. It was so loud you couldn't hear yourself think. They put heavy fire within fifteen meters to our front and worked it over to the tree line. Hot brass from their miniguns came raining down on our position and all around us. That stuff stings and burns, if you get in its way.

Patton arrived in the area and was circling overhead in his helicopter when he asked me for a sitrep. I told him I was going to attack the bastards as soon as the Cobras rolled off.

After the Cobras rolled off, I radioed their pilots:

"Red Two-One, Red Two-Two, this is Six. We are going to attack into the tree line. Stay close. I want you to be able to see us and shoot dinks trying to run, over."

"Two-One, roger."

"Two-Two, roger."

I climbed out of the crater, stood, and yelled to the ARPs, "Follow me!"

Andy O'Meara comments.

"Dozier and I had been firing at the enemy right along with the ARPs. All of us ducked when the gunships came in, trying to avoid getting hit by falling brass, which was impossible. I could see Doc talking on the radio but couldn't hear what he was saying. Then the gunships stopped firing and it was suddenly quiet, except for sporadic fire coming our way. I didn't see Doc talking to his men, but just as soon as the gunships pulled up, he stood up, raised his hand, and shouted, 'Follow me!' as he motioned forward and leaped out of the crater. Some NVA were still shooting at us!

"I had seen Doc in action before and knew him to be a fighter. But his leadership and bravery at that moment was unbelievable. He was unarmed, we were in the middle of a firefight, and he was directing his gunships and ground forces with calm and confidence. He understood the tempo of battle. He could intuit the enemy's next action and instinctively knew how to defeat him."

Doc resumes.

Our assault shocked the NVA. Even though there was a hell of a lot more of them than us, they started running back into the jungle. I then realized I was not armed and started yelling at my ARPs to kill the bastards. They did, quickly killing ten and capturing three.

Andy O'Meara continues.

"I was now concentrating on collecting POWs, looking for documents, and so forth. There was still a lot of shooting going on. As I made my way toward the wood line, I saw movement in the underbrush and aimed my weapon toward it. I heard him groaning in pain before I saw him: an NVA captain who'd been shot in his hips and couldn't walk.

"Fearing for their own lives, his soldiers had left him behind when they retreated. He was bleeding and wouldn't have survived long. You don't capture an NVA captain every day. He was a prize catch and I wanted him interrogated as soon as possible.

"He didn't weigh much, not more than one-hundred-ten pounds. I picked him up and carried him on my shoulders back to a LZ. An ARP medic met us there and got my prisoner's bleeding stopped."

Doc resumes.

My ARPs linked up with the PRU platoon within minutes of our counterattack and led them back to a LZ, where Dozier put them on lift ships and sent them back to their parent unit. The PRU platoon leader was the only friendly casualty.

As promised, four ACAVs loaded with an infantry platoon from the 2nd of the 2nd arrived in time to help us sweep the area. We killed a lot more enemy than just those left behind and took three POWs. Between what the POWs told us and the documents we picked up, O'Meara was able to learn much more about this area than the PRUs would have been able to find out.

I had dismounted my helicopter in haste. I was unarmed, didn't have a radio, and wasn't wearing my steel pot. No way around it, no excuses for it: I was totally unprepared for the action that took place.

I chewed Bates's ass, but to his credit, he remained overhead and directed the gunships. He did the right thing, leaving me on the ground, and clearing out before our helicopter got shot up. When I got back to my base camp, I got together with my XO, Pete Noyes, and told him to write Bates up for the Distinguished Flying Cross, which he later received.

Colonel George Patton, Major Jim Dozier, and Major Andy O'Meara, and others witnessed Doc's leadership during this rescue mission. O'Meara wrote it up and Patton signed the award recommendation, recommending Doc for the Distinguished Service Cross, which was downgraded by II Field Forces to a Silver Star, first oak leaf cluster. This was Doc's second Silver Star for conspicuous courage and gallantry in action.

∗ Chapter 52 ∗

29 October 1968—vicinity of Chan Luu, west of Bien Hoa Air Base

Early in my command, I experimented with different ways of doing things, trying to improve the troop's combat effectiveness. I had never attempted to command combat actions while flying a Cobra and wanted to give it a go.

On this particular morning, I decided to fly in a pink team. I climbed in the rear seat of Warrant Officer Jim Noe's AH-1G Cobra and had him ride in the front seat as my gunner. Warrant Officer Guy Ballou flew with us in his OH-6 Cayuse. He was our scout pilot for the routine aerial recon we were conducting in the vicinity of Chan Luu. This area was prime hunting ground when we were looking for action.

We didn't spot anything of interest in the morning. Hoping to increase the odds of spotting the enemy in the afternoon, I decided to search an area next to the one Ballou was working.

Shortly after I stopped trailing him, Ballou flew over a cluster of three or four isolated farm hooches nestled among banana trees in the middle of a very large dry rice paddy area. He went in to take a closer look and got his chin bubble hosed down with AK-47 fire. He moved to the side of the contact area and called me with a sitrep. Ballou said that he'd taken fire and had several holes in his canopy, but neither he nor his observer was hit and his aircraft was not seriously damaged. He had returned fire, dropped red smoke to mark, and cleared the area.

Noe and I were very close to his location and immediately flew to him. As soon as we saw his smoke, we rolled in with rockets and the nose minigun. I banked and came back for a second firing pass. Looking down, I could see VC running like rats deserting a sinking ship. I had no intention of letting them escape. I broke from my gun run and started circling the area.

While Noe proceeded to gun the VC down, I radioed my TOC and told them to scramble ARPs. They sent two squads and held two in reserve. Meanwhile, Ballou found a slot in my flight pattern and joined Noe and me in gunning down VC attempting to flee the hooches.

Two lift ships loaded with ARPs were over the contact area within thirty minutes. I told Ballou to drop a smoke grenade two hundred meters north of the hooches to mark what looked like a safe LZ. However, the lift ships came under fire as they inserted the ARPs. We saw where the green tracers were coming from, and Noe worked it over with our minigun, temporarily suppressing the VC's fire.

The ARPs hit the ground and took cover behind a rice paddy dike just before the VC started shooting at them. Deciding that it was time to quit playing cat and mouse, I called my TOC and had them scramble the two standby ARP squads.

Former first lieutenant Dennis Reardon comments on working for Doc and this mission.

"Doc and I didn't see eye to eye on anything. We got off on the wrong foot and that footing never changed. I didn't get along with him on a work level but I didn't dislike him on a personal level. My differences with him were professional—how my platoon's missions were best accomplished. But he was the boss.

"I went out with the first squads on this mission. Our lift ship took fire from automatic weapons before we landed, and there was no cover once we were on the ground. I knew what had to be done and was trying to maneuver my men without getting them killed while Doc was telling me what to do from the air."

Former staff sergeant and ARP squad leader Dave Summers recounts joining the troop and this action.

"I was in the Nine-nineteenth Engineer Company attached to the Eleventh Armored Cavalry Regiment. In early September, when the Air Cavalry Troop was transitioning its LRRP platoon to ARPs, I was sent to teach them how to use explosives.

"I liked the troop right away. It was such a great place that I soon indicated my desire to stay. Someone conveyed my desire to Major Bahnsen and he got me permanently assigned to the ARPs.

"My squad was one of the two squads held in reserve during the initial phase of this mission. I was sitting in the rear door of a D-model Huey as we approached this island of hooches in the middle of a large dry rice paddy area. I could see green tracers coming out of the hooches and red tracers going in. The green tracers were landing in a field behind the dike and in front of the other two ARP squads. I was thinking, 'Please God, don't let us land in that field.' But that was exactly where we landed. If the Cobras hadn't rolled in on the hooches just as we started to land, our helicopter would have taken fire.

"As soon as we were on the ground, we ran behind the dike and joined up with the other squads.

"Major Bahnsen was on the radio, telling Lieutenant Reardon where he wanted him to position us for an assault on the hooches. Major Bahnsen dominated the radio during battles and was doing so in this one, so much so that Reardon was having difficulty communicating with his teams. Not long after the two teams I was with inserted, Reardon told us to switch to the alternate push, taking us off the command net."

Scout pilot Guy Ballou recalls this action.

"The ARPs were pinned down and couldn't get up to advance. Doc was trying to get them to move but they wouldn't. Nobody could have gotten across that field in the beginning. Still, Doc was trying to make the transition from LRRPs to ARPs with this contact.

"I had the ability to move, so I got off to the side, between the ARPs and the hooches, and minigunned the hell out of those dinks. About that time Jim Noe and Doc rolled in with rockets and guns. I kept firing until I ran out of ammo."

Doc resumes.

I radioed Lieutenant Reardon and told him to make a full assault on the village to his front. As I continued to circle, I noticed he wasn't moving out. As best I could tell no fire was coming from the village, but Reardon continued to stay behind the dike. I gave him a second order to move out and nothing happened. He didn't even roger my transmission.

I was getting agitated. Reardon had twice before refused to follow my instructions during a firefight, and he ignored my third order to move out. That really pissed me off! I proceeded to land between the hooches and in front of the dike.

Dave Summers continues.

"It was my impression that Lieutenant Reardon didn't care for Major Bahnsen from the first moment he arrived. There were times when the tension between them was so thick you could cut it with a knife.

"Major Bahnsen exited his aircraft and came stomping toward us. He didn't have to say a word. He was not a happy camper and it showed. We didn't want Reardon to do something unmilitary, so all of us NCOs instinctively moved in shoulder to shoulder with him in case that happened.

"Major Bahnsen walked right up to Reardon and started screaming at him. I can't remember the exact words he said, but at the time we thought it was in bad form.

"All of us NCOs were already standing in a huddle, so Major Bahnsen told our platoon sergeant what he wanted us to do, and asked him if he understood and if he could get it done. Our platoon sergeant said, 'Yes, sir!'

"Just then, a Huey landed by Major Bahnsen's Cobra, and he left to go meet it. We didn't wait for him to return. His orders were clear. We broke into squads and started our assault on the hooches."

Doc resumes.

Colonel Patton landed near my Cobra and I walked over and reported to him. I told him I had relieved my ARP platoon leader, which came as no surprise to Patton, and asked him to take him off my hands. Patton looked over at Reardon and told him to mount his helicopter.

I gave Patton a quick sitrep and watched the ARPs start their assault before getting back into my Cobra and joining the other aircraft circling the hooches.

The ARP assault resulted in their finding dead bodies, wounded, and weapons. They took no casualties themselves. After I got the all clear from the ARP platoon sergeant, I landed on the opposite side of the village for the mop up. Patton had been watching this whole action. He landed by my ship and came over to talk again. As we were looking the area over, I pointed out the dead VC in the paddy area, then someone spotted another VC trying to crawl away. He was a hundred fifty to two hundred meters from our location.

Patton yelled out, "He's mine, he's mine! Don't anybody shoot!"

We all watched Colonel Patton attempt to shoot the VC with a single-shot M-79 grenade launcher. Patton had carried that M-79 for several weeks and this was his first real chance to use it. He launched seven to eight rounds, coming close, but never hitting the man. He finally gave up with a lot of profanity about the lucky bastard and his crappy shooting. I told the ARP platoon sergeant to send some guys to pick the VC up, which they did, and we took him prisoner.

I learned that troop command in a Cobra was not the way to go and never used it for that purpose again.

First Lieutenant Dennis Reardon's relief from command during this enemy contact was a huge turning point for the ARPS, who soon started to become the kind of aggressive fighters Doc wanted and expected them to be.

Warrant Officer Guy Ballou received the Silver Star for his gallantry during this hostile engagement. Several ARPs were awarded the Bronze Star with Valor device. Colonel Patton observed much of this action from the air. Based on his recommendation, Major Doc Bahnsen and Warrant Officer Jim Noe received the Distinguished Flying Cross.

✴ Chapter 53 ✴

30 October 1968—Alpha Pad and 11th Armored Cavalry Regiment officers' mess, Bien Hoa Air Base

Former staff sergeant Dave Summers reflects on Lieutenant Reardon's relief from command.

"Soldiers tend to see the same things differently based on the perspective their rank, duties, and experience provides. The vast majority of the enlisted men in Vietnam were young fellows trying to perform very dangerous tasks by killing a very determined enemy and trying to avoid having their name etched on a future black granite wall.

"In some cases, the feeling among enlisted men in Vietnam was that some NCOs and officers were being cavalier with their lives by taking unnecessary risks.

"My fellow ARPs and I felt that Reardon was one of the good guys. He avoided situations that put us at risk unnecessarily. Having him relieved was quite a blow. But now that I look back on it from a command standpoint, Major Bahnsen did the right thing.

"Major Bahnsen gave us enough rope to make us feel like we had some autonomy but kept a tight enough rein to keep us under control. That was a unique quality in an officer. Reardon wanted more rope than Major Bahnsen was willing to give. That got him relieved. Unit cohesion and leadership suffer when platoon leaders don't follow their troop commander's orders."

Attending West Point was the answer to my childhood dreams.

I was one of the first in my West Point class to attend the Command and General Staff College.

My family lived in East Point, Georgia, while I went off to war. *Front, left to right:* Leeanne, Jimmie, and bradley; *back, left to right:* Chris and Pat.

I had to dig in my heels to keep from flying Caribou transports during my first tour in Vietnam. I wanted to fly Huey gunships. Fortunately, I got what I wanted. *(Official U.S. Army photo)*

Thach Thi Hung, a.k.a. "The Dragon Lady of Bien Hoa."

My brother Peter visiting me at Bien Hoa Air Base.

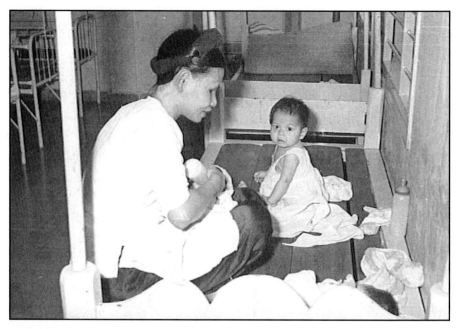

This blind nurse at the Bien Hoa Catholic orphanage was a loving caregiver to the children, many of whom had American fathers. *(Warren George)*

Bags of rice taken from enemy bunkers often wound up feeding the children at the Bien Hoa Catholic orphanage. *(Warren George)*

The Bandit platoon gathered around me at Bien Hoa Air Base. When it came to flying gunships, the Bandits were the best of the best. *(Official U.S. Army photo)*

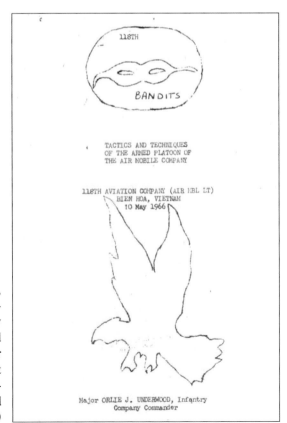

Much of the Bandit book, issued as a hasty "lessons-learned" guide on 10 May 1966, is still being used today. You can build better gunships but it's difficult to improve on battlefield-validated gunship tactics and techniques. *(Larry Mobley)*

118TH

BANDITS

TACTICS AND TECHNIQUES
OF THE ARMED PLATOON OF
THE AIR MOBILE COMPANY

118TH AVIATION COMPANY (AIR MBL LT)
BIEN HOA, VIETNAM
10 May 1966

Major ORLIE J. UNDERWOOD, Infantry
Company Commander

Bandit gunships parked alongside Marine H-34s on the beach at Ky Ha during Operation Double Eagle. *(Warren George)*

U.S.S. *Valley Forge*. All Bandit pilots became carrier-qualified, flying on and off this ship during Operation Double Eagle. *(Official U.S. Navy photo)*

Deckhands painted a red USN and anchor on top of the white thunderbird on the side of our helicopters as soon as we touched down on the U.S.S. *Valley Forge*.
(Warren George)

The 118th's "Georgia Boys." Capt. Jerry Cubine, me, and Capt. Johnny "Al" Phillips.

Viet Cong dead policed up from a nearby battlefield where they were killed by ARVN ground forces supported by U.S. Air Force fighters and U.S. Army gunships. *(Warren George)*

Warren George, Larry Mobley, and other Bandit pilots traded Prince Albert tobacco cans for machetes, axes, and other native-made goods at a Montagnard village near Dong Xoai. Thunderbird helicopters were used to temporarily relocate these people when they were threatened by advancing enemy forces. *(Warren George)*

Lt. Col. Horst Joost pins on my major's leaf, March 1966. *(Official U.S. Army photo)*

Joost presented me with my first Silver Star based on the recommendation of Marine Air Group 36 for my actions during Operation Double Eagle. *(Official U.S. Army photo)*

Addressing the Air Cavalry Troop, 11th Armored Cavalry Regiment, at Bien Hoa Air Base during change of command ceremonies on 24 September 1968. Col. George S. Patton, the regimental commander, is behind me, observing. *(Public Information Office, 11th Armored Cavalry Regiment)*

Phyllis "Fif" Shaughnessy worked in the pacification program during her "second tour" of Vietnam. We were later married and divorced. *(Rex Saul)*

Left to right: Me, Warrant Officer Guy Ballou, and Warrant Officer Mike Bates. Ballou was one of the best and bravest scout pilots in Vietnam. Bates was my pilot in the Air Cavalry Troop. He knew no fear. Both received direct commissions to second lieutenant. *(Rex Saul)*

Col. George S. Patton was the 39th colonel of the Blackhorse and its 6th commander in Vietnam. Patton was a highly respected and courageous battlefield commander who fought fiercely. Two Distinguished Service Crosses top the long list of medals of gallantry awarded to him during the Vietnam War. *(Public Information Office, 11th Armored Cavalry Regiment)*

Leaders of the Air Cavalry Troop. *Left to right:* Me, Capt. Earl Moore, Maj. Ed Underwood, 1st Lt. Al Moore, and 1st Lt. Duke Doubleday. *(Public Information Office, 11th Armored Cavalry Regiment)*

1st Lt. Tom White was a superb ARP platoon leader, the first in his West Point class to make general officer, and appointed the 18th Secretary of the Army by President George W. Bush. *(Rex Saul)*

ARP Specialist 4th Class Rex Saul catches a ride back to an LZ after an enemy contact. *(Chris Gunderson)*

Heroes of the 1 December 1968 action. *Left to right:* Sgt. Wade Butler, Sgt. Bob Roeder, 1st Lt. Duke Doubleday, Specialist 4th Class Mozelle Starkey, and Sgt. Dave Summers. *(Rex Saul)*

South Vietnamese national policemen Nguyen Van Rang and Tien Trang with one of the three Honda motorcycles we captured from Viet Cong messengers.
(Rex Saul)

My flight crew in Air Cavalry troop, Fall 1968: Mike Gorman, Mike Bates, me, and Jim Gray.
(Rex Saul)

Air Cavalry troopers built a stage for the Australian rock band that played at the troop's New Year's Eve party on 31 December 1968. *(Rex Saul)*

The weekly feeding of the boa always drew a crowd. *(Rex Saul)*

Sgt. Bob Roeder was an outstanding soldier whose tour in Vietnam was cut short by an enemy mine. Since retirement, I hunt birds in eastern Kansas with him every fall. *(Rex Saul)*

ARP Sgt. Dave Summers looking at a pile of monkey skulls found during the sweep of a Viet Cong base camp. *(Official U.S. Army photo)*

ARPs during a search for Viet Cong in a small village. *(Rex Saul)*

Col. Patton often joined me on the ground during enemy contacts but always let me run the fight. *(Public Information Office, 11th Armored Cavalry Regiment)*

Col. Patton landed to show me where he had seen enemy soldiers from the air. We captured six Viet Cong within 100 meters of our position shortly after this photo was taken. *(Public Information Office, 11th Armored Cavalry*

Col. Patton and I toasting our idea of "peace on earth." The photo shows nine North Vietnamese Army soldiers killed by ARP Sgt. Lynn Sowder. *(Public Information Office, 11th Armored Cavalry Regiment)*

ARP Specialist 4th Class Otis Darden protecting a downed Cobra helicopter until it can be extracted. Sadly, this fine young man was KIA only days later. *(Rex Saul)*

None of my medics wore red crosses on their uniforms and, like Specialist 5th Class Donald "Doc" Southwell, they always carried a weapon and grenades. *(Rex Saul)*

ARP Specialist 4th Class Jim Weller was in over 300 enemy contacts during his one-year tour in Vietnam. Here, he clears a weapons cache for demolition. *(Rex Saul)*

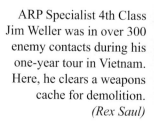

ARP Sgt. Chris Gunderson escorts Viet Cong POWs back to Regiment for interrogation. *(Rex Saul)*

ARPs searching enemy dead after a firefight in heavy jungle. *(Rex Saul)*

An ARP pulls a North Vietnamese Army soldier killed by Specialist 4th Class Rex Saul out of a bunker. *(Rex Saul)*

An M Company tank stopped in a bomb crater during an assault on North Vietnamese Army bunkers near the Michelin plantation. *(Rex Saul)*

Sgt. Joe Oreto talks on a radio behind a G Troop ACAV during an air strike on 3 February 1969. Regrettably, this outstanding soldier was KIA just over a month later. *(Rex Saul)*

2nd Squadron tracks and Air Cavalry Troop ARPs join a pile-on operation. *(Rex Saul)*

Casualties being medevaced during a fight near Lai Khe. *(Rex Saul)*

ARPs protecting a tank's flank and rear during a jungle busting operation. *(Rex Saul)*

An M Company tank burns after being hit by a RPG during a fight near the Michelin plantation at Dau Tieng, April 1969. *(Rex Saul)*

Warrant Officer Guy Ballou was shot down trying to pick up wounded ARPs from a bomb crater. Luckily, everybody survived the crash. *(Rex Saul)*

Air Cavalry Troop pink teams and ARPs wait for an air strike to lift before assaulting a heavily fortified North Vietnamese Army base camp. *(Rex Saul)*

ARPs moving to contact. *(Rex Saul)*

Patton and his commanders just before his tour ended. *Left to right:* Col. George S. Patton, Lt. Col. Merritte Ireland, Lt. Col. Lee Duke, Lt. Col. John McEnery, and me. *(Public Information Office, 11th Armored Cavalry Regiment)*

Maj. Don Snow and a Vietnamese interpreter provide cover during the fight on my first day of squadron command. A fierce fighter, Snow received the Silver Star for his gallantry in this counter-ambush action. *(Rex Saul)*

Col. Jimmie Leach landed to help us sweep enemy bunkers after my squadron was ambushed on my first day of command. *(Rex Saul)*

Col. Leach and I discuss the ambush on the first day of my squadron command, 17 April 1969. *(Rex Saul)*

Two of the six North Vietnamnese Army POWs captured during the counter-ambush action on my first day of squadron command. We also killed 20 NVA soldiers. *(Rex Saul)*

1st Squadron attacking north of Lai Khe. *(Rex Saul)*

1st Squadron troopers put a North Vietnamese Army soldier on an ACAV so that he can lead us to his friends. *(Rex Saul)*

ARPs securing an LZ for a medevac helicopter near Quan Loi. *(Rex Saul)*

1st Squadron troopers inspect RPG damage to my command and control ACAV during operations in the Iron Triangle.

A Huey lift ship, working medevac, arrives to extract ARPs near Quan Loi. *(Rex Saul)*

Gen. Creighton Abrams presenting me
with the Distinguished Service Cross
at Quan Loi, August 1969. *(Rex Saul)*

Command Sgt. Maj. Frank
Zlobec, a great soldier and
a great friend who shared
a tent with me during
some tough times. *(Public
Information Officer, 11th
Armored Cavalry Regiment)*

1st Squadron Executive
Officer Maj. Bill Good,
me, and 1st Squadron
Operations Officer Don Snow
at Quan Loi, August 1969.

Heroes of 9 August 1969. All eight of these ARPs received the Silver Star. *Front, left to right:* Pfc. Rothie Brackens, Specialists Bill Fergerstrom and Ed Cook; *middle row, left to right:* 1st Lt. Doug Rich and Specialist Dan Bock. *Back, left to right:* Pfc. Robert Lamdin, Pfc. Bruce Stephens, and Specialist John Montgomery. *(Rex Saul)*

A Cobra being rearmed on the runway at Quan Loi. *(Rex Saul)*

Col. Jimmie Leach and I visited Capt. Art West at the 93rd Evacuation Hospital, Long Binh, where Leach awarded West his third Purple Heart. *(Rex Saul)*

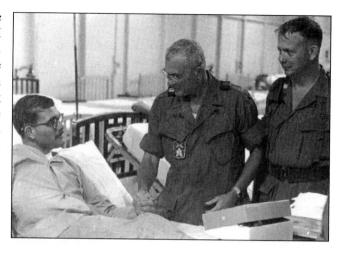

I was awarded my fifth Silver Star and the Legion of Merit during 1st Squadron's change of command ceremony at Loc Ninh, September 1969. *(Rex Saul)*

Relinquishing command of the 1st Squadron, 11th Armored Cavalry Regiment to Col. Jimmie Leach. Master Sgt. David Wolff is standing to my left. He was filling in for Command Sgt. Maj. Frank Zlobec who was WIA a few days earlier. *(Rex Saul)*

The first TRADOC Systems Management team for attack helicopters, Ft. Rucker, Alabama, 1977. *Left to right:* Maj. Chuck Crowley, Maj. Joe Beach, me, Lt. Col. Joe Moffet, and Maj. Jerry Hipp. *(Official U.S. Army photo)*

Quail hunting in west Texas while I was Chief of Staff, III Armored Corps, Ft. Hood, Texas, 1985. *Left to right:* Lt. Col. Jim Noles, me, and Lt. Col. Tommy Franks.

Brig. Gen. John C. "Doc" Bahnsen, Jr., and Maj. Peggy Miller Bahnsen, Ft. Hood, Texas, 1986. *(Official U.S. Army photo)*

At the 40th class reunion, USMA '56. *Left to right:* Ann Prather, Norm Schwarzkopf, Brenda Schwarzkopf, me, and Judy Lehardy. *(Peggy Miller Bahnsen)*

USMA '56 alumni awarded the Gold Order of St. George at Ft. Knox, Kentucky, May 2000. *Left to right:* Bob Sorley, me, and Rick Brown. *(Official U.S. Army photo)*

My children and grandchildren. *Front, left to right:* Lea Harvey, Derrick Bahnsen, J. B. Bahnsen, and Lana Harvey; *middle row, left to right:* Leeanne Bahnsen, Brad Bahnsen, and Lauren Bahnsen; *back, left to right:* Robert Johnson, Jimmy Bahnsen, Chris Bahnsen, and Wendy Bahnsen.

My son Minh and his wife, Linh Bahnsen.

Peggy and me at home on Miller Farm. *(Fred Miller)*

Doc talks about replacing his ARP platoon leader.

Relieving Reardon was a drastic, but necessary, action as I saw it. I never discussed relieving him with my ARPs. Nor did I realize he had them switch frequencies during the contact. The ARPs all knew what I expected of them and Reardon wasn't meeting my expectations or following my orders. Relieving him was something I had to do to instill discipline and convince any doubters that I meant business.

Patton agreed.

At his evening briefing, Patton announced that the Aero Rifle Platoon leader's job was open and that I would interview interested lieutenants for it the next day.

Although he'd been relieved, neither Patton nor I wanted to smear Reardon's record or reputation. He was a skilled officer and deserved the chance to serve elsewhere—where his talents could be put to good use.

Patton offered Reardon two options: go back to a Special Forces unit or take an assistant S-5 job under Captain Lee Fulmer, the regiment's civil affairs and psychological operations officer.

Dennis Reardon reflects on his choice.

"I chose to work with Lee Fulmer. As it turned out, I spent almost as much time in the field in that job as I did with the LRRPs or the ARPs. We did civil affairs work by day and psyops by night.

"The work was interesting and often dangerous but I enjoyed it, picked up a Bronze Star with 'V' while participating in a nighttime psyops mission on 5 January 1969, and I came home feeling good about myself and my time in Vietnam.

"As for Doc, we made our peace over twenty years ago. There is no ill-will between us today. If there was, I wouldn't have a picture of us hanging in my office."

Doc resumes.

Like all other ARP jobs at this point in my command, the platoon leader position was open only to volunteers. Being qualified wasn't good enough. You had to want the job to get it. After I got things going the following morning, I drove to regiment and took up a table in the officers' mess, where I interviewed three outstanding officers for the position: First Lieutenants Charles "Duke" Doubleday, Jerry "J. W." Thurman, and Thomas "Tom" White.

Former captain Duke Doubleday, who later became Georgia's civilian aide to the secretary of the army, recalls why he applied for the position.

"I was an ACAV platoon leader in F Troop, Second Squadron, for a short time before becoming its XO as the result of a high attrition rate of junior officers in the unit. My squadron had come out of the field about three weeks earlier to take its turn at providing security for Blackhorse base camp at Xuan Loc. I was going stark raving mad shuffling papers and chasing down gold-bricking NCOs who were trying to skate by.

"I didn't know Doc, but I knew exactly what the job was and that I could do it. I saw the ARP platoon leader's job as an open door of opportunity, even though I didn't meet its specs, being armor, not infantry branch. I knew I would have to sell myself and went for it full of piss and vinegar because landing it would get me back in the field."

Retired Colonel, then First Lieutenant, J. W. Thurman tells why he tossed his hat into the ring.

"I didn't know what an air cav unit was. I assumed the job to command the Aero Rifle Platoon had something to do with infantry and that it had flight status. I'd been in the infantry as an enlisted man, and was a field artillery aviator at the time—assigned to Second Squadron's Aviation Section. For all I knew, this was some new type of gunship platoon, and that made me curious enough to go see what this job was all about.

"I didn't get far into my interview with Doc before I realized this job had no flight status, and that killed my enthusiasm for it."

Retired Brigadier General, then First Lieutenant, Tom White, who became the eighteenth secretary of the army, talks about his interest in commanding the ARPs.

"When I first interviewed for the ARP job, I was a platoon leader in the Third Squadron's M Company. Doc was refocusing the Aero Rifle Platoon away from the LRRP concept to the ARP concept. It was clear that Doc would get you a lot of action and I wanted to get more in the center of things.

"This was the first and only time I ever interviewed for a job in the Army that I didn't get. It wasn't as ego-crushing as it sounds. I went on to another platoon leader job in K Troop."

Doc resumes.

When I told him he would have to give up flying if he got the job, J. W. eliminated himself from further consideration. I understood his thinking and had no problems with it.

That left me with two good choices: Doubleday or White.

White was a West Pointer, I liked that. Doubleday was an Armor OCS graduate who'd lost his draft deferment during his first year of law school.

I was leaning toward White, but Doubleday's smooth-talking Georgia-boy charm and self-promoting salesmanship won me over.

If you were casting a movie about ARPs, and Doubleday auditioned for the lead role, you'd cast him in it. Plain and simple. He looked the part, said all the right things, and said them in the right way. He sold me on his ability to do what I wanted my new ARP leader to do, and told me that he was eager to get back into the fight. One more day of garrison duty was one too many for him.

Doubleday cleared his troop and reported for duty as my Aero Rifle Platoon leader within a few days.

✳ Chapter 54 ✳

31 October–17 November 1968—Bien Hoa Air Base, Long Binh, and Cam Ranh Bay

I woke up in the middle of the night and barely made it outside to the portable latrine before I puked my guts out. Vomiting until my stomach was empty left my mouth dry and throat burning. Thinking it would settle my stomach down and cool my throat, I drank some water, but puked it right back up.

The next few hours were pure torture. I was hot one minute, had the chills the next, and started sweating the next. I was dizzy, weak, and dehydrated. I had no idea what brought this on, but felt like I had been shot at and missed, then shit at and hit. I was a sick, sick boy.

I don't know how, but I managed to get out of bed and over to see the regiment's surgeon, Captain Jerry Noga, early the next morning. He checked my vital signs. My temperature was 101 degrees. He quickly diagnosed my problem as malaria and had me driven to Long Binh immediately, where I was admitted at the 93rd Evacuation Hospital for treatment.

Before being moved to a curtained-off section of the infectious disease ward, doctors gave me quinine and started me on a saline IV. They also drew some of my blood for lab tests. When the results came back, they told me I had *plasmodium falciparum*—the most morbid and fatal type of malaria.

My temperature remained high for the next several days, and my diarrhea wouldn't let up. I was losing weight fast but the doctors kept pumping me full of fluids through an IV. Before long, the veins in my arms and hands collapsed from dehydration to the point where the doctors couldn't obtain a successful cannulation in them and they had to insert the cannula needle in my toes. Damn that hurt! I had to bite my lip whenever they poked me.

Every Monday morning, all soldiers in the theater took the big orange pill to prevent malaria. This had been going on for years. It was normally performed in formation to ensure compliance. This antimalarial pill often gave you terrible cramps closely followed by diarrhea about the middle of the afternoon. You had to go immediately. Many a soldier messed in his trousers before he could get to a place to relieve himself. I once landed in bandit country to keep from messing in my pants.

Colonel Patton came to see me in the hospital soon after I was admitted. He was livid over my coming down with malaria and accused me of not taking the big orange horse pill that we were required to take every Monday.

Patton was wrong. The doctors told me that *p. falciparum* malaria was resistant to chloroquine—the active ingredient in the big orange pill, which was very effective against *plasmodium vivax* malaria.

I took my pill every Monday, but I could have cared less about what Patton thought. I was too damn sick to argue and there was nothing I could've said that would have changed his mind.

Former ARP platoon leader Duke Doubleday recalls arriving at the Air Cavalry Troop and meeting his men for the first time.

"Doc was hospitalized with a serious bout of malaria when I reported in at the Air Cav Troop. Major Don Peters was running the show in his absence. I stowed my gear in the officer's hooch and went to the ARPs' hooch to meet my men.

"The ARPs were really pissed at Doc for relieving Lieutenant Reardon. These guys stuck together. They really liked Reardon and weren't happy about there being a new sheriff in town.

"I talked with them for about thirty minutes. I told them I was not trying to undo anything. I had a job to do and needed them to support me in it. When I left their hooch, I said something like, 'Let's carry on.' "

Former ARP squad leader Dave Summers recalls Lieutenant Doubleday's coming to the ARPs' hooch to meet them.

"What happened out in the field never really hit us until we returned to base camp. Officers got relieved in Vietnam but rarely, if ever, the way Lieutenant Reardon was relieved—during a firefight.

"Shell-shocked isn't the precise way to describe our emotions, but none of us felt like being ARPs any longer.

"I don't remember who brought Lieutenant Doubleday to our hooch. We were all lying around on our bunks pouting and sulking. If Major Bahnsen had been around, there'd have been none of that. He would have kicked our asses for acting like a bunch of spoiled brats who suddenly can't have their way. We were young, but Major Bahnsen treated us like men, and he expected us to act like men.

"Lieutenant Doubleday was a sharp-looking officer. He seemed confident in his ability to lead us and only wanted us to give him a chance.

"After he left, I spoke up. Although we were all about the same age, late teens to early twenties, I'd been in the Army for five years before going to Vietnam. I'd seen more and knew more about how the Army operated than most of the guys. Reardon was gone and we needed to snap out of it. Not one to beat a dead horse, I told the guys that, rather than sitting around on our asses, we ought to give Doubleday a chance.

"We were scrambled for a mission within a very short time, and that put an end to our sulking."

Doc continues.

It took about a week for the doctors to stabilize me. There wasn't anything more they could do for me at the 93rd Evac, so they had me flown up to Cam Ranh Bay to recuperate at the 6th Convalescent Center. I felt damn lucky to have escaped death. The type of malaria I came down with killed people in Vietnam, and there were fellow soldiers in the infectious disease ward with me who didn't make it out alive as the result of whatever infection they'd come down with.

The 6th Convalescent Center was a cluster of buildings built on the Cam Ranh Bay peninsula. It always seemed to be sunny in that part of Vietnam. The sand on the beach was white as could be, and the ocean water was clear blue and warm. Patients at the center were there to relax and recuperate. We wore light blue hospital pajamas and put on white hospital slippers when we got out of bed. The staff did everything they could to take our minds off the war.

I suppose most of the patients were thankful to have a hiatus from the war. I wasn't one of them. I didn't go to Vietnam to lie around on the beach while my troopers were fighting. I didn't like being away from the action.

Initially, I worried about how the troop was doing in my absence. However, some reflection on the people running the show while I was recuperating lessened my worries.

Major Pete Noyes, my executive officer, was a New Englander and a graduate of Norwich University. He played hockey in college, was as rough as a cob, and was totally guileless. Noyes was a self-starter and a real workhorse. He didn't quit until the job was done, and he did his best on every assignment, every duty. He always maintained a great sense of humor. His personal loyalty to me was second to none and he quickly became "my man."

I soon developed an unquestioning trust in Noyes's ability to handle matters that required discretion and judgment. More than once, he got things done in ways I didn't want to know about. He made the supply system cough up things we needed in ways I was afraid to ask about. But I knew whatever he did was justified in the end.

Major Don Peters became my ops officer after I fired the one I inherited when I took over the troop. Peters was a solid leader, excellent pilot, and a hell of a fighter.

Senior to Noyes by date of rank, Peters was second in command and assumed command of the troop in my absence, giving him two hats to wear at times. Even though he never complained to me about it, I knew this was hard on him. But he bore his burdens well and I knew he'd be providing solid leadership while I was recovering.

Together, I was fully confident that Noyes was keeping the troop's administration squared away and that Peters was running its operations proficiently.

Sergeant First Class A. C. Cotton was my first sergeant. He was top of the line. A big, tall, and imposing soldier, the troops listened to and respected him. He was a cavalryman and a fighter first and foremost, but quickly adapted to the administrative role of a first sergeant.

Cotton was one of those rare guys who get things done quietly. We did not have enlisted problems with him in charge—only one Article 15 (Jim Weller's) and no court-martials that I can remember.

We did ship people out quickly and quietly when they didn't perform. This was done with only a high sign from me. I knew Cotton would be taking care of the enlisted troopers and assisting Major Pete Noyes with his duties.

Captain Earl Moore, my Lift Ship Platoon commander, was a superb pilot and a well-grounded armor officer. He was a man of sterling character and absolutely trustworthy. His flight crews could get people on and off of the battlefield with ease. He didn't run when the bullets flew. I could count on Moore to be there where he was needed.

Lieutenant Duke Doubleday assumed command of the ARPs the day I went to the hospital. I felt good about selecting him. He was smart, aggressive, and glib. I believed Doubleday's way with words and people would go a long way in getting the ARPs to accept him as their leader. And I was confident that Peters, Moore, and the experienced ARPs would get him off to a good start.

Major Ed Underwood replaced Lieutenant Gary Worthy as my Aero Scout Platoon leader. As I remember, he came to the troop fresh out of flight school. Underwood had a good armor background but very little flying time. He was generally timid as a scout pilot and did not "hunt" aggressively. He was much more interested in aircraft maintenance than leading aerial recon missions. That was fine with me. What Underwood lacked as a scout was more than covered by an aggressive group of "hunter" pilots in his platoon.

After I moved Don Peters into the ops officer job, First Lieutenant A1 Moore became the senior officer in my Aero Gun Platoon. He was a tall, handsome, personable, and socially adept young man. People liked Moore and he liked being one of the boys. Our personalities clashed at times. I thought he lacked the personal maturity to lead at that point in his career, but the platoon leader's job came his way by default and he never did anything to cause me to relieve him.

I also reflected on my personal pilot.

Warrant Officer Mike Bates flew with me almost every day. He was the top in his class and commanded the cadet brigade during his final weeks of flight school. He attended the Cobra transition course right out of flight school—en route to Vietnam. He arrived in-country in August 1968 when the troop still had C-model Huey gunships, and he ended up being assigned to fly the troop commander.

Bates was totally proficient as a pilot and understood intuitively how the fight should go once we made contact. He was smart and accepted responsibility readily. He showed initiative and followed orders. He was great with the crew chiefs and door gunners. He understood quickly why we needed two UH-1s for the command and control mission, and he kept them flying and everything working. He never made excuses about anything and showed leadership in everything he did.

I was fortunate to have such a competent group working for me, and I wanted to get back working with them as soon as possible.

Celebrities of one sort or another often visited soldiers in Vietnam. We appreciated them being there and always tried to make their stay pleasant. They did their best to brighten our day and lift our spirits. Plus, they made us feel good about what we were doing and appreciated for doing it.

Coach Woody Hayes, Ohio State's football coach in those days, visited the 6th Convalescent Center while I was there. I was still sick, but I really appreciated him being there and talking to me. He was a caring, great guy in my view.

The troop fought while I healed, but not without misfortune.

On 10 November, about a week before I got well enough to return to the troop, Specialist Four John Paul Murphy, one of my ARPs, was killed in action. He was a Pennsylvania boy, just a young kid, really. He was married and had big plans for the future. My stomach knotted up when I learned of his death.

Former ARP Dave Summers recounts the day Murphy was killed.

"We had the whole platoon out that day. Our mission was to recover rice we found at a VC base camp a day or two earlier. This rice was in bags stamped with 'shaking hands' and inscribed with something like 'a gift from the USA to you.' It was meant to feed South Vietnamese friendlies, but like a lot of stuff sent to aid our allies, it had ended up in enemy hands. Bummer.

"We flew across the Dong Nai River and headed west to somewhere in southern Binh Duong Province where the base camp was located. We didn't expect any action but this was Indian territory. Two squads set up a perimeter around the base camp while the other two squads humped sacks of rice back to slicks sitting in the LZ.

"It took us a couple of hours to pack all the rice out; the slicks were shuttling it back to Bien Hoa as quick as we loaded them up.

"Once the last of the rice was loaded, Lieutenant Doubleday signaled for the guys on perimeter to pull in and link up with the rest of us at the LZ. We always counted heads before heading to the LZ. It was basic combat discipline—a good way to make sure you didn't leave anyone behind. But we didn't that day. I don't know why.

"Our platoon sergeant counted heads when we got to the LZ. We were one short. Someone asked, 'Where's Murphy?' just before we heard a couple of gunshots coming from the edge of the jungle.

"A bunch of us took off running toward the sound of the gunshots.

We were ready for a firefight but didn't see even one dink in the area. We made it just inside the trees and saw Murphy, he was sitting up against a tree with his head keeled over and blood pouring out of his chest. No question, Murphy was dead."

Then Specialist Four Chris Gunderson recalls what happened next.

"We found an empty AK-47 magazine about twenty yards from Murphy's body. It was on the edge of a trail. Somebody on a radio yelled and told us that one of the Loaches thought they saw movement just ahead of us along the trail going into thicker jungle.

"Sergeant Bill Emanuel and I went down the trail looking for dinks but gunships started rolling in. We didn't have a radio and didn't want the gunships to mistake us for the enemy, so we turned around and headed out.

"We carried Murphy's body back to the LZ and lifted off without further incident. It was a damn shame, losing him like that."

Doc resumes.

I had lost about twenty-five pounds and looked lean and mean by the time I returned to Bien Hoa and reported to Patton. Doctor Noga had squared Patton away on the difference between *p. falciparum* and *p. vivax* malaria.

The moment he saw me, Patton apologized profusely for falsely accusing me of not taking the weekly antimalaria pill. (We later started taking the daily white pill that was supposed to prevent you from coming down with *p. falciparum* malaria.)

After giving me a quick briefing on the regiment's actions during my absence, Patton sent me back to my troop. He wanted me back in the fight without further delay.

☆ **Chapter 55** ☆

18 November 1968—Alpha Pad, Bien Hoa Air Base

After nearly three weeks of hospital and convalescence time, I was eager to get back to the war. Peters and Noyes had covered my duties well. I got an update from Lieutenant Doubleday. He seemed to be getting along with his ARPs just fine.

While I was recuperating, I decided that I would no longer suffer the ARPs' attitude that they were volunteers who could unvolunteer at their convenience. I put out the word that, from that point forward, there'd be no more volunteer shit. Joining the ARPs would be an assignment, not a choice. ARP vacancies would be filled by people we selected.

There wasn't a pipeline from which we could draw trained ARPs, so I created my own. I instructed Noyes to be on the lookout for young, eager, physically fit soldiers who'd grown up out in the country. I wanted soldiers coming into the platoon to have a long history of hunting, using weapons, and getting around in the woods. If they played high school football, even better.

Leaders have to learn how to make do with the resources available to them, particularly when commanding in combat. I was well aware of the burden that would be borne by the experienced ARPs to train new personnel on the job, but I couldn't see any other way to keep the platoon up and running.

Former ARP Dave Summers comments on Doc's decision.

"I didn't second-guess Major Bahnsen's decision at the time and wouldn't today. I will say it changed things. Our esprit de corps was higher when we were all volunteers. Volunteering to be part of something makes you more committed to it than when you are ordered to be part of something that may not be high on your list. And, based on my experience, volunteers bond faster emotionally.

"We stopped sending new guys to the Recondo course. The only training they received was on the job. Consequently, things got a little sloppy anytime we took two or three new guys on a mission. It wasn't their fault, but they didn't know how to do things the rest of us did second nature—based on our training and experience. That could put you at risk in situations where you'd be perfectly safe with experienced ARPs.

"And, I have to admit that Major Bahnsen's doing away with the volunteer aspect of ARP-hood never kept us from going on missions or doing our job. We were adrenaline-driven, full of brio, and serious about our business. Once newbies got the hang of it, most of them became damn good ARPs.

"Bottom line, we saw a lot more action as ARPs than we did as LRRPs, and we had a lot to show for it. Major Bahnsen had a marvelous way of getting the best and the most out of his soldiers no matter the circumstances."

Doc resumes.

Commanding in combat involves more than taking the fight to the enemy. You have to take care of your soldiers' needs the best you can and do whatever you can to help them keep their spirits high. The importance of things like decent chow, mail call, comfortable living quarters, recreation facilities, a PX, religious services, and so forth cannot be overstated.

And, whether commanding in combat or a garrison, leaders are never equals with their soldiers. One minute you're a father, the next you're a big brother. You can't be one of the boys and an effective leader at the same time. The dividing line between a leader and the led must always be maintained for the sake of military discipline.

There are times not to let on things you know. Patton was good at this. You have to be aware, yet uninvolved, or involved without appearing to be too aware. It's an art, really. And you shouldn't be petty when your soldiers screw up. If they need chewing out, chew them out and forget it. If they slip and fall, pick them up. If you stand behind them when they need you, your soldiers will be there when you need them.

Three former Air Cavalry troopers recall life in the troop.

Former Cobra pilot Jim Noe recalls Doc getting him out of jail in Saigon.

"After a particularly stressful mission, Doc gave me a three-day pass to Saigon. I got drunk, stole a motorcycle, and got arrested by the MPs. Doc came to Saigon and took me back to Alpha Pad. As punishment, he had the *audacity* to restrict me from the officers' club for one day. It could have been a bad situation for me had I been serving under a different commander."

Former Lift Ship Platoon commander Earl Moore recalls his additional duty as the club officer and talks about Crazy Frank's python.

"Doc put me in charge of the officers' club. All of us pitched in and refurbished an empty building for it. Once the club was up and running, my job was to keep the bar stocked, clean, and the price of beer cheap.

"The ARPs called one of my pilots 'Crazy Frank.' He was an excellent pilot and feared nothing, but this guy had been in-country too long. He was crazier than a shithouse mouse.

"Crazy Frank flew down to Saigon one day and bought an eleven-foot python. He kept his monstrous pet in a cage inside the officers' hooch. Scary looking as it was, the snake was docile, unless hungry. It had to be fed once a week and, oh, did its feeding times ever provide prime entertainment.

"Pythons don't eat anything that is already dead. They have to kill their dinner. This snake was fed after supper on Thursday evenings. Usually, its feeding ritual took place between the officers' and the ARPs' hooches. We'd gather round in a large circle and watch the snake let loose just before a duck or a chicken was released. It didn't matter if it was a chicken or a duck, the bird wouldn't try to get away. It just stood there, like its feet were nailed to the ground, and trembled uncontrollably—making no effort to escape its fate.

"Whenever I could, I got the snake feeding moved inside the officers' club and opened it up for enlisted men and NCOs. We'd turn the tables on their sides and push them together in a makeshift rectangular ring, keeping the hungry snake inside.

"We sold a lot of beer before, during, and after snake feedings. The profits went back into the club, which kept the price of beer down—one of my more important duties as the club officer."

Former Thunderhorse pilot Mike Bates recalls how power was supplied to the troop's hooches after it relocated from Xuan Loc to Bien Hoa Air Base.

"When we first arrived at Alpha Pad—outside the northern perimeter of Bien Hoa Air Base—the base engineers hadn't strung power out that far. The only power we had was a small generator for the TOC. Unacceptable!

"I got together with fellow pilots Ray Lanclos and A1 Moore and drove around the base looking for generators that weren't being used. It took a while but we found one: a trailer-mounted five-kilowatt generator. Of course, we found it in an Air Force unit. Those guys always had more than they needed or could use.

"We returned later that evening with a larger truck, hooked the trailer up, and drove back to Alpha Pad. That was how Bates, Lanclos, and Moore Power Company got started.

"We didn't charge for our power, but any group that wanted a line strung to their hooch had to participate in keeping the enterprise going. The ARPs built a wooden shed around the generator to keep it out of sight. Other groups provided fuel or serviced the generator.

"A nonprofit enterprise from start up to shut down, Bates, Lanclos, and Moore Power Company remained in business until power lines were strung out to our base camp."

Doc resumes.

Unfortunately, on 25 November Lieutenant Johnny W. Benton was killed in action, when a random sniper shot hit him during an aerial recon just north of Bien Hoa. Benton was a great young man from Idaho and had only been in the troop for a couple of weeks.

✶ Chapter 56 ✶

1 December 1968—southern sector, War Zone D

As the Blackhorse intelligence officer, then Major Andy O'Meara frequently flew with the troop's scout pilots. His observations about scout pilot Larry Spencer provide some background on this combat action.

"Mister Spencer was a sergeant in the infantry prior to attending flight school. The training and experience he received during that period of his career provided excellent background for his days as a scout pilot in the Air Cavalry Troop.

"Spencer knew the ground, what it looked like undisturbed, and how to make out the slightest irregularities. This skill was very unique. If the enemy was in his area, Spencer had an uncanny ability to find him."

Retired CW3, then CW2, Larry Spencer recounts finding a large enemy base camp.

"I flew out at first light to recon an area near a big bend in the Song Be River in the southern sector of War Zone D. I reconned this area routinely. VC were always in it and easy to find, unless they were trying to avoid contact.

"I flew very low and slow, hovering at times, about two feet above the elephant grass in the large open fields interspersed between patches of dense jungle. Employing the standard technique used by all of our scout pilots, I orbited in tight circles, looking for places where the morning dew was brushed off the grass, where the grass was matted down by soldiers sleeping in the area, fresh trails, and other signs of recent enemy activity.

"I didn't spot anything unusual over the open fields, so I reconned over the surrounding jungle. This was dense growth jungle. It was hard to see anything on the ground that was camouflaged. Dense jungle also gave the enemy plenty of places to hide anytime they heard you coming.

"After a two-hour recon that turned up nothing, I returned to Bien Hoa to refuel. While my ship was being refueled, a Cobra pilot by the name of Jim Noe came over to talk with me. He told me he'd flown the max hours in a Cobra for the month and wanted to know if he could fly with me as my observer—just to see what it was like. I didn't have any problem with his request, so I gave my crew chief, who normally flew as my observer, some time off.

"Early afternoon, Noe and I resumed recon over the same area where I'd been that morning. We'd been out about forty-five minutes when I noticed enemy troops moving around in the jungle below us. I circled back over the area and made out what looked like a huge bunker complex. Noe confirmed what I saw."

Doc picks up the story.

I listened to Spencer call in a sitrep. I radioed to tell him that I was en route and to stay clear of the bunkers: I was going to call in a tactical air strike.

I contacted the FAC on station. He had two fast movers with high drag bombs available. Bates flew us in low and close to the bunkers, and my crew chief marked the spot where I wanted the air strikes concentrated with a white phosphorous grenade. The FAC re-marked with a white phosphorous rocket. Spencer moved in behind me as Bates went into an orbit north of the bunker complex to be clear of the fast movers' flight path.

Two F-100s were circling overhead. When they saw the FAC's rocket explode, they came screaming in tandem, flying east to west, and each released two five-hundred-pounders. Their bombs hit close, but not on the bunker complex. I radioed the FAC and got him to bring them back for another strike. Their bombs hit closer this time, but not close enough for my liking. I had the FAC bring in two more F-100s that put eight additional five-hundred-pounders on the bunker complex. After the air strike lifted, I sent Spencer back in for a recon and damage assessment.

Larry Spencer resumes.

"There was still a lot of shooting going on when I went back in to take a look at the bunker complex. I made several passes over it and got shot at each time without being hit. On my last pass, I made out the entrance to one of the bunkers. I couldn't see any enemy around it, so I moved in for a closer look. Just when I was directly overhead, an enemy soldier stepped out and sprayed my bird with automatic weapons fire. One round came through the right side of the chin bubble, hit the cyclic, then slammed into me just above the knee. The searing pain caused me to flinch involuntarily. I looked down and saw blood spilling out of my leg . . . so much blood that it made me think I might bleed to death."

CW5, then CW2, Jim Noe, who remains on active duty at the time of this writing, remembers this action clearly.

"With much of the first and second level of the triple canopy jungle blown away, the enemy knew they were exposed and stopped trying to hide after the air strikes. Spencer took us in so close to the ground that I could see faces in the trenches and muzzle flashes from spider holes.

"The enemy really lit us up. The noise created by their barrage of small-arms fire voided the noise of the helicopter's turbine—even Doc's loud and clear orchestration of the air-land battle over the radio was lost in the din. It was shocking and confusing.

"The aircraft snapped violently up and over when Spencer got hit. Besides having his primary flight control knocked out by enemy fire, he was in no shape to fly. Although not qualified in the OH-6 and there only as an observer, I instinctively dropped my weapon and grabbed the flight controls to at least try to level the aircraft before we hit the ground, which I was sure we were about to do.

"Gaining control, unexpectedly, I looked for a place to put her down and radioed our situation. I glanced over to see how badly Spencer was hurt and there he was, clutching what was left of the cyclic stick, trying, I think, to control his own fate: he was tough, he was seasoned—plus I don't think he trusted a Cobra pilot to fly his bird. Together, we put the LOH [Loach] on the ground in an open area close to the battle.

"Doc landed and his crew got Spencer out of the helicopter and placed a tourniquet around his leg while I covered the perimeter with Spencer's M-16. Another scout ship landed within seconds and Doc's crew put our wounded brother in its observer's seat. The scout pilot lifted off and made a mad dash to the Ninety-third Evac at Long Binh—about a ten-minute flight.

"As soon as Spencer was on his way to the hospital, Doc asked me if I could fly the six out of there and I said something like 'Well, it's still running.' I didn't really assess the chances of getting this shot-to-hell LOH back to Alpha Pad; I was more concerned about getting it out of the LZ before Charlie realized I was there by myself.

"Later, we counted over seventy holes in the aircraft, most of which were grouped in the cockpit area. We aligned entrance and exit holes with string and it became very apparent how lucky Spencer and I had been."

Doc resumes.

I could see the VC who shot Spencer. I wasn't about to let them live to fight another day. I called in more bombing runs and followed them with a heavy volume of artillery fire, which pounded the hell out of the general area, but none of it hit dead center of the bunker complex.

The air and artillery strikes were holding the enemy in place, but I could see that ground forces would be required to destroy the VC. I called the TOC and had them scramble all available ARPs. I could get my ARPs to the contact area quickly, but figured I needed additional infantry to assist them in assaulting such a large bunker complex.

Colonel Patton was backing me up on this operation. Company B, 1st Battalion, 18th Infantry, 1st Infantry Division was on standby. Patton had it chopped to him at a nearby fire base.

While ground forces were en route, I brought in my gunships and had them circle the area to make sure no VC got away.

Two lift ships carrying eleven ARPs, including Lieutenant Doubleday, soon arrived. I found a small LZ nearby and guided them in. The ARPs didn't have any missions scheduled that day. The rest of the platoon was at the PX or otherwise out of the area when I made the alert call.

Doubleday, Roeder, Summers, Starkey, Butler, and the other six ARPs immediately moved to the area fronting the bunkers and launched an assault. Between their weapons fire and the grenades they threw, they began to kill the enemy.

Former ARP squad leader Dave Summers comments.

"Starkey, a medic, and I were fighting side by side when we attacked. We were taking a very heavy volume of fire. The noise was so loud I could barely hear anything he said. It was a good thing that Lieutenant Doubleday got us organized before the action started, because once it was underway, there was no way we could have heard him.

"We were going from bunker to bunker, tossing grenades through the entrance, waiting for them to blow, then storming in with our Car-15s on full automatic.

"At one point, we rushed into a bunker and were met by two VC who had their AKs pointed at us. We opened up on them without a second's hesitation. The noise inside that bunker got so loud that I was reading lips until my ears cleared.

"There were enemy dead in every bunker. Their blood and guts were splattered everywhere. The floors were littered with shell casings, weapons, eating utensils, personal belongings, and all kinds of papers.

"Live VC used to get under one of their dead buddies and play dead. To get around this ruse, we picked the enemy dead up and carried them outside."

Former ARP sergeant Bob Roeder recounts attacking the enemy bunkers.

"Butler and I had our own sector to assault. We had to be aggressive but cautious at the same time. Lots of bullets were flying in our direction and there was one ChiCom .51 that kept our heads down.

"We'd fire our weapons, crawl forward some, fire again, and crawl some more. We did this until we were within grenade-throwing range. The VC were using plywood to cover the entrances to their bunkers. Grenades that hit the plywood bounced back and blew without doing any real damage. We needed to improvise!

"We started getting on top of the bunkers. Butler would reach down and pull the plywood out far enough for me to toss a grenade inside. After it blew, we leaped to the ground and made our bunker entrance behind short blasts of Car-15 fire. We switched roles from bunker to bunker.

"In one bunker, I found one live VC trying to hide under a dead one. He started moving when I got close to him. Bad mistake. I shot him with my pistol.

"There were a lot of bunkers and the VC were putting up a good fight. As the action wore on, Butler and I got between two bunkers and took a break.

"We sat down against one of the bunkers and drank some water from our canteens. After about ten minutes, I told him, 'Well, let's get back to work.'

"It was surreal. Fighting became a job like hauling hay. I really didn't think that much about what I was doing, things happened too fast."

Doc resumes.

Those eleven ARPs were magnificent. They killed over thirty enemy soldiers before reinforcements from the 1st Infantry arrived.

Captain Earl Moore and his lift ships picked the infantry up and I guided them to a LZ close to the bunker complex. I put artillery fire on the north side of the bunkers as the infantry moved up from the south where they joined Doubleday. Captain Richard Holden, B Company's commander, then took over command of the ground fight.

Mike Gorman comments.

"Our gunships were providing very close combat support. The VC were pinning our guys down with machine gun fire. One First Division guy was shot in the head by a .51 caliber. The First Infantry put out smoke to mark their position and radioed the Cobras to minigun the bunkers on the other side.

"One of our Cobras rolled in on the bunkers and mistakenly hit and wounded two First Infantry guys. An RTO, with a heavy Spanish accent, was on the radio when this happened. We heard him shout to the Cobra pilot, 'Why you shoot at us? Why you shoot at us?' We could hear screaming in the background. All I could think of was how horrible it was that we'd shot our own men."

Doc resumes.

It got dark about this time, making it too dangerous to bring in more B Company soldiers and too dangerous for an extraction. Captain Holden pulled his soldiers back to a crater area about one hundred fifty meters from the bunkers, where he set up a night defensive perimeter (NDP).

Mike Gorman continues.

"The sky was still bright in the setting sun when Martinez's—my crew chief buddy —helicopter went down after inserting a load of First Infantry soldiers. The pilot called in a sitrep, reporting where he'd gone down and that his crew was okay—no serious injuries.

"Mister Bates took us in a slow orbit looking for the crash site. The long shadows made anything on the ground doubly difficult to see. After perhaps five to ten minutes of desperate searching over the approximate area, I caught sight of the orange flashing on top of the rotor blade, but then lost it. It was getting darker by the minute, and I was just beginning to feel a little panic. I told Major Bahnsen what I had seen. We zeroed in on the area where I'd seen the orange flashing. After a few minutes, we had them in sight and this time we kept them in sight.

"Major Bahnsen got on the radio, called Lieutenant Doubleday, and told him to bring his ARPs out to secure the wreckage and its crew."

Former ARP platoon leader Duke Doubleday picks up the story.

"By the time Doc got hold of me it was too dark to see where we were going. I knew the general direction of the crash site, which was about seven hundred meters from my position, but that wasn't going to get us there any time soon.

"I asked my ARPs if any of them had a strobe light. Summers did, but he wasn't excited about holding it over his head while Doc guided us to the crash site. No one wanted to be anywhere near him. There were a lot of VC in the area and a strobe light would give them something to shoot at.

"Summers looked around for a long stick. He wanted to strap the strobe light to it and hold it out in front of him. No such stick could be found. Summers just held the strobe above his head and we walked single file to the crash site, following directions Doc gave as he circled overhead."

Dave Summers continues.

"I was damn happy to reach the downed helicopter before the enemy got a chance to zero in on my strobe light. Evidently, the helicopter was coming out of a LZ when it flew between two big trees and sheared its rotor blade off. When we got there, the helicopter was tilted to its port side with its left skid poking through its fuselage. Luckily, it didn't catch fire and the crew was okay.

"We set up an NDP around the aircraft and stayed very alert for the rest of the night, which passed without any further action in our area."

Former captain Earl Moore talks about resupplying the ground forces before calling it a day.

"Captain Holden was with one of his platoons holed up in a couple of bomb craters. They were thirsty, hungry, and virtually out of ammo. It was too dark to make out their exact location. Doc lifted the harassing and interdiction (H&I) artillery fire he was putting in on the bunker complex and brought in an Air Force spooky (a special ops AC-47 aircraft) that provided cover and illumination for me during the two resupply missions I flew for them.

"I couldn't land safely, so I hovered over the craters and dropped in water, C-rations, and M-16 ammo that had already been loaded in magazines by ARPs back at base camp.

"It was twenty-two thirty hours when I made the last drop. Doc remained on station for another half-hour before heading back to Bien Hoa for the night."

✳ Chapter 57 ✳

2 December 1968—southern sector, War Zone D

I had an artillery battery put H&I fire around the complex all through the night in an attempt to hold the enemy in place. That tactic proved unsuccessful. During the night, the VC slipped away through the artillery. However, the H&I fire may have kept the VC from attacking Holden and his men.

I went back out to the contact area at first light. I put an air strike on the bunker complex before sending my scouts in for a recon and aerial damage assessment. After my scouts reported the bunkers appeared to be safe to enter, I sent Holden and his platoon in to sweep it.

Dave Summers continues his account of this action.

"I had a hangover when we got this mission. We ran out of water during the night. The next morning, my mouth was dry and I was very thirsty. Furthermore, we hadn't had anything to eat and were all about to drop from the lack of sleep.

"Just as dawn broke, slicks appeared on the horizon. We popped smoke to identify our position—even though there were no signs of the enemy, we still had our perimeter defense in place.

"As soon as the first slick landed, its crew chief started handing out ice-cold beers—two each. I am certain that was Major Bahnsen's way of thanking us for a job well done. I got mine and drank them while lying in the grass between two small mounds. Beer never tasted better before that morning and hasn't tasted as good since.

"We helped rig the mangled helicopter for a sling-ride back to Bien Hoa. The crew loaded up on another slick and headed home. I would have liked to have gone with them, but I had one last thing to do.

"We made our way back to the bunker complex. The night before, dozens of enemy dead were strewn very close to the craters where we'd left the First Infantry. By the time we returned, only a couple remained. I don't know how, but Charlie managed to sneak in, pick up their dead, and sneak out undetected. That was a really unusual trick, and they were good at it.

"I was the demolition expert for the ARPs. That made blowing the bunker complex my job. I got started on it while everyone else searched the bunkers for anything of intelligence value, weapons, ammo, and other such material.

"This was a very large bunker complex—at least forty maybe as many as seventy of them. I didn't count. I had what I needed choppered out to me: lots of C-4, detonation cord, rigging tape, and blasting caps.

"I rigged a main ring of det cord in the center of the complex then ran branch lines through all of the bunkers. Our hand grenades didn't do any real damage to the bunkers, so I placed more than enough C-4 in them to get the job done right the first time.

"It took me a while to get all set. Captain Holden cleared everybody out of the bunker complex and I blew it. It was a spectacular sight. Poles, dirt, furniture—all kinds of stuff—went flying into the air."

Doc resumes.

Earl Moore's lift ships extracted Captain Holden and his men back to their base and got all of our ARPs back to Alpha Pad.

B Company had one KIA and a couple of soldiers wounded—by friendly fire, no less. Damn shame, but it happens in the fog of battle. Spencer was wounded but alive. He was my only casualty in what was a long fight with a numerically superior force.

We had armored units in the AO, but Patton and I figured it would take too long to get them there before sunset. Bad decision. An ACAV troop would have overrun the bunkers without much difficulty. We learned from this.

Documents collected from the VC killed in this battle revealed that this bunker complex was MR5 HQ (the VC's regional command for military and political activities). Elements from the VC Dong Nai Regiment, a traditional foe of the Blackhorse, were in the area as security forces.

This action was Doubleday's defining moment as the ARP platoon leader. He earned a lot of respect that day. His performance was flawless. Overall, I have to say it was one of the bravest fights I ever saw by a small group of soldiers during my time in the war.

⋆ Chapter 58 ⋆

3 December 1968—southern sector, War Zone D

Major General Orwin C. Talbott, the 1st Infantry Division commander, held an impact awards ceremony for the ARPs, others of my troop involved, and soldiers from B Company who got into the fight two days earlier. This was unusual but not unheard of.

Holden, Doubleday, Roeder, and several others were awarded Silver Stars. A larger group that I think included the rest of the ARPs and several soldiers from B Company were awarded Bronze Stars with Valor device.

I don't recall what awards my pilots received, most likely a Distinguished Flying Cross—the same medal Talbott pinned on me.

After the ceremony, Patton and I went to the 93rd Evacuation Hospital to visit Spencer. While we were there, Patton awarded him an impact Silver Star.

Unfortunately, Spencer's wounds necessitated his being evacuated stateside for further medical care. I lost an outstanding soldier and one of my best scout pilots on his departure.

✶ Chapter 59 ✶

4–12 December 1968—Alpha Pad, Bien Hoa Air Base, and War Zone D

The days following our fight at the big bunker complex involved hunting the enemy and piling on. Based on intelligence reports indicating nighttime trail activity, I sent out a squad, maybe two, of ARPs to conduct a night ambush along a heavily used trail in War Zone D.

Former ARP Dave Summers talks about this mission.

"We inserted midafternoon and made our way into the jungle, where we found an excellent ambush site alongside a bend in a well-traveled trail. Just as it was getting dark, we laid out claymores in an overlapping pattern that made for a good-sized kill zone and took up interlocking firing positions.

"All through the night, we waited and waited. We heard distant background noise but couldn't make out what it was or pinpoint where it was coming from. Just as it was getting light, the noise got louder and louder and it was coming our way.

"Within ten to fifteen minutes, a team of Zebu oxen pulling a bull cart loaded with rockets and sacks of rice came round the bend and triggered our claymores. One ox was slightly wounded. We killed that team's handlers and moved up the trail. We soon ran into two more ox teams that made up this supply column. We shot those teams' handlers quickly and took cover, waiting to see if any VC soldiers came along to see what was going on. They didn't. We radioed our TOC with a sitrep and asked what we should do with the oxen.

"Before our troop's ops people had the chance to say anything, someone from regimental ops came up on the net and ordered us to burn the bull carts, blow the rice, destroy the rockets, and kill the oxen."

Doc resumes.

I was in my helicopter, not far away from the ARPs position, and proceeded to it immediately. By the time I arrived, the ARPs were in a circular field about fifty to sixty meters in radius. The rockets were stacked in one big pile, bags of rice in another, bull carts lined up side by side, and the oxen standing at the edge of the field.

Mike Bates, who was flying Doc's aircraft, talks about what happened next.

"The ARPs didn't have many limits on what they would do in battle, but there was no way they were going to shoot those oxen—too senseless a slaughter for their stomachs. And there was not a chance in hell that Doc would allow our door gunners to fire at them.

"There are stories about U.S. soldiers killing domesticated water buffalo during the war, but I never saw any such thing in the Blackhorse's AO. Other than being cruel without cause, that would have been taking food out of the Vietnamese peoples' mouths—not something we would ever do."

Doc resumes.

Being an old country boy, I had no intention of killing those oxen. They were beautiful animals.

Zebu cattle have large pendulous ears, and a big throatlatch and dewlap. They also have a camel-like hump over their shoulders and neck that stores water. They can go for a good while without being watered. They are hardy animals, able to survive insect bites, parasites, extreme heat, and disease. All of which makes Zebu oxen prime draft animals for the environs of Southeast Asia.

It takes a long time to train oxen to work in teams. I suspect the Zebu in this supply column had been teamed in pairs from a very young age. Even from the air, I could see these animals were well cared for. They were absolutely beautiful.

The idea of killing these animals was enough to make me sick. We were in a time and place where local farmers could not afford tractors. Ox teams were valuable. The order to kill them didn't come from Jim Dozier, the S-3, and I knew it. He wasn't the kind of guy who'd give that kind of an order.

I was in no mood to explain myself and didn't feel like arguing with the dumb shit who ordered the ARPs to kill those oxen.

I told the ARPs to move the oxen in under the trees and hold them there. I then radioed Pete Noyes and told him to locate a cargo net. I was going to sling-load the oxen under a lift ship and haul them back to my base camp. I did not tell regiment about my decision.

Noyes located a cargo net at a Navy facility at Vung Tau and sent a lift ship down to pick it up. In the intervening time, the ARPs blew the rice with C-4 and used white phosphorous grenades to set the bull carts on fire.

When the lift ship arrived, the ARPs used the cargo net to sling-load the oxen one at a time for a ride to our troop area. They didn't get it quite right on the first one. The helicopter was about twenty feet in the air when the net came undone and the ox slammed to the ground. It got on its feet, shook the dust off, and stood there—no worse for the wear. The ARPs got it back in the net and the helicopter lifted off without further incident. Five round trips later, all six oxen were safely grazing inside a makeshift corral on the edge of our base camp.

We tried to keep this quiet, but Colonel Patton knew about it by the time I arrived at his evening briefing. He asked why the ARPs hadn't killed the oxen as ordered. I told him why. "Sir, we aren't in Vietnam to kill cattle. It was a stupid order. My ARPs don't follow stupid orders."

Patton chuckled over my explanation and nodded his head in agreement. Others present shook their heads in disbelief.

Patton then asked me, "Doc, what the hell are you going to do with those damn things now that you have them?"

"Well, sir. I'm going to have a rodeo with Zebu riding as the main event. I'm going to have my cooks slaughter and roast the wounded one and serve it up to my troopers. We'll wash it down with cold beer."

He laughed at my answer, and that was that.

A few days later, my cooks did just what I told Patton they were going to do. My troopers really enjoyed it. Fresh beef was an extremely

rare commodity in Vietnam. During the Zebu riding event, one partici-
pant was thrown and dislocated his shoulder. Nothing serious, all good
fun. He was back to work in a couple of days.

Colonel Patton didn't attend the festivities. Instead, he waited until
dark and came to my hooch for a barbecued Zebu sandwich and cold
beer. Patton was that way. He didn't want anyone to think he was con-
doning the capture of these animals.

☆ Chapter 60 ☆

13–20 December 1968—Hong Kong, and Bangkok, Thailand

I took very little time off during my troop command other than a week of R&R in Hong Kong and Bangkok with Fif. We had a great time, but I was hobbling when I got back to Bien Hoa.

The hotel where we stayed in Bangkok had a nice swimming pool with a diving board. I'd been drinking and started showing off my diving skills. On my second or third dive, my heel crashed into the edge of the diving board, splitting it open. It wasn't that big of a gash, but it bled like crazy.

I went to a U.S. Army medical detachment in Bangkok to have my cut treated. It took seven sutures to close it, and my heel was left swollen and tender to the touch. Did that ever make it hard for me to dance!

✻ Chapter 61 ✻

When I returned from R&R, my foot was so swollen that I couldn't get a boot over it. I couldn't allow that sorry condition to prevent me from doing my job. I just hobbled along in a slipper I wore inside a plastic bag to keep dirt, grime, and water out. It made me feel stupid and limited what I could do on the ground during enemy contacts.

One of the first things I noticed was that the Zebu oxen were gone. I asked Noyes about their whereabouts. He told me they'd been loaded up in the back of deuce-and-a-half trucks and hauled into Bien Hoa, where they were sold to some local farmers. He said they fetched a good price, which was paid in piastres.

The proceeds from the sale were used to pay for the troop's New Year's Eve party. However, the Australian rock band hired for the party demanded payment in U.S. dollars. U.S. forces in Vietnam were paid in military scrip. Possessing U.S. currency was strictly forbidden. So the band's demand presented a problem. I don't know who or how, and I wouldn't tell if I did, but arrangements were made for a meet with a black market money changer to swap enough piastres for U.S. dollars to pay the band.

Nobody in the troop personally profited from the sale of those oxen. Monies from their sale not spent on the party paid for the beer my troopers drank during the early part of January.

About this time, I received one of Colonel Patton's infamous Christmas cards.

Patton landed during the sweep of a contact area where a bunch of dead, black pajama–clad Vietcong soldiers had been placed in a big pile. He took a black-and-white picture of this pile of enemy dead that he later had made into a simple Christmas card that read: "Peace on Earth." He signed the cards with a short handwritten greeting.

I recall him having about thirty cards printed. He sent them to a short list of people he considered to be his close friends, including General Creighton Abrams, the commanding general of MACV.

Knowing Patton's sense of humor, most recipients got a kick out of the card. Not so for General Abrams. He was furious. He got Patton on the phone and told him, "George, you dumb sonofabitch! You get every one of these cards back! I want them all accounted for, including mine!"

Patton sent someone to Saigon to bring back General Abrams's card and personally went about retrieving the rest. He got them all back, except one . . . the one he sent to his old friend, retired Major General Art West.

West's son was serving in the Blackhorse and had been relieved from duty as a troop commander. Patton didn't intervene on young West's behalf. He stood behind the squadron commander's decision. I can only assume that General West used the card as an opportunity to retaliate. Instead of sending it back to Patton, he leaked the card to the media. I've always thought this was spiteful, chickenshit, and petty revenge.

As you might expect, stories about Patton's morbid Christmas card quickly appeared in several newspapers. These accounts sensationalized and overhyped the whole affair beyond its news value simply because Patton was involved and because it could be used to put a racist face on American soldiers in Vietnam.

Any notion that Patton was a racist is absolute bullshit! He was a combat commander in a war where Vietnamese serving as VC or NVA soldiers were his enemies. He treated the Vietnamese people in general exceptionally well.

✶ Chapter 62 ✶

30 December 1968—north of Bien Hoa, between Lai Khe and Tan Binh

We continued to send out three to four pink teams for daily aerial recons in the regiment's AO that resulted in some small contacts. The big action of this day broke out when First Lieutenant J. W. Thurman, an aircraft commander in the 2nd Squadron's flight section, decided to go looking for an enemy soldier to take prisoner.

Retired Colonel, then First Lieutenant, J. W. Thurman describes his action.

"We were operating out of Fire Support Base Bandit Hill, about eight kilometers due east of Lai Khe. I was flying a UH-1C Huey that was overdue for inspection and had a lot wrong with it. I planned to fly it to Blackhorse base camp at Xuan Loc for maintenance and repairs later in the day.

"Before heading to Xuan Loc, I went out on an early morning recon around our area with my copilot Warrant Officer Randy Willer, crew chief Specialist Four Vince Gambino, and door gunner Specialist Four James Graham. This was Willer's first mission in Vietnam.

"We didn't see anything unusual and went back to base camp to refuel, get some C-rations, and see if anybody was hanging around for a ride to Xuan Loc.

"I had seen bunkers the evening before while flying a mortar-watch recon. The Rome plows were just getting down to them. Sergeant Maury Pledger, our ops sergeant, suggested I might want to fly a quick recon over the area before heading to Xuan Loc. Because I wasn't in any big hurry and it was only ten hundred hours, I decided to do just that.

"We'd just arrived over an area where a steam ran through a field of very thick and tall elephant grass at the edge of a wooded area when my door gunner started opening up on someone in the stream.

"I hadn't had an early morning brief on where the friendly forces were located, so I started to pitch my helicopter to throw off Graham's aim. I wanted to be sure we knew who we were shooting at. About the same time, Gambino started blasting away with his door gun. I looked down and saw two or three Vietcong fall over in the water, and two or three more pulling back to take cover.

"I called my TOC, 'Bingo. I've got about eight in a stream bed, at least three knocked down, I am continuing to engage.'

"Lieutenant Colonel Lee Duke, my squadron commander, who was up in the air but not near my contact area at that time, got on the radio.

" 'Eagle One-Eight Tango, are you receiving fire?'

" 'That's a negative, over.'

" 'Cease-fire. I want a prisoner, over.'

" 'Roger, I've got about three knocked down. I'll land and get one, over.'

" 'Roger, One-Eight Tango, out.'

Major Gus Johnson, our XO, was in our TOC and heard what I said. He immediately got on the radio and told me, 'I wouldn't advise you to do that. Over forty enemy soldiers are reported to be in that area.'

"I couldn't see forty, but I knew we had a few right below us trying to hide in the stream.

"I had Willer put down and hover right over the middle of the stream. I jumped out of our helicopter and landed waist-deep in water. Graham and Gambino followed after me.

"I was wearing a .38-caliber pistol and had a box of ammunition for it in one of my pockets. Graham brought his M-16. Gambino was armed with a .45-caliber pistol but didn't have any extra ammo. We were lightly armed but loaded with spirit and stupidity.

"We were moving toward a dead VC who was sort of floating on his stomach when I stumbled over a live one. He stood up with his AK between us. I bear-hugged him, grabbed him by the hair of his head, stuck my .38 behind his ear, and pulled the trigger. Within a second or two, we came under intense small-arms fire from VC we had not detected.

"I turned and signaled Willer to pull pitch and get out of the area. No way did I want my helicopter shot up.

"During the brief firefight that followed, we killed two and wounded two who had been hiding in the stream. We captured the wounded. I left them with Gambino and led Graham farther down the stream, toward the tree line. It was tough going because all the grass in the water restricted our movement.

"Gambino was not far from us, guarding our POWs, and I'll be damned if he didn't start taking sniper fire from a tree about ten meters away. I crawled under the tree and saw the sniper's ass hanging over a limb. I had just reloaded my revolver and put all six rounds in that dink's ass. It killed him right away. When he fell from his perch, his feet got tangled in some branches, leaving him hanging upside down.

"Graham started running toward me and fired into the tree. Another dink fell out of the tree and landed next to me. Graham slid in next to me. He started to put a new magazine into his rifle right before he started frantically pointing over my shoulder. I turned and saw an AK barrel poking up out of the water and gave it a good yank. The dink on the other end of the barrel came up out of the water and Graham shot the shit out of him—full rock 'n' roll—with the muzzle of his rifle about a foot away from the dink's head.

"I thought we'd better get the hell out of there. We were in the middle of bad juju. By that time, we'd cut a path in the reeds from our wallering through them, which made slogging back to Gambino's location easier.

"About this time, a second lieutenant, his RTO, and two or three other infantrymen from a unit working in the area arrived to give us a hand. Before Graham and I headed back into the fray, I traded my pistol for the RTO's M-16 and told him to follow me. It didn't register with me that he was carrying the radio, and that was a big mistake. The radio antenna singled him out as a target. I should have grabbed another soldier and left the RTO behind.

"We hadn't taken but a few steps when a dink jumped out of some reeds and shot the RTO in the head, killing him instantly. That scared the fuck out of me! I couldn't see exactly where the shots came from, but I emptied most of a magazine in the general vicinity.

"Within seconds, Graham shot another VC in the shoulder. He surrendered, and Graham took him back to Gambino. Moments later, another VC got up and surrendered to me just before we came under intense small-arms fire from more VC hidden on higher ground. Outmanned and outgunned, we started out of the area, slogging down the stream with our POWs. Lieutenant Gruber, a platoon leader in G

Troop, saw us, dismounted his ACAV, and came sloshing down the steam to assist.

"The firing had pretty much quit by this time. Graham looked around and asked me, 'Where the hell are all the dinks?' I told him the best I could figure out, they were in that one tree where everything seemed to be taking place.

"Moments later, dinks jumped up out of the water and shot in Gruber's direction, hitting him in the arm pit. However, Gruber was not in danger of dying and kept going strong.

"I had two prisoners under my arms and stumbled over another VC hiding in the water. Instead of killing him, I just kept going and left him for Graham to capture.

"When we reached the LZ, Major Dozier, the regimental S-3, along with several other Blackhorse soldiers, was waiting for us. I turned my POWs over to him. He turned them over to soldiers from G Troop for the time being.

"I had just walked behind one of the ACAVs when Willer landed with two new door gunners on board. He'd flown to Lai Khe to refuel and a couple of First Infantry soldiers volunteered to fly back to the contact area with him.

"By this time, the fighting had resumed and we were in the middle of a pitched battle. I didn't know how big the VC force was, but I wasn't worried. We had ACAVs and infantry on the ground, and Doc and Cobras from his pink teams were providing combat assault fire from the air.

"I got back in my helicopter and we stayed in the area, providing what cover fire we could with our door guns, and landing twice to pick up friendly casualties that we medevaced to Lai Khe.

"The contact ended about eleven thirty hours. Our guys picked up the dead RTO during the sweep of the area. Someone found and returned my pistol to me, as well. Nothing pretty about that battle. Just a lot of shooting, one friendly killed, several more wounded. I don't know how many VC were killed in all. Some of their dead probably went undetected in the thick, thick grass in the stream. But we made it out with five prisoners."

Doc resumes.

By the time we cleared J. W.'s contact area, Warrant Officer Guy Ballou had an action going in a nearby area. The ARPs had set up a blocking position on the edge of a flooded rice paddy near a river to prevent a sizeable number of enemy being chased by ACAVs from crossing the river.

I flew to the rice paddy. Our guys had killed several enemy soldiers and had a large group of them scattered over a wide area. I brought more pink teams for the search and kill.

Colonel Patton was in the area and joined the hunt. In an attempt to flush out hiding VC, Patton popped a CS (2-Chlorobenzalmalononitrile, a nonlethal substance used as a riot-control agent) gas grenade and threw it out the door of his helicopter. My helicopter was downwind, and along with my crew, I got a snout full of CS gas. Bates quickly sat our helicopter down in the rice paddy, so we could clear our eyes and noses. I called Patton and told him what he'd done. He flew to my area, sat down near my helicopter, and asked me to meet him on the ground, knowing full well that I had a plastic bag over my foot.

I got out and waded over to his helicopter for a parley. I told him that he had gassed us instead of the enemy.

"Sorry to hear about that, Doc. I'll bet it hurts like hell to walk around on that foot of yours. Does that bag keep it from getting wet? Must sting, if it doesn't."

Some rat bastard told Patton how I injured my foot, and he was giving me a good ribbing. He never approved of my seeing Fif while I was married to Pat and thought I deserved to get hurt for trying to impress her with my diving skills.

Patton kept me standing in the water for a few more minutes, making idle talk. When he was good and sure that I was suffering, he said, "Goddamn, Doc. You shouldn't be bullshitting with me when you've got a fight to finish." He'd had his laugh, and we climbed into our helicopters to rejoin the hunt.

Guy Ballou comments on this action.

"While Doc was on the ground talking to Patton, I was going full throttle after a bunch of dinks trying to escape across this river, ten feet deep and half a football field wide. There were a lot of dinks down there, and I was shooting every one I could.

"Before long, I expended all my minigun ammo, so I started shooting my pistol out my door. My crew chief, Sergeant Hepler, was shooting his M-60 along with me. We got in some low-level killing of scattered enemy trying to hide in the river.

"All too soon, we were both plumb out of ammo and there were still dinks to be killed.

"I proceeded to hover over enemy soldiers until my skids were directly over them. I then lowered my helicopter until the water came up to the bottom of my seat. I got so carried away with drowning dinks that I forgot about my radios being situated under my seat, and they shorted out. Now, I was out of ammo and out of commo. There were other aircraft in the area, but I couldn't get their attention.

"We had ARPs on the far side of the river shooting at dinks in the water not far from my location. They were doing their job and I continued doing mine. That is, until these ACAVs came up the other side of the river and started shooting their .50 cals at those same dinks. Some of their .50-cal rounds were skipping on the river and hitting near the ARPs. Not a good situation.

"I had no commo with the ACAVs and they didn't realize the ARPs were in their line of fire.

"I flew and got between the ACAVs and the ARPs and hovered. No way were the ACAVs going to shoot me, and it got them to stop shooting in the ARPs' direction.

"Major Dozier arrived on the scene and was leading the ground element from the ACAVs into the water for the final assault. There were at least thirty dinks in the water. Dozier was one of a half-dozen friendlies. Another bad situation; they were way outnumbered. I started doing three-sixties, using my tail rotor blades to keep them from going into the water.

"Dozier was pissed. He walked into the water until it was chest-deep and tried to grab hold of my aircraft. I pointed down and raised my skids up, releasing some dinks I'd just drowned. Dozier saw them floating up. He then understood."

Doc resumes.

Ballou was a very excitable young man who really liked to get into the fight. I do not know how many enemy he killed in the water—had to have been a dozen or more. When he finally told me the story, he was still pissed about no one helping him out.

✶ Chapter 63 ✶

Former sergeant Robert Roeder recounts a mission that took place while Doc was hospitalized as a result of wounds incurred during the New Year's Day contact, when Rodney Yano was killed in action.

"This was a bad day for the ARPs.

"Around fourteen hundred hours, seven or eight of us, one team, were scrambled out to the Heart-Shaped Woods, way out in the boonies, where a VC prisoner was supposed to lead us to a big weapons cache.

"After securing the LZ for a brief time, we searched an area of tall grass and thick brush where the POW indicated the cache was located. Our search was a bust. We found nothing. That pissed us off, and the POW took notice of our mood. He excitedly pointed to another area, and we were told to head in that direction by whoever was controlling the action from the air. There were a lot of helicopters in the air, but it was someone from the troop.

"Sergeant Wade Butler was walking point. I was backing him up. Sergeant Bill Emanuel was behind me. The POW was near the rear of our single-file formation.

"It was starting to get late in the afternoon, we'd been on the ground for close to an hour. We were told to hurry up in order to find the weapons cache before dusk. There was a well-beaten trail leading in the direction the POW kept pointing to, and we were directed to sweep down it.

"If you had any experience on the ground, you knew two golden rules: never get in a hurry in enemy territory, and never, ever walk down a trail. Either one could get you killed. Doing both at the same time was acting out a death wish.

"Following orders, we hurried down that damn trail but didn't get far. It was a mistake that we should never have made.

"Nobody knows for sure what it was or how it was detonated, but some sort of explosive device blew, hitting Butler and me almost straight on. Emanuel and some other guys behind him were also hit, including Specialist Mozelle Starkey and Lieutenant Duke Doubleday.

"One of Butler's legs was damn near blown off. I was hit from head to toe. Luckily, I was wearing an NVA AK-47 ammo vest and an SKS ammo belt, both filled with two magazines in each pocket. They took most of the impact and saved me from dying on the spot.

"I remember lying on my back and looking up. The sky was as blue as I've ever seen it. I didn't know if I was dead or alive. I'd never been dead before and sure didn't feel like I was alive. I don't remember hearing any shots fired, but I doubt the POW survived."

Former ARP Bill Emanuel picks up the story.

"Mister Ballou, one of our scout pilots, was overhead and saw the explosion. The smoke hadn't cleared before he used the rotors on his Loach to cut back enough brush to make a LZ. The next couple of minutes were a blur of activity.

"The four linch pins securing the minigun were pulled, dropping it into the mud to give the helicopter more lift and speed. All of its ammo was tossed to make room to put one person in the cramped compartment behind the cockpit.

"Despite being wounded himself, Starkey—our medic—put a tourniquet on Butler's leg and sat him in the observer's seat. Roeder was tucked in back of the observer's seat and up under it.

"Blood was spilling out of Butler's torn-up leg and onto the floor. Roeder was lying in it. They were both covered in blood and their uniforms looked like they'd been put through a shredder. The rest of us wounded were in much better shape.

"Leaving his observer, Sergeant Hepler, on the ground, Mister Ballou pressed the manual override for the governor before pulling pitch, pushing the engine beyond its normal max power. From what I heard, he kept one finger on that button all the way to the Ninety-third Evac at

Long Binh. He likely burned out the engine. Stuff like that didn't worry Mister Ballou. I'm totally confident that if he hadn't flown Butler and Roeder to the hospital so quickly they would have bled to death. I was lifted out on the same ship as Starkey.

"Business was too damn good at the hospital that day. Doctors and medics were busting their asses to take care of wounded arriving in droves. I don't remember the details but understand that a bunch of them were from the Big Red One.

"The triage nurse put all those needing emergency treatment and urgent surgery at the head of the line. My own wounds were not life threatening. Hell, I sat in the hall on a gray metal chair for two hours before being treated. I didn't mind. A lot of other guys were in far worse shape, and way too many of them died that day."

Former ARP squad leader Dave Summers comments on this action.

"Our platoon took it in the shorts that afternoon. Butler and Roeder were two of our best and most experienced ARPs. They'd both made the transformation from LRRPs and were very qualified. They ended up being evacuated out-of-country for further treatment. We lost two of our best, and that hurt our capability.

"Why they were wounded in the first place is nothing more than fucking stupidity. It had nothing to do with risk-taking. Whoever ordered them to go rushing down a trail in Indian country ought to have been caned by a Singapore prison guard in front of a troop formation.

"This fuck up would never have happened had Major Bahnsen been controlling the mission. He was aggressive and expected the same from us, but he would never place our lives in jeopardy over a weapons cache that wasn't going to disappear overnight. And so what if it did? There were way too many weapons caches out in the boonies for one platoon of ARPs to get them all. We were good, but not that good."

Doc concludes.

I didn't see my ARPs when they came to the hospital, and wouldn't until a couple of days later. The news of this action hit me like I'd just stuck my finger in a live electrical socket—I was shocked as hell! These guys were important to me, not just as ARPs, but as young men I'd grown to admire and respect. Replacing them wasn't going to be easy.

Colonel Patton visited the wounded ARPs the night he returned from R&R but didn't drop in on me—he wanted to talk to the 1st Infantry first. He later told me that when he arrived at the hospital, he saw a doctor standing next to a soldier, whose head was completely bandaged, lying on a gurney. Turns out that soldier was Sergeant Robert Roeder, who had over two hundred shrapnel wounds, many of which still had small pieces of shrapnel in them.

Patton asked the doctor how the soldier was doing. The doctor said, "Not good. I don't think he's going to make it." Before Patton could say anything, Roeder yelled, "Fuck you, doc. Fuck you, doc."

Patton really got a kick out of Roeder's determination to live, and so did I when I heard that story.

✶ Chapter 64 ✶

5 January 1969—Alpha Pad, Bien Hoa Air Base

No matter who'd been killed, attending memorial services was tough, gut-wrenching duty. One morning you're eating breakfast with someone and the next thing you know, they're killed in action before supper. It's that unexpected and sudden, and an ugly thought to boot, but an accurate depiction of the brutal reality of war.

Attendance at memorial services wasn't mandatory. You attended them out of respect for the dead and to honor them for making the supreme sacrifice a soldier can make for our country.

Rodney Yano's memorial service was particularly disheartening for the troop. I wrote his family a letter expressing my great sorrow for their loss and lauded his meritorious service to the troop and his heroism during that fateful mission on New Year's Day.

☆ Chapter 65 ☆

My reprieve from my actions on 1 January gave me a new lease on life and motivated me to do well in Patton's eyes.

Most of our actions at the time were routine operations north of Bien Hoa in War Zone D north of the Dong Nai River. Others were just northeast of Lai Khe. If the enemy didn't make contact with us, we literally went hunting for the enemy.

Routine actions usually started with a pink team, the scout pilot making visual contact and the gunship crew taking the area under fire. If the contact proved lucrative, we put the ARPs on the ground to mop up or to hold the enemy until further reinforcements arrived. By this time we had perfected the pile-on operation and everyone knew what was expected of them.

Pete Noyes comments on Doc's leadership and gallantry during these "routine operations."

"Neither the length of the battle nor the size of the enemy force mattered to Doc. He fought fiercely all the time. Indeed, he was as gallant during what we considered routine operations—brief fights with small enemy elements—as he was in extended engagements against a superior enemy force.

"Those of us who fought under Doc's command more than once or twice grew accustomed to his way of fighting. His battlefield leadership was second to none. Undaunted valor was normal for him. We didn't always think to write him up for one medal or another, although his actions probably warranted it. Moreover, many of the troop's hostile engagements were fought and finished before officers from higher headquarters arrived in the contact area. As a result of their not witnessing these engagements, they didn't recommend Doc for medals they may have if they'd been on the scene during the fight.

"Neither of these conditions bothered Doc. I never knew him to seek personal glory or do something courageous just to draw attention. Doc was a warrior. He led the troop in dispensing with the enemy as quickly and soundly as possible. On the other hand, he always did his best to have his soldiers' gallantry recognized. I can't recall how many times he came into the TOC after a fight and handed me three-by-five cards with the names of soldiers written on them. It was my job to interview eyewitnesses to the fight to determine what medals he should recommend them to receive."

Doc talks about how he dealt with Patton's orders not to have Fif in his troop area after taking her into an enemy contact as an unauthorized passenger.

Until you become a general officer, your jeep driver pulls double duty. He drives you and also acts as your aide. You have to trust your driver. He hears things that aren't meant to be repeated. He sees things that shouldn't be talked about.

Sergeant Mack McCluskey was everything I could have asked for in a driver. He was absolutely trustworthy, loyal, and dependable. He'd been an ARP for a good while and had proved himself in battle. He was a damn good soldier and always looked sharp.

My driver was going home and I needed a new one. I chose McCluskey to replace him.

Because Patton had banned Fif from flying in any troop helicopter, I made arrangements with McCluskey to drive her back and forth between Bien Hoa and Saigon every now and then.

Former sergeant Malcolm "Mack" McCluskey comments on this arrangement.

"Major Bahnsen used to send me down to pick Fif up in my jeep and bring her back to Bien Hoa. He always gave me spending money. I usually left in the afternoon, took one of my ARP buddies with me, and stayed the night.

"Fif was a nice lady and always treated us well. I remember one time when Dave Summers went to Saigon with me. Fif took us out to dinner at a very good French restaurant. After taking Fif back to her apartment, Summers and I went out and sampled the local 'cultural attractions,' then returned to our hotel room and went to bed.

"We picked Fif up the next morning and drove her to our base camp. She spent the day and the night, after which I drove her home. I don't remember how many times I did this, but it was more than a couple and I didn't mind at all. It was easy duty and I always enjoyed it."

Doc resumes.

When Fif came to visit, she had to use one of the outhouses used by my troopers. Wanting her to have more privacy, I talked with Sergeant Dave Summers about getting an outhouse placed next to my hooch.

Dave Summers recounts his almost successful quest to fill Doc's request for an outhouse.

"A couple of us ARPs were standing around smoking and joking when Major Bahnsen walked over.

" 'You an engineer, Sergeant Summers?'

" 'Yes, sir.'

" 'I need a shithouse to put by my hooch.'

" 'Do you want me to build it or steal it?'

" 'The end justifies the means,' he said, smiled, and went about his business.

"Not wanting to disappoint my commander, I rounded up Specialist Fours Scott Van Della and Charlie Prater, and we conducted a total recon of Bien Hoa Air Base looking for a shithouse. We spotted a really nice one in the regimental headquarters area. They had a lot of outhouses; we didn't think they'd miss one. The one we decided to steal was in fact the best-looking two-holer outhouse I saw in Vietnam. It was well built, painted nicely, and sitting on a platform with skids, making it convenient to move from place to place.

"We returned to our hooch, changed out of our tiger fatigues, put on regular ones, took off our black berets, and put on those goofy baseball caps. With a hundred-foot rapelling rope in hand, we commandeered the troop mess truck. Because our 'snatch the commander a shithouse' op called for incognito tactics, we used soot from the truck's exhaust pipe to black out the unit numbers on its bumpers.

"We drove over to regiment, pulled up next to the outhouse, and found a private standing next to it. I told him to help me take the waste cans out. He did, without questioning why or what we were up to. He even helped us secure the outhouse with one end of the rope and tie the other to the truck's rear bumper.

"With Prater behind the wheel and Van Della riding shotgun, I stood on the passenger side running board as we headed out of the area, dragging the shitter behind us. We'd only gone about twenty yards when a captain comes running out of a tent and yells, 'What are you doing?'

"I told Prater to keep going, stepped off the running board, and saluted the captain. 'Sir, Sergeant Summers, Nine-nineteenth Engineers.'

"He didn't return my salute, just snarled and said, 'Come with me, sergeant.'

"I followed him into a GP-medium tent. There was a desk with a phone. A private was sitting behind it. Command Sergeant Major Squires was standing next to him.

"The captain glared at me and told me that was Colonel Patton's private outhouse. That was news to me! Was I ever up the proverbial creek without a paddle.

"The private called the motor pool and told whoever answered that he needed a deuce and a half right away. While he was on the phone, I took out a cigarette and asked the captain if he had a light. He growled, 'I don't smoke.'

"I asked if it would be okay to get a drink of water. He said, 'You can get one in the mess hall. It's next door.'

"I proceeded to the mess hall and ran straight out the back door. There were two guys sitting in a deuce and a half a short distance away. I ran over and jumped on the passenger side running board and said, 'Get me out of here! I just stole Colonel Patton's shitter!' The driver said, 'Congratulations! Get in.'

"He was moving before I had the door closed. I told him to drive me to Alpha Pad.

"I got back to my hooch, changed into my tiger fatigues that didn't have name tags sewn on them, put on my beret, and started getting the materials I needed to paint the shitter a different color. Less than an hour later, someone ran into my hooch and told me that I'd better get lost, some of Patton's people had just pulled up, and they were looking for his shitter. Evidently, they had followed the shithouse's skid marks all the way to the troop area.

"I beat feet to the armorer's shack and remained there until the coast was clear. Whoever came from regiment found Patton's shitter where my accomplices had left it: beside Major Bahnsen's hooch. I didn't see them take it, but from what I was told, the guys from regiment brought in some equipment and loaded it in a truck to haul it back. I guess they didn't want to risk damaging the colonel's private outhouse."

Doc resumes.

I didn't expect my ARPs to steal Colonel Patton's outhouse for me. Patton called me over the field telephone and told me that I must have needed a shithouse bad to send my people to steal his. He chewed my ass a little, but I didn't take him seriously. I was glad he did it over the phone because I couldn't have kept a straight face if he'd been looking me in the eye.

Notwithstanding this "failed" attempt to get an outhouse placed next to my hooch, another one soon showed up. Mission accomplished!

On a more serious note, soon after my short stay in the hospital, I had to bring in a new leader for my ARP platoon.

Duke Doubleday had earned a lot of respect for the superb job he was doing in leading the ARPs. He returned to duty within a few days after being wounded in the 3 January 1969 action, but hadn't fully recovered. Patton liked Doubleday and, thinking he might like a change of pace, offered him a staff job as an assistant S-3. Doubleday snapped up Patton's offer without a moment's hesitation.

Doubleday was a first lieutenant. Patton thought he would have more impact as a captain, so he frocked him: made Doubleday a brevet captain. Frocking enlisted men was common during the war. However, it was rare for company-grade officers. Not to imply that anyone ever stymied Doubleday's ability to do his staff job, Patton's frocking him didn't go over well with a lot of people.

I sensed the ARPs being let down by the choice Doubleday made. He damn well surprised me by quitting. He was a damn good soldier and platoon leader and was later appointed the state of Georgia's civilian aide to the secretary of the army.

I told Patton I wanted First Lieutenant Tom White as Doubleday's replacement. He concurred with my choice and White became my Aero Rifle Platoon leader—the best platoon leader I commanded in my Army career.

✳ Chapter 66 ✳

Former specialist four Mike Gorman, Doc's crew chief at the time, talks about events of this day.

"No unit can fight all the time. Equipment can't hold up under constant use. If you don't take care of your equipment, it breaks down—sometimes when you need it most.

"The crew typically maintains its own aircraft, but there was nothing typical about how Major Bahnsen operated. The line or the intermediate inspection crew usually handled the maintenance on our helicopters. Major Bahnsen never rested, so neither did his crew. He often flew twelve or more hours straight, making it almost impossible for us to keep our ship maintained. If his primary helicopter was being serviced or repaired, he'd switch to his backup helicopter.

"The troop was on stand down, pulling maintenance and repairing damaged equipment, mostly helicopters, but Major Bahnsen was itchy for action and took Mister Bates, Sergeant Walt Peterson, and me on a routine reconnaissance patrol.

"Major Bahnsen always rode in the left seat and let Mister Bates fly. His personal M-16 rifle was always in his lap loaded with solid red tracer. He was very particular about the cleaning of his weapon and the loading of his magazines, which he loaded with red tracer rounds. His extra magazines were in an open box right beside his seat. He was deadly accurate with an M-16 from treetop up to a couple hundred feet of altitude. He always test fired it and had my door gunner and me test fire our M-60s as we flew over Bien Hoa's outer perimeter. Woe be unto us if our weapons didn't operate properly. Major Bahnsen was a hunter through and through, always ready to shoot, and he expected the same of us.

"We carried his LBE over the rear of his seat for quick use. When we landed and he dismounted, it was my job to give him his steel pot, LBE, and the sack of hand grenades he always carried.

"His grenade sack was usually empty when he returned to our ship. The ones he didn't lob at the enemy, he generally passed out to soldiers on the ground. Something like, 'How ya doin', soldier? Good to see you. Here, have a grenade. Kill some dinks with it.'

"We had a PRC-25 radio ready for him to carry if he thought he might need it, and he often carried his motorcycle on our ship in case he might have use for it as a ground vehicle. He was no Evil Knievel, but he learned how to do an acceptable wheelie and was game enough to attempt other stunts with that motorcycle that we always got a kick out of watching.

"As we approached the Tan Uyen River, Mister Bates took our ship in low, flying a few feet above the river. Our prop wash was spraying water in all directions and beating the bushes unmercifully. We were looking for enemy footprints in the riverbank and trying to draw fire, just doing our best to stir up some action, but the enemy wasn't taking our bait. A pink team was also working the surrounding area doing what it could to make contact.

"Late in the afternoon, we received a radio call asking us to look for a company from First Infantry Division that was not sure of its position and needed help locating its position on the map. We were told it was in an open field covered with elephant grass along the west bank of the river.

"I had eyes like a hawk in those days and quickly spotted the disoriented company standing in a long line waiting for help to arrive. We landed and Major Bahnsen got out and conferred with a young lieutenant who was holding a map.

"When Major Bahnsen got back in the helicopter, he told us we were going to fly back and forth along the side of a nearby hill. The hill was quite steep and covered with a dense stand of tall hardwood trees. Major Bahnsen thought NVA soldiers might be hiding in them, waiting to ambush the infantry once we left the area. He wanted to see if we could draw fire and thwart any ambush on our guys. He radioed the pink team to come and give us a hand. We then flew low and slow back and forth along the hill, seeing what we might scare up.

"After half an hour, and no contact, we broke off and landed at a nearby battalion command post area. It had an extremely tight LZ surrounded by tall trees, denuded by napalm strikes. Major Bahnsen talked to Lieutenant Colonel Leroy Suddath, his West Point classmate and the battalion's commander, for about ten minutes before they both returned to our bird. Colonel Suddath wanted a lift back to the infantry company Major Bahnsen helped orient earlier in the day.

"As I mentioned earlier, we landed in an extremely tight LZ, which meant we'd have to liftoff vertically. Major Bahnsen decided to fly us out. However, with the colonel's added weight, our helicopter started losing lift after we were about twenty feet in the air. We couldn't sit back down safely, so Major Bahnsen powered the ship forward to gain altitude. We were just about to clear the LZ when our helicopter smashed into the top of a tree and broke the left side of the chin bubble, just in front of where Major Bahnsen was sitting. Big chunks of Plexiglas sprayed all over the place, some of it hit Major Bahnsen and bloodied him up some. He wasn't hurt badly, just a few scratches.

"No doubt, this got Colonel Suddath's attention and probably shook him up, but he didn't say or do anything to show it. He just hung tough like infantry guys are supposed to in a crisis.

"Me? I was scared to death and really thought we'd bought the farm. But Major Bahnsen said nothing and kept powering our ship through the tree as if it wasn't there and flew directly to the infantry company's location. I was shaking nonstop when we landed and dropped Colonel Suddath off, and kept on shaking all the way back to Alpha Pad.

"After getting out of our helicopter, I took a good look at the damage. It was bad. We should have crashed. I've always believed we had a guardian angel flying with us that day. Nothing else can explain why we didn't crash and die.

"As I stood there staring at the damage, I had a panic attack. I started ranting and raving about almost getting killed. I told everyone in the area that I would never fly again. That was it for me. No way was I getting killed for a measly one hundred twenty-four dollars a month.

"Because flying with Major Bahnsen was always such an imminent danger-filled adventure, panic attacks were virtually a nightly ritual for me. My fellow crew chiefs and door gunners were always amused by them. If I was especially rabid, like I was every time our ship took hits during a fight, they would convulse with laughter and tears would roll down their cheeks.

"Our backup ship was down, so we had to fix the one we'd been flying that day. We couldn't replace the chin bubble on such short notice, so we ordered a new one and repaired the one on our helicopter the best we could by using wire and heavy clear plastic. As we worked on the helicopter, I swore to God that I was through with flying."

✶ Chapter 67 ✶

22 January 1969—Tan Uyen River, War Zone D

Mike Gorman continues with events of the following day.

"In the morning, my panic now under control, I got back on the helicopter and we flew out to the same location where a fight had started during the night.

"The NVA were on the side of the hill and the infantry company was trying to sweep them off. They weren't having much success because the NVA held the high ground and were bringing in more troops to oppose them. From where I was sitting, it looked like those crazy dinks had decided to make a fight of it.

"What started as a small firefight had turned into a pretty big battle. Major Bahnsen brought in four pink teams and the Aero Rifle Platoon. That gave the infantry some much-needed help. All day long there was a continuous series of probes, assaults, firefights, artillery fire missions, and air strikes. We landed a number of times, and Major Bahnsen got out and took direct control of ground operations.

"The way he took charge of a fight was truly amazing, a spectacle to behold. As I watched him on the ground, I was thinking it was just another typical day for Major Bahnsen. When we arrived at the contact area it was a shitty mess but, as he had a special knack for doing, Major Bahnsen took charge of the mess and quickly brought order to chaos. There he was, totally calm, simultaneously directing gunship fire, positioning friendly forces, and calling in artillery fire and air strikes. Even more amazing was that in the middle of all that was taking place, he was unruffled by the constant stream of enemy small-arms fire directed our way.

"By day's end, Major Bahnsen got the infantry off the field and into the wooded hill without taking any casualties. That was a pretty good trick. I'm sure the dinks thought so, too.

"As night fell, the dinks quieted down. I thought they were leaving the hill now that the infantry was edging closer to their position. Major Bahnsen stayed on the ground 'til after dark, directing this and that.

"We got back to Alpha Pad late that night. Major Bahnsen went over to the TOC to see if anything else was happening. Thankfully, nothing was or we'd have flown right back out. I was really exhausted, so I asked some other crew chiefs to look after my helicopter, and I went to sleep."

✶ Chapter 68 ✶

23 January 1969—Tan Uyen River, War Zone D

Mike Gorman continues with events of this day.

"The next morning, we went back out to the same spot. Things had gotten hot again and our troops were pushing the NVA farther up the hill. NVA dead were mounting up. They were still making a fight of it though, and bringing in more and more troops. Major Bahnsen called for more air strikes, but they had to wait because our guys on the ground had used all their yellow smoke grenades and couldn't mark their positions with the color being used that day.

"However, Major Bahnsen wasn't about to delay the air strikes until supply ships arrived to rearm the infantry. He told Mister Bates to sit down near their position. We came under heavy fire as Mister Bates landed our helicopter on the bottom of the hill and we handed off a case of yellow smokes to some riflemen."

Doc begins.

This was First Lieutenant Tom White's first combat action with the Air Cavalry Troop. I inserted him and his ARPs in another nearby area. Bates flew our aircraft in low and slow counterclockwise circles to the left while I further assessed the ground situation. It wasn't long before I spotted some of the NVA force just in front of White's position. I radioed him immediately.

"Raider Six, Thunderhorse Six, over."

"Raider Six, over."

"Move due northeast and stay spread out. There are dinks less than fifty meters to your front, over."

"Roger, Six. My point just spotted movement and is taking them under fire. We're in contact, over."

"Roger, Raider leader. Keep me posted."

We continued flying in counterclockwise circles, and soon spotted NVA moving in the trees below us. I immediately engaged them with my M-16. Following the trail of my tracer rounds, Peterson and Gorman joined in the fray, blasting away at the NVA with their M-60s.

Mike Gorman recounts what happened next.

"You have to understand that we were flying very close to the hill, about fifty meters from these dinks—about fifteen of them. I could see their faces clearly and make out things like details on their uniforms. While we were circling overhead, our ship was hit by six rounds of small-arms fire, including one round immediately in front of and another right behind Major Bahnsen's head. This didn't faze him. He just kept shooting at the dinks and Peterson and I did the same. Major Bahnsen killed several of the enemy while we were circling the area. The rest of the dinks were running in panic, except one. He was down on one knee and firing back at us.

"On our second pass, I spotted this one unpanicked dink because of his muzzle flash, a bright, electric blue twinkle at the end of his AK-47. I turned my M-60 toward him. I was going to blow the bastard away, but my gun jammed. I was trying to clear the jam when he fired at us, spraying our helicopter from nose to tail, hitting me in the left shoulder with a single round."

Doc picks up the story.

Bates told me Gorman was hit and quickly leveled the helicopter. I looked back over my shoulder and saw Gorman. He wasn't moving, just lying in the rear of the chopper. Blood was gushing out of his wound and onto the cabin's floor. It was a gruesome sight.

Peterson put a four-by-four pressure bandage directly over the bullet hole. He knew Gorman would bleed to death if he didn't stop the bleeding. Bates turned the chopper over to me, unstrapped, and climbed in back to assist Peterson.

I pulled pitch to quickly gain altitude and get out of enemy small-arms range. I looked back to see what was happening and saw Gorman look up at Bates and start apologizing about his gun jamming, but he passed out before he finished. I thought he was dead.

As I looked forward again, I glanced at the instrument panel and saw that the oil pressure gauge was dropping dramatically, indicating a serious problem: we needed to land soon. I'd just started looking for a LZ when I noticed smoke streaming out of the engine compartment. Our serious problem had taken a turn for the worst! I headed for an open field nearby. Just before sitting down, I called in another troop helicopter as a replacement, and radioed Lieutenant White.

"Raider Six. We just got the crap shot out of us. My crew chief is hit bad. Will return when I get him taken care of."

"Roger, Six. We'll keep up the chase."

Once we landed, Bates checked our helicopter. It was too severely damaged to fly, so he called in another chopper to medevac Gorman to the 93rd Evacuation Hospital, about fifteen minutes away. Bates remained on the ground with our disabled helicopter and called in a backup helicopter. I took to the air in a replacement aircraft.

I was mad as hell! I thought those bastards had just killed my crew chief. As soon as I got back over the contact area, I radioed White.

"Raider Six, Thunderhorse Six, over."

"Raider Six, over."

"Raider, give me a sitrep, over."

"Roger, we've got a good-sized force here and they appear to want to fight. Recommend we start a pile-on operation, over."

"Roger, Raider, will make that happen shortly. Hunker down. Pop smoke. I'm bringing in air strikes to your front, over."

"Roger, Six, give me a few minutes to warn everyone. Smoke is out, call color, over."

"Roger, Raider, I've got yellow and purple smoke."

I then proceeded to call in an air strike.

"Sidewinder Four-Four, this is Thunderhorse Six, over."

"Four-Four, over."

"Four-Four, we've got enemy troops in the trees. What do you have on station?"

"Six, I have two flights of two with high drag, nape, and twenty mike-mike. Show me where you want it, over."

"Roger, Four-Four. Have you got the colored smoke in the trees? Over."

"Roger, Six. Yellow and purple."

"I want you to make north-to-south passes a hundred meters west of that smoke. I'll mark with white."

We then made a low-level pass over the trees and my crew chief dropped a white phosphorous grenade where I wanted the air strikes concentrated.

"Four-Four, did you see my mark? Over."

Before he acknowledged my mark, the FAC flew his 0-1 Birddog in a "split S" maneuver and fired a 2.75-inch white phosphorus rocket to confirm.

"Roger, Six. My mark is on the way. Will put in high drag followed by nape, over."

"Roger, Four-Four. Hold the twenty mike-mike."

"Roger, Six. Stay clear of the air space over the strike area."

Two F-4 Phantom fighter-bombers swooped down at about three-hundred knots and dropped general-purpose bombs that proceeded to tear up everything in front of the ARPs. A second flight of two F-4s roared in right behind the first flight, dropping napalm bombs as they passed. Explosions sent large chunks of shrapnel flying through the air, followed by enormous orange fireballs that consumed a vast area of tall trees and underbrush. Some of the general-purpose bombs landed much closer to the ARPs than the requested hundred-meter safety buffer.

Then First Lieutenant Tom White recalls what happened next.

"I looked up and saw bombs slowly spiraling down. They looked like great big knuckle balls, and they were coming in very close to our position. I yelled at my ARPs, telling them to take cover. I wanted to crawl inside my steel pot.

"A couple of the bombs landed within twenty-five meters of our position. The concussion lifted us up and tossed us into the air. No one was hurt, but it was a bit close for comfort."

Doc resumes.

I proceeded to adjust a total of five air strikes. The napalm cleared the area of foliage. I also brought in several pink teams to look for moving targets around the edges of White's position.

Fighter-bombers fly parallel to the front line of the unit in contact, if at all possible. During rapidly developing situations, it's extremely important to other aircraft to stay clear of that lane. All the pink team pilots were experienced and competent. I didn't have to remind them to keep up with the air strikes on the command net in order to stay clear of the "fast movers."

About this time, our backup helicopter arrived. Bates called it in and took over for its pilot and copilot. People from the Maintenance Section arrived shortly and repaired the shot-up helicopter well enough for the backup helicopter's pilot and copilot to fly it out. As soon as Bates was circling over the fight, he called me. I was still airborne in the replacement helicopter.

"Thunderhorse Six, this is Six Alpha, over."

"Six Alpha, this is Six, over."

"I'm right above you, over."

"Six Alpha, I'm going to land. Come and pick me up, over."

"Roger, Six, I'm right behind you."

We landed and I climbed in with Bates, who took us back over the fight.

Early in the contact, I asked regiment to give me a reinforcing unit of infantry. The area was too tough for armor. About this time, an infantry company from the 1st Infantry Division arrived at a remote LZ. I radioed Captain Earl Moore and told him to have his four lift ships begin shuttling them to my location, one platoon at a time.

Bates followed the lift ships to a LZ at the bottom of the hill and landed. I dismounted and ran over to the first platoon to hit the ground. I didn't have time to stand there and brief the platoon leader. I took point and told him to follow me, briefing him as I headed for White's position at a fairly fast pace. I really wanted the bastard who killed my crew chief.

Colonel Patton and Major Dozier arrived on station and were now circling high overhead, listening to the fight over my troop command net, ready to call in more reinforcements if necessary, or do whatever else they could to assist.

I led the infantry platoon as we rushed to an area that had been hit with napalm. Brush and trees were still smoldering. As we searched the area, I saw an NVA soldier attempting to hide in a hollowed out tree. He was holding an AK-47 against his chest. I thought about shooting the bastard but decided to take him prisoner instead.

I didn't want him to know I'd spotted him. That might have caused him to start shooting. I ran ahead as if I was going to bypass the tree, but just as I came alongside it, I stopped, reached into the tree, grabbed him by the throat, and yanked him out. I handed him over to some of the platoon's riflemen, and told them to make sure he was interrogated thoroughly.

I was still on point, leading the infantry toward White's position, when I spotted a small group of NVA soldiers running away from us. I began firing right away and the rest of the platoon joined in. We killed some and captured the rest by literally running them down.

We pressed forward and soon caught up with White and his ARPs. They'd been fighting fiercely and had cleared their area of enemy forces. White told me they killed the NVA soldier who shot up my helicopter and crew chief. That made me very happy.

Bates continued to circle overhead while I remained on the ground. The rest of the reinforcing infantry company eventually caught up with me. I had them help sweep the battlefield, gathering up enemy weapons and searching dead NVA soldiers for documents that might provide useful intelligence information.

After the battlefield was thoroughly cleared, I assembled all the troops. I took point and led them, POWs in tow, on a two-kilometer withdrawal back to the pickup area. Moore's lift ships shuttled the infantry back to their base camp, then returned to fly the ARPs and their POWs back to Alpha Pad.

It was late afternoon when Bates landed to pick me up. After we got back to base camp, we were informed that Gorman was alive but had sustained irreparable damage to his spinal cord. He was paralyzed below his waist. I really felt sorry for him. Gorman was a good soldier and just a young kid starting out in life. His girl friend was pregnant and I was working on getting him an emergency leave to marry her in Hawaii. He was excited about getting married and having a baby. Whatever plans he had for his future would now have to be worked around a big-time disability that he could never shake; one he would have to learn to deal with in the best way possible. Bates and I went to visit Gorman in the hospital as soon as we could.

Major Pete Noyes recalls talking to Tom White that evening in the troop's orderly room.

"Lieutenant White was tired and dirty and in remarkably good spirits for a guy who looked like he'd been dragged through a briar patch. He got straight to the point of why he'd stopped by.

" 'Sir, does Major Bahnsen fight like this everyday?'

"In truth, Doc didn't fight this fiercely every day. But I wasn't about to pass up an opportunity to yank White's chain.

" 'Nothing out of the ordinary, Lieutenant. The troop has hostile engagements, like today's, everyday. Major Bahnsen? Well, he fights like that every day. Every damn day.'

"White didn't flinch. I was sort of hoping that we'd have a good laugh together. But he didn't catch on to my sophistry.

" 'Well, if that's the case, I better keep up with my life-insurance premiums.'

"I guess his first day in combat with the troop must have made a big impression in White's mind, because over the next ninety days he led his ARPs in fifty or more hostile engagements. That's an incredible amount of fighting for a unit of any size or any one person. He took it all in stride and proved himself to be an exceptional combat leader and fighter."

Doc sums up this action.

No friendlies were killed in this fight. Other than Gorman, none incurred a serious wound. There was a lot of valor shown that day. Although it was White's first mission with the ARPs, he performed skillfully and with the calm resolve in a crisis that marks a seasoned fighter.

Several of my troopers and soldiers from the 1st Infantry were awarded medals for gallantry in this battle, including Tom White and Mike Bates. Mike Gorman was awarded the Air Medal with Valor device and a Purple Heart.

Gorman was popular among his fellow soldiers. Bates and I were just getting used to having him fly as our crew chief. It was a sad moment for me when Gorman was medically evacuated out of Vietnam, never to fight again.

During an awards ceremony at the 11th Armored Cavalry Regiment's headquarters at Quan Loi in August 1969, General Creighton Abrams, Commanding General, USMACV, personally presented Doc with the Distinguished Service Cross for extraordinary heroism during this combat action against a numerically superior enemy force.

✷ Chapter 69 ✷

Retired Colonel, then Major, Andy O'Meara describes routine reconnaissance missions performed by the troop's pink teams.

"As the S-2, I ran reconnaissance for the regiment. I flew with the troop's pink teams often, but always in an observer status. I didn't interfere with its chain of command.

"After Colonel Patton got the go-ahead to call in B-52 strikes on the free-fire zone south of War Zone D, I delegated routine aerial recon missions of this area to each of the troop's eight pink teams when they weren't otherwise needed. Scout pilots flew low and slow, looking for newly constructed buildings and bunkers, new or recently improved trails, troop movement, and other signs of enemy activity. Because they reconned the same area over and over again, scouts spotted changes almost as soon as they occurred.

"The by-the-book procedure for reporting intelligence on enemy activity called for scouts to prepare a written report and submit it to my section for analysis. After we analyzed the report, we would prepare a written summary for Colonel Patton and his staff to use in formulating future missions. As you can imagine, this was a very time-consuming process. Doc didn't like written reports. He had a genius for handling intel reports in a more timely and effective way.

"When one of the troop's scouts saw something that needed to be reported to my section, he would drop off his observer then pick me up at the regiment's pad. He would fly me out to the area and take us down low so I could make an eyes-on assessment of the situation. After I made my assessment, he would fly me back to regiment, and I'd report to Colonel Patton, or the S-3 in his absence, and tell him, 'Here's what we found,' and then summarize the situation.

"This unorthodox procedure provided the regiment with actionable intelligence in a timely manner. It also gave us a leg up on nipping a lot of enemy activity in the bud, before it grew into something larger.

"Subsequent missions would be launched as the situation warranted. If the intel pink teams developed included a target good enough to justify it, B-52 strikes would be worked up. However, B-52 missions required coordination with several higher headquarters, resulting in a delay of several days to a week before the actual strike took place."

Doc begins.

I sent several pink teams out on routine reconnaissance at first light. The morning passed without a single report of enemy activity. Late in the afternoon, one of my scouts was shot at by a .51-caliber heavy machine gun and quickly moved to the side of the contact area. The gunship pilot spotted the signature green .51-caliber tracers firing on the scout ship and rolled in to take it under fire. However, before he could get in position to launch rockets on the gun's location, the antiaircraft fire got heavier and he had to get out of the way. Both ships took hits but no serious damage resulted from them.

The gunship pilot radioed our TOC with a situation report. I was in the general area and heard the transmission. I called pink team immediately. Both pilots told me what they'd seen. I asked them if anybody else in the contact area had shot at them. They told me negative. They spotted a single machine gun nest but no signs of other enemy soldiers in the area.

Bates had us to their position in a matter of minutes. We flew all around the area, scoping it out, being very cautious to keep out of the machine gun team's sight. If a .51-caliber gunner could see you, he could hit you. We were shot at every time we got close to this gun's position. If we'd stayed in the gunner's sight, he would have used tracer fire to adjust his aim, and we would have bought the farm.

After fifteen minutes of sorting the situation out, we determined it was indeed a solo antiaircraft team. This was very unusual. When the NVA went hunting for unsuspecting helicopters, they normally hunted in a pack of three to four teams, a minimum of two. They liked to get you in a triangle, so no matter which way you turned to run, you'd be running toward one of their gun positions.

We had one antiaircraft machine gun team at the end of a quarter-mile long erosion wash, six to seven feet deep, situated between rolling hills covered with patches of low scrub brush. Even though it was partially camouflaged beneath limbs from bushes in the immediate vicinity, I could see the AA team's emplacement clearly.

After looking the area over very carefully, I called my TOC and told them to scramble ARPs. For whatever reason, the ARPs were taking the afternoon off and the only ones available were recent additions to the platoon. Experienced ARPs knew better than to hang around the troop area when they had time off.

A lift ship carrying one squad of inexperienced ARPs arrived over the contact area within minutes. I told the pilot to orbit until I could get suppressive fire on the machine gun's position, making it safer for an insertion. By this time I had another pink team on station. The two pink teams placed a heavy volume of minigun and rocket fire around the enemy location. Due to defilade, the .51-caliber crew survived this onslaught.

I then decided to land with the ARPs behind the enemy's position. We would seal off the wash, and I would have the pink teams bring in another dose of heavy rocket and minigun fire from their front. The way I saw things developing, the machine gun team would turn and run, and we'd be waiting for them.

At very low level, Bates led the lift ship into a LZ right beside the wash, flared, and landed. I dismounted my aircraft at the same time the ARPs hit the ground. Bates and the lift ship pilot pulled pitch and flew out of the LZ at low level to avoid becoming a target for the enemy machine gun team.

I had my M-16 rifle, PRC-25 radio, and a sack of fragmentation grenades with me. I led the ARPs to a position just above the wash and told them to get ready to throw some grenades. I supplied grenades to those who didn't have any and to those who only had one or two. I then got on my radio and ordered the gunships to attack the enemy's position with long-range rocket fire.

Shortly after the rockets splashed, the lead scout radioed me.

"Six, this is White Two-Four. Three dinks are headed your way. Be aware, they have their .51 cal with them. Doesn't look like they know you are there, over."

"Roger, Two-Four, we'll be ready for them. Keep me posted."

The ARPs and I were lying on the edge of the wash with grenades ready. I told them to be prepared to throw their grenades into the wash on my command.

"Two-Four, how close are those dinks to my location?"

"Less than a hundred meters, and closing rapidly, over."

"Roger, stay clear of their line of fire. I don't want you getting shot."

I ordered the ARPs to pull pins and toss their grenades in the wash.

I didn't know it at the time, but we heaved our grenades into the wash before the machine gun team was within range. As soon as our grenades exploded, I rose up and yelled, "Follow me," then jumped into the wash. It was deeper than I thought. I landed on my ass and lost my steel helmet. I looked to my rear and found out I was all alone. No one had followed me!

I looked down the wash. Three NVA soldiers were about twenty-five meters away, dragging their machine gun mounted on a two-wheeled frame behind them. Lucky for me, I surprised them and their gun was pointed the wrong direction. They looked at me and stopped dead still. Still sitting on my ass, I brought my M-16 up and shot three short bursts, killing them where they stood.

I yelled up to the ARPs, chewed their ass for not following me, and told them to get their butts down in the wash. They quickly jumped into the wash and joined me in policing up the machine gun and searching the dead NVA.

It then dawned on me that these particular ARPs did not know me very well. They were so new to the platoon that this could have been their first enemy contact, which explains why they hesitated when I said, "Follow me."

We returned to Alpha Pad within the hour after initial contact was made. Those young ARPs put the captured .51-caliber machine gun on display for all to see, and stood by it with the pleasure you see young country boys take in showing a prize pig at a county fair. They got all excited when telling other troopers the story of how it came to be in our possession.

Pete Noyes comments.

"I was working in the orderly room when Doc returned from this contact. He came in and told me they'd brought back a .51-caliber machine gun—the enemy weapon most feared by helicopter pilots in Vietnam.

"I went out to see it and the ARPs started telling me about Doc's actions. They were absolutely amazed by their commanding officer's fearless flair in taking out the NVA machine gun team.

"I talked with the pink team pilots to get their input on the action. Their report, along with what the ARPs had said, indicated this was definitely a medal-worthy action on Doc's part.

"If one of the ARPs had done what Doc did, I most certainly would have written him up for a Silver Star. However, even though his actions warranted a higher recognition, I put Doc in for an Army Commendation Medal with Valor device for no other reason than the fact that he didn't have one. And he got it! That surprised me. I expected regiment to upgrade my recommendation. They must not have read my write-up closely."

✳ Chapter 70 ✳

3 February 1969—K4 Woods, seven kilometers northeast of Lai Khe

The Air Cavalry Troop was assigned routine reconnaissance for an area known as the K4 Woods. We were familiar with this area in general, but had never reconnoitered it thoroughly.

Fairly close to the 1st Infantry Division's Headquarters at Lai Khe, the K4 Woods was a heavily wooded area east of the old railroad line built by the French that ran north to south through this part of Vietnam. The railroad was long abandoned but remained a visible terrain feature from the air. Running east to west, the woods were about a kilometer wide and were bordered north to south by open fields.

I was working with two pink teams, getting more familiar with the area and hunting for signs of recent enemy activity. Four lift ships loaded with ARPs were in the air not far behind me. If my scout pilots spotted enemy forces or active bunkers, I was ready to start a pile-on operation right away.

Sergeant First Class John Ryan had recently replaced A. C. Cotton as the troop's first sergeant. He'd been ribbing my new crew chief, Specialist Four Enrique Enrico, and door gunner, Sergeant Walter Peterson, over what he told them was "easy duty."

Former sergeant Walter Peterson remembers Doc and the ribbing Enrico and he had been getting from their first sergeant.

"I reenlisted for a six-year hitch just before leaving Germany for Vietnam. Not long after I started flying with Major Bahnsen, I told him

I was tired of being a spec four. He asked, 'How long have you been in the Army, Son?' I told him, 'Two years.' He told Mister Bates that it wasn't right for someone to reenlist for six years and not be promoted to sergeant. Mister Bates said he would talk with our XO and get that taken care of. I was soon wearing sergeant stripes.

"I mention this because it's a good example of how Major Bahnsen treated me, and he treated me better than any commander I had before or after the Air Cav Troop. He was a Georgia boy but treated me, a black man, like he was from California. That was very unusual for a southerner in those days. He made me feel important as a member of his personal crew, the troop, the Army, and as a man.

"Sergeant Ryan was new to the troop and had never flown on a mission. In the evenings, he used to hear Enrico and me talking about what we'd done that day. We'd tell him, then he would tell us we were full of shit. He'd say stuff like, 'I bet all you do is fly around, drink ice water, and bullshit.'

"Enrico and I would come back at Sergeant Ryan and tell him he was a pussy—that he just sat on his ass in the orderly room all day shuffling papers and growing hemorrhoids, and that he didn't have the balls to fly with us."

Doc resumes.

I didn't know what motivated Sergeant Ryan to ask if he could come along on this mission, and I didn't question him about it. He knew he was welcome to fly with me anytime his schedule allowed. He said he had time on this particular morning. I told him, "Okay by me. Go get in my helicopter. Sit in the jump seat. You can get a good view of what's going on from there."

We hadn't been out too long when one of the scouts took fire from an unknown-sized enemy force and called me. We proceeded to his area. When Bates took us over the target, we also took small-arms and automatic weapons fire. Several rounds came up through the cabin floor. One hit the jump seat behind me where Ryan was sitting and some metal fragments hit him in the ass. Another round hit Peterson.

Walter Peterson talks about being wounded.

"There were bullets zinging all around the cabin. I felt a sharp, burning pain in my arm and yelled, 'I'm hit! I'm hit!'

"Major Bahnsen looked over his shoulder and asked, 'Where?'

" 'In my arm! In my arm!'

" 'Show me.'

"I rolled my sleeve up over my elbow. I was bleeding, but not bad. The bullet just nicked me.

" 'That's nothing, Peterson, you'll live,' Major Bahnsen calmly said. 'Enrico, get in the first aid kit and find something to put over Peterson's wound. Stop the bleeding. That's good enough for now. We'll have it looked at later.' "

Doc resumes.

I looked at Ryan. He had the look of terror in his eyes. I thought he must have been thinking he was a dead man. He wasn't wounded all that bad, even though he needed some patching up, and I didn't want him going into shock.

Bates headed our aircraft straight to Lai Khe, where we dropped Ryan off at the 1st Division's MASH. We were back over the contact area within ten minutes.

We didn't know how large of an enemy force was in the woods at this point, only that we'd taken fire.

While my pink teams assessed the situation, I radioed Captain Earl Moore, my Lift Ship Platoon leader, and told him to insert the ARPs in the open field two hundred meters south of the wooded area. The enemy knew we were there, but I wasn't about to let them shoot at my ARPs while they were in the LZ. I radioed my gunships and told them to put suppressive fire on the wood line and stand by for close support if the ARPs took fire.

I then got on a frequency with a field artillery unit and called in H&I fire on the north end of the wooded area. With gunships watching the east and west ends of the woods for fleeing soldiers, and ARPs moving in from the south, this fire effectively blocked the enemy in place.

The ARPs took a few rounds before clearing the LZ, but Lieutenant White quickly organized them and moved to contact. The gunships lifted their suppressive fire just as the ARPs entered the woods. I kept the artillery fire coming, about a thousand meters in front of the ARPs.

Then Sergeant and ARP squad leader Chris Gunderson talks about taking fire.

"The shots came from a LZ watcher who didn't hang around, but we knew we were going to make further contact. I'd been training Spec

Four Darden to walk point. And even though it was going to be risky, he wanted to walk point on this mission."

Then First Lieutenant Thomas E. White Jr. talks about what happened next.

"We set out in two parallel columns. Specialist Four Otis James Darden was walking point for one. I was about three feet behind him. Just as we went into the tree line, we took heavy fire from a trench line and well-fortified bunkers. Darden was hit before we could take cover. He dropped right in front of me. The rest of us quickly took cover and returned fire while two of my ARPs recovered Darden and started moving him to the rear for evacuation.

"This was a very well-concealed bunker complex and based on the enemy's initial volume of fire, I thought we were seriously outnumbered. I was fully expecting the NVA to close with us, but they didn't. For some unknown reason, they shut down their fire. If they hadn't, several more of us would have been killed.

"Based on what I'd discovered and my estimate of the situation, I radioed Doc with a sitrep. He told me to move back to the LZ and hunker down; he was bringing in air strikes. I signaled my platoon to pull back."

Doc resumes.

White informed me his ARPs had run head-on into a large enemy force and they were lucky to have only one casualty.

I got hold of the FAC on station and asked him what he had. He told me he had two birds with high drags, nape, and twenty mike-mike. I told him to hold the twenty mike-mike and that I was going to mark.

Bates took us in low over the southern edge of the woods; Peterson dropped yellow smoke to mark where I wanted the air strike concentrated. The FAC called color and I rogered color. He then proceeded to re-mark with a white phosphorous rocket.

Within thirty seconds, two F-4s that had been circling the contact area came swooping down like hawks after a rabbit, leveled off, dropped their high-drag bombs, pulled up, then circled back to hit the enemy position with napalm. As soon as the fast movers were clear of the area, I brought in more H&I artillery fire on both sides of the woods.

I then called the regimental TOC and asked for ground reinforcements. Colonel Patton was in the air nearby. He heard my call and joined me at the scene. Our pilots orbited our ships at low level while I briefed him.

Patton agreed that a pile-on operation was in order. He very shortly chopped me the 2nd Squadron's H Company, commanded by Captain Tom Montgomery, and E Troop, commanded by Captain Tom Templer.

H Company was equipped with M-48A3 Patton tanks. M-48A3s had gasoline engines and were armed with a 90mm main gun, a .50-caliber heavy machine, and a coaxial .30-caliber machine gun. They could travel at speeds of up to forty-eight kilometers per hour over open terrain and had a formidable presence in battle.

E Troop rode in M-113 ACAVs. As I understand it, the acronym ACAV (armored cavalry assault vehicle) was coined by someone in the 11th Armored Cavalry Regiment. ACAVs were modified M-113 armored personnel carriers. They were versatile mobile-fire platforms armed with a .50-caliber heavy machine gun and side-mounted M-60 machine guns. M-60s were also sometimes mounted on the rear of the vehicle. Gunners operated their weapons from behind protective gun shields. Some ACAVs were armed with a 4.2-inch mortar mounted in their open bay. ACAVs had a crew of two and carried up to ten riflemen, who could fight from inside the track or dismount and follow beside or behind it.

My plan was to soften the enemy position with more air and artillery strikes then overrun it with ACAVs and tanks, followed by a sweep of the area using my ARPs and reinforcing infantry—a typical pile-on operation.

Retired Lieutenant General, then Captain, Tom Montgomery, who later became deputy commander UN Forces and commander U.S. Forces Somalia, talks about this mission.

"My company was located at Fire Base Jim at the time, about two to three kilometers south of the contact area. We were pulling maintenance that day. We also had some Donut Dollies visiting us. It was a special treat to have these dedicated women visit your unit at places like Bien Hoa Air Base. But having them visit us out in the field was a really special treat—so we weren't looking for something to do.

"Around fourteen hundred hours, I was alerted by my squadron TOC to reinforce a U.S. unit in contact with the enemy. The regiment was opconned to the First Infantry and this contact was very close to its base camp at Lai Khe. I assumed we were going to reinforce an infantry battalion from the First Infantry.

"A large portion of the area we were operating in was Rome plowed rubber, which made it suitable for tanks. My company, minus one tank platoon, was almost always task organized with an attached ACAV platoon. I quickly scrambled my tanks and got moving to the contact area in a single-file column behind Tom Templer's ACAVs."

Retired Colonel, then Captain, Tom Templer recalls this enemy contact.

"My troop was on standby to reinforce the ARPs anytime they were in our area. We were also at Fire Base Jim that day. A few days earlier, we had been out on a mounted ambush patrol in the same area as this contact. About dusk, an NVA soldier crawled up to our position and Chieu Hoi'd. We turned him over to regiment for interrogation and they'd just returned him to our custody to use as an intel source in future operations.

"When the mission came down, I had this POW put on board my track before I headed to the contact area with two platoons—sixteen ACAVs. I rode with a Vietnamese interpreter in my track. He didn't get along well with the POW. I quickly put an end to their bickering. They could get back to arguing after we returned from the mission.

"My troop led the armor column through brush and across dry irrigation ditches in what appeared to be abandoned rice paddies. The ground was almost perfectly flat and the brush fairly tall. We couldn't see that far ahead and were following a sky spot's straight-shot directions to the contact area. I didn't realize it at the time, but the sky spot was Doc Bahnsen, the Air Cavalry Troop commander. Nor did I know he was running this operation."

Doc resumes.

I knew Templer from his days as an assistant in Glenn Finkbiner's S-4 shop, and I worked with him on a previous mission. I did not know Montgomery.

I spotted the reinforcing armor column from the air not long after it departed Fire Base Jim. I made radio contact with both commanders and started directing them to where I wanted them to come on line.

It was getting late in the afternoon, and I wanted to sweep the bunker complex before dark. I kept yelling at Templer to hurry up, and prodding Montgomery to stay right on Templer's trailing ACAV. Neither one of them appreciated my goading and told me so. These young captains knew their business and were capable combat leaders. I only needed to tell them what I wanted them to do. They could take it from there, and they did.

Walter Peterson continues.

"After Major Bahnsen talked with Colonel Patton, he called in a second air strike. He was really pissed over Darden being hit, and it showed. In all my flying days in Vietnam, I never saw heavier bomb strikes on one area. I was pissed, too. Seeing those bombs rain down on the enemy made me feel better."

Doc resumes.

When the tracks started arriving in the contact area, I brought them up on an assault line well clear of the woods on line—ACAVs to the left, tanks to the right.

Tom Templer continues.

"We formed up for the assault and Doc told us to wait up. He was bringing in one more air strike. I got on my command net and told my guys to get their heads down. It was a good thing I did. The air strike came in very close to us, maybe twenty or thirty meters inside the tree line. Mud and debris from it hit our tracks. That was very scary. They made several passes before Doc gave us the all-clear, brought in artillery fire north of the base camp, and ordered Montgomery and me to attack.

"The air strikes knocked down a lot of trees and set fires that were still burning as we rolled toward the tree line. I had two riflemen from each track dismount and walk behind their vehicle. That put them in a good position to place grenades and small-arms fire inside bunkers as we advanced through the complex. The ARPs fell in behind Montgomery's tanks for the same reason. This conventional war assault formation was unusual for Vietnam, but there was nothing usual about fighting under Doc Bahnsen's command. He could sense what would work and did it. No one with any brains ever questioned his orders in the heat of battle. If you want to go to war, go with Doc."

Doc resumes.

I placed the gunships and scouts over the open field north of the woods, where they could kill anyone fleeing the woods. At one point, Patton's pilot, Charlie Watkins, started orbiting just below my aircraft. No one got inside my circle or lower than me during a contact. That obstructed my view and hindered my ability to control what was going on below. Patton could do his job from a higher altitude. Bates became irritated at Watkins and started yelling at him over the radio. When Watkins didn't respond to my pilot's instructions to get above his orbit, Bates flew right at him to emphasize his message. That caught Watkins's attention, and he climbed to a higher altitude.

Tom Templer continues.

"We assaulted until we reached a trench line. By that point, we'd already overrun several bunkers, and part of my unit and most of Montgomery's tanks halted pretty much in the middle of the bunker complex. But the fighting wasn't over. I still had guys shooting people in bunkers and pulling others out. While all of this was taking place, my previously captured POW dismounted my track and ran over to a bunker where some enemy soldiers had just been captured. He obviously knew these guys and wasn't very happy with them. He started raising hell with them right away—yelling at and kicking them for not surrendering earlier, like he did. My soldiers put a quick end to that nonsense.

"We were still clearing bunkers when Colonel Patton and Doc both landed and came walking up in front of my ACAVs to talk to me. My riflemen were still taking prisoners and picking up all kinds of stuff.

"While I was giving Doc a sitrep, Patton started using his Car-15 to put holes in canteens and metal plates scattered on the bottom of the trench. The situation was still dangerous. I turned and spoke to him. 'Sir, please don't do that. My guys have itchy fingers on their .50-cal triggers. I'd hate one of them to mistake your firing as enemy activity.'

"I don't recall what he said, but he stopped firing. I was relieved when he did. Shit would have hit the fan if one of my guys would have opened up on him.

"About this time, A Company, First of the Eighteenth Infantry, and a platoon from B Company, Second of the Twenty-eighth Infantry arrived. They helped us sweep the bunker complex while some of Montgomery's tanks pushed farther north before turning around and coming back through the bunkers."

Doc resumes.

I got back in my helicopter and Bates flew us to the north side of the woods, where we watched for enemy soldiers fleeing into the open field. We weren't there long before two NVA darted out of the woods. Bates landed and I dismounted. I quickly shot one of them and a couple of ARPs helped me chase the other one down.

The pile-on operation went without a hitch. We destroyed what turned out to be a hospital bunker complex, killed eighteen and captured seven NVA in a couple of hours, start to finish. I don't believe many, if any, enemy escaped. There weren't as many of them as we initially thought. As Tom White later pointed out to me, this was a caretaker force, not a platoon of hard-core NVA.

The 1st Infantry Division's leaders were surprised to find out that an enemy hospital had been located right under their noses for some time. Although it had gone unnoticed, this was a poor location for a base camp. The wooded area wasn't expansive and had open fields on all sides, leaving no safe escape route.

It was dark by the time the action ended. I had the ARPs flown back to Bien Hoa. It was too dark for the tracks to travel back to Fire Base Jim safely. I left Montgomery in command of the task force. He set up an excellent NDP around the bunker complex, positioning the reinforcing infantry between tracks. All units returned to their base early the next morning.

When we landed at Alpha Pad, Bates and I took a good look at our helicopter. It was full of bullet holes, but not damaged mechanically.

This contact serves as a good example of how the Blackhorse operated and how quickly it could respond with flexibility and fury. We didn't always outnumber the enemy, but we could overwhelm him with our maneuverability, speed, and firepower. pile-on operations like this one saved a lot of our soldiers' lives and resulted in a significant number of enemy dead.

However, no matter how effective the tactics and techniques a combat commander employs may be, warfighting results in casualties among his own forces.

Darden was a very handsome young man, physically fit, and a hard-core soldier. He had a lot going for him. Unfortunately, he was dead on arrival at the MASH in Lai Khe. Walter Peterson took Darden's death hard. They'd become close friends in the short time Darden had been in the troop.

White recommended Specialist Four Otis J. Darden for a posthumous Silver Star for his gallantry in action during this enemy contact. I endorsed his recommendation. Darden also received a posthumous Purple Heart.

Besides recognizing Darden's gallantry and sacrifice, other troopers received medals for distinguishing themselves in combat.

I recommended Montgomery, Templer, White, and several ARPs for the Bronze Star with Valor device for their heroic achievement during this action. I wrote up Bates for a Distinguished Flying Cross for extraordinary achievement while participating in aerial flight, and several of my pilots for Air Medals with Valor device for meritorious achievement while participating in aerial flight. Patton recommended me for the Silver Star.

* Chapter 71 *

Two of my best scout pilots, Warrant Officers Guy Ballou and Phil Mohnike, spotted a company-plus-sized NVA force, marked its location with a red smoke grenade, then engaged it with miniguns. Mohnike killed two NVA soldiers before Ballou and he moved to the side of the contact area to assess the situation.

During pink team operations, Cobra gunships' higher altitude afforded them better line-of-sight communications with our TOC at Bien Hoa. For this reason, one of the gunship pilots normally called in a sitrep when enemy contact was made. Depending on my location, I could hear the sitrep as it was being reported. If not, the ops shop would run me down and let me know what was going on.

I heard this particular sitrep and took immediate action. First, I radioed the TOC and told them to launch the ARPs. While they were en route, I contacted the Air Force FAC in the area to find out what he had available.

Bates had us over the contact area in a matter of minutes. The lift ships carrying ARPs arrived shortly after. I directed the lift ship team leader to a LZ about one hundred fifty meters from the enemy's position.

Former ARP platoon leader Tom White talks about this mission.

"We inserted without incident but came under fire soon after. Specialist Gene 'Fruit Cake' Tschirren was walking point. We called him

'Fruit Cake' because he cut off the lid to a C-ration can of fruit cake, punched a hole in it, and used a string to attach it through the button-hole on the right breast pocket on his jungle fatigues. That C-ration lid became his personal identity badge.

"Tschirren grew up in the Midwest and spent a lot of time outdoors, most of it hunting and shooting. He had an incredible knack for seeing people and objects in the shadows and in the bush, and was a dead-eye shot. Because it fired a larger projectile and had greater knockdown power, he carried an M-14 rather than an M-16 or Car-15. And he preferred walking point. That was unusual because it was dangerous. But he was exactly the kind of guy you wanted out front.

"We hadn't been on the ground more than a minute or two before the enemy's lead element came running down a trail toward us. Tschirren killed three of them from a distance of about a hundred meters. That stopped the enemy in his tracks and gave us an opportunity to pull back for an air strike."

Doc resumes.

White marked his front with smoke. A flight of two F-100 fighters then proceeded to drop five-hundred-pound, high-drag bombs. The bombs hit right on target. The ARPs were close to the target area and hunkered down to avoid being hit by shrapnel or flying objects—rocks, limbs, whatever. Unfortunately, Sergeant Ron Bishop took cover with his feet toward the strike area, and a piece of shrapnel hit his crotch.

White called me and reported that he had one wounded. Bates took us down immediately. By the time I got on the ground, the shooting had stopped but the pink teams continued to chase enemy soldiers as they ran for their lives.

White had the situation under control before I caught up to him. A couple of ARPs helped Bishop to his feet. The seat and crotch of his pants were soaked with blood. He dropped his pants so our medic could assess his wound. It wasn't a pretty sight: the shrapnel severed one of his gonads. He was in a lot of pain, but he handled it extremely well. He looked down at his wound then and calmly said, "I've got a really bad hit here, sir. I'm sorry I faced the wrong direction during the air strike."

"No apology necessary, Bishop. I'm damn happy you didn't get killed. We're going to get you to a hospital right away. Don't worry. You're not going to die. Not now. You'll be fine."

Bishop was a courageous young man whose lot in life had just taken a dramatic change. He took it all very well, better than I would have. As soon as the medic got the bleeding stopped, a couple of troopers in his squad walked Bishop to one of our lift ships that medevaced him to the 93rd Evacuation Hospital at Long Binh.

The ARPs then moved forward to see if any of the enemy were still there. I remounted my helicopter. We tried for the next hour, but were unable to spot any enemy stragglers from the air or on the ground, so we called it a day and returned to Alpha Pad.

Except for the one wounded, this was a typical day of Air Cavalry recon: we usually made contact, got shot at, killed some enemy soldiers, routinely took prisoners, and returned to Alpha Pad without casualties.

I never took having my men killed or wounded lightly. War is dangerous. Soldiers get killed and wounded, it's unavoidable. Notwithstanding, I always did my best to prevent either from happening. If an air strike or an artillery fire mission, or both, would kill the enemy and prevent friendly casualties, I called it in and kept it coming until I was damn sure it got the job done.

I never concerned myself with the price of bombs or artillery shells. My job was to lead men in battle and bring them out safely, not to save the government money. If a battlefield commander gets caught up in the cost of bombs and artillery shells, he is going to get distracted from his primary mission: to kill the enemy and protect his own forces.

⋆ Chapter 72 ⋆

13 February 1969—east side of the Catcher's Mitt, northeast of Tan Uyen

Retired Colonel Andy O'Meara Jr. describes this sector of the Blackhorse AO and its significance to the U.S. war effort at the time.

"The Catcher's Mitt was an area south of the Testicles, a land shaped by a series of prominent bends in the Song Be River—south of War Zone D and about five miles northeast of Bien Hoa. Terrain features made both areas near impossible for track vehicles.

"A large trail ran south out of War Zone D through the Testicles and into base camps in the southern sector of the Catcher's Mitt. The enemy used these base camps as staging areas for assaults on Long Binh during both the first and the second Tet Offensive.

"We observed a large VC base camp in the Testicles for a long time before we went in and bombed it. We followed the air strike by a large-scale gunship assault.

"As a result of our pounding them hard and heavy, the VC moved in a southeasterly direction along the major trail leading to base camps in the eastern sector of the Catcher's Mitt. This movement was known to the regiment, and we conducted several ambushes along that trail that resulted in a large number of enemy kills.

"The east side of the Catcher's Mitt was virgin timber. Some areas had been defoliated by Agent Orange, and these were the only places where you could see much of the ground from the air. The infamous VC Dong Nai Regiment was very active in this area and provided assistance to NVA units moving through it."

Doc begins.

O'Meara routinely flew with the troop's aero scouts. Early in the afternoon, one of my scout pilots, Warrant Officer Phil Mohnike, picked O'Meara up and flew him out to the east side of the Catcher's Mitt to make a firsthand, eyes-on-the-ground intelligence assessment.

Andy O'Meara vividly recalls this recon mission.

"Mohnike wanted to show me where he spotted evidence of heavy trail activity earlier in the day. Based on what he'd seen, he estimated that at least a battalion-sized force moved through the area the previous night.

"We flew over defoliated timber and could see the trail clearly. This wasn't the main trail in this area, but it was well worn and recently used. We followed the trail until we ran into forest that hadn't been sprayed with Agent Orange. Mohnike flew his Loach under the jungle canopy, following the dusty, fresh-footprint-covered trail winding its way through the trees. He flew very low over the trail until its powdered dust came to an end in a small clearing.

"We were very low and flying very slow. I was looking out my door for signs of the enemy when I saw a Ho Chi Minh sandal–covered foot sticking out from behind the far side of a tall tree. I told Mohnike what I saw. He turned the helicopter to give me a clear shot. I'd just stuck my Car-15 out the door when the enemy I was about to shoot, shot at us.

"Several rounds riddled our bird. None of them hit anything vital mechanically, but a single armor-piercing round came up through the floor and struck me just above the rear of my left ankle and traveled up my calf before exiting just below the knee.

"My calf muscle virtually exploded! The pain was horrible, almost too much to bear. The bullet ripped out most of my calf muscles and tore up the tendons behind my knees. Blood, hair, and meat from my leg splattered the cockpit, making a real mess. The blood gushing out of my horrendous wound started to puddle on the cockpit floor beneath me. I was in terrible shape.

"Mohnike realized right away that I was in dire need of medical care. He also realized that he couldn't get me anywhere in a hurry: we were surrounded by trees. He had to do some meticulous maneuvering to keep the helicopter's rotor from striking large branches. It was slow work and we were still vulnerable.

"The enemy soldier evidently emptied his magazine, got scared, and climbed into a spider hole when the Cobra covering us rolled in. That gave Mohnike enough time to get us out of there safely. It seemed to take forever, but it was only a few minutes. I used this time to remove my left boot lace and used it as a tourniquet above my left knee. I was still bleeding afterward, but not as much.

"Doc was in the area and heard the Cobra pilot call in a sitrep. He called Mohnike immediately."

Doc resumes.

Mohnike told me that his helicopter was full of holes but still flying with no noticeable problems. He reported seeing only the one VC, and that O'Meara was in bad shape. He had already set course to Twenty Ducks. I told Mohnike I would have one of our scouts trail him in just in case he encountered problems en route.

I was mad as hell! Andy was a good friend, a super soldier, and fearless in the toughest actions. I thought the world of Andy's hard-charging, fighting spirit. I was pissed and obsessed! I wanted to kill the bastard who shot him!

Mohnike's wingman remained on station to keep an eye on the spider hole. On hearing the sitrep, other pink teams flew to the contact area without delay. They didn't have to be told to assist in situations like this one. When I arrived over it, several pink teams were circling the contact area like a pack of wolves ready to pounce on prey. Most helicopter pilots were disciplined enough to await instructions from whomever was controlling the action. If they hadn't been, there would have been rockets and bullets flying every which way.

I got on the radio with Mohnike's wingman. He told me generally where the spider hole was located. Even standing next to one, spider holes were difficult to spot. But this one was in a clearing small enough to spot it with a little help from the Cobra pilot.

The Communications and Electronic Operating Instructions (CEOI) were issued during the morning briefing. They included the call signs and command net frequencies for all units in our AO. I personally kept up with the general locations of all units in the area.

As soon as I pinpointed the clearing's grid coordinates on my map, I called the nearest artillery battery and requested a precision fire mission.

Precision fire missions involved one gun firing to destroy a single small target, such as a bunker, abandoned vehicle, or any other object. Being the most precise and accurate artillery piece, the eight-inch howitzer was preferred for precision missions. These were large and heavy weapons, which made them more difficult to get in and out of fire bases. We had eight-inchers in our AO, but the easier-to-move-around 155mm howitzers were much more plentiful, and they did the job very nicely.

Helicopters orbiting the contact area had to be warned to stay clear of the incoming artillery fire. Depending on the situation, I would use one of several commands to give them a heads up over the UHF guard frequency. I might say something such as, "All helicopters in the area. I want you to move your orbit west of the contact area. Artillery fire coming from the east." Or I might say, "Everyone in the air on this channel move north of the yellow smoke. Artillery coming from the south."

The artillery unit responded very quickly and had my signature two-hundred-meter height-of-burst white phosphorous round on the way within a few minutes. I proceeded to adjust the fire into the small clearing one round at a time, each round getting closer to the spider hole. Thirty-two rounds later, a round hit dead center of the spider hole. The VC who shot my friend took to the air . . . in pieces! I was ecstatic!

I called check fire. Bates took us in low and slow. We could see the dead VC's body parts strewn all over the ground. It made me feel better about the situation. Not every soldier would have felt that way, but it was how I felt then, and still feel today.

Andy O'Meara continues.

"I woke up in post op to find I still had my leg. I was grateful, but I didn't know how close I came to losing it until Doc visited me. He told me the doctors were all set to amputate when Patton intervened. Doc said he didn't know the details, but evidently Patton arrived just before the doctors were coming into the OR to cut off my leg. In their opinion, the damage to my muscles and tendons was too severe to save it. Patton told them he wanted a second opinion.

"I was sedated at that point, but stable enough to delay the surgery long enough for Patton to fly in a doctor he knew when he was on MACV staff in Saigon. That doctor, a highly skilled surgeon, performed the delicate and tedious surgery necessary to save my leg. The guy must have been some sort of miracle worker because the Ninety-third's doctors were all very competent and didn't amputate unless there was no other option."

Doc concludes.

For extraordinary heroism in aerial flight during this enemy engagement, I recommended Phil Mohnike for the Distinguished Flying Cross.

I felt bad for Andy but was glad he'd survived. He was an exceptional intelligence officer. Patton totally trusted Andy and thought highly of him. We all did.

Patton awarded Andy the Silver Star for this action. I don't know how the citation reads and wouldn't second-guess Patton's write-up. However, I am certain this award was merited by the cumulative valor and heroism Andy showed in combat more than it was for the sole action of this particular day. Nothing wrong with that.

Andy was evacuated out-of-country three days later. It took several subsequent operations and months of convalescing before he returned to full duty.

✶ Chapter 73 ✶

When it became difficult for us to get the enemy to come out and fight, we found other ways to remain useful. The identification of targets suitable for B-52 strikes and BDAs of those strikes were such useful activities.

During slowdowns in enemy activity, I had the troop step up its reconnoitering efforts to locate targets for B-52 strikes. Once regiment had a chance to review our target lists, they were routed through channels to the Air Force. As soon as possible after the strike went in, the troop conducted BDAs to gather fresh and timely intelligence information.

Although BDAs regularly turned up useful intel, the regiment lived on the solid intelligence POWs provided. The troop took POWs routinely, but we hadn't captured a single dink for at least a week. This wasn't unusual; the enemy often took to hiding when refitting, resupplying, training, or otherwise standing down.

During this POW dry spell, Patton started to hassle me over not providing him with fresh POWs during his evening briefing. Initially, he was jesting, but he brought it up again and again. I got a little testy but said nothing. I did let the troop know we needed POWs, if only to get Patton off my back. Over the next few days, we made a concerted effort to run some down, but ended up getting kills only.

On this particular day, the ARPs went on a late-afternoon BDA out in War Zone D. Minutes after they put boots on the ground, Lieutenant

Tom White radioed to tell me that they'd found a naked VC wandering around the edges of a bombed out bunker area in the jungle.

Then First Lieutenant Tom White relates what he remembers about this incident.

"If you like to see things blown up, you would have loved seeing a B-52 air strike. They were a spectacular display of firepower that caused a lot of damage and left huge craters. The intensity and volume of the ordnance dropped during a B-52 strike created a tremendous overpressure that magnified its explosive effects.

"We first spotted this naked dink from the air as we were being inserted. I sent a couple of my guys to pick him up as soon as we hit the ground. He was unarmed and didn't offer any resistance. They bound his hands behind his back, put a rope around his neck, and brought him over to me. He was just a kid, a teen I would guess, but no less an enemy soldier.

"I should point out that putting ropes around POWs' necks was common in Vietnam. It was an efficient and effective way to get them to do what you wanted them to do. Out in the boonies, we didn't have a more effective way to control or prevent them from taking off at first chance. What's more, I never knew of a single instance when this practice harmed a POW.

"This particular POW was wandering around in a stupor when we first saw him. I suspect he had been close to the strike and his clothes caught on fire, so he took them off. He had some blood trickling out of his ears, an indication that he was suffering from a concussion. He could not hear, but was unmarked otherwise. He wasn't in the best shape and would have died wandering around alone in that neck of the woods. He was damn lucky to be alive and very lucky we came along. On examination, my medic determined this dazed enemy soldier would live and that he didn't require medical treatment before interrogation."

Doc resumes.

The regiment's evening briefing was due to start about this time. I told White to have the POW delivered to me as they found him at the regimental helicopter pad. The briefing was under way by the time I got to regiment. I waited at the pad until White and a couple of his ARPs arrived in one of our lift ships with the POW.

As soon as they got him on the ground, I took hold of the rope and led this POW straight to the briefing room, less than seventy meters away. With the naked POW in tow, I walked straight down the center aisle to where Colonel Patton was sitting, causing a little commotion along the way. Patton turned around to see what all the commotion was about, and stood up when he saw me. I walked up to him and said, "Colonel here is the prisoner you wanted." Then I gave him the rope.

Patton looked this scrawny, scared, and naked dink up and down, then said, "Sonofabitch, Doc, he's got the smallest pecker I have ever seen."

People in the room roared! Patton then asked me what happened to his uniform. I told him that was the way the ARPs found him. As I recall, Patton handed the rope to Captain Ralph Rosenberg, the 541st Military Intelligence Detachment commander who temporarily became the S-2 after O'Meara was wounded.

Rosenberg took the rope and led the POW off to be interrogated, clothed, fed, and given whatever further medical care he might require. I found an empty chair and sat down and the meeting continued, amid occasional snickers.

Retired Major General Jim Dozier comments on this incident.

"Patton developed lifelong and extraordinarily loyal relationships with several officers who served with him in the Eleventh Armored Cavalry Regiment in Vietnam. However, no other person in the regiment had the balls to present a POW to Patton during the evening briefing, fully clothed or naked. No other officer could have gotten away with doing something like that.

"Doc knew what he could get away with with Patton and he got away with a lot because he was so effective in combat. I don't recall Patton ever giving Doc a bad time about not bringing him enough POWs again."

✯ Chapter 74 ✯

One of my scout pilots located a sizeable and occupied enemy bunker complex. His gunship immediately rolled in with rockets and minigun fire. I was in the general vicinity and heard the sitrep as it was being called into my TOC.

As Bates turned our helicopter toward the contact area, I got on the radio with my TOC and told them to scramble the ARPs. Meanwhile, another pink team arrived over the contact area. Maneuvering through heavy small-arms and automatic weapons fire, the pink teams contained the enemy in place.

When we arrived over the contact area, Bates took our helicopter into a counterclockwise orbit so I could size up the situation. I quickly decided to start a pile-on operation. I called the regimental TOC and asked for ground reinforcements. They chopped an ACAV troop from the 2nd Squadron to me. ACAVs could maneuver through the trees and were very effective at crushing bunkers. The infantrymen ACAVs carried generally did a very good job of clearing bunkers.

Lift ships packed with ARPs arrived over the contact area within twenty-five minutes. I guided them to an open spot about two hundred meters away from the bunker complex. The ARPs moved toward the bunkers very carefully, but took cover about fifty meters out to size-up the situation. The ACAVs pulled into the area about this time.

Sergeant Lewis Sowder, a skinny-as-a-rail country boy who stood just over six feet, took point and led the ARPs toward the bunker complex. Sowder was an outstanding soldier and a religious young man of the highest character. His actions over the next several minutes were both courageous and heroic, meriting him a Silver Star in the process.

Former sergeant Lewis Sowder talks about becoming an ARP and his actions during this mission.

"I grew up in Kentucky. We didn't have TV in my part of the country, so we had to make up our own games. As kids, we played Cowboys and Indians in my cousins' barns. By the time I got to Vietnam, sneaking up on gooks in bunkers came naturally to me. But I didn't go to Vietnam to sneak up on gooks: I went to drive trucks.

"Driving trucks got boring and I decided I wanted to do something more for the war effort. My friend James Ard, another Kentucky boy, helped me get into the ARPs. I wanted to fight and nobody fought more than the ARPs.

"We were scrambled and choppered out to the area about midday. I think all four squads went out. The weather was good and we flew about a hundred fifty feet above the ground as we approached. I loved riding in Hueys. Their exhaust fumes smelled better than perfume to me.

"We inserted and made our way to the tree line with two squads walking in tandem on each flank. I was walking point for my squad. I was about a hundred yards into the trees and a hundred feet in front of everybody else when I saw gooks running in all directions. They were ducking into bunkers and jumping into spider holes.

"I just started to 'Machine Gun Kelly'—shooting my Car-15 off my hip at them. I saw two or three gooks fall dead before I emptied my magazine. I didn't reload. I could see where the gooks were dropping out of sight. I could throw a pretty good baseball in my time. I just started running toward the gooks and throwing grenades into their bunkers. Several grenades went right in the gun ports, some missed and blew up outside. The ones that missed kept the gooks in spider holes from rising up and shooting me."

Doc resumes.

I brought the ACAVs on line. They assaulted the bunker complex in a very tight formation and disciplined manner. My ARPs and the ACAV troop's infantry thoroughly cleared the bunkers, making damn sure no live enemy was left behind to shoot them in the back.

Lewis Sowder continues.

"After the shooting stopped, we started pulling dead gooks out and stacking them in a pile. I pulled this one out and turned him over. The back of his head was gone! All that remained of his head was the skin of his face. No eye balls, no nothing. His face looked like a Halloween mask—the kind of image that gives you nightmares.

"We called them gooks and dinks because they were the enemy, but they were human beings, too. They had mommas and daddies, brothers and sisters . . . children—just like we did. But if you didn't kill them, they would kill you. It was just like a game of Cowboys and Indians, only with real guns and deadly consequences."

Doc concludes commenting on this mission.

We didn't take any friendly casualties during this operation, and none of our helicopters or ACAVs sustained serious damage. When the fighting stopped, we found twelve NVA dead and took another one prisoner. A search of the area just west of the bunkers turned up a large cache of rice and ammo. All in all, it was an efficient and effective hunt.

Specialist Four Rex Saul took a photo of Sowder searching the bloody bodies of the nine VC he'd killed. It is a very graphic and vivid image of the realities of war. People die in war. Better the enemy's people than your own. That's how I saw it then, and still see it today.

✴ Chapter 75 ✴

Everything the Air Cavalry Troop accomplished revolved around the skill of its pilots to find the enemy, engage him from the air, and insert ground forces.

Officers commanded the helicopter platoons and sections. Warrant officers, though they were more often proficient and experienced pilots, led teams or missions only when no officer was available.

Gunship pilot Ray Lanclos, scout pilot Guy Ballou, and my pilot Mike Bates were exceptional pilots, fearless under fire, and self-starters who required little supervision. They were also dependable and quickly earned my confidence. I viewed them as pilots who had what it takes to lead in combat. To do that, they had to become commissioned officers.

Colonel Patton knew these pilots well and saw them in action almost daily. I talked with him about recommending them for direct appointments as second lieutenants. He unequivocally supported my idea.

All three knew they were being recommended for direct commissions. They didn't balk, so I figured they had no problems with becoming second lieutenants.

Major Noyes prepared the necessary paperwork for my and Patton's signatures and sent it to DA. We had no control over what branch would accept them, but I recommended them for armor. Mike Bates's paperwork came back approved with a commission date of 6 March 1969. He was commissioned in infantry. Ballou and Lanclos received commissions in armor with a commission date of 31 March 1969.

I was then, and am today, pleased to have played a part in them receiving commissions as officers. All three of them left Vietnam with a bunch of medals for gallantry. Bates was the most decorated of the bunch. Along with Silver and Bronze Stars, he was awarded seven Distinguished Flying Crosses, a distinction matched by very few pilots in the history of our armed forces.

Bates and Lanclos fulfilled the two-year obligation resulting from accepting their appointments as commissioned officers and separated from the service. Ballou remained in the Army and later commanded the 25th Infantry Division's Aviation Brigade before retiring as a colonel. They were then, and remain today, three of the best men I have ever known.

✯ Chapter 76 ✯

9 March 1969—east of Phouc Vinh, War Zone D

Former ARP specialist four Rex Saul talks about BDA missions.

"Some nights we'd be sitting around in our hooch, smoking and joking, and all of a sudden we'd hear the groaning sound of B-52s flying over a few minutes before the whole earth started shaking from the concussion of multiple five-hundred- and seven-hundred-fifty-pound bombs blowing, followed by some eerie clicking noise that I never figured out. This was a telltale sign that we were going out on a BDA the next morning.

"We always had air cover during BDAs, usually a couple of pink teams. Doing BDAs was like walking up to your knees in a freshly plowed field. We had to get around all the downed trees and shredded brush. We looked for documents, equipment, weapons, and whatever else we could find of intelligence value. We often saw pieces of charred human flesh dangling from trees and bushes. This was hard evidence that the strike had hit enemy troops.

"If there was a fine film of dust over the ground and vegetation, we didn't make contact during a BDA because that meant the enemy hadn't come back into the area. If we saw footprints, it meant the enemy had come back and we were going to make contact.

"Charlie was very good at clearing his dead from the battlefield. If he was in a hurry, it was not unusual for him to bury his dead in bomb craters. You could always tell when he'd done this. The bottoms of undisturbed bomb craters were churned up like mashed potatoes. If you saw one leveled off with footprints all around, you could dig down a few feet and find dead bodies."

Then First Lieutenant Tom White talks about the BDA mission his ARPs were given for this day.

"We had been going to this area almost every day for the past week or so. It was out in the boonies; a heavily wooded area and a hotbed of enemy infiltration, resupply, refitting, and staging activity, which made it a prime sector for B-52 strikes.

"The strike we were assessing on this particular day went in the previous night. It reduced a rather large east-to-west rectangular boxlike site to rubble. We inserted on the east end of the box midmorning without incident, then spread out in squads and started making our way west."

Retired Colonel and former scout pilot Guy Ballou recalls this BDA.

"There is a side story to this action. Early in the day I was told to report to Doc in the field. I went to his location and was told that Patton had a couple of ACAV troops that needed action. I was told to go find a base camp. I knew of one not far from the ACAV troops' location.

"The pink team I was part of went over to the area and determined the base camp had activity. I could not tell how many gooks were there, but I could tell it was active from the smell and the shine of the trails in the area. I could also see some tarps on the ground with fresh camouflage. I radioed Doc with a sitrep.

"Doc called Blackhorse operations and reported that we had an active base camp in sight. Operations chopped the Third Squadron's L Troop, under the command of First Lieutenant Jim Steele, to him. L Troop's move to the location would take some time as this was a heavily wooded area, so we had a pause in action. Doc wanted Steele's ACAVs on line and ready to assault the bunker complex before he brought in the ARPs.

"I was checking the outer area when I noted a couple of gooks hiding under some bushes probably two hundred meters from the base camp. Another pink team had shown up by this time, and Doc decided to have some target practice.

"I dropped smoke and the Cobras rolled in with guns and rockets. The other scout pilot and I maneuvered to a position where we could pound the enemy position with our miniguns while the Cobras circled to make a couple of firing passes. Rockets exploded all around the gooks and heavy smoke temporarily blocked our view. Once the smoke cleared, we could see that the two gooks were still alive. I don't remember who finally killed them. Most likely, it was my observer Robert Hepler, who was the best shot I have ever known."

Rex Saul continues.

"The previous night's B-52 strike walked bombs right up to the edge of the base camp and partially destroyed it. There were still bad guys in it. That was not unusual. Charlie was prone to hang around nearby and reoccupy—rebuild if necessary—base camps as soon as he thought the coast was clear. Sometimes he wouldn't leave at all and would put up a hell of a fight and regiment would send in tracks to help us sweep the complex. This was one of those times."

Tom White continues.

"I was in radio contact with Doc and knew what was happening. As it turned out, we arrived ahead of Jim Steele and his tracks and made contact with the enemy, who was still well entrenched in the bunker complex. The pink teams had killed some of the perimeter guards and stirred up their buddies. Charlie was ready and let us have it with everything he had. As we closed on the bunker complex, we were met with a fusillade of small-arms and automatic weapons fire. We took cover in bomb craters as soon as we could get to them and returned fire as best we could without getting our heads shot off. Several of my ARPs were wounded during this initial onslaught. Others were wounded later in the action. We were clearly outgunned at this point but held our ground.

"I wanted to evacuate my wounded ASAP but the only LZ within a safe distance was too small for a Huey. Guy Ballou was listening to me talk with Doc on the radio and heard I had wounded. He decided to assist. This wasn't the first time he volunteered to medevac wounded; it didn't seem to bother him that he would be taking enemy fire all the while."

Guy Ballou resumes.

"There were a lot of folks wounded in that very large crater. I started taking fire even before I began hovering to pick up the most critical. My seat was armor plated, so I turned my back to the enemy and went in to the crater 'til my head was ground level. I stuck my right skid against the wall and used the cyclic to keep the aircraft level.

"People were trying to get the wounded on board, but the gooks riddled my engine with AK-47 fire before I could pick them up, and my aircraft fell to its left side into the crater. We were very lucky no one got hurt badly and that my chopper didn't catch fire.

"One of my skids pushed an ARP with a head wound face down into the mud. A couple other ARPs quickly grabbed hold of him and pulled him out. He didn't seem to be any worse for the wear.

"It didn't take long to figure out that we were pinned down. The gooks had machine guns set up. Every time we looked over the edge of the crater, their fire had us covered. It took a lot of guts, but the ARPs and Hepler returned fire.

"I believe Hepler was one of only two in our crater not wounded and did a great job of keeping the gooks back. There wasn't going to be an easy way out. We were lucky that L Troop showed up and quickly overran the bunkers. They killed a bunch of gooks."

Tom White resumes.

"Doc brought Jim Steele's ACAVs in from the west. Even though I had several wounded, we kept the enemy from escaping to the east and killed several who tried, but we didn't avoid taking wounded ourselves. Sergeant Lewis Sowder rose up on the edge of a bomb crater to shoot at some dinks in an emplacement to his front. A dink to his flank shot him in the left leg, hitting a camera in his side pocket about midthigh high. He fell back in the bomb crater and one of the medics immediately cared for his wound. It did not hit any arteries—pure luck!

"As soon as the ACAVs overran the base camp, the fire coming our way let up and several of us advanced to help clear the bunkers and sweep the area."

Former sergeant Lewis Sowder recounts being wounded.

"This was the second time I'd been wounded in combat. The first time, I was shot through a can of red smoke I was carrying on my NVA ammo vest while I was pulling one of our guys out of an enemy-infested bunker. I took some shrapnel but was back to duty right away.

"I wanted some pictures of us in action. I didn't have an Instamatic, so I borrowed one from Spec Four Kenneth Green. He was from Tennessee and even more of a country boy than me. I put the camera in the side pocket of my fatigues as we were loading up for this mission.

"The helicopters were putting in a lot of rocket and minigun fire that was hitting very close to us. It was scaring me to death. I was thinking I was going to get killed by friendly fire.

"When I got hit, it felt like somebody hit me in the leg with a sledge-hammer. The bullet went right through the camera's lens, hit my leg bone, turned up, and went right into my crotch. I went down thinking I was going to die. I had on an NVA ammo vest filled with magazines loaded with a total of four hundred rounds. ARPs rarely wore steel pots. I took off my ammo vest and put it over my head to protect me from all the bullets that were still flying around."

Guy Ballou resumes.

"During the detailed search of the overrun base camp, I asked someone to take a look at the two gooks we were doing target practice on. About thirty minutes later, one of the NCOs from the ACAV troop came up to me with a large cloth case full of money, mostly U.S. currency. He wanted to know what he should do with it. I told him to keep it, and I didn't tell anyone 'til now. I figured those ACAV soldiers saved my life and deserved every penny."

Doc begins.

As soon as the action quieted down, White got his wounded to a LZ large enough for troop lift ships to come in and evacuate them to the 93rd Evacuation Hospital, where they were patched up. Miraculously, no one was seriously injured when Ballou crashed, and luckily there was no fire. Someone was really looking out for my guys.

White and I went to the hospital the next day to visit our wounded. I carried two eight-by-tens of the photo Specialist Rex Saul had taken after the action when Sowder killed nine VC.

All of my wounded were doing okay and were generally in good spirits. A doctor showed us X-rays of Sowder's wound. The bullet hit his femur, turned and traveled up his leg, hit his crotch, severed one of his testicles, and lodged in his penis. Sowder was joking about all of this! I found that amazing.

"He told us Patton came to visit him earlier. Patton told him that one ball was all he needed and he was gonna have a hell of a war scar on his whacker! A doctor told him the same thing. Sowder found that reassuring.

Sowder autographed the photos I brought along; one for Patton and one for me. Patton always hung his in his private latrine when he returned from Vietnam. I still have my framed copy hanging on the wall in my garage.

Lewis Sowder continues.

"During an earlier contact, I was within fifty feet of Sergeant Bishop when, out of the clear blue sky, a piece of friendly bomb shrapnel hit him and cut off one of his balls. I couldn't believe it. Guys got wounded but not like that. I suffered the same fate from a gook bullet shortly after. I still have that camera and the slug. They are constant reminders that sometimes guys do get their balls shot off in war."

Tom White resumes.

"Sowder was one of several ARPs who'd spent time in the woods hunting as a teenager, if not before. He was an expert marksman and a natural for what we did. He was a hell of a good soldier and a good young man. I hated to see him go home this way. But I was very happy to learn recently that he is the proud father of three children and still married to the same gal he married before coming to Vietnam."

Doc wraps up this action.

The enemy paid his soldiers in cash, which explains why their paymasters carried bags of it. It wasn't uncommon to kill or capture enemy paymasters en route to either NVA or VC units.

I can't speak for other units, but I can say that I never knew of any Blackhorse trooper who ever padded his wallet or enlarged his bank account with captured money.

Whatever money that didn't get turned in made its way into unit funds and was used to help build morale—stock the bar, pay for parties, or help out soldiers who needed some extra cash for one reason or another. Some of this money also found its way into various civic action projects in the Blackhorse AO.

Looking back on it now, this was a very traumatic day, although it didn't seem that way at the time because we experienced enemy actions like this one on a frequent basis.

Among others cited for heroism in this action, Tom White was awarded the Silver Star for conspicuous valor—the same kind of conspicuous valor he led and fought with in every action as the ARP platoon leader. White was mature beyond his years as a soldier. He got the job done in every action. He was a very controlled combat leader who stood fast in this hot and heavy action where a lot of people got hurt.

✷ Chapter 77 ✷

This week had several days of pile-on actions with the Air Cavalry Troop finding the enemy and setting them up. The ARPs also conducted several BDAs.

On 10 March, the troop led a pile-on operation against a NVA bunker complex near Lai Khe. The jungle in this area was triple canopy and thick. This limited my visibility of the ground, so it took me a bit longer to guide the reinforcing armor elements—tanks and ACAVs—to the contact area than it would have in more open terrain.

As they arrived on the scene, I directed the tracks into a formation surrounding the enemy bunker complex and told them to circle the complex until they knocked down enough trees and brush to clear a swath around the bunker complex.

After making the swath, I lined the tracks up in three-vehicle wedge formations for the final assault. They went through the complex killing NVA as they found them, out in the open and in bunkers. I don't remember the total number of enemy kills. I personally killed two NVA attempting to run across the swath, shooting them with my M-16 out the door of my helicopter as we flew at low level.

During this action, one of our Cobras had engine failure and crashed with a very hard landing. The crew claimed it was shot down. Later that evening, the troop maintenance officer informed me that six .38-caliber slugs were found in the armor plate over the engine turbines along the left side of the helicopter. I called the crew in and chewed their asses for being so damn dumb as to put self-inflicted holes in their aircraft. It was an idiotic attempt to disguise what really happened. They then admitted that they ran out of power at low level and had a hard landing that simply spread the skids, damage that could be easily repaired. I quickly forgot about the crew's dumb action and they continued to fly and fight.

On 11 March, my pink teams caught NVA in the open but couldn't kill them before they took cover under some trees. The 1st Squadron's D Company was chopped to me, and I sent its tanks in to flush them out. The NVA saw the tanks roaring in and ran toward a swampy creek bed area to get away from them. The company commander lined his tanks up, raced after them all the way to the creek's grassy edge, and halted. His tanks proved too heavy for ground conditions and got stuck in the muck under the high grass. On retrieval, almost all of his tanks had crushed NVA under them. Enemy soldiers making it to the creek were killed by gunships. We were fighting like this everyday, but strategic changes in how the war would be fought were in the air.

Richard M. Nixon had been elected president in November 1968, in part because he promised to get the United States out of the war and to help South Vietnam remain free of communist rule. Upon taking office, Nixon instituted changes that stepped up pacification operations and Vietnamization.

Then Major Jim Dozier talks about pacification and Vietnamization.

"The Blackhorse took considerable effort to win the hearts and minds of the Vietnamese people. Although we built schools and community buildings, most of our pacification efforts were one- or two-day affairs. I remember a well-drilling platoon attached to the Nine-nineteenth Engineers drilling wells in several villages that didn't have a source of fresh water. We were also involved with medcap [medical civil action program] and sent our medics out to villages to provide locals with medical attention. Much of this effort involved giving locals inoculations and medicines. We never handed out more than a day's worth of meds because we didn't want them to fall into enemy hands. This was difficult for some medicos to understand, but we didn't want outlying hamlets to become pharmacies for the enemy.

"Vietnamization called for the ARVN to take on a more significant role in prosecuting the war. We had always fought with and supported ARVN units, CIDG [Civilian Irregular Defense Group] companies, and PRU platoons operating in our AO. Nixon's emphasis on Vietnamization had no effect on the regiment's day-to-day operations."

Jim Dozier continues. Here, he talks about increased enemy activity in the Michelin Rubber Plantation.

"Intelligence gained from radio intercepts, POW interrogations, and captured documents revealed that over eight thousand soldiers from the NVA's Seventh Division and its supporting units were moving into the rubber and the jungle surrounding the Michelin to prepare for a large-scale attack on Saigon—forty miles to the south.

"The Michelin plantation covered an area approximately eight miles north to south and six miles east to west, and was surrounded by jungle on all sides. The rubber trees stood fifteen to twenty feet apart. A number of streams ran through the plantation, some fordable, others spanned by bridges too small and feeble to handle armor traffic. The once-pristine condition of the Michelin had deteriorated in recent years as the result of the many battles fought in it and because, by this time in the war, there weren't enough men left in the area to properly care for all the rubber trees."

Doc resumes.

Sometime during this period, I was out with White and his ARPs on a BDA when I spotted a small group of NVA going into a base camp. Bates took our helicopter into an orbit high enough that I could see both the base camp and the ARPs. I radioed White and told him what I saw and gave him directions for getting into the base camp.

As the ARPs moved out, I fired my M-16 at the leading edge of the bunkers. My door gunners followed the trail of my red tracer rounds with a heavy volume of M-60 fire. We circled back around to lay down another dose of suppressive fire. On this pass, we also tossed hand grenades at enemy soldiers who came out of their bunkers to shoot at us. When we lifted our fire, the ARPs assaulted.

It was a quick action. The ARPs killed a dozen or so NVA and captured two or three others before sweeping the bunkers. I called in three or four lift ships to extract the ARPs and their POWs. They landed in a LZ located at a ninety-degree angle from the approach the ARPs used going into the base camp.

Making his way to the LZ, White noticed a solitary bunker located a good thirty meters from all the others. It appeared to him to have a smoke pipe coming out of its roof. Rather than send ARPs in to clear the bunker, White decided to clear it himself. He had all the ARPs around him hit the ground before dropping a fragmentation grenade into the pipe. A couple of the more experienced ARPs, who were walk-ing to the rear of the formation, recognized the bunker for what it was and yelled at White to stop. Their warning cry came too late. The bunker housed a latrine for the base camp. The pipe was its source of ventilation. The resulting explosion blew shit all over the place, cover-ing White and eight to ten of his ARPs with human excrement from head to toe. I landed shortly thereafter, intending to have White ride with me. I changed my mind when he approached my helicopter. He smelled awful and looked dreadful!

Tom White talks about this incident.

"I was totally taken by surprise. Doc wouldn't let me near his heli-copter. The lift ship pilots weren't keen on letting my guys get in their helicopters either. I was afraid we were going to have to walk out and hike all the way to Alpha Pad.

"I stood there, shit dripping from my fatigues, smelling like a sewer, begging and pleading with Doc to give me a ride. I told him over and over that I had mistaken the latrine for a regular bunker. Doc sat in his helicopter and laughed and laughed. I was just about to give up trying when he said, 'White, if brains were dynamite, you wouldn't have enough to blow your nose. Go get your guys loaded up and get in with me. You need to get cleaned up. You look like shit!'

"As soon as we touched down at Alpha Pad, we all ran straight to the showers, laid our gear down, stripped, and washed thoroughly. I don't remember anyone trying to salvage his filthy, stenchful uniform. I think we all just put them in a burn barrel."

Doc resumes.

On 16 March, I flew recon missions with four pink teams for most of the day, covering the 1st and 3rd Squadrons as they moved into a staging area on the southeastern edge of the Michelin plantation, not far from Dau Tieng, in preparation for spearheading the major search and destroy mission known as Operation Atlas Wedge. This multidivisional operation involved units from the 1st Infantry, 25th Infantry, and 1st Cavalry.

✶ Chapter 78 ✶

The French government paid the South Vietnamese big bucks not to damage its rubber trees. It also paid the North Vietnamese not to use the rubber plantation for hiding. Obviously, the North Vietnamese did not honor their part of the deal.

We were not generally allowed to bomb in the Michelin plantation or in any way destroy its rubber trees unless we had clearance from the South Vietnamese government. This clearance was normally granted to regiment by the senior South Vietnamese leader in that region. Having to get permission to protect ourselves, friendly forces, and local villagers from NVA attacks staged out of the Michelin plantation made my blood boil. It was time consuming and difficult to get. Worse yet, word of our pending assaults were passed on to the enemy, giving him time to get out of harm's way before our requests were granted. Pure bullshit in my eyes!

I sent my pink teams out early in the morning to see if they could find the NVA who were supposed to be holing up in the Michelin plantation. It didn't take long for the action to begin.

Captain Bert Dacey had recently joined the troop as a scout pilot. As he flew low level over the plantation, he spotted NVA soldiers lounging up against the rubber trees. One of them rose up and put rounds in his aircraft. Dacey marked with red smoke, pulled off to the side, and called in a sitrep. I was nearby and flew to his location to take a look. Sure enough, there was a large NVA force in the edge of the plantation, all of them wearing full-body camouflage nets laced with twigs and leaves. They made no effort to hide when we flew over them. Obviously, the NVA were well aware that we were restricted from attacking them at will so long as they were inside the Michelin plantation.

Then newly commissioned Second Lieutenant Mike Bates comments.

"I looked down as we orbited. There were a lot of rubber trees down there, and at least one dink was resting against every one of them. They knew they were off limits to us because they were in the rubber. A few feet of fucking turf was protecting those bastards.

"I was flying low enough that I could see their faces. They just looked up and smiled. A couple of them flipped us off. That really pissed me off!

"Doc told me to circle back around and those dumb shits took up arms and put holes in our helicopter's tail boom. That may not have mattered to commanders reluctant to return fire into the rubber without permission, but those dumb fuckers shot at Doc Bahnsen."

Doc resumes.

I called regiment and reported that we had taken fire from a large enemy force located just inside the Michelin plantation. I told them that I wanted to bring in air and artillery strikes. Colonel Patton and Major Dozier were in the air and out of radio contact range. The people on duty in the TOC wouldn't grant me clearance without first getting either Patton's or Dozier's approval. All they would give me was a "Wait, out." Well, I wasn't about to wait.

I got on another frequency and talked to the FAC on station. I told him what I had going on, and he started bringing fighters on station.

The NVA weren't even trying to hide. They just sat against the rubber trees looking up at us, giving us the finger, and taking pot shots as we orbited overhead.

I was losing my patience while waiting for clearance to bring in air strikes. I made one last request and was told "Wait, out." Fully confident that Patton would stand behind me, I did exactly what he would have done if he were in my situation.

"Niles Five, this is Thunderhorse Six, over."

"Go ahead, Six."

"I'm going to mark. I want you to bring in everything you've got. If your fast movers have enough fuel to hang around, have them use their twenty mike-mike on anyone they spot out in the open, over."

"Roger, Six."

Bates took us over to the edge of the rubber plantation, and we marked the spot where I wanted the air strikes concentrated with a white phosphorous grenade. There were five flights of two F-4s stacked up and circling overhead by this time. Their pilots were listening to the FAC and me talk and clearly saw my mark.

One by one, the F-4s came screaming in over the plantation, making two passes each, dropping a good mix of high-explosive and napalm bombs.

Mike Bates resumes.

"I don't remember Doc getting around to calling in artillery that day. The air strike was absolutely devastating. It ripped up a lot of rubber and killed a lot of the enemy. There were huge plumes of smoke, and fires raged everywhere. That made me very happy. It was one of those moments that made me proud to be serving under a commander who had the balls to do what needed to be done, with or without approval. It was one of the ways Doc stood out as a warrior and leader."

Doc resumes.

Two-and-a-half hours after I spotted the first NVA in the plantation, clearance to shoot into the Michelin plantation came through the regiment's TOC. They had been monitoring my frequency and knew what I'd done, but said nothing.

Colonel Patton finally got my message and called me. He directed me to come up on secure radio. I briefed him on my decision to shoot without clearance and my reasons for doing it. I told him we had a regimental-sized force hiding in the rubber plantation and that we needed ground elements as quickly as he could move them to the area.

Patton told me not to worry about the clearance. He backed my decision. He then proceeded to move tanks and ACAVs into the surrounding area. They made enemy contact in short order, killing them as they fled out of the Michelin plantation and into the adjacent jungle. The troop's pink teams shot enemy soldiers running ahead of the advancing tanks and ACAVs.

Bates and I flew fourteen hours on this date. Our helicopter's rotor blades never stopped turning. We pissed standing on the skids when we hot refueled at the small base of Dau Tieng, and went right back to the action.

✳ Chapter 79 ✳

18 March 1969—Michelin Rubber Plantation, and Blackhorse headquarters, Bien Hoa Air Base

Widespread and fierce fighting was taking place throughout the regiment's AO. Every unit in Operation Atlas Wedge was involved. The 1st and 3rd Squadrons continued search and destroy operations along the eastern edge of the Michelin plantation and in the adjacent jungle.

At one time, the Blackhorse's 3rd Squadron was engaged in three separate firefights. The 1st Squadron kept its units together for a series of brief contacts. The Air Cavalry Troop's pink teams conducted aerial recon along the edge of the Michelin plantation and provided air assault support to the squadrons as needed.

After flying for fourteen hours, I returned to Bien Hoa to attend the evening regimental briefing. Reports were made on the day's activities and assignments were given for the following day. We also planned B-52 strikes on the northeastern edge of the Michelin plantation, where my scout pilots had seen large numbers of NVA moving into bunkers.

∗ Chapter 80 ∗

My scouts began aerial recon at first light and soon reported enemy troop movement in and around the Michelin plantation. They also reported seeing columns of enemy soldiers headed in the direction of Cambodia—a long hike to the west.

The Minh Than CIDG Company, led by U.S. Special Forces advisers, was placed under my control. I had the troop's lift ships insert them in places where they could organize ambushes for enemy forces on the move. We also provided lift ship and air assault support and worked up plans for B-52 strikes.

This was Major Jim Bradin's first day with the troop. He was slated to replace me when I assumed command of 1st Squadron in June. In the interim, he was coming in to replace Major Pete Noyes as my executive officer.

Retired Colonel James W. Bradin recalls his arrival.

"It was midmorning when I arrived at Tan Son Nhut Air Base. I was greeted by Captain Mike Barnes, an assistant S-1, as I came down the ramp from the plane that brought me back to Vietnam for my second tour. After my baggage was located and loaded in a three-quarter-ton truck, I was whisked away in a jeep to the troop's headquarters at Bien Hoa Air Base.

"I was greeted in the orderly room by Major Pete Noyes, an old friend and neighbor at Fort Stewart, Georgia. Pete explained that Doc had a fight going on the edge of a rubber plantation northwest of Lai Khe. Pete suggested I might want to walk over to troop operations and listen to it over the radio.

"There were several troopers in the ops shack. Each one introduced himself. Moments later, the ops sergeant told me Doc was inbound, about three minutes out. A few moments later, I heard the distinctive sound of a Huey, and I went outside.

"A C-model Huey approached the pad, turned toward the troop revetment area, hovered, and set down in the revetment closest to the ops shack. Doc jumped out of the left side and ran to a nearby latrine. A few minutes later, he was running back. I approached him as he was putting on his chicken plate and gloves. His greeting was short, 'Get your ass in the right seat and let's go!'

"Doc's pilot, Second Lieutenant Mike Bates, climbed out of the right seat, pulled off his Nomex gloves and CVC helmet, handed them to me, then climbed into the jump seat. I was stunned and hesitated momentarily. I was in a short-sleeve khaki uniform, low-quarter shoes, an overseas cap, and still pissing stateside water.

" 'If you're going, and you are, get your sorry ass in and let's go!' Doc bellowed.

"I pulled on the damp loaned gloves, climbed into the right seat, and strapped myself in. Placing my head in Bates's very damp helmet, I concluded that Bahnsen's pilot sweated a lot.

" 'Crank her up and let's go!' Doc ordered over the intercom.

" 'Hell, I can't fly this thing,' I said. 'I've never even sat in a C-model before. I don't know where the switches are.'

"Doc leaned over and grumbled, 'I guess you don't know how to fly,' as he flipped switches and cranked the engine. Once everything was up and in the green, Doc said, 'You've got it. Let's get the hell out of here!'

" 'Doc, is there a special technique to get out of a revetment?' I asked. I spent my first tour in Nam flying Caribous and had never been in a revetment.

" 'Jesus!' Doc shouted. 'Just pick the damn thing up and move out!'

"Okay, I thought. There is a first time for everything.

"Making sure all the needles were where I thought they should be, I pulled up on the pitch, all the while working hard to keep the helicopter in the center of the revetment. When I was pretty sure the skids were above the revetment, I dumped the nose. The helicopter staggered forward and down. The toes of its skids hit the ground twice before we leveled. I checked the airspeed and saw we needed a bunch. The needle was barely crawling up when we were about to hit the perimeter fence.

" 'The cyclic!' Doc shouted. 'Pull back on the goddamn cyclic!'

"I did. The helicopter floated up and cleared the fence but began to settle on the far side. I am not sure what I did to gain altitude but suddenly the helicopter was no longer straining to stay airborne.

"Now assured that I was not going to crash his war bird, Doc began a long rapid-fire briefing on what was going on and worked to assure me that this was serious business. Once, while he paused to take a breath, I recall thinking that I'd been in-country less than three hours.

"There was a steady and heavy volume of radio traffic taking place over the three radios in our helicopter. I was amazed at how easily Doc kept up with it all. We hadn't been out long before Doc pointed to a large clearing and ordered, 'Put me down there. I need to talk to that unit.' I looked down and saw an infantry company on the edge of a tree line.

"I made my first C-model landing without using all the clearing. As he was putting on his ground gear, Doc told me to stay overhead. If refueling was required, I was to do it, and get back ASAP. He dismounted our aircraft and jogged toward the infantry. I didn't know it then, but I quickly learned that Doc routinely landed to assist units on the ground.

"Bates got in Doc's seat and I lifted off, making my second C-model takeoff. We orbited overhead, listening to the contact over the FM radio. We could hear Doc issuing orders to the infantry and calling in artillery strikes to its front. We moved out of the gun-target line. Doc brought in a lot of artillery before calling check fire. The next thing I knew, he radioed for us to pick him up in the same LZ where we'd dropped him off about an hour earlier. We spent the rest of the afternoon assisting units engaged in what Doc told me were minor contacts, as if there was such a thing when bullets started flying.

"It was late in the evening when we returned to Bien Hoa. Doc was tired and dirty. Bates and I were just tired. My sweaty khakis told me that I had shed the last of my stateside water through my pores. But I no longer cared. I had seen more action that afternoon than I had during my entire first tour. It was clear that I had joined a fighting outfit and that I was understudying the best warrior I would ever meet.

"After some cold food and a cold shower, I went to bed. My biological clock was still on Eastern Standard Time. I didn't know if I'd be able to catch any sleep. Pete Noyes was abed on the other side of the room.

"We'd just turned off the light, when Pete abruptly jumped out of his bed and raced out of our hooch, almost taking the screen door with him. I sat up and peered through the dark, trying to figure out Pete's strange behavior. Then I heard a whooshing sound of something passing over the building followed with a loud explosion just outside the front door. I joined Pete in a small sandbagged container. We both stood silent in our underwear. After hearing nothing else for a few minutes, I followed Pete as he walked to the front of the orderly room door. There was a smoking crater in the road.

" 'What was that?' I asked.

" 'A 122mm rocket.'

" 'What made you get up and run?'

" 'I heard it fire.'

" 'I was awake and I didn't hear anything.'

" 'It won't take you long to learn.'

" 'How come you didn't warn me?'

" 'Forgot you were here.'

"Welcome back to Vietnam, I thought to myself. I climbed back in bed and stared at the ceiling until daylight filled the room."

✶ Chapter 81 ✶

20 March 1969—Michelin Rubber Plantation

This was a tough day of fighting for the Air Cavalry Troop. I had a couple of newly assigned officers in key positions. That hampered me some, but it can neither justify the fact that we didn't fight as effectively as we knew how nor rationalize the ARPs taking a significant number of casualties, nineteen in all: eighteen wounded and one killed.

After sixty days of nonstop action with the ARPS—on top of all the combat he'd seen earlier while successively leading ACAV and tank platoons—I decided to pull Tom White out of the field and have him assist Pete Noyes with the troop's administration. I replaced White with one of his West Point classmates: First Lieutenant Marty Harmless. Harmless had been serving as aide-de-camp to Brigadier General George Cantlay, the 1st Infantry's assistant division commander. This was Harmless's first mission as the ARP platoon leader and his first combat action.

I was leading the troop on a BDA mission and decided to have Jim Bradin fly with me for the day. He needed to gain firsthand experience with how the troop fought and to get more flying time in a Huey—even though he was helicopter rated, he was not fully checked out in the UH-1.

Three B-52 strikes went in on the northeastern edge of the Michelin plantation at about 0400 hours. Although payloads varied from time to time, normal B-52 strikes consisted of a flight of three aircraft, each dropping eighty-four internally carried five-hundred-pound and twenty-four externally mounted seven-hundred-fifty-pound general-purpose bombs into a "box" one thousand meters wide by three thousand meters long. Anything and everything inside one of these boxes was blown up, torn up, chewed up, crushed, burned—you name it. Gigantic orange fireballs could be seen for miles against the darkness of the predawn sky. Tremors from the concussion of bomb clusters pounding the earth rumbled in every direction.

Our BDA mission was preempted en route to the strike site. My scouts spotted a huge bunker complex in triple-canopy jungle bordering one of the B-52 boxes. They suspected the bunkers were occupied, but couldn't estimate how many enemy soldiers were in it. I had ARPs in lift ships trailing my helicopter and put them on the ground on the edge of the B-52 box about a kilometer from the bunkers.

Former specialist four Rex Saul talks about this mission.

"We had the whole platoon out. It was Lieutenant Harmless's first mission with us. Nguyen Van Rang and Tien Trang, our Special Field Force National Police interrogator and interpreter, respectively, were with us. Rang and Trang were both very good at their jobs. We were required to have them with us when we went into a village, but they routinely joined us on BDAs and assault missions as well.

"The ABC war correspondent Don Baker and his Korean cameraman were also with us. Baker was one of the few correspondents who reported the war objectively. He spent a lot of time with the troop. We liked him and didn't mind taking him on missions.

"This bunker complex was set a ways back in the tree line and well camouflaged. We couldn't see it as we approached, even though we knew it was there."

Then First Lieutenant Martin Harmless talks about joining the ARPs and this mission.

"I accompanied General Cantlay on a visit to the Blackhorse's mobile headquarters in early March. While the general spoke with Colonel Patton, Major Jim Dozier struck up some small talk with me. He mentioned that the ARPs didn't have a platoon leader and asked if I knew of anyone who might like the job. I told him that I'd ask around.

"I thought about it for a few days. I arrived in-country in June of '68, just after Tet. I had led three platoons in the First of the Twenty-sixth

Infantry, First Infantry Division. Nothing was happening in our AO at the time. No one fired at us. We shot at no one. After about three months of no action, I became General George Cantlay's aide.

"Being a general's aide was good duty in a war. I got to wear clean uniforms and shined shoes. I flew around in a helicopter for about eight hours a day, ate in the general's mess, slept between sheets in a comfortable cot, and never got shot at.

"On the other hand, I was a first lieutenant who hadn't gone through the rite of passage as a soldier: no combat, no medals. It was a duty thing. I felt a strong pull to get in on the action. I told General Cantlay I wanted the ARP platoon leader job. He said he would arrange an interview for me.

"I hadn't met Major Bahnsen prior to interviewing with him. He was pleased to hear that I wanted to fucking kill gooks and told me the job was mine.

"My first combat experience began when our lift ships landed in a hot LZ pocked with bomb craters. It took us a while to reach the wood line fronting the thickest jungle I ever saw in Vietnam. I was walking with Sergeant Frank Saracino's squad.

"Saracino was walking backup to his point man. His point man yelled something soon after entering the jungle. I looked toward him and saw the muzzle of an AK-47 poking out of a spider hole a split second before it started shooting into the air. The dink pulling the trigger could have easily shot our point man, Saracino, my RTO, and me. But for reasons I can't fathom, he didn't.

"I told my guys to back off. We withdrew about twenty meters and took cover. I called Doc with a sitrep. He told me to move back into the bomb crater area and hunker down; he was going to call in fast movers. I got the platoon into the craters where we waited for the air strike. It was a big one. The jets made several passes. Their thousand-pound high-general-purpose and five-hundred-pound napalm bombs devastated the jungle in front of us. The noise from the jets and the explosions was almost deafening. The concussion bounced us around a bit. It was an awesome and terrifying experience for me. Through it all, I managed to use some of this time to talk with Saracino. He was raring to go and talked a lot about his future plans.

"After the air strike lifted, we went back into the jungle from a different direction. I don't remember our point man's name but I can picture him. He carried a twelve-gauge shotgun, an M-79 grenade launcher, and a .45-caliber pistol. Coming up on the outer ring of the bunkers, he motioned for us to go down and then went into a partially destroyed bunker where he found two enemy dead—the air strike got them. While our point man pulled the dead enemy out, Saracino decided to move ahead and took point. My RTO and I fell in about fifteen feet behind him.

"We hadn't gone far before Saracino yelled, 'Gooks!' and the shooting started. He was on the other side of a trench fronting the bunkers to my left. Saracino's flanker was hit in the arm. He rolled into the trench and scooted backward. The trench had about a foot of dirt piled all along its outer edge for added protection during a firefight. My RTO and I took cover behind it. I peered over the brim. Saracino was trapped in the open looking at dinks in a bunker no more than twenty feet away.

"The scene that followed played out in slow motion before me. Saracino looked to his left and right, then straight ahead. He shrugged his shoulders as if to say 'What the hell, if I'm a dead man, I might as well take some of them with me.'

"He then charged the bunker, firing his weapon on full automatic. An awful noise rang in my ears; it was the sound of AK-47s returning fire. I watched him take a round in the head and saw his boonie hat fly into the air and land in a bush next to me. I stared at it for the next four hours.

"What Saracino did was a very, very brave thing. He died fighting, and he saved my RTO's and my life. If he hadn't attacked the bunker, all three of us would have been killed.

"Lying flat on the ground, I told my RTO to pass me the radio. I called Doc with a sitrep. I had one dead. Even though he was only fifteen to twenty feet in front of us, we couldn't get to him without getting killed. My RTO and I were pinned down. Doc told me to stay put, he was maneuvering forces toward my location. I radioed Staff Sergeant Rollie Port, my platoon sergeant, and told him to position the rest of the platoon. He spread them out; the closest to my RTO and me were about twenty yards to our rear."

Former specialist four Jim Weller talks about this action.

"This was very thick jungle. You couldn't see more than twenty feet in front of you except where there were trails. This bunker complex was enormous—the largest one I saw in over three hundred missions with the ARPs. Its forward edge was on flat ground. It went down a gentle slope into a valley to its rear. It was surrounded by a series of interlocking trenches together with I don't know how many spider holes, providing the enemy with well-concealed firing positions. The bunkers were connected by a network of tunnels. There was no way this complex could have been cleared one bunker at a time. Of course, we didn't know any of this as we made our way toward this enemy stronghold.

"All hell broke loose when Saracino was hit. We took heavy fire from our front, flanks, and rear. It was the greatest volume and intensity of fire I ever experienced. They were shooting everything—AKs, RPGs, machine guns. We were scattered out all over the place and couldn't really make out where all the enemy fire was coming from. We thought we might have walked into a trap. Our main concern was staying alive. We had to pull back out of the kill zone or be slaughtered."

Rex Saul continues.

"I was walking in the rear of my squad, escorting Don Baker and his cameraman. When we pulled back, Baker asked me to take them back to a safer area, which I did. I rejoined my squad only to reassume the pinned-down-by-enemy-fire position. Bullets were flying everywhere! I remember thinking I was going to die. The more I thought about it, the more I started to think dying wasn't all that bad. I lost my fear of dying within the hour. I decided that, if I was going to die, I should take some pictures of my last moments alive, so I took my camera out of the side pocket on my pants. From that point on, until the battle was over, I shot my Car-15 at the gooks with one hand and shot pictures of the action with the other."

Doc resumes.

I had a hell of a situation on my hands. The ARPs were spread out and pinned down. Harmless was calling me repeatedly to come in and save them. The ARPs needed help, but I couldn't land because Bradin was flying with me and he wasn't ready to takeoff and land a UH-1 on his own. We had one dead that we couldn't get to. The only way I was going to straighten this mess out was to bring in tracks and infantry. I called the regiment and asked for reinforcements.

Retired Lieutenant General John W. McEnery talks about reinforcing the Air Cavalry Troop during this action.

"I was commanding Third Squadron. I knew there was going to be action around the area where we were putting in B-52 strikes, and I wanted my squadron to get in on it.

"After the evening briefing on the nineteenth, I started begging Colonel Patton to let me move my squadron up to the Michelin. The First Squadron was already close and Patton was planning on using it to reinforce any action the Air Cav Troop stirred up.

"Finally, around twenty-two hundred hours, Patton caved in and told me I could move my squadron up to the Michelin. I had my tracks ripping up Highway Thirteen at oh-four hundred hours, just as the B-52 strike got underway. We went roaring past First Squadron about oh-six hundred hours. They were just getting up.

"I established my temporary headquarters where a dirt road leading west to the Michelin takes off from Highway Thirteen. Anticipating that we would need infantry reinforcements, Patton had an infantry company from the First of the Eighth Cavalry, First Cavalry Division opconned to me for the day."

Doc resumes.

McEnery was a superb soldier and as good a squadron commander as there was in Vietnam. He didn't run from fights; he ran to them. He could be counted on when you needed his help, in or out of combat.

McEnery came up on my command net. I gave him a sitrep and told him that I needed tanks and infantry right away. He chopped a tank platoon from M Company and an ACAV platoon from L Troop to my control, along with the rifle company opconned to him.

I flew to McEnery's position and located the tank platoon. The platoon leader came up on my command frequency. I started guiding him cross-country on a four-kilometer course leading to the edge of the B-52 strike box, where I inserted my ARPs earlier that morning. Meanwhile, I had my lift ships pick up the infantry company and chop them out to the same spot.

Jim Weller continues.

"We didn't know any of this was going on. We were pinned down. We couldn't move or do anything. We all felt helpless and stuck. We were praying like hell that we wouldn't run out of ammo before somebody came to our rescue.

"I suppose that somewhere in the back of my mind there was a spark of assurance that Major Bahnsen wouldn't leave us out there to die. He had gotten us through some ferocious contacts before. Thinking about that helped me believe he would get us through this one."

Doc resumes.

The ARPs were pinned down for a good four hours before reinforcements arrived. The tanks got there ahead of the ACAVs. I didn't want to wait for the ACAVs to arrive before sending reinforcements in to relieve my ARPs. I ordered the tank platoon leader to link up with the infantry company and be prepared to assault through the bunker complex.

I orbited overhead until the tank platoon got lined up. I gave the platoon leader the command to move out with five tanks on line closely followed by the infantry. Only the tanks moved out! The infantry just stood there like bumps on a log.

The tanks moved into the jungle without infantry coverage, and in spite of their enormous firepower, three were hit in the rear and immediately disabled by RPGs when they passed the first bunkers containing enemy soldiers. Luckily, their crews evacuated safely.

The platoon leader's tank rolled into a bomb crater just inside the jungle after he was hit in the face and blinded by RPG fragments. He radioed me immediately and repeatedly told me what had happened to him and pleaded for help.

Just as I'd been telling Harmless earlier, trying to calm him down, I kept telling this young lieutenant that he was not going to be left there to die. I would get him out and to a hospital as quickly as possible. He was in a great deal of pain and his calls were hard to bear. They lowered the morale of everyone on our radio net.

Jim Weller continues.

"I remember hearing tanks approaching. It seemed like we'd been pinned down forever. We couldn't see the tanks, initially. Nor could they see us. There was a damn good chance their gunners would mistake us for the enemy. That worried us, especially if the tanks cut loose with canister rounds packed with small steel pellets. Ammo like that doesn't discriminate between friend and foe. We already had small-arms and automatic weapons fire, along with a steady stream of RPGs, coming in all around us. It wasn't until the infantry reached our position that I stopped thinking if the gooks didn't get us, friendly fire would.

"When the infantry got to us, Lieutenant Harmless talked to their commander. They took over for us so we could get our wounded out. I carried eight hundred rounds with me that day. I had one twenty-round magazine left when we swept the bunkers."

Doc resumes.

I directed the commander of the single tank that made it through the complex in a wide circle back to the LZ where I was holding L Troop in reserve. I also directed the rifle company commander to move his men back to the LZ.

I looked down at the battlefield. What a fucking mess! Three tanks on fire, a fourth disabled, and no leader down there who had a fucking clue about getting things straightened out. I was pissed and frustrated over not being able to land and take charge of the action. On top of that, my helicopter was running on fumes and needed to be refueled immediately.

I got on the radio and contacted McEnery. He was in a Loach, orbiting above me in a wide circle. I gave him my estimate of the situation and told him what I thought needed to be done. I then turned the battle over to him and flew to Dau Tieng to refuel.

John McEnery talks about what he did next.

"I landed, gathered up the ground commanders, and told them what we were going to do. I put the tank in the middle, four ACAVs on my left, five on my right. I told the rifle company commander to have his men follow right behind the tracks. They were to clear each and every bunker as the track they were following passed over it. I then got on the rear deck of the tank and ordered the assault.

"The tank gunner fired canister rounds while the tank commander blasted away with his .50 cal. The ACAVs laid down a steady stream of machine gun fire to the front and flanks of the bunkers. We moved past the burning tanks and the one disabled tank and into the complex. The First Cavalry riflemen got the job done right, shooting NVA caught in the trench network and tossing hand grenades into bunkers. We swept through the entire complex, turned around, and came back through. Enemy dead lay in trenches, spider holes, and bunkers. What little remained of the bunker complex by that time was blown using C-4 charges

"I took shrapnel in my back, just below my chicken plate, during the initial assault. I don't know whose shrapnel it was, ours or the enemy's. It burned and bled just the same. I didn't pay much attention to my wound when I got hit, but I knew I needed to get it taken care of by the time we came back through the bunkers.

"I dismounted the tank and briefed my people on sweeping the complex and surrounding area. Doc had refueled and was orbiting overhead. It was safe enough for him to land, and he did. We had a brief conversation about what needed to be done before I got in my Loach and flew to the 93rd Evacuation Hospital at Long Binh for treatment."

Doc resumes.

I was back over the area in time to see most of McEnery's assault. It was one of the bravest actions I ever witnessed. We thought the area was secure when we started a police of the battleground, but one of my ARPs was wounded by a NVA who came crawling out of a spider hole. Needless to say, that bastard was killed instantly.

We were credited with killing over 131 NVA on this date. Specialist Weller told me that he and the few unwounded ARPs who helped sweep the bunkers saw what they took to be dead Chinese soldiers dressed in NVA uniforms. He said they were bigger than Vietnamese with fuller and rounder faces.

I have no reason to doubt Weller's observation. We knew the Chinese were providing the NVA with arms, ammunition, supplies, and technical assistance from sanctuaries just across the border in Cambodia. However, we were never able to confirm that the Chinese were also supplying the NVA with soldiers.

This was a hell of a day of fighting, and several people distinguished themselves during it. Patton and I put McEnery in for the Distinguished Service Cross and recommended Saracino for a posthumous Distinguished Service Cross. Other troopers in all units were also decorated for their gallantry in action, including Harmless, who was awarded the Silver Star.

The 1st Cavalry rifle company took a lot of casualties during this action. I don't remember exactly how many. The 3rd Squadron also took casualties, but none of its people were killed. Eighteen ARPs were wounded. Many of them were the more experienced soldiers in the platoon. Some had to be evacuated stateside for further treatment; some returned to duty shortly; and some returned to duty but not in the ARPs.

I flew fourteen hours on this date. It was after dark when I went to see my wounded in the hospital. They were brave young men, one and all. I was proud to be their troop commander. I also saw McEnery. The small hole in his lower back was a bit larger after surgery to remove the shrapnel. He healed quickly and returned to duty just over a week later.

✴ Chapter 82 ✴

**21–24 March 1969—area north and northeast of the Michelin Rubber Plantation
and Alpha Pad, Bien Hoa Air Base**

The 7th NVA Division moved into the Michelin plantation and base
camps in the surrounding jungle. It stood and fought gallantly during
the first few days of Operation Atlas Wedge.

Over the past few days, we had fixed the 7th NVA in place and
kicked it pretty well. Our devastating firepower disrupted its plans, destroyed its equipment, and disordered its ranks. The 7th NVA could not
defeat us militarily and continuing the fight would result in its destruction. Its only hope for survival was to break contact and withdraw back
into its sanctuaries just across the Cambodian border.

Heavy casualties temporarily limited my use of the ARPs. The
troop's role during these few days was to provide pink teams to locate
bunkers for B-52 strikes and lift ship support for units operating on the
north and northeast sides of the rubber plantation.

On 22 March, we started early and found a column of NVA in the
open. As they were carrying several stretchers, my initial thought was
that we had a hospital unit in the open. What we actually saw were
stragglers from recent contacts who were headed northeast toward the
Cambodian border. I joined my pink teams in routing them.

I also landed a squad of ARPs to hold up a company-sized enemy
force while I brought in 1st Squadron's C Troop with its ACAVs and
D Company with its tanks for the pile-on. They killed fifteen and captured six enemy soldiers during this contact that took up most of the
morning.

In the afternoon while running down isolated pockets of NVA, one of my scouts spotted a small enemy force—a platoon or less. I decided to send a squad of ARPs after them.

Captain Kenneth Bailey was the first man in his flight school class and a super young soldier. He had just taken over as my Lift Ship Platoon leader. I hardly knew him and knew very little about his background other than that he was from Burlington, Vermont. The ARPs were aboard Captain Bailey's helicopter. He inserted them in a small LZ in the jungle but was mortally wounded before he could get out.

Former specialist four Mike Gorman tells what he heard about this event.

"I'd been medically evacuated prior to this action, but my good buddy Specialist Five John Godek told me about it after he returned from the war. We talked about it several times before he passed away.

"Godek dismounted during the insertion and was still on the ground when his ship took heavy enemy small-arms fire from the tree line. The ARPs had already cleared the LZ, but Bailey hadn't lifted off. Bailey was hit in the head and died instantly. Warrant Officer Bill Wisenor, the copilot, was hit in both feet, and bullets continued hitting the helicopter.

"Wisenor was bleeding profusely out of both feet and realized he was about to lose consciousness. He also realized he had to get out of the LZ. It was a matter of life and death. He didn't hesitate. He lifted off before Godek could climb back in. Wisenor flew about five hundred meters and sat down in an open field near some American forces.

"Godek was stranded, armed only with a .45-caliber pistol, trying to burrow into the ground to avoid being shredded by AK-47 fire. Much to his good fortune, Wisenor radioed the ARPs and told them what happened. The ARPs returned to the LZ and placed a heavy volume of fire on the tree line. The dinks stopped shooting within seconds, and the ARPs picked Godek up. He remained with them for the rest of this contact.

"Godek told me he was terrified that he was going to be captured. These were hard-core NVA. They had no use for enlisted POWs. Worse yet, Godek was a helicopter crewman, and helicopters were the bane of the enemy. We could easily spot them. We could follow them over any terrain. We could bring overwhelming fire on their asses. The enemy hated aircrews! If they would have captured Godek, I have no doubt that they would have strung him up in the nearest tree and skinned him alive.

"We used to talk about getting captured while sitting around in our hooch at night. Never allow yourself to be captured and never surrender were quasi-religious tenets with us. We always vowed to save our last bullet for ourselves."

Doc resumes.

I landed in the open field shortly after Wisenor sat down and helped get Bailey out. We evacuated Wisenor immediately. I brought in another crew to fly the helicopter back to Alpha Pad.

By 23 March, the largest part the NVA units had made it across the Cambodian border, but stragglers remained. I still had C Troop and D Company attached to me until noon. They assisted my troop in a sweep of its assigned area. My gunship crews were credited with four NVA killed during the cleanup, after which Operation Atlas Wedge was shortly brought to an end.

I went to the hospital in Long Binh later that afternoon to visit my wounded. The next morning, I stood the troop down for maintenance and to give my troopers a much needed break from battle.

✷ Chapter 83 ✷

25 March–6 April 1969—Blackhorse AO, Saigon, and Bien Hoa Air Base

During Colonel Patton's last days as colonel of the Blackhorse, the troop's pink teams conducted routine aerial recons, but they didn't have any major contacts.

I remember this being a time when Patton joined my scouts in making dusk patrols over Bien Hoa Air Base's northern perimeter. Patton euphemistically called these aerial recons the Children's Hour in a tongue-in-cheek play on Henry Wadsworth Longfellow's classic poem. These patrols often resulted in minor contacts with NVA setting up nighttime mortar and rocket attacks on Bien Hoa.

During this period of slow down, I made late-evening calls to see Fif. The procedure was simple, but confidentiality was involved. The requirement for these missions included guaranteed good weather for the evening and no major operations planned for the next day. Majors Noyes, Bradin, and Peters knew about these missions and their purpose.

After the evening briefing at regiment, I returned to the troop and made plans for the next day and signed all the paper work Noyes had ready for me. I then had one of my secondary pilots, along with a backup crew chief and door gunner, fly me to Free World Heliport in Saigon.

The crews selected were all volunteers. I briefed them on what was required but did not give details. Pilots Jim Noe, Tom Mandelke, and Earl Moore usually flew me, with Noe being my closest confidant.

My motorcycle flew with us for use as my ground transportation in Saigon. After landing at the Free World Heliport, my crew unloaded my motorcycle while I put on my steel pot, checked my sidearm, put my PRC-25 radio with long antennae on my back, climbed on my bike, and rapidly drove to Fif's apartment.

I normally arrived at Fif's around 2100 hours. The first thing I did was hang my radio's antennae out of her second-story window. I made certain that my TOC could reach me, if needed, and had radio checks when I first got out of the helicopter and as it flew back to Bien Hoa.

At about 2300 hours, another crew would fly down to pick me up, calling me as they overflew Fif's apartment. I would get on my bike and be at Free World Heliport ready for pickup within ten minutes.

One night, a little after midnight, we were returning to Alpha Pad when the Bien Hoa Air Base came under mortar attack. We saw the flashes of the mortars firing from the north side of the base. I quickly pinpointed the enemy's location, called the local artillery FDC, and had rounds falling within five minutes. After a couple of adjustments, I called in one last minor adjustment, "Drop five-zero, fire for effect." That command brought thirty-six 155mm artillery rounds in right on top of the enemy. Obviously, their mortars shut down.

The regiment's TOC duty officer was monitoring this action by radio. He woke Patton up and told him there had been a mortar attack on the base and that I was in the air adjusting fire on the shooters.

The next day, Patton commended me on my quick action. He made the comment, which was later passed on to me, "That damn Bahnsen never sleeps. He doesn't want to miss any chance to kill dinks."

When he saw me later that day, Patton wanted to know how the hell I got into the air so quickly at midnight. I said something to change the subject, and he let it go at that. Patton knew I went to Saigon on my days off, but to my knowledge he never found out that I was going to see Fif in the evenings.

Just before Patton departed, I visited Fif and was a little late in meeting my helicopter at the Free World Heliport. Around midnight, under blackout conditions, I was speeding along when a large dog broke in front of me. I broadsided the damn thing with my motorcycle. My steel helmet went flying, and my radio hit me in the head. I sprawled on the ground and landed hard on my left shoulder. I got up hurting badly. My shoulder was obviously dislocated. I was a real mess with more than a few skinned places.

I found my helmet and put it on, and then I put my radio over my good shoulder. Starting that motorcycle was always a bitch. I normally did a running jump-start. Not being in any condition to do this, I resorted to the kick-start. It took me several tries to get it going. The bike's handle bars were tilted almost ninety degrees to the left. I had to steer with one hand and drive very slowly from that point to the Free World Heliport.

We flew back to Alpha Pad and woke our senior medic to look at my shoulder. He said he knew how to get it back in the socket, if I wanted him to, or I could go on sick call the next morning and have the regiment's surgeon do it.

I told him to give it his best shot. He did, and my shoulder slipped back into place. It was not a pleasant experience. I never missed a day of duty over this accident, but I flew with my arm in a sling for over a week.

Patton wanted a command photo before he departed. My left arm is in a sling in this photograph. Everyone just assumed I had been wounded. No one, and I mean no one, ever asked me where, or how, I was hit.

I also rode my motorcycle to regiment headquarters for the evening briefing. It added the right touch to my persona and became my signature personal ground vehicle.

While my left arm was still in a sling, I was riding it back from the evening briefing using my one good arm to steer. The 2nd Squadron CP was located about fifty meters off the road leading to Alpha Pad. Lieutenant Colonel Lee Duke and Majors Dale Hruby and Gus Johnson, my West Point classmate, were sitting outside the tracks having a beer. They all three yelled to me, "Hey, Doc." I thought they were just hailing me and raised my right arm to wave at them. Wrong move!

I lost control of my motorcycle, hit a big hole in the dirt road, tumbled to the ground, and landed square on my ass. That got the hogs to barking! They weren't expecting such a grand gesture. The three of them rushed over to help me get back on my feet. I was bruised but not broken. They dragged my motorcycle off the road and invited me to stay for a cold beer before getting back on my way.

One evening, on a dark and absolutely black night, I had a drink with Colonel Patton after the evening briefing and had two more drinks while we ate supper in the regimental officers' mess. I was feeling pretty good when I left.

It was late, so I decided to use a shortcut. Unbeknown to me, my shortcut road had been black topped that afternoon. The engineers put three fifty-five-gallon drums in the middle of the road topped by several rolls of concertina wire as a barrier to keep traffic off the fresh blacktop. However, they didn't place flashing lights or warning signs in front of the barrier. I generally did not use any lights at night and was going at a pretty good clip when I hit this barrier head on. My motorcycle got all tangled up in the concertina wire and stopped suddenly, sending me headfirst into the wire.

I tried to extract myself from the wire but to no avail. I couldn't see anyone in the immediate area to yell at for a little help. Not knowing what else to do, I pulled my Smith and Wesson .38-caliber pistol out of its shoulder holster, slowly fired three shots, and called for help as loud as I could. No one answered. I repeated the same, then realized I was out of ammo. I'd shot all six rounds.

Despite my shots for help, no one came to my rescue. After a long struggle, I got out of the mess. My motorcycle was stuck in the wire. I just left it and walked back to my troop area.

Noyes and the guys were astounded by my sorry-ass appearance. I was a damn mess. My uniform was ripped to shreds. I had cuts all over my hands and arms. I looked like a big cat had gotten hold of me. Noyes retrieved my bike while I went to the medics to get patched up. My troopers got a big hoot out of all this, as did Patton and his staff when they heard about it.

I had never carried extra ammo for my .38-caliber personal side arm, but I started after this incident. I also started using the lights on the bike when riding it at night.

Patton's tour was winding down. His record as colonel of the Blackhorse was impeccable, and the regiment evolved into a fierce fighting force under his leadership.

Shortly before his departure, the 3rd Tactical Fighter Wing FACs threw a farewell party for Colonel Patton. This outstanding Air Force outfit had a FAC on station during our daytime missions and could be called out at night. They also had fighter-bombers circling high over our operations that we could count on to drop their payloads on enemy positions within a matter of minutes.

Everybody in the regiment who routinely worked with the 3rd's FACs was invited to the party, as were all the FAC pilots and possibly all the wing's fighter pilots, making for a good-sized crowd. I arrived at the party ahead of Colonel Patton. There was a bar setup, a buffet, and, in one corner of the room, an 8mm projector was playing a skin flick.

We were standing around, snacking on finger food, knocking back beers, and shooting the shit when Patton arrived. He came through the door and was looking around the room when the guy in charge tried to introduce him. Patton said something profane to the effect that he wasn't going to be party to this kind of an affair, turned around, and walked back out the door. He was mad as hell that a skin flick was being shown during a party in his honor. He took it as an insult.

The Air Force guys were really embarrassed. They hadn't meant to offend Colonel Patton. The skin flick wasn't the main event. In fact, I don't remember many guys paying much attention to it. At any rate, the guy in charge turned the projector off as soon as Patton left. I stayed, had a couple more beers, and went back to the troop.

On the evening of 6 April, a farewell supper was held for Colonel Patton at the regimental officers' mess. It was an informal affair, lots of small talk, and no speeches—they would come the following day. Other than the presence of his squadron commanders and me, Patton's farewell supper was not noticeably different from a typical evening in the regimental officers' mess.

Retired Colonel Glenn Finkbiner recounts an event that took place just as Patton's farewell supper ended.

"We'd just finished eating when we heard a ruckus outside and stepped out to see what it was all about. What we saw was akin to an ancient Greek funeral rite, only better, no one had died.

"Patton's outhouse garnered a lot of attention in a time and place when the oddest things seemed normal. There was widespread agreement that it was the primo private outhouse on Bien Hoa Air Base. People coveted it. No one other than Patton used it. The ARPs swiped it once but to no avail.

"Well, some people in Headquarters Troop organized a little sendoff ceremony for Colonel Patton that involved his outhouse. They hooked it behind a truck with a long piece of rope, set fire to it, and dragged it down the dirt road that ran through the regiment's area—horn a-honking, whooping it up, having a jolly time. Patton was leaving, but his outhouse would be left to no one.

"Patton may have laughed the loudest. I remember the humorous irony in this symbolic sendoff. It was a real hoot."

✳ Chapter 84 ✳

During Vietnam, American combat unit commanders were generally rotated every six months or sooner. Just when you were getting used to your commander's way of doing things, he left.

Patton's warfighting tactics inflicted heavy losses on the enemy and prevented reckless loss of life in the regiment. His sterling leadership created high esprit de corps and made him very popular with the vast majority of his soldiers. Nevertheless, he had detractors. Most notably, Major Gordon Livingston, our regimental surgeon.

When Patton assumed command of the Blackhorse, Major Gerry Noga, a West Pointer, good soldier, and fine surgeon was the regimental surgeon. When Noga rotated out-of-country, Patton overemphasized the importance of his replacement being an Academy graduate, and he selected Livingston entirely on that basis.

Retired Colonel Lee Fulmer recalls Gordon Livingston.

"Livingston was on a premeditated mission to get Patton from day one. Right from the start, he endeavored to turn me against Patton by agreeing with his antiwar views. I particularly remember that he tried to get me to say that Patton didn't support pacification, which wasn't true. Patton was a warrior and worked hard at it. At the same time, while I was his S-5 civil affairs officer, Patton supported my pacification efforts one thousand percent, as did his staff and the entire regiment.

"Soon after he arrived, Livingston confided in me that he would not finish his tour in Vietnam: he would be relieved and sent home because he didn't agree with Patton on how the war should be fought. Carrying an antiwar chip on your shoulder while serving in the Eleventh Armored Cavalry Regiment was no way to make friends. Livingston knew that, but didn't care in the slightest. The only thing he seemed to be interested in was spending enough time in Vietnam to gain the credibility needed to give him a prominent place on the antiwar platform once he left the Army."

Doc resumes.

Livingston accused me of violating the Geneva Convention because I did not force my ARP medics to wear red crosses on their steel pots and allowed them to carry weapons. That's not the way I saw it. My ARP medics didn't wear a red cross anywhere on their bodies. That would have made them targets for the enemy. And going into a combat situation unarmed is grounds for being locked up in the nut house.

Livingston intensely disliked Major Andy O'Meara and repeatedly accused him of interrogating wounded POWs before allowing them medical treatment. Somehow, possibly through Livingston, Associated Press reporter Peter Arnett caught wind of this bullshit allegation and visited the Blackhorse. In his dream of dreams, Arnett hoped to find evidence of our mistreating POWs. He found none. A big disappointment to him and I'm sure to Livingston. After Arnett left, Patton told us, "I don't want that sonofabitch allowed in the regiment's area again." He got no argument; we all felt the same way.

Livingston never understood that Patton, and soldiers like him, could clearly distinguish the Vietcong from ordinary Vietnamese. The former being enemy soldiers, the latter being friendly people we were there to help. Nor did Livingston ever grasp the need to vilify the enemy in such a way that you wouldn't hesitate to kill him. This was of special importance when you fought virtually every day and could not afford to have guilty feelings over the killing part of war. Our mission was to kill the enemy, pure and simple. If we could capture them, okay. But our main mission was to kill them. We weren't there to mistreat POWs, and we didn't.

Livingston fairly earned the Bronze Star for valor while providing medical aid to my troopers during a night assault mission that I led. My recommending him for that medal took the Blackhorse's senior leaders and staff officers by total surprise. They worked closer with him than I did, and the more time they spent around him, the easier it became for them to recognize Livingston's antiwar sentiments.

Colonel James H. Leach became the fortieth colonel of the Blackhorse in a change of command ceremony attended by General Creighton Abrams and virtually every senior American and Free World commander in II Field Forces.

Leach's heroic actions in combat merited him the Distinguished Service Cross while serving as a tank company commander under Abrams in the 37th Tank Battalion, 4th Armored Division during World War II. Abrams served under Patton's father during World War II, and Patton served in Abrams's tank battalion in Germany after the war in the late 1940s. It came as no surprise that both Patton and Leach were favorites of Abrams.

Livingston attempted to use Patton and Leach's change of command ceremony as an opportunity to make a big antiwar statement and embarrass Colonel Patton in front of General Abrams, but ended up shitting in his own shorts.

Retired Colonel, then Major, Glenn Finkbiner recalls Livingston's antics during the change of command ceremony.

"We were standing in formation, waiting for the ceremonies to start, when Livingston came running in and out of ranks passing out flyers printed with what he maliciously referred to as the Blackhorse Prayer. I mistakenly thought he was passing out copies of the prayer our chaplain was about to offer. I glanced at the flyer but didn't pay much attention to it right away.

"As our chaplain began to pray, I looked at the flyer to follow along. Much to my astonishment, it was totally unrelated to our chaplain's prayer. Livingston had written a blasphemous parody on the Twenty-third Psalm, hoping to embarrass Colonel Patton and turn the ceremony into an antiwar circus. I was livid!"

Retired Colonel Jimmie Leach remembers this incident.

"Livingston handed that flyer out to everybody at the ceremony, including General Abrams. I glanced at the first few words and thought it was rather innocent. I had no reason to read along while the chaplain prayed. I just folded it and put it in my pocket. I noticed Abrams and Patton doing the same."

Glenn Finkbiner continues.

"Fortunately, the ceremonies went without disruption. General Abrams took Colonel Patton with him on his return flight to Saigon. Neither of them read Livingston's prayer before leaving.

"After they'd gone, and people were returning to duty, Jim Dozier and I talked about what Livingston had attempted to do. We agreed that it was very serious misconduct and decided to talk it over with Lieutenant Colonel James Tuberty, who replaced Bill Haponski as XO when he took over 1st Squadron, 4th Cavalry Regiment, 1st Infantry Division.

"A lot of people had read Livingston's prayer by this time. The very thought of someone in the regiment, especially a field-grade officer on Patton's staff, doing something like this was enough to raise the hackles on the back of our troopers' necks. Livingston's actually doing this was enough to make a whole lot of people want to do him fatal bodily harm.

"Tuberty wasted no time. He placed Livingston under arrest and had him locked up in the trailer where he slept. If Tuberty hadn't placed guards outside, Livingston very well may not have survived the night. Livingston was relieved of his duties and shipped stateside right away, and he soon left the Army under a very dark cloud."

Jimmie Leach continues.

"I was unaware of what Livingston had actually done until later that evening when Jim Tuberty came to see me. He asked if I'd seen Livingston passing out flyers. I told him 'yes,' and that I had one in my pocket. He asked if I'd read it. I told him 'no.' He told me that I should.

"I got my copy of the flyer and read it. What a bunch of crap! It was a vicious attack on Patton, the Blackhorse, and the war effort.

"Livingston was a West Pointer, and the Army paid for his medical schooling. You'd expect someone with that background to have sufficient character to constrain his antiwar feelings while wearing a soldier's uniform. My blood was boiling by the time I sat the flyer down.

"Tuberty told me that, acting on my behalf, he relieved Livingston and sent him packing. I was delighted to hear that news. Livingston was lucky; he wouldn't have gotten off that easily with me."

Doc resumes.

Before Patton left, he called me to his quarters one evening and gave me my OER. Off the record, he counseled me to get my personal affairs in order. He did not approve of my relationship with Fif and advised me to repair my deteriorating marriage to Pat. On the record, he was effusive in his praise of my duty performance.

Colonel Patton awarded Doc the maximum point rating possible and entered the following comments on Doc's OER dated 4 April 1969.

The rated officer is the best, most highly motivated and professionally competent combat leader I have served with in twenty-three years of service, to include the Korean War and two tours in Vietnam. It is emphasized that the fine reputation this Regiment now enjoys is due primarily to the actions, reactions, and methods of operation of Major Bahnsen. . . . He is one of those rare professionals who truly enjoys fighting, taking risks and sparring with a wily and slippery foe. He is utterly fearless and because of this, demands the same from his unit. He is however, a personal leader, commanding both in the air and often on the ground by example as opposed to direction. He contributes over 80 percent of the intelligence processed by this Regiment. In this connection, his B-52 targeting procedures, and the results they have obtained, have set the pars for excellence in the entire III CTZ. His scout aircraft and gunships fly lower and slower than any I have seen. His Aero Rifle Platoon enjoys a 130:1 kill ratio. His aircraft availability rate in all models is well above the USARV average. The rated officer is a master of improvisation in combat. Equipped with a quick and nimble mind plus an unusual degree of imagination, he is able to transform scattered unrelated units into a cohesive fighting force within minutes of first contact. He is a master of "pile-on" tactics. This officer's overall contribution to the combat capability of the 11th Cavalry is priceless . . . I cannot praise Major Bahnsen too highly for his fantastic performance in battle.

Doc resumes.

I met Colonel Leach when he was the senior adviser to the ARVN's 5th Infantry Division. We got along well from the first day I met him. Just before he assumed command, Leach interviewed me. He told me that although I was not scheduled to be promoted to lieutenant colonel until later that summer, Colonel Patton had recommended that I assume command of 1st Squadron in June when Lieutenant Colonel Merritte Ireland was due to depart. That suited me just fine. I'd been looking forward to commanding an armored cavalry squadron in combat.

✳ Chapter 85 ✳

13 April 1969—1st Cavalry AO, northwest edge of the Michelin Rubber Plantation

The regiment was opconned to the 1st Cavalry Division on 12 April. This had no significant impact on its day-to-day operations. It just meant the regiment would be fighting in the 1st Cavalry's area instead of the 1st Infantry's. Both AOs were north of Bien Hoa; 1st Cavalry was west of the Michelin plantation and, 1st Division was east of it. Not all that far apart by air.

On the second day of operations under the 1st Cavalry, the troop's scouts spotted a bunker complex northwest of Lai Khe. This area teemed with hot action during Operation Atlas Wedge. We chased the NVA operating in it back into Cambodia. However, despite ongoing B-52 strikes, it appeared they were moving back in. While I was en route to the contact area, I called my operations and told them to scramble ARPs.

Former first lieutenant and ARP platoon leader Martin Harmless talks about this contact.

"I scrambled four squads totaling twenty-eight men and boarded our lift ships within ten minutes of the alert. At least half of those going on this mission were fairly new to the platoon, including me. It was the first ARP mission for some of them—my second.

"We arrived at Doc's location within thirty minutes. He was not quite ready for us to start the assault, so he had us take up a temporary position in jungle a few klicks out from the bunker complex. We set up a perimeter and remained there for forty minutes to an hour.

"Just as I heard helicopters approaching, I received a radio call telling me to prepare for extraction. We boarded the lift ships and inserted between the rubber and the adjacent jungle in a hot LZ within two hundred meters of the bunker complex."

Former specialist five, then specialist four, Dan Bock talks about joining the Army, his first assignment in Vietnam, and his first mission with the ARPs.

"When I volunteered for the Army, I requested infantry and airborne training. Got infantry; no jump school. I was disappointed but sucked it up and went off to the war.

"My first assignment in Vietnam was in C Troop, 1st Squadron, 11th Armored Cavalry Regiment. I spent a few months riding around in the back of an ACAV without seeing any real action. That bored me. I wanted to do more and volunteered for the ARPs—they were real infantry who saw action routinely. The older ARPs—those who'd been in the platoon for over three months—were good about teaching new ARPs the ropes, but it took time to get to know them personally.

"I was eager and anxious as we flew out to the contact area. I wanted to experience a firefight, but I really didn't know what to expect or how I would make out. Because I was a cherry, I got stuck carrying the radio for my squad. I worried about that making me a target. The jungle was very thick. That limited our visibility and made walking hard. Lieutenant Harmless split us into right and left flanks of two tandem squads. I was in the rear squad on my side."

Marty Harmless continues.

"Specialist Four Kenneth Jensen was walking point for one of the lead squads. Sergeant Joseph Oreto was also toward the front. They hadn't quite made it to the second ring of bunkers when the dinks let loose with a violent volley of small-arms fire. We all hit the ground and returned fire. Oreto and Jensen were caught in the open, right in the middle of a kill zone.

"Oreto was hit in the heart and died instantly. We succeeded in picking up his body before I moved the platoon back out of the bunkers. Jensen took several rounds and bled to death before we could get him out. A couple of my men were still pinned down on the other flank, watching over his body. There wasn't anything I could do to help them."

Retired Air Force master sergeant, then Army specialist four,
Bruce Stephens talks about his buddies being killed.

"I was not far behind Jensen. He screamed, 'I'm hit! I'm hit!' I hit the ground and hollered for help. It took Doc Southwell ten to fifteen minutes to crawl up to where I was pinned down. There was nothing he could do. He couldn't get up to Jensen without getting killed himself.

"The guys on the other side got to Oreto and carried his body out. I was taking fire from my right side and could not move. That was okay with me, I wasn't about to leave Jensen to the gooks. I watched over him for the next couple of hours—until the tracks and infantry swept the bunkers. Once the area was secure, I picked up Jensen's body and carried it out for evacuation. I was mad as hell! It was my most terrible day in Vietnam! I don't like to talk about it!"

Doc resumes.

Based on the ARPs' initial contact, I thought we had a sizable enemy force by the ass. This would prove incorrect later, but I proceeded on that basis.

I instructed Harmless to maintain contact and stay hunkered down until I got reinforcements on station. I then instructed my gunships to start placing rocket fire into the bunkers from the rear of the complex to avoid hitting the ARPs, whom they could not see through the jungle canopy. I then called the regimental TOC and requested infantry and armor reinforcements.

Two rifle platoons from the 8th Cavalry Squadron, 1st Cavalry Division were chopped to me along with 1st Squadron's A Troop. I sent my lift ships to pick up the rifle platoons and had them inserted in the second LZ where I'd landed the ARPs. Meanwhile, I flew to A Troop's location and began guiding it cross-country to the contact area. It took me about an hour to bring them in.

The regiment started receiving M-551 Sheridan tanks in early 1969. They were assigned nine per troop, beginning with the 1st Squadron. The 2nd and 3rd Squadrons didn't receive their Sheridans until later in the year.

The Sheridan was a lightly armored reconnaissance track with heavy firepower. Its 152mm cannon fired both high-explosive and canister rounds filled with thousands of tiny darts (flechettes) that were deadly on personnel. Its main gun also served as a launcher for the MGM-51

Shillelagh antitank missile, although, to my knowledge, these missiles were never fired during the war. A few test shots, perhaps, but none during a contact. One reason for this may have been that the Sheridan's main gun recoil shook its chassis so violently it fouled up the missile launcher's electronics.

Besides the main gun, the Sheridan was armed with an M-2 .50-caliber and an M-240 coaxial 7.62mm machine gun. This tank's major drawback was its thin aluminum armor that could be penetrated by heavy machine gun fire and offered very little protection against anti-tank mines. Its deficiencies aside, the Sheridan was a fast, highly mobile, and deadly weapons platform.

My first mission for A Troop was to have its ACAVs and Sheridans make a large circular swath around the outer boundary of the bunker complex. This took quite a while, but the resulting swath made a superb kill zone for my gunships. They could easily kill enemy soldiers trying to get across it.

A Troop was still working on the swath when the rifle platoons arrived and linked up with my ARPs, who were still engaged with the enemy.

An artillery forward observer with less than two weeks left in-country arrived with the rifle platoons. Tragically, this young lieutenant was killed by small-arms fire shortly after he took up a position to assess the feasibility of a fire mission.

Despite our casualties, things were going well at this point. I called Harmless and told him to withdraw and link up his ARPs and the rifle platoons with the tracks for an assault.

Once A Troop finished making the swath, I instructed its commander, Captain John C. F. Tillson IV, to mass his ACAVs and Sheridans in front of the riflemen and ARPs, then assault the bunkers. Secured by riflemen and ARPs protecting his flanks and rear, I told Tillson to overrun the bunkers and kill every NVA he found.

I had employed this modus operandi with most of the regiment's troops and tank companies. It was a proven technique for situations like the one we were developing.

Marty Harmless resumes.

"A Troop's tracks roared out much too fast for us to keep up. We were walking over and around downed trees and brush. Hell, we couldn't have stayed up with them if we'd been walking on asphalt."

Doc resumes.

Bad things happen when troop commanders don't have tight formations and tight control. Through some miscommunication, Tillson's unit started moving through the bunkers piecemeal and widely separated. Worse yet, he moved out too fast for the ARPs and 8th Cavalry riflemen to keep up and protect his rear. Consequently, when the lead Sheridans moved into the bunkers, the enemy rose up and shot several tank commanders in the back. This all happened very quickly and was very upsetting to Tillson.

Dan Bock comments.

"To put it in Army slang, this was a real cluster fuck. I hadn't seen anything this screwed up in all my days in C Troop and didn't experience anything this fucked up again. We got our asses kicked because the dumb shit captain leading the charge didn't know what he was doing."

Marty Harmless resumes.

"The 8th Cav took heavy casualties during the initial assault. The NVA were still shooting as my medic, Doc Southwell, did his best to patch up the wounded—nine in one pile. Like all ARP medics, Southwell always carried a weapon and grenades. The dinks saw him working on our wounded and started taking potshots at him. Much to their surprise, every time one of the dinks popped out of a spider hole to shoot at him, Southwell lobbed a grenade at him, and went back to work. I don't know how many he threw, but it was a lot. He had to use some of our wounded's grenades before it was over. It was really a heroic action for which he was awarded the Silver Star."

Doc resumes.

It took me a while to settle Tillson down over the air and to get his casualties out of the line of fire. I then brought him back through the complex and lined him up with my ARPs and what remained of the 8th Cavalry's riflemen. This took some time, but Tillson led the assault the right way the second time around.

If you measure battlefield success by the number of enemy you kill in proportion to how many of yours he kills, we lost this combat action even though we destroyed the bunker complex and killed or chased out every enemy soldier in it.

We killed eleven NVA by body count. The friendly toll was higher: nineteen in all, including two of my superb ARPs. That pissed me off to no end. This was my only combat action during two tours in Vietnam where friendly casualties outnumbered those of the enemy.

✶ Chapter 86 ✶

17 April 1969—Dau Tieng and areas east and northeast

Operation Montana Raider was initiated by overflights of areas west of Nui Ba Dien and north of Tay Ninh. These flights dropped fictitious operational maps and sent bogus radio messages to mislead the enemy into believing U.S. forces were moving into this vicinity. However, the initial reconnaissance in force began east of it.

Montana Raider was a joint operation intended to locate and destroy NVA forces operating in the Crescent northwest of Dau Tieng, the area south of the Fish Hook on the western bank of the Saigon River, and the area in and around the Minh Thanh Rubber Plantation. We did not have sufficient intelligence on the exact locations and identities of enemy units in this region, but we believed it contained two North Vietnamese divisions. The terrain was not particularly rugged, but dense jungle areas hampered track vehicle movement and made spotting enemy soldiers from the air difficult.

Colonel Leach was moving his TOC and 1st and 2nd Squadrons into the 1st Cavalry Division's AO. The 3rd Squadron was opconned to the 1st Infantry Division. My pink teams were already up on aerial recons for the 1st and 2nd Squadrons when I reported to him to discuss my plans for the day. Much to my surprise, those plans went by the wayside.

Retired Colonel James H. Leach comments on the whys and wherefores for changing Doc's plans.

"A few days earlier, Lieutenant Colonel Merritte Ireland, the 1st Squadron's commander, collapsed from encephalitis and was medically evacuated. I put Major Bill Privette, the executive officer, in command without delay only to have him come down with encephalitis. With the regiment fully engaged in Operation Montana Raider, I could not afford 1st Squadron to be without a commander, even for a day, so I placed Major Don Snow, the operations officer, in temporary command.

"Before Patton left, he gave me the names of three Blackhorse officers to consider as squadron commanders in an emergency situation: Major Doc Bahnsen, the Air Cavalry Troop commander; Major Jim Dozier, the S-3; and Major Glenn Finkbiner, the S-4. Well, I had an emergency situation and considered all three officers in terms of what I wanted.

I wanted a fighter and a proven combat leader who could hit the ground running. All three were fighters, but Doc fought on a daily basis. All three were exceptional leaders, but Doc was the only proven combat leader, and over the past six months he had commanded elements of the 1st Squadron during several enemy contacts. On top of these considerations, Doc was already scheduled to take command of 1st Squadron in June and had been training Major Jim Bradin to assume command of the Air Cavalry Troop. The way I saw it Doc, was the logical and best choice."

Doc resumes.

Colonel Leach told me to pass command of the Air Cavalry Troop to Jim Bradin and go out and take command of the 1st Squadron. Major Don Snow knew I was coming to relieve him. There wasn't time for us to hold a formal change of command ceremony at either unit. I got the location of the 1st Squadron's CP and marked it on my map.

Jim Bradin was with me. I told him that I was flying our helicopter out to the 1st Squadron and would return it later that day. He would have to get another helicopter to fly him back to the troop.

I flew directly out to the 1st Squadron's CP, where I met with Major Don Snow. He introduced me to all the key players before giving me a quick update on the location of the squadron's units. Those units included a Headquarters Troop, including an aviation section with two UH-1s and two OH-6s; A, B, and C Troops; D Company; a Howitzer Battery; and the attached 1st Platoon of the 919th Engineers. D Company's 2nd and 3rd platoons were opconned to the 1st Squadron, 8th

Cavalry, 1st Cavalry Division for the duration of Operation Montana Raider. The Howitzer Battery was opconned to 1st Infantry Division's artillery.

I studied the map briefly. In my opinion, the CP was too far to the rear of the maneuver units. I asked Snow to help me choose a more suitable location for it. We picked a new spot located on a trail farther north. I then gathered my staff around, pointed to the CP's new location, and gave my first order as a squadron commander: "Move the CP forward."

I told Snow that he would command the ground elements during our move. I would provide him support from the air.

While Snow supervised the loading of equipment and supplies and got our convoy lined up, I made an aerial recon of the site selected for my CP. When I returned, Snow had our vehicles lined up in a close column.

A 919th Engineer platoon M-48 tank commanded by Staff Sergeant Arthur Strahin was the lead vehicle. At the relatively young age of thirty-six, Strahin was one of the oldest NCOs in the squadron. I talked with Snow and him briefly, telling them about the terrain in and around our new position and the ground leading to it. All set, I gave Snow the go-ahead and mounted my helicopter to oversee the march forward from the air.

Retired Lieutenant Colonel, then Major, Don Snow picks up the story.

"We were in Indian country and prepared to fight, but we weren't looking for or expecting one, especially one so close to our NDP.

"Unbeknown to us, there were enemy holed up in a relatively small and hastily constructed bunker complex built within the past week, ten days tops. We'd only been moving for a few short minutes when they ambushed us without warning, hitting us with a heavy volume of RPG and automatic weapons fire.

Doc resumes.

Strahin's tank took seven or eight hits, but he led his crew in returning fire. I saw the largest volume of RPG fire coming from what I then recognized as a bunker complex on the column's right, and gave my second command as a squadron commander: "Action right! Action right!"

All tracks immediately turned ninety degrees to their right and opened fire with 90mm canister rounds and .50- and .30-caliber machine gun fire. Snow was mounted on top of an M-577 Command Post Vehicle. Without a second's hesitation, he led the charge into the bunkers, blasting away with his .50-caliber machine. I radioed regiment and informed them that we'd been ambushed by an unknown-sized enemy force in bunkers and were engaged in a fierce firefight.

Don Snow continues.

The RPGs stopped after the initial barrage, but we continued to take automatic weapons and small-arms fire as we stormed the bunkers, relentlessly pounding the enemy with canister and machine gun fire. There was a lot of shooting going on, but the whole affair was over within thirty minutes.

"The enemy was outmatched from the beginning. There was only a platoon of them, and they were dumb enough to try and take out a troop-plus-sized armor column. Curiously enough, if they hadn't fired at us, we may never have seen them."

Doc resumes.

I landed as soon as I could to help the ground force press the fight forward. I'd only been on the ground for a few minutes before Colonel Leach arrived over the area. I radioed him with a sitrep.

Retired Major General Jim Dozier comments.

"I remember this day clearly. The whole regiment was on the move. I was riding with Leach in his command and control helicopter, listening to radio traffic, and watching troop movements. Just as soon as Doc's sitrep came over the air, Leach told his pilot to head for Doc's location. He wanted to see what was going on."

"Leach got energized when he orbited above contacts. He really liked to get on the ground and join the battle. Bullets didn't scare him, and he was a tough soldier.

"During his many years of combat, going back to World War II,

Leach was wounded six times, awarded five Purple Hearts, and never went to a hospital for treatment—being tough enough to heal on his own, or so it would seem."

Doc resumes.

My troops were just wrapping up the final sweep of the bunkers and surrounding area when Leach dismounted, with M-16 in hand, and came running up to Snow's ACAV, where six POWs were being held. Dozier also joined us and made arrangements to evacuate the POWs back to regiment for interrogation.

Snow and the CP folks did a great job and took no casualties. They killed twenty and captured six NVA. I suspect this was an advance party sent to receive prepositioned supplies for an upcoming operation.

Snow's leadership and valor under fire during this contact was absolutely spectacular. He received a Silver Star for his actions. Except for holes in the lead tank, we took no vehicular damage. Snow brought another tank forward to tow Strahin's tank. As soon as we got the column lined up again, we resumed our march to our CP's new location and set up camp.

On arrival at the new CP, I sent a helicopter crew to Alpha Pad to pick up some clothes and the rest of my gear. Midafternoon, I flew out to meet the line troop commanders, all of whom I knew.

Captain John Tillson was commanding A Troop, Captain Lee Fulmer was commanding C Troop, and Captain Ron Caldwell was commanding D Company. He was detached with his 2nd and 3rd platoons to the 1st Cavalry and wouldn't return for about thirty days. The 1st platoon remained with the squadron to work with the three ACAV troops. First Lieutenant Tim Kerns, the 1st platoon leader, was filling in for Caldwell.

Captain Jarrett Robertson had been commanding B Troop since early November when he replaced Captain John Hays, who had been killed in action. The first thing Robertson told me was Ireland had told him that he was going to make him the S-3 and that First Lieutenant Bill Hanna would take command of B Troop in mid-April. The second thing Robertson told me was that they'd just held a change of command ceremony and Hanna was B Troop's new commander. This had been done without Leach's or my approval. I could have had Robertson's ass. He'd acted way beyond his authority. Nonetheless, as I had no reason to question this move, I let this stand for the time being. I told Robertson that Snow was going to be my S-3; he would be one of Snow's assistants.

Robertson was a tremendous soldier and took this turn of events in stride.

I sensed Robertson was ambitious at the time and was not wrong. Robertson went on to become deputy commanding general, 1st Armored Division during Operation Desert Storm. In 1993, while serving as deputy commanding general, V Corps at Frankfurt, Germany, Major General Jarrett Robertson was tragically killed when the helicopter he was riding in crashed.

Looking back on the situation today, I am damn glad that I didn't make a fuss over Robertson's hubris in Vietnam because it would have truncated the course of his distinguished career.

That evening I finally got a chance to talk to Don Snow. We were already acquainted from our days attending the Armor Advanced Course together. He was a tough little guy from Idaho who grew up riding broncos competitively. I was on the secondary zone promotion list for lieutenant colonel but Snow was senior to me by virtue of date of rank.

There is a provision in Army regulations that allows an officer to command someone of the same grade who outranks him by date of rank. It requires the assumption of command orders to be by order of the commander in chief—the president of the United States. This provision is so rarely employed that I never heard of it being used during my thirty-year Army career. Time didn't allow Leach to request such orders, so he approved Snow as my S-3 on an ad hoc basis. I would be Snow's commanding officer but not his rating officer. However, my input would serve as the starting and ending point for his OER. The regimental S-3 would be Snow's rater on paper. Jim Dozier had no problem with that arrangement.

Don Snow comments on this talk with Doc.

"I knew Doc was coming to take over the squadron, but I wanted to serve under him. I didn't care about rank. Doc was a breed apart from Army officers of the day. Nothing about him struck me as typical and he was certainly anything but a typical combat commander. I saw having the chance to serve under someone like Doc Bahnsen as a rare opportunity. I didn't want to pass it up, and I told him so.

Doc resumes.

Snow wanted to stay on as my S-3, if I wanted him. This was a no brainer for me. He was fully capable of running the squadron, but was accepting of my being selected for the job. Honest, fearless, blunt, energetic, smart, loyal, and more, I couldn't have found a better soldier to serve as my S-3.

Snow and I established a great relationship from day one. He handled both the XO's and S-3's duties until I brought in a new XO several weeks later.

✶ Chapter 87 ✶

18–19 April 1969—east of Tay Ninh

Recons in force for Operation Montana Raider jumped off with a bang on the second day of my squadron command.

C Troop was detached to a 1st Cavalry infantry unit. D Company's 2nd and 3rd Platoons were opconned to 2nd Squadron. My squadron task force for the day consisted of A and B Troop with three platoons each and D Company's 1st Platoon of five M-48 tanks. The platoons in A and B Troop were equipped with five ACAVs and three Sheridans each. Neither of the squadron's two UH-1s was available, so I used an OH-6 as my command and control aircraft for the day.

Our assigned AO was a very heavy jungle area where intelligence reports indicated one (possibly more) NVA base camp was located. Early in the morning, my task force ran into a large well-concealed and heavily fortified NVA bunker complex. The action was hot and heavy right from the get-go. Enemy fire came at us from the front and both flanks. All tracks returned fire immediately. M-48 canister rounds shredded trees, exposing parts of the bunker complex. Flechette rounds fired by M-551s peppered the bunkers and surrounding area with thousands upon thousands of tiny darts. A heavy volume of .50-caliber and M-60 machine gun fire caused the enemy to hunker down. It was an impressive counterattack. However, I couldn't see through the triple-canopy jungle, so I had damn little control or influence over what was taking place on the ground.

I was able to talk to my maneuver element commanders. Based on what they told me and plumes of colored smoke rising through the canopy, I was able to get a pretty good idea of their locations before calling in artillery and tactical air strikes to set up an assault on the bunker complex. The artillery fire went in after the fast movers made two passes over the contact area. Everything was going according to plan when .50-caliber tracers created a firestorm in the dry bamboo thickets, making it impossible for my task force to see its way around trees and thick brush. Once the smoke cleared, the assault on the bunkers resumed amid a heavy firefight that continued until dusk.

Although we killed a lot of NVA during the initial assault, we incurred casualties of our own.

I landed and walked into the contact area to have my aircraft evacuate D Company's casualties. I remember standing there talking to First Lieutenant Tim Kerns, the platoon leader. During a close-support firing pass, a gunship fired rockets too close to his men and wounded several of them. That upset Kerns, and I don't blame him. He was also agitated over having men killed during the initial contact.

I sensed Kerns to be a little overwhelmed. He wanted to quit. It would have been wrong for me to let him off the command hook. He had a job to do and he was going to do it. Words don't mean much in these situations, but I tried to buck up his spirits by telling him that his men needed him and that he needed to hang in there. Kerns understood and went back to work.

As darkness fell, we medevaced all the remaining wounded. I then ordered my maneuver elements into night laager positions for resupply operations.

Several tracks were destroyed at various times during the day. I had them blown in place. I never hesitated in this regard.

If the commander on the ground believed salvage or recovery of a track was impossible, he told me, and I gave the order to destroy it. For disabled tanks, the procedure was to pull all weapons and radios, then put a thermite grenade in its tube to render it useless, and hopefully start a big enough fire to burn it in place. We also put a white phosphorous grenade in the turret to make sure all ammunition was destroyed. For disabled ACAVs, we pulled weapons, radios, and ammo. We then placed a thermite grenade in the engine compartment, and that usually did the trick.

We killed ninety-three enemy soldiers in this fight, which was the longest battle in Phase 1 of Operation Montana Raider. Unfortunately, nine of my troopers were killed in action. B Troop lost Specialist Four James Baka, Specialist Four Robert Morgan, Specialist Four Thomas

Fitzpatrick, and Second Lieutenant Daniel Leahy, its artillery forward observer. A Troop lost Specialist Four Charles Chandler and Specialist Four Ronald Pongratz. D Company lost Specialist Five Roy Maas, Sergeant Don McAtee, and Specialist Joseph Morrow.

The entire task force fought fiercely that day. Troopers from all units received medals of valor, including Distinguished Service Crosses awarded to Sergeant First Class Francisco Rodriquez, from D Company, and Platoon Sergeant Donald Kelly, from B Troop.

Lieutenant Hanna left one of B Troop's disabled ACAVs out in the contact area without destroying it. He didn't know it at the time, but one of his dead was still inside. I didn't find out about this until the evening briefing.

Pissed off is an understatement. I had to restrain myself from doing something I would later regret. Hanna felt horrible and I didn't blame him personally. This incident wasn't talked about and I never reported it. It was just one more screwup on a really bad day.

The next morning, I sent Hanna back out to recover his trooper's body and destroy the disabled ACAV. I then lined up my task force and got it moving south, where I established my CP in a rubber plantation near Dau Tieng.

✶ Chapter 88 ✶

Retired Lieutenant General Tom Montgomery makes the following observation about Doc and maintenance.

"Doc scared a lot of people because he didn't know when to quit. I never heard about him sitting around on his ass while his troops were fighting. He led them into battle and stayed on the battlefield until the last man was out. Many of us believed he would have fought day and night if possible. He didn't worry about abusing equipment, if necessary, to accomplish a mission. It was not uncommon for him to push his people to the max. He also had a sixth sense for standing down individuals and units at the very moment they were literally on the verge of collapse."

Doc begins.

Our tracks had taken a beating over the past few days, busting jungle and overrunning bunkers, and really needed a lot of work. Our weapons were in serious need of a good cleaning and oiling. The troops needed some time to look after their bumps and bruises, get cleaned up, write letters, read their mail, have a hot meal, and so forth. Without a doubt, both machine and man needed some tending to after several days of constant battle. After moving into the rubber plantation, I ordered my unit commanders to laager their vehicles and stood the squadron down for two days of maintenance.

During this time, I got a chance to walk about and meet my soldiers and my leaders and get a better handle on the squadron's equipment and operations.

Squadron headquarters had six M-577 Command Post Vehicles, four M-113 ACAVs, one M-578 Light Recovery Vehicle, one M-88 Heavy Recovery Vehicle, three M-132 Flamethrowers, one M-577 Medical track, three M-113 Medical tracks, three M-60 Armored Vehicle Launched Bridges, and two or three ACAVs mounted with radar. The aviation section had two UH-1Ds and two OH-6s. None of them were armed.

A, B, and C Troops all had an M-577, three M-113s APCs, one M-113 ACAV, and an M-578 in their headquarters section. Each of their three platoons was outfitted with three M-551 Sheridan tanks, five M-113 ACAVs, one M-113 Armored Personnel Carrier, and one M-106 self-propelled 4.2-inch mortar. They also had an M-578.

D Company had three platoons with five M-48 Patton main battle tanks each. Its headquarters section had two M-48s (one equipped with a front-mounted dozer blade), an M-88, and three M-113 ACAVs.

The Howitzer Battery had one M-577, six M-548 ammo carriers, three M-113 ACAVs, one M-578, and six M-109 self-propelled 155mm howitzers.

In addition, all units had jeeps, trucks, and trailers that were used for support purposes.

The three ACAV troops were the squadron's key maneuver elements. Two of D Company's three platoons were normally attached to one of the troops. Its tanks incurred heavy battle damage, blew engines, busted transmissions, and quickly wore out tracks. Consequently, on a normal day D Company had five of its seventeen tanks down for repairs.

When not being used for their primary purpose, I had the Headquarters Troop commander make a small combat team out of three M-113s, the Surveillance and Radar Section track, and the Flamethrower Section.

Former 1st Squadron S-3 Don Snow talks about this improvisation.

"I had only heard about Doc's penchant for improvising his assets to create additional combat elements before he arrived at the squadron. He really didn't care about how things were supposed to work according to our TO&E, but invented ways of optimizing the use of the resources our TO&E provided.

"If a piece of equipment wasn't being used, Doc put it and its crew to work killing the enemy. If matériel not in our TO&E could broaden his fire and maneuver base, he'd find a way to get hold of it. The Army had standard ways of doing things and Doc had his way of doing things. Doc's way was the better of the two. At least for his squadron."

Doc resumes.

I asked Lieutenants Bates and Ballou to transfer to the squadron because I liked them and had total confidence in their flying ability. They politely said "no," but never told me why.

Mike Bates reveals why he and Guy Ballou opted to remain with the Air Cavalry Troop.

"Doc did a lot for me personally, as he did for Guy Ballou, Ray Lanclos, and a lot of other guys. That didn't obligate us to follow him to First Squadron.

"The way Ballou and I saw it, going to the squadron was like giving up a nice home to go camp in the woods. The squadron's pilots lived in the field with the rest of its frontline troopers. They had no hooch, no maids, no PX, and no club like we had at Alpha Pad. I guess we were just too comfortable with the 'good life' to trade it for 'primitive life,' even if working with Doc came with the trade."

Doc continues.

I did persuade two of my Air Cavalry Troop pilots to go to the squadron with me: Warrant Officers Steven Little and Tom "Cool Hand" Mandelke. They were my primary pilots. Captain August "Gus" Daub, my Aviation Section leader, had no problem with that. He understood my desire to fly with pilots I knew.

Although the Air Cavalry Troop provided pink team and lift ship support to all regimental units, the value of an aviation section under squadron control was tremendous. We always had someone over the troops on the ground, scouting and helping see the battlefield.

I stopped wearing flight suits when I joined the squadron and started wearing fatigues, a steel helmet, and LBE all the time. As a matter of routine, I rode on the left outside seat in the back of a UH-1, where I could see and shoot my M-16 out the door. I wore a headset and used a floor mike switch to transmit radio messages. I also operated my own radios, which were mounted right above my seat. I normally flew with an airborne battle staff that included an artillery liaison officer, an assistant S-3, and my command sergeant major. I only flew in an OH-6 when both UH-1s were down for maintenance. Just a pilot flew with me in the OH-6.

Former captain and 1st Squadron Aviation Section leader August "Gus" Daub comments.

"I'd been in the squadron a while before Doc arrived. He liked doing things his way, which was fine with me because it didn't interfere with how I ran the section.

"He brought two excellent pilots with him. Doc loved those two. He flew with them most of the time because he'd flown with them before and didn't like breaking in new pilots. I mostly flew with Major Snow or one of his assistants in one of our Little Birds. I did fly with Doc on occasion. Flying with him was an adventure. He always found a way to get us into the heart of the action."

Doc continues.

My command sergeant major from day one until the day he was wounded (one day before my last fight in September) was Frank Zlobec. He came to Vietnam from Germany, where he was a command sergeant major of the 3rd Brigade, 3rd Armored Division.

Zlobec was an old friend of Colonel Donn Starry. He had been slated to become Starry's command sergeant major when he took over the regiment many months later. However, Colonel Leach was commanding the Blackhorse when Zlobec arrived. Leach had already put Don Horn in as his command sergeant major, and Zlobec was assigned as 1st Squadron's command sergeant major. Going from a brigade to a squadron command sergeant major's slot is a step backward. Zlobec was let down about this unanticipated turn of events, but he quickly got over it.

A soldier's soldier, Zlobec talked to everyone easily and freely. He confided his every observation with me, as I did mine with him. Unless he had other things to do, Zlobec flew with me. When we landed in a troop area, he would seek out the first sergeant and other NCOs to get their view on how things were going and how he could help. If we landed in a hot area, he stayed with me. He told me over and over that I was going to get us killed, but he never showed fear or hesitation in a firefight.

Another key NCO from start to finish of my squadron command

was Master Sergeant Dave Wolff, my ops sergeant. Wolff had a rare military background. He served in the Navy during World War II, the Marine Corps during the Korean War, and then became a career Army man. He rarely flew with me, as his duty normally kept him in the ops track. When he did get to the field, Wolff was a cool hand when the bullets flew.

Soldiers in the field normally got one hot ration a day, usually supper. Two times a day, I ate C-rations just like everyone else. I preferred the fruit and the ham and eggs. Nearly everyone hated ham and eggs, but they were my favorite. I also liked the spaghetti ration. When these two items were hot, they were tolerable. I lived on fruit when we could not get them heated. Hot meals were cooked in our rear area, packed in mermite cans, and flown out by helicopter with the log pack (helicopters transporting water and POL bladders, ammunition, cases of C-rations, and other supplies).

My CP consisted of three M-577s placed back to back in a T-formation with other tracks laagered around them. Zlobec and I shared the same GP-small tent with Major Don Snow. We slept in sleeping bags laid out on cots. I had a shop van for my living quarters in the rear area, as did Snow and Zlobec, but I rarely spent the night there.

My jeep driver, Sergeant Franklin, worked under Zlobec's supervision. He generally stayed with my jeep in the rear area. His main mission was to keep me in clean uniforms, underwear, and shined boots. He sent these items to me daily, packed in a waterproof .50-caliber ammo can that was delivered by helicopter to my location.

Although the XO was officially second in command, the way I operated, the S-3 was my number two. My S-3 helped me with the fight and my XO oversaw administration and logistics in the rear area. When I first arrived, the squadron's rear area was located at Blackhorse base at Xuan Loc.

☆ Chapter 89 ☆

This was day one of Phase 2 of Operation Montana Raider. The entire regiment was relocating to Quan Loi, an area of old rubber plantations located about a hundred kilometers north of Saigon. This was a 149-kilometer road march for some units, about eighty for my squadron. The move took the better part of two days.

I laagered my units around Quan Loi before moving southwest to a new NDP (designated "Jamie" for Leach's son) midway between Tay Ninh and Quan Loi. We conducted troop-sized recons in this area for two days without stirring up significant enemy contact.

I then received orders to set up new joint NDP with one of the 1st Cavalry Division's infantry battalions. To my delight, this battalion was commanded by Major "Ski" Ordway, a fellow West Pointer and an old friend.

I moved the squadron to an area near the new NDP from where I watched Ordway's infantrymen dig in behind a concertina-wire perimeter. I then placed my tracks in spots around the perimeter with good fields of fire and fronting open space.

Ordway and I spent two days talking about old times while our units reconned out of our joint NDP. We were majors commanding units normally commanded by lieutenant colonels. Majors besides us did command battalions and squadrons, but we considered our good fortune to be a career-enhancing opportunity. In fact, I was the only major to command a squadron in the 11th Armored Cavalry Regiment during the Vietnam War.

During this period, First Lieutenant Doug Starr joined the squadron, and I placed him in my S-3 shop. A fellow West Pointer, he commanded a troop in the 14th Armored Cavalry Regiment in Germany before coming to Vietnam. From the beginning, he impressed me as a solid soldier and a good man. He thought I should give him troop command right away. I told him he would have to wait his turn. The next command slated to change was my Headquarters and Headquarters Troop. Captain Jim Vance, the S-4 and another West Pointer, was slotted for the job. For the time being, I was assigning him to work as an assistant S-3.

On 27 April, two Air Cavalry scout crews went down over a bunker complex west of Quan Loi. I did not see this action, but it took place in my AO. An OH-6 flown by Warrant Officer Phil Mohnike was hit during a low-level recon of bunkers housing an NVA field hospital. The helicopter crashed instantly and burst into flames. Mohnike and his observer, Private First Class Jeffrey Harvey, were killed instantly.

Another scout pilot, Captain Bert Dacey, witnessed this incident and flew in over the crash site to see if he could assist. His OH-6 was shot down almost immediately. Dacey and his observer, Specialist Four Lorne Sipperley, died on impact.

I knew all of these men very well and thought highly of them.

Dacey was serving as the Aero Scout Platoon leader. He was from New York City and a religious young man who went to mass every day he could. He was awarded a posthumous Distinguished Service Cross for his actions above and beyond the call of duty during this mission.

Harvey was from Burlingame, California. When I first reported to the Air Cavalry Troop, Harvey was an OH-6 mechanic on permanent KP. He was uncomplaining, but being screwed for some reason. Putting someone on permanent KP is chickenshit and demeaning. I let my leaders know that there would be none of this in my troop and immediately sent Harvey back to the scout platoon.

Mohnike was from Visalia, California. He was a superb scout pilot who earned a number of medals of valor under my command.

Sipperley was from Grand Rapids, Michigan. I remember him as being an all-American soldier who did his duty and more. He was wounded badly on an earlier tour and went home to recover. As soon as he got a clean bill of health, he came back to the troop to soldier with the scouts.

Early in the morning of my third day with Ordway, Leach ordered me to move my squadron further south into Tay Ninh Province, where considerable enemy movement had been reported. Ordway was not happy to see me go. We didn't have any major actions while our units were jointly located. I felt the NVA were avoiding us. He told me that as soon as I left the bastards would hit him. I noticed his soldiers digging deeper as we left. One night later, the NVA mortared them and attacked their perimeter. Ordway's soldiers were ready and waiting and killed the better part of their attackers.

✶ Chapter 90 ✶

29 April 1969—Tay Ninh Province

Retired Colonel Lee Fulmer, C Troop's commander at the time, describes the battle in which Staff Sergeant Arthur Strahin was killed in action.

"This part of Vietnam was bustling with NVA and VC activity. The dinks weren't more than a stone's throw away in all directions. But we had a lot of good guys in the area helping us put the kibosh on the enemy wherever and whenever he stood to fight.

"There was no way we could get an accurate count, but by all estimates the enemy had us outnumbered. No big deal. Our superior firepower, maneuverability, and speed gave us superior advantage over his numbers.

"B-52 strikes played a huge role in thinning enemy ranks and destroying base camps and supply routes. More often than not, these strikes compelled the better part of a surviving enemy force to didi mau, leaving a lesser part behind as a security force to cover its withdrawal. We routinely encountered enemy security forces during BDAs of base camps hit by B-52 strikes.

"We had just reentered the Tay Ninh area when a First Cavalry infantry company became pinned down in heavy contact at a partially destroyed NVA base camp. Tom Montgomery's H Company was dispatched to assist this unit. En route to the contact area, Montgomery made contact and decided to develop that action. I got the call to take his place and quickly moved out.

"The contact area had been chewed up by a B-52 strike, making it very difficult to maneuver our tracks, but cavalrymen are not deterred by difficulty and we arrived in short order. This particular base camp was an interlocking series of heavily fortified bunkers that could withstand most anything short of a direct B-52 strike.

"The infantry was glad to see us. We had water and ammo and they were running short. Even with bringing in a steady stream of air and artillery strikes, they'd been shot up badly—several dead and many more wounded.

"I talked to the infantry commander. He wanted us to help him evacuate his casualties right away. My tracks laid down suppressive fire to cover those of us who went in to carry out the dead and the wounded. Several of my troopers were wounded in the process. After we got the first group out, evacuation of casualties continued while I launched an assault.

"The air smelled of exhaust fumes and cordite. Smoke hung over some parts of the battlefield as if tethered to an anchor. The deafening din of machine gun and small-arms fire, exploding grenades, and the roar of track engines made it hard for me to hear what was being said over the radio. Times like this were what I call the 'fog of war' and they always seemed to move in slow motion.

"A Nine-nineteenth Engineer M-48 commanded by Staff Sergeant Art Strahin was positioned between another ACAV and mine as we maneuvered toward the bunker complex. We were taking heavy fire from the wood line when an RPG crossed the front of my track, hit the turret on Strahin's tank, bounced back, and exploded. My left gunner was hit in his face and shoulder, and tiny pieces of shrapnel hit me in the face.

"We both dropped down and started flopping around like a couple of bass landed on the deck of a boat. We were bleeding like crazy, but neither of us was hurt as much as we or my assistant track commander thought. When he saw us on the deck, lying in a pool of blood, he got all excited and made a net call, repeatedly shouting that his commander was down.

"I quickly realized that I wasn't going to die and stood up. Strahin was slumped over in his turret. His tank was on fire but not in a roaring blaze. My assistant track commander and the track commander on the other ACAV were using .50-caliber fire to make toothpicks out of the trees fronting the wood line. Other tracks moved up and fired away, making quick work of the enemy.

"Doc heard my assistant tank commander's call and got on the radio with me. He wanted to know if I was okay.

" 'Yes, sir. I'm fine. Just a couple of scratches.'

" 'Don't try to be a fucking hero, Fulmer. You'll get yourself killed.' A surprising admonition, coming from Doc Bahnsen.

" 'Roger. I am continuing the assault.'

"What followed isn't exactly clear in my memory. So much was going on, it's impossible for me to remember it all. The fight raged on for a good three hours. In the end, my tracks and the infantry overran the base camp and killed every dink still in it.

"I got out of my track and helped pull Strahin out of his tank. We extinguished the fire and laid Strahin out on the rear hatch. I vividly remember him looking up at me and saying, 'Sorry, sir, I've got to rest. I can't fight no more.'

"I had my medics bring their track up to an area a hundred meters to my rear where they set up a temporary aid station. The infantry had a lot of soldiers wounded in this fight. I had thirty casualties of my own, and that really upset me. The aid station was close to an open area large enough to bring in medevacs. We got the most seriously wounded out first, Strahin being one of them. I didn't expect any of them would die.

"Tiny pieces of shrapnel covered my face like face razor nicks. I bled plenty, but was not seriously wounded. My medics wrapped my face with gauze. I looked like a kid dressed up as a mummy for Halloween.

"I decided to keep my troop in place to rearm. I was at the medic track, talking to my troopers, when Doc came walking up. He was damn glad that none us had been killed and that I was up and talking. I gave him a sitrep.

"The base camp was the headquarters of an NVA unit, possibly a division, large enough to have its own hospital complex. The B-52 strike set off a mass withdrawal toward the Cambodian border. The enemy soldiers we'd killed were part of a security force covering the withdrawal. We scored a significant victory in killing most, if not all, of them.

"After I wrapped up, Doc asked about my wounds.

" 'Just how bad are you hurt, Fulmer?'

" 'I've got a bunch of shrapnel cuts on my face. That's all.'

" 'Let's have a look.'

" 'Trust me. I'm okay.'

" 'I want to see for myself.'

" 'No, I'm okay.'

" 'I just want to make sure.' More out of curiosity than anything else, Doc reached out and unwrapped my bandages before I could back away. He took a look at me, started laughing, and announced, 'Hell, Fulmer. You're not hurt.'

" 'No shit, sir. That's what I've been trying to tell you.'

"We then talked about some pressing business for me: I was scheduled for R&R starting the next morning. The question was, do I stay with my unit for a couple of days or do I leave right away?

"One of the unwritten rules in Vietnam was, 'Never postpone an R&R. You might not live to take it.'

"Doc told me to turn my troop over to my XO and go on R&R. By the time I was finished speaking to my XO, Doc had a helicopter waiting on the ground for me."

Doc begins.

From everything I heard, Strahin was magnificent in keeping up the fire. He killed more than a dozen NVA with canister and .50-caliber fire. He was a top-notch soldier who'd proven himself a fierce fighter over and over again in previous actions. Strahin was initially expected to live, but died later that day.

I recommended Strahin and Fulmer for the Silver Star. I don't recall the other people I wrote up for medals of valor, but it was more than a handful. Purple Hearts were also awarded, too many for any of our liking.

C Troop remained with the infantry in that base camp for several days to go through every bunker with a fine-toothed comb. They picked up quite a few maps and documents that contained timely intel. They also discovered several caches of rice and miscellaneous supplies that included a significant stash of weapons and ammo.

✴ Chapter 91 ✴

30 April–13 May 1969—vicinity of Tay Ninh and Quan Loi

The regiment continued the reconnaissance in force actions known as Operation Montana Raider for the next two weeks. During this operation, we pushed the NVA back into their Cambodian sanctuaries and destroyed dozens of their base camps in War Zone C, resulting in Free World forces gaining control of areas previously dominated by the enemy.

Many of the brief, but fierce, contacts during this period occurred in the heavy jungle of the eastern sector of War Zone C. Jungle busting and constant maneuver punished our tracked vehicles unmercifully. We took this in stride, dealt with it the best we could, and pressed the hunt for the enemy relentlessly.

On 11 May, A Troop's Private First Class Samuel Patterson was wounded somewhere near Quan Loi. He died two days later. I didn't know Patterson and was never told about the circumstances of his death. But whether or not I knew a soldier personally, I took every trooper's loss personally.

The regiment logged slightly more than sixteen hundred kilometers during this Montana Raider. Lieutenant General George I. Forsythe, who commanded the 1st Cavalry Division for about half of the operation, later wrote, "In effect, this amounts to the distance between the Normandy Beaches and the environs of Paris. . . . Translated into World War II terms, such maneuverability of a combat unit was indeed brilliant."

✶ Chapter 92 ✶

Retired Colonel Jimmie Leach talks about the regiment's need to pull maintenance on its equipment.

"Shortly after assuming command of the regiment, I presented Lieutenant General Julian Ewell, the II Field Force commander, with a maintenance plan. He rejected it. If he would have backed me on it, the regiment's tracks would have been in a better state of repair and wouldn't have been breaking down as often.

"The regiment was essential to operations throughout the III CTZ, and the II Field Force commander wouldn't give me time for maintenance! How nutty is that? I should have done what I wanted to do without asking his permission.

"After maneuvering through jungle from one flank of the III CTZ to the other during Operation Montana Raider, I went to see General Ewell and told him I needed a full week to get my tracks repaired. He pointed his finger at me and said, 'Don't you tankers want to fight? All you want to do is maintain, maintain, maintain. I'll give you three days.' Three days wasn't enough time to get all the parts we needed, ordered, delivered, and installed, but I accepted what time I could get.

"The regiment had over two hundred and fifty tracked vehicles. A lot of miles were put on every one of them that could move on its own during Operation Montana Raider. All these vehicles needed maintenance. I didn't have a direct support ordnance unit. The nearest place where I could get my tracks the kind of maintenance they needed was Long Binh, a two-day road march away, much of it through hostile territory."

Doc begins.

When Patton commanded the regiment, he stood down a platoon a week, when possible. He had the direct support ordnance people come in and help. When the platoons rolled back on line, they were in top-notch condition. Patton never asked anyone's permission to do this because he couldn't have gotten it. Like many generals in Vietnam, Ewell was a light infantry guy and didn't understand armor maintenance.

Moving out early on 14 May, I led my squadron on a two-day convoy from the Quan Loi area back to Long Binh, where we were scheduled for a three-day maintenance stand down. On the second day of this road march, D Company's Private First Class Ralph Ramirez was killed in an ambush.

Former specialist five Charles "Chicken Man" Stewart recounts this ambush.

"We had a breakdown and got separated from the main convoy. Once we were up and running, we joined four tanks from Third Platoon and resumed rolling to Long Bien. I was driving the tank. Sergeant Robert Oracz was the track commander. Ralph was our gunner. He was sitting on top of the turret with his feet hanging down through the hatch. We entered a small village and had just about cleared it when an RPG came across our tank, hitting Ralph in the gut.

"I had lost five tanks during previous contacts and wasn't about to stop. I floor-boarded my tank; Oracz immediately popped a flare and returned fire with the .50 cal. It was almost dark. We couldn't make out any VC, but they were there. Several other tanks joined in. While all of this was going on, someone on the radio was yelling, 'Don't shoot in the village. Don't pop flares.' That was bullshit. We always returned fire no matter where it came from.

"As soon as we were safely out of the village, I pulled into a clearing and we called in a medevac to take Ralph's body out."

Doc resumes.

My three days of maintenance became two. The third day was preempted when I received a mission to assist an ARVN unit that was getting beat up by NVA near Xuan Loc.

✴ Chapter 93 ✴

We got an early start and road marched east, where we bivouacked near Xuan Loc, the regiment's old base camp. The ARVN 18th Division was having problems with the 33rd NVA Regiment in this area.

Working under regiment control, my squadron was to conduct search and destroy missions in support of the ARVN 18th Division.

By this time in my command, I had cross-reinforced the squadron by putting ACAV platoons in D Company and some of D Company's tanks in the ACAV troops. The next morning, we started reconnoitering southeast of Xuan Loc in troop-sized formations.

During this period, jungle busting was a daily event and wet areas were causing tremendous problems for our tracks.

Former captain Ron Caldwell talks about a reconnaissance mission in a particularly wet area.

"I took two of my platoons and a platoon of ACAVs on a joint reconnaissance with an ARVN infantry company quite a ways out from Blackhorse base camp. We quickly began having problems with our tracks.

"The soil in this vicinity was very moist and tended to cake up on the sprockets and lift the track off. We'd have to stop every time one of our vehicles threw a track. This was really slowing us down.

"Doc became agitated by this unavoidable circumstance. He told me to leave a security force with disabled tracks and continue reconnoitering with what was left of the company.

"After dropping several tanks, my company was so severely limited in firepower that an encounter with the enemy would have been very dangerous. There were times when I had half to three-quarters of my company strung out behind me.

"One day, Colonel Leach overflew us and saw what was going on. He called me and wanted to know what the problem was with our maneuvering. I told him the tracks on my company's vehicles were stretched so far out that we needed new ones for most of them, and that we were having problems with road wheels, torsion bars, and track pads. Leach said he would get with Doc and arrange for my company to have a stand down to work on our vehicles.

"The next day we were told to pull into a flat area where Chinook helicopters started bringing in supplies for us to repair the tracks.

"We began to break the tracks down, remove road wheels, and so on. We stopped when it got dark and assumed a defensive position. I didn't realize it at the time, but we were in a dry rice paddy.

"It began to rain and rained hard all night long, causing a nearby creek used to irrigate the rice paddy to flood. When I woke up in the morning, there was about a foot of standing water around our vehicles. The ARVN soldiers with us were sitting on the back deck of our tanks fishing for breakfast.

"We chained up road wheels, reattached the tracks we could, and headed for high ground. One tank was still partially disassembled and bogged down about a foot in the mud. We pulled it out with another tank and towed it about twenty or thirty meters before it got bogged down again. Another tank went in even deeper. We couldn't pull the first tank out with one tank, so we maneuvered some other tanks out front and created a freight train sort of affair to get enough tugging power to get it moving again.

"We would make a little progress, and then our freight train of tanks would bog down. Before long, three tanks were bogged down pretty good, and we began breaking pulling cables right and left. Doc sent my M-88 heavy track recovery vehicle with additional pulling cables out to help me get out of this mess.

"The slow progress toward high ground went on for two days before I received a message to hurry up: a nighttime B-52 strike was set to come in near our area in a couple of days. We weren't moving fast enough, so Doc sent the squadron's M-88 out to help us. About five hundred meters short of our position, its engine caught fire and disabled it. So, now I was forced to use my M-88 to pull the squadron M-88 and use my tank train to pull bogged down tanks out of the mud.

"Working through the night, we made progress but not enough to clear the designated danger zone before the B-52 strike was scheduled to begin. There was some debate about whether to go ahead with the strike or not. Someone up the chain of command above regiment decided to do it anyway. We were given the time of the strike and told to button up during that period.

"It was very dark when the strike began. Out in the boonies with bombs exploding about a thousand meters from our position, we experienced some of the terror that the VC must have felt when B-52s dropped hundreds of bombs on them. The overpressure wasn't too bad where we were, but we were too close to the strike area for comfort; our fifty-two-ton tanks were literally bouncing like basketballs on a playground.

"The next day, we continued inching out and breaking more pulling cables. We were operating in dense jungle where no LZs were available, so Doc had lift ships drop pulling cables to us. The lift ships hovered near our position while their crewmen pushed the cables out. The trees were tall, which meant they had to drop the cables from a fairly good height.

"I remember one drop in particular. A lift ship was hovering for a drop when one of my troopers panicked and ran right into the path of a falling cable that struck the back of his legs, breaking both of them. A real tragedy. It was the worst thing that happened during this weeklong and futile operation. Every minute of it was miserable.

"Within the next day or two, we reached high ground and rejoined the squadron, where it was bivouacked in a large field. We were filthy. I arranged for my troopers to take showers. Their need to wash away the mud and grime they'd accumulated in the bog took precedence over repairing our vehicles at the moment."

Doc comments.

At times, the war wasn't about fighting the enemy but fighting to keep your men and equipment operational.

I found out very early in my career that there are two great secrets to success in the military. The first is perseverance. You have to keep going when going seems impossible. The second is a sense of humor. You have to have a sense of humor to keep things in perspective, particularly when stress has you surrounded.

I didn't know the ground conditions before sending Caldwell into that area. Had I known, I would have found another way to recon it. To his credit, Caldwell showed superb leadership during this fiasco. He never lost his head and kept his troopers working hard. They didn't have time to think about their misery; they persevered through it all, and later laughed over jokes about "Caldwell's Bog."

This period was not without casualties. Staff Sergeant Roger Oliver of A Troop was killed in action on 24 May. Staff Sergeant Forrest Smith of D Company was killed on 28 May. As I remember, Oliver was killed by a sniper; Smith was killed when he stepped on a mine while guiding a tank through thick jungle. They were both good men and outstanding soldiers.

☆ Chapter 94 ☆

29 May–7 June 1969—vicinity northeast of Xuan Loc

We continued to support the 18th ARVN Division for a week or longer, particularly in the jungle five to seven kilometers north of Xuan Loc from where the 33rd NVA Regiment was staging its operations.

On 29 May, I was doing my own scouting from the left seat of a UH-1 piloted by Captain Gus Daub. The morning passed without success. Toward the middle of the afternoon, Captain John Tillson's A Troop made contact with elements of the 33rd NVA Regiment near the village of Ap Cu My. This contact immediately turned into a big firefight. I radioed D Company and told Captain Ron Caldwell to move out with two of his platoons: A Troop needed help.

Former captain Gus Daub recalls this action.

"When A Troop reported contact, Doc told me to put us in orbit over its location. He talked with Tillson over the radio as he sized up the situation. We could not see the enemy's location through all the foliage, but our helicopter was hit in nonvital areas by small-arms fire as we circled at about fifteen hundred feet."

Doc continues.

This was a fairly dense jungle area with lots of tall trees. The troops on the ground were having difficulty sorting out the enemy's exact location. After a few orbits over the contact area, I spotted it. The enemy was hunkered down in a fairly big bunker complex that covered an area about a hundred by two hundred meters. I could spot individual and small groups of NVA milling around, but I could not determine how many more of them were in there. I suspected it to be the base camp for at least an NVA battalion.

I got hold of a FAC and had him bring in two flights of fast movers that dropped high-drag and napalm bombs on the base camp. The napalm started a big fire that burned foliage off the trees, allowing me a better view of the ground.

Tillson and Caldwell were still having difficulty making visual contact, which slowed their progress toward getting their tracks lined up. I could see them clearly and started giving them directions. Even with my help, they continued to have trouble forming an assault line because their tracks were being forced to maneuver around and through trees and brush.

Conditions like this are very dangerous during a firefight. You can't tell where enemy fire is coming from. You start worrying about getting hit from your flanks and rear. Everyone with a weapon is returning fire or ready to shoot at anything he sees moving around him.

Both Tillson and Caldwell were still operating far enough away from the bunker complex that it was safe for me to bring in as much artillery fire as I could. I called in fire from every artillery unit that could reach the contact area, including a battalion of 175mm guns out of Long Binh. Those guns were capable of shooting their 174-pound projectiles almost thirty-three kilometers. I also got hold of regiment and had a couple of Air Cavalry pink teams opconned to me.

Gus Daub resumes.

"I moved our aircraft off to the side of the gun-target line to stay clear of friendly artillery fire. The pink teams were out there with us, waiting for the go ahead to attack the base camp.

"Doc called in a massive amount of artillery fire, adjusting it from one end of the bunker complex to the other and all around its edges. Whenever the artillery let up, if only for a few minutes, he directed the pink teams to make rocket and minigun runs over the bunkers. It was really quite amazing to be up there with Doc. He was bringing in air strikes, telling the tracks where to maneuver, calling in artillery from several units, and directing pink teams—all with perfect precision.

"With artillery fire still coming in, Doc told me to move in low and slow so he could get a better view of what the tracks were doing. I hesitated to get as low and go as slow as he wanted. But the more I hesitated, the more he kept telling me to get lower.

"I soon found myself flying thirty to forty feet above the treetops, too low for what was taking place, but when you flew with Doc, you usually had to throw caution to the wind. This time, Doc's caution-be-damned flying got us in trouble. A 175mm round exploded right beneath us and sent an eight-by-two-inch piece of shrapnel up through the floor of our cockpit and destroyed one of my foot pedals. I could no longer fly the helicopter from the right seat, so Doc took over flying it from the left seat."

Doc resumes.

Losing a foot pedal in flight can lead to a crash. Fortunately, neither of us was hit. While I was looking for a LZ, I got on the radio and had my backup helicopter sent out.

Gus Daub resumes.

"We landed safely in a LZ a klick or two south. As soon as his backup helicopter landed, Doc gathered up his belongings and started toward it. I was still checking out my aircraft and yelled at him to wait for me. He looked back over his shoulder and yelled, 'No, you stay here.' Next thing I knew, Doc lifted off in the backup aircraft, headed back toward the contact area, and left me on the ground."

Doc continues.

I got back over the contact area and saw that Tillson and Caldwell still hadn't gotten together. Shadows were starting to fall and it would be dark within a couple of hours. I didn't want to chance breaking contact. They were doing as good a job as possible under the conditions. However, I was getting a little agitated and told them I was going to come and show them where to go. I couldn't see any better than they could on the ground, but I knew where the bunker complex was located.

Retired Lieutenant Colonel, then Captain, Frederick "Bear" Palmer picks up the story.

"I was working in the S-3 shop where I'd been monitoring this fight. I decided to form several of our Headquarters and Headquarters

Troop's vehicles, which included an M-132 Flamethrower, into a small combat team and go see if we could give a hand.

"I was heading down a trail in an M-577 command track when Doc radioed me and said that he had my column in sight. He told me to stop; he wanted to get on the ground. He landed and switched to the M-132 in very short order. We were back rolling toward the bunker complex in less than two minutes."

Doc continues.

The firefight had been going on for over two hours at this point. Unbeknown to me, the main body had already withdrawn from the base camp, leaving a small security force behind.

I had Palmer put his small combat team between A Troop and D Company's assault formation. The flamethrower I was riding on was smack dab in the middle. I then gave the order to move out. The tracks roared forward and were closing on the base camp when I ordered the M-132's track commander to move us within range of the first row of bunkers.

The moment we were in position, I ordered him to ignite the flamethrower. In a matter of seconds, he started roasting the occupants while the other tracks laid down a heavy volume of canister and machine gun fire. Realizing just how outgunned they were, all of the enemy still able to run broke contact and ran into the surrounding jungle, just like many of their comrades had done earlier in the fight.

I dismounted the flamethrower. With my M-16 in one hand and a sack of grenades in the other, I led a small group of troopers in clearing the bunkers.

Meanwhile, ACAVs and tanks went back and forth throughout the complex, busting bunkers and looking for stragglers. We killed the enemy until dusk—over thirty by actual body count. No telling how many more enemy dead were carried out by the main body when it withdrew into the jungle.

Leach had been orbiting overhead and observed the action from the air. As soon as the shooting stopped, he landed and came to talk with me.

Retired Colonel Jimmie Leach comments on Doc's leadership during this enemy action.

"I could see the action quite well from the air and listened to Doc talking to his commanders over the radio. He was a tremendous fighter, always on the air giving instructions and shouting orders using colorful language—a real dynamo.

"He was also a courageous soldier, particularly so during this fight. Watching it was like watching a training film on combat leadership. He was flawless, killed a good number of NVA, and orchestrated the destruction of a sizable base camp without any of his troopers being killed.

"I have to say this was one of the bravest actions and one of the most inspiring demonstrations of combat leadership I've ever seen, and I've seen a lot of war. I recommended Doc for the Distinguished Service Cross. General Ewell sent my recommendation back downgraded to a Silver Star, the third highest medal of valor. That really pissed me off. Doc's gallantry and leadership in this fight was clearly worthy of the Distinguished Service Cross."

Doc resumes.

I laagered the task force in the bunker complex for the night. We conducted a thorough search of the bunkers the next morning. Weapons were found scattered all over the place. We also found ammo and supplies and picked up maps and documents that I turned over to the regiment's S-2 for analysis.

We remained in the Xuan Loc area for another week before the regiment redeployed to Quan Loi and nearby environs.

Unfortunately, three of the squadron's troopers were killed during small firefights with the 33rd NVA Regiment during this time. Sergeant Darwin Labahn of C Troop was killed on 3 June. He was from South Dakota. Private First Class Alf Eriksen and Sergeant Kenneth Pitre of B Troop were killed during an enemy contact on 7 June. Eriksen was from New York; Pitre was from Louisiana.

✳ Chapter 95 ✳

8–9 June 1969—Iron Triangle, southwest of Lai Khe

Several changes in my squadron's leadership and operations occurred during early June. I pinned captain's bars on Jim Vance. I had confidence in Vance and considered him to be a capable leader, so I made him my Headquarters and Headquarters Troop commander. Captain Lee Fulmer's tour was up, but he extended it to serve on the MACV staff at Saigon. Fulmer's performance during his time in the regiment was outstanding. Captain Art West replaced him as C Troop's commander. Several lieutenants also arrived in the squadron, including First Lieutenants Bill Nash and Paul Baerman. I assigned Nash to A Troop and Baerman to C Troop as platoon leaders.

The squadron was opconned to the 3rd Brigade, 1st Infantry Division, commanded by Colonel Bob Haldane. Haldane, who retired as a three star, was a company tactical officer at West Point during my days as a cadet. He had the reputation of being a good man and superb combat leader. I was looking forward to working with him.

My initial AO was in the Iron Triangle located west and southwest of Lai Khe and stretched southward to a point almost due west of Bien Hoa. The Iron Triangle was a free-fire zone that was free of friendlies and heavily mined in places. Parts of it had been Rome plowed and sprayed with Agent Orange (a powerful herbicide). Scrub brush thrived in other areas, and there were lots of abandoned rice paddies.

I knew the Iron Triangle was definitely hostile territory for us but a haven for the NVA and VC. They frequently staged attacks on Saigon and Bien Hoa out of it. I asked Leach for a reinforcing unit; he opconned 3rd Squadron's L Troop to me. I also relocated my rear area from Xuan Loc to Lai Khe during this time.

On 9 June, we conducted troop-sized recons in the western sector of the Iron Triangle. We were searching for base camps and supply routes. I spent the morning observing my recon teams weave their way through brush and trees and landing occasionally to talk with my troop commanders.

Sometime in midafternoon, L Troop spotted an NVA company on the move down a trail in the woods and began to chase it. I called in a pink team and headed for L Troop's location. Within five minutes, my helicopter was orbiting the contact area at eight hundred to a thousand feet. The woods were fairly thick, making it hard for the tracks to maneuver at high speed and impossible for track commanders to keep the enemy in constant sight. From the air, I could see NVA soldiers scattered out and sprinting toward a stagnant stream, literally running for their lives.

The stream's banks were fairly brush-free. I directed L Troop's commander to bring his tracks into the open area fronting the stream, an ideal position to make quick work of the NVA as they came out of the woods. However, the NVA made it to the wood line ahead of L Troop. They didn't slow down a bit. They just kept running straight for the stream and jumped in. I was watching one NVA in particular and kept my eye on where he'd gone into the stream.

By the time L Troop's tracks were out of the woods and the pink team arrived, the NVA were all in the stream. I knew from experience that the enemy took refuge under overhanging edges of river banks, stayed there until we gave up hunting for them, and then regrouped and went back to their bunkers or resumed their march toward their objective.

I brought the scout ship in very low and slow over the stream. Its prop wash beat the water back but did not reveal any enemy in hiding. I told the scout pilot to pull up and move to the side.

I did my damnedest to tell the troop commander where the NVA had gone into the stream. I ordered him to get his troopers out of their ACAVs and into the water after the NVA. He halted his tracks, but not a one of his troopers dismounted. They just sat there like bumps on a log. I was all pumped up and told the troop commander that I was coming down to show him and his troopers how to get the NVA out of the water.

I hadn't taken my eye off the spot where I saw the one NVA soldier

I'd been watching go into the stream. As soon as I was on the ground, the troop commander and several of his troopers joined me as I walked straight to that spot.

I laid my M-16 down, took off my LBE and helmet and laid them beside it, and started walking very slowly along the edge of the water. The brown and murky water was waist-to-chest deep on me and littered with floating patches of thick algae. No doubt, it was full of leeches.

It didn't take me long to find the bastard even though his head was covered with a mat of algae. I jumped into the water, grabbed his AK-47 with one hand and his throat with the other, and threw him up onto the bank. Two troopers took custody of my prisoner and tied him up.

The entire troop was amazed by what they'd seen, and I climbed out of the stream to congratulatory cheers. Based on my example, a dozen or more troopers then jumped into the stream and grabbed additional prisoners. Meanwhile, L Troop's interpreter got the NVA soldier I caught to talk on the spot. He was an NVA lieutenant but didn't provide us with actionable intelligence. I left him with L Troop to bring back to my CP with the rest of the POWs they were rounding up.

L Troop's commander wrote me up for a Bronze Star. He also told someone from the Public Information Office (PIO) about the crazy sonofabitch he saw jump into a stream unarmed and grab an armed NVA officer by the throat. Although I was not interviewed for it, a brief article about my "fishing for the enemy" was published in the August edition of *Blackhorse,* the regiment's monthly newspaper.

★ Chapter 96 ★

10–18 June 1969—Iron Triangle, K4 Woods, and Lai Khe

I didn't have the opportunity to meet with Colonel Haldane before we made our first contacts with the enemy. His operations officer was providing my missions and I was providing sitreps to him about our actions.

Retired Lieutenant General Robert Haldane recalls his first face-to-face meeting with Doc in Vietnam.

"Doc wasn't in my company at West Point but I knew who he was. I think everybody did. Doc had a way of making himself known and was hard to ignore, even as a cadet.

"The Eleventh Cav was famous for developing contacts then asking for reinforcements from the First Infantry. It didn't matter if the commander of our reinforcing unit outranked the Eleventh Cav commander whose unit was in contact, the Eleventh Cav always took control and told our guys what to do.

"This is how, as a major and troop commander, Doc often took charge of one of our lieutenant colonel's battalions during an enemy contact. I used to fight with George Patton and Jim Dozier over this. Although our fights were closer to friendly disagreements than divisive, bitter arguments, I often felt like I was fighting more with them than the enemy. Of course, we got along and fought side by side just as if we were all in the same outfit.

"Soon after Doc's squadron was opconned to me, I was in my helicopter with several staff officers, including my artillery fire support co-ordinator. Doc was also in the air and radioed my fire support coordi-nator. Doc started telling him in colorful terms that he needed rapid reaction to his fire missions and wanted his Howitzer Battery back. Doc wasn't about to take no for an answer. He was an aggressive guy known to have a hot temper, and he got a little abrasive with some people. That didn't worry me. I liked guys like Doc. They were the ones who did most of the fighting.

"I interrupted and told Doc to land so we could have a face-to-face meeting. We stood in the middle of a field and talked the situation over. It was a good conversation. I fully supported him in getting his How-itzer Battery back under his command. I told him I would talk to the di-vision artillery commander. In the meantime, I told him I'd give him my fire support coordinator right then—'You can keep him all day.'

"Doc was pleased with our agreement. I told my fire support coor-dinator to get in the back of his helicopter. I monitored the radio chat-ter for the rest of the day but never heard my fire support coordinator call in a fire mission. When he returned that evening, I asked him what he'd done all day because he hadn't been calling in artillery fire. He stood there, proud as a peacock, and told me that Doc let him shoot dinks out of his helicopter all afternoon: 'We must have killed fifty of them!' That didn't surprise me. That was Doc, and Doc had made an in-stant ally in my fire support coordinator."

Doc resumes.

The Squadron's Howitzer Battery had been emplaced in a fire sup-port base (FSB) for many months. As I recall, it was FSB Holiday Inn. Rather than providing direct support to the squadron, it was covering a sector of the 1st Division's overall fire support plan.

The 1st Division's artillery commander did not like the idea of giving up direct control of any artillery unit. What he thought didn't mean dick to me. I was taking my Howitzer Battery back. I softened his resistance by promising him that no matter where we bivouacked for the night, I would always tie my battery into his fire support plan. From that time on, my Howitzer Battery marched with the Headquarters Troop ele-ments.

The Howitzer Battery had maintenance problems from being static too long. Its howitzers required some repairs and tuning up to keep up with the squadron's frequent moves. This took a few days.

Shortly after my Howitzer Battery began marching with the squadron, C Troop made contact and called in with a fire mission. The enemy's location required the battery to shoot "danger close, line over." It was a classic hip shoot and should have been no problem. However, a short round wounded a dozen of C Troop's soldiers—one man lost his arm. I broke into the fire mission and called, "Check fire!" C Troop's commander radioed me and reported that he was breaking contact to evacuate his casualties as quickly as possible.

I was furious!

I flew back to the guns to find out what the problem was. I landed, grabbed the battery commander, and started walking the gun line. The first thing I noticed was that none of the guns had its spade grips down. I couldn't believe my eyes! Spade grips prevent howitzers from incurring recoil shift during fire missions. I then started checking powder lot numbers by gun and found another problem: they changed powder lot numbers on one gun during the fire mission—a major fuck up in shooting artillery "danger close, line over" friendly troops.

I called regiment to get our senior artillery liaison officer flown out immediately. I wanted him to confirm what I had found. He confirmed my findings in short order.

The battery commander worked in the regiment's artillery liaison shop before taking command of the Howitzer Battery. We all liked him. Likable or not, I couldn't risk further friendly casualties while he got his shit together. I relieved him on the spot.

I put the XO in temporary command and went looking for a new battery commander. After reviewing all of the 1st Infantry's available field artillery captains' files, I interviewed Captain Ed Plymale, an Army National Guard officer from Kentucky, and hired him for the job. He did an outstanding job for me from day one.

Retired Lieutenant Colonel Ed Plymale recalls his interview with Doc.

"I was initially assigned to the First Battalion, Fifth Field Artillery, one of the units in the First Infantry Division's direct support artillery. I was running an FDC out in the middle of an area being cleared by Rome plows.

"Doc walked into the FDC and asked me to brief him on the artillery coverage for his AO. He listened, but didn't ask questions about artillery support. Instead, he started chitchatting and asked me if I'd like to command his artillery battery. I told him, 'Yes, sir.' He told me, 'Okay, I'll make that happen.'

"Sure thing, about eight to ten days later, I was picked up by helicopter and flown to the First Squadron's Howitzer Battery, which was located on the end of a runway.

"Doc was direct, to the point, a real 'let's go, get the job done' commander. I highly respected and enjoyed working for him. I listened to his command net for entertainment as much as I did to do my job. When the shit hit the fan, Doc's command net was the best show in Vietnam."

Doc resumes.

Sometime around 17 or 18 June, our recons started to payoff when C Troop's ACAVs and Sheridans swept an area of jungle near the K4 Woods. They made contact and killed nineteen of the Vietcong Dong Nai Regiment's soldiers and ravaged its base camp. Other small actions started occurring daily.

⋆ Chapter 97 ⋆

Based on intel reports, I moved the squadron out of Fire Base Jim early in the morning to sweep an area where NVA were located. This was Captain Jim Vance's first operation as my Headquarters and Headquarters Troop commander. Unfortunately, he was seriously wounded in it.

Retired Colonel Jim Vance talks about being wounded in action.

"I was leading a provisional combat element consisting of a mixed bag of tracks that made up a fine fighting force. We were positioned on the right wing of the squadron formation. A couple of the Air Cav's pink teams were working with us.

"A little after noon, we crossed a creek and were climbing up the other side when we stumbled into a classic L-shaped ambush. Small arms fire hit both my right-side gunner and me right away, dropping both of us to the deck of my M-113 command track. I had two Sheridans loaded with 152mm canister rounds and an M-132 Flamethrower right behind me. My assistant track commander took over my position and joined them in cleaning the NVA's clock.

"The canister rounds not only killed a lot of dinks, they shredded the brush of leaves. The flamethrowers charred a lot of dink bodies. The initial engagement was over in a flash, leaving around thirty of the enemy dead. None of my guys were killed, just a couple of us wounded."

Doc resumes.

I flew to Vance's site and landed. He was a bloody mess. An AK-47 round had ripped open his right arm from wrist to elbow. After a medic got Vance and his wounded gunner stabilized, we put them in the back of my helicopter and flew them to the MASH at Lai Khe, just minutes away.

Newly promoted Captain Doug Starr was flying as my assistant S-3 for the day. He had been itching for a troop command to open up. Before we lifted off, I gave him command of my Headquarters Troop.

Retired Colonel Doug Starr talks about this action.

"I heard the contact happen over our command net. Vance was badly wounded and needed immediate evacuation. A scout ship going in to pick him up took heavy ground fire and crashed into the jungle, but our helicopter managed to land safely.

"A medic was treating Vance in his track when we made it to him. He was covered in blood, but alive. Doc told me to take command. Vance handed me his map. It was sopping in my West Point classmate's blood and splattered with pieces of his flesh. The first thing I had to do was wipe it off.

"I picked up Vance's CVC helmet and put it on so I'd be able to communicate over the radio. Vance's blood started trickling down the back of my neck, and I was standing in a pool of his blood. I didn't bother to take the helmet off and wipe the rest of Vance's blood out, or worry about getting his blood on my boots; I was too caught up in the moment and focused on going after the dinks who had survived the ambush."

Doc continues.

I escorted Vance into the MASH facilities. On the way in, Vance asked me several times not to let them cut off his arm. I reassured him they would not do that. I grabbed the doctor in charge and told him to save the kid's arm. He gave me some bullshit about that being his prerogative as he saw it.

I had Vance's blood all over my uniform and was in no mood to take shit from a doctor. His arrogance made me hostile and mad. I jumped down his throat.

"I've got a fucking fight to get back to, but I'll be back. When I get back, my man's arm had better still be on him, or I will personally have your ass."

He got the message; I went back to the fight.

Doug Starr resumes.

"Other than the killing that took place during the ambush, this firefight was relatively inconsequential. By the time Doc returned, we had chased the surviving dinks into their nearby base camp, and the fight was tapering down.

"Doc's helicopter went into a low orbit over the contact area from where he could see our tracks idling in the middle of the base camp. The next thing I heard was Doc calling me over the radio. I answered his call and he started in, 'What the fuck's going on? Why aren't you guys moving?'

"Doc was very demanding and aggressive and he expected the same from his subordinate leaders. If you weren't up to his standards, you didn't last long with him. I learned very early that if you let him intimidate you he'd run all over you. I answered his questions accordingly, 'We're searching the base camp. Soon as I have something, I'll call you, over.' He gave me a 'Roger, out,' and I went back to searching the base camp."

Doc resumes.

I was impressed by Starr's aggressiveness in chasing down and killing the NVA who shot Vance and his gunner. Hunting and killing the enemy would be Starr's specialty for the remainder of his tour of duty under me. He was one of the best troop commanders I ever saw in combat, and he later proved to be a fantastic armored cavalry regiment commander during Desert Storm.

I checked on Vance later that day. He was stabilized and would not lose his arm, but the doctor avoided me just the same. Two of our troopers were not so fortunate. Private First Class James Nesselrotte of A Troop and Specialist Five Victor Shaffer of D Company were killed during this operation. They were both Ohio boys. Nesselrotte was from Painesville; Shaffer was from Toledo. They were first-rate soldiers and good young men.

Jim Vance resumes.

"I was really pissed off over being shot. I was a bloody mess before my medic got a tourniquet around my arm and wrapped my forearm with sterile gauze. I was never in any real pain but was damn worried my arm might be amputated, which might have happened if Doc hadn't intervened. I wanted to stay, but the extent of my wound necessitated my being medically evacuated out-of-country.

"I was just twenty-four years old when I was in the squadron and had a lot to learn about leadership. Doc had a formative influence on me. He personified the adage, 'Fortune favors the bold.' The lessons I learned from Doc were ones I tried to teach officers who served under me for the rest of my career."

✴ Chapter 98 ✴

20 June 1969—northeastern sector of the Iron Triangle

Our recons in force were resulting in brief, hot actions but not turning up the intelligence we needed on the size and disposition of the enemy force operating in our AO. There was no better way to get that kind of intel than by taking POWs and getting them to talk.

I put the word out for several days, during my evening briefings, that I wanted some POWs. It wasn't long before one was hand delivered to me.

Retired Colonel, then First Lieutenant, Paul Baerman recounts his capture of a POW.

"I have to go back to my first conversation with Doc to put this event in context. Bill Nash and I were classmates at West Point. We arrived at the Eleventh Armored Cavalry Regiment within a week of each other and were subsequently assigned to the First Squadron.

"I first met Doc at the regiment's Xuan Loc base camp, where I caught a helicopter ride with him out to C Troop's NDP. As soon as we were at altitude, Doc started asking me about West Point. In particular, he wanted to know where I'd graduated in my class. I told him thirty-ninth out of seven hundred eight. I thought he might be impressed by that, but instead, it just pissed him off.

" 'Goddamn it! I need fighters and get fed smart bastards. The trouble with you smart bastards is that you don't want to fight. You just want to avoid getting killed so you can go back for a graduate degree and teach at West Point.'

"He never let up until we sat down at C Troop. As I picked up my gear to dismount, I made a vow to myself that I was going to show Doc that 'smart bastards' are also fighters.

"The opportunity came when we moved into a new area to conduct search and destroy missions. We'd all been told that Doc wanted POWs. I was looking for the opportunity to deliver one to him.

"We were working the area thoroughly when we came upon an NVA soldier that my side gunner shot and wounded. He was lying on the ground about fifty meters from my track. I ordered my driver to stop.

"I took off my CVC helmet, hopped off my track, and started running toward the wounded soldier with only my holstered .45 to protect me. I didn't get far from my track before dust started flying all around me! The wounded dink's buddies were shooting at me!

"I don't know what I was thinking, but I picked up my pace and zig-zagged my way to him. He saw me coming and was bringing his AK-47 up to shoot me. I saw what he was doing and kicked him in the chest, knocking the wind out of him. I grabbed his weapon with one hand, the back of his shirt collar with the other, and started dragging him toward my track. Thankfully, my platoon sergeant and troopers put a lot of suppressive fire on the area where they saw enemy soldiers shooting at me, so my return trip was less eventful.

"Doc landed and was standing by his helicopter by this time, so I traipsed right past my track, dragging my POW behind me, and handed him over to Doc and said, 'So there.' Doc gave me a thumbs up and told me, 'That's good.'

"I walked back to my track to get a drink of water and critique my troopers on how to capture wounded enemy. After I'd finished, my platoon sergeant took me aside and told me, 'If you ever do something that stupid again, I will kill you personally.' It wasn't until that very moment that I realized what a great risk I'd taken to prove myself worthy to Doc."

Doc resumes.

I have to admit my bias against academic types at that time. My experience with the majority of the ones I'd served with was that they wouldn't do anything that would get their hands or uniforms dirty. You can't lead effectively that way.

From the first time I read it, I was inspired by Teddy Roosevelt's famous speech in which he said:

> The credit belongs to the man who is actually in the arena, whose face is marred by dust and sweat and blood; who strives valiantly; who errs, and comes short again and again, because there is no effort without error and shortcoming; but who does actually strive to do the deeds; who knows the great enthusiasms, the great devotions; who spends himself in a worthy cause; who at the best knows in the end the triumph of high achievement, and who at the worst, if he fails, at least fails while daring greatly, so that his place shall never be with those cold and timid souls who know neither victory nor defeat.

I've always taken these words as praise for doers not thinkers.

I can still picture Baerman and his POW today, nearly forty years later. He was wearing a sweat-stained T-shirt, no helmet, had an AK-47 in hand, and came huffing and puffing, dragging a POW behind him, to where I was standing. He was proud of himself and had every right to be. I was proud of him, too. What he'd done was very brave and could have easily gotten him killed. And he'd delivered me a POW who sang like a bird.

That was a defining moment that redefined what I thought about "smart bastards." Baerman defined himself as a fearless fighter and that changed how I thought about guys who graduated from West Point in the top of their class.

Retired Major General Bill Nash's first encounter with Doc was similar to that of his classmate.

"I went through the regiment's in-country school at Xuan Loc before reporting for duty with First Squadron. The S-1 picked up a couple of other guys and me in a helicopter and flew us out to the Squadron CP located at Fire Base Thunder One, near Lai Khe. En route, the S-1 told me in no uncertain terms that the First Squadron's commander was a tough bastard. 'If he gets on you and you back off, he's going to chew you up.'

"I went to the CP and reported for duty. Doc was there. He told me to come with him. We walked outside and stood in the middle of the fire base, and then the interrogation began. He wanted to know where I'd graduated in my class. I told him about thirtieth. He told me that was too high.

" 'All smart guys like you want to go to grad school so you can teach at West Point. Do you know what I want to do?'

" 'No, sir.'

" 'Kill dinks. That's what I want to do.'

"While we were engaged in our conversation about personal aspirations, the Howitzer Battery commander came walking by. It appeared to me that he wanted to pass unnoticed, but that was not to be. Doc chewed his ass about something, and then went back to chewing me out for graduating too high in my class.

"About this time, Captain Frederick 'Bear' Palmer, A Troop's commander, suddenly appeared. Doc introduced me to Bear, and told him that I was going to be his new First Platoon leader, as he was pulling First Lieutenant Skip Gill off the line to make him an assistant S-3.

"Bear wasn't one bit happy about this news. Doc hadn't mentioned anything about moving Gill to Bear prior to this. Gill was a proven combat leader. Doc was taking Gill and replacing him with an unknown that Bear had just met.

"Bear started to argue, but Doc cut him off and chewed him out in front of me. I don't remember all that was said but Doc ended it by looking Bear square in the eye and telling him, 'It's a decision! It's a decision! No discussion!'

"Bear just rolled his eyes and told me to come with him. And that was how my working with Doc began.

"Little did I realize that working for Doc in Vietnam would become the most important and formative experience of my career. He taught me how to be aggressive. He gave me a reason to wake up in the morning—to go out and fight! And he taught me how to fight.

"That was the only time in my career when I knew exactly what I existed for—to go out and fight, everything else was secondary.

"There is an old adage, 'Those who lead from the front show slow soldiers how to die.' Well, Doc led from the front and didn't die. There were times when I thought Doc was trying to get us all killed, but his casualties were relatively few given the squadron's incredible number of enemy contacts.

"I have a great deal of respect and admiration for Doc as a combat commander and as a man whom I could always count on to be there when I needed him."

✷ Chapter 99 ✷

Our time in the Iron Triangle was tough duty. Colonel Haldane gave me anything I needed to ensure my success, including an AN/TPS-25 Ground Surveillance Radar and crew. The radar itself was mounted on an eighty-four-foot tower, which gave it an eighteen-kilometer range. I kept that radar with me in my CP area. Haldane also opconned a rifle company to me. It played a significant role during our assaults on enemy bunker complexes.

We had a number of contacts during this period where we were literally sitting on top of tunnels that housed enemy soldiers. The enemy would come out to fight and then disappear back into their tunnels. We could hear them down there, but couldn't locate their tunnel entrances and never did get a POW to show us the entrance to one. This was very frustrating. We were out there "alone" to kill or capture the enemy where we found him, but we couldn't find him in this network of tunnels.

We had a lot of tracks damaged by mines in the Iron Triangle. Many of them could be repaired in the field. Those requiring major repairs had to be towed to the rear area down a road that crossed over a bridge at Ben Cat. There was a sign at either end of the bridge stating that only one fifty-ton vehicle was allowed on the bridge at a time. There were also Vietnamese guards at both ends of the bridge, who were supposed to enforce this restriction, but they were ineffective—the bridge collapsed when several vehicles with a collective weight exceeding the max weight limit tried to cross it sometime before we started using it.

D Company had a motor sergeant named Sergeant Dorothy. He was quite a character and tank repairman par excellence. He kept our M-48s running better than those in any other unit in the regiment. No matter when you saw Dorothy, he was covered in grime and grease. That didn't bother me; he could fix tanks.

Dorothy used an M-88 Tank Retriever to tow disabled tanks to the repair area. These vehicles were very powerful and could tow two tanks in tandem at a time. During the middle of our time in the Iron Triangle, two of our M-48 tanks needed to be towed to our rear area at Lai Khe.

Sergeant Dorothy hooked the tanks up to an M-88 for the trip. He was driving at max speed as he approached the Ben Cat Bridge, ignoring the warning sign. He made it across with the M-88 and one tank before the bridge collapsed, leaving the second tank hanging by its tow bar in the river.

This incident was reported immediately to the 1st Division's TOC and subsequently to me. The 1st Division's engineer flew to the bridge right away and got hold of Dorothy. I landed very quickly thereafter. The engineer, a lieutenant colonel, was eating on Dorothy when I arrived. I dismissed Dorothy and this lieutenant colonel started chewing on me. Another time, I would have gone toe to toe with him, but under the circumstances, I just ignored him and walked away. The damage had been done.

In talking to Dorothy about why he attempted the crossing with two tanks in tow, he told me that the week before he had made it with one tank behind the M-88 and had no problem. Somehow that made him think he could make it across the bridge with two tanks in tow.

Major General Talbott was damn mad when he heard about the bridge collapse. So damn mad that he let it be known that he did not want to see me for a while. I got the message and stayed away from his headquarters for quite a while.

On 2 July, C Troop entered a base camp and took two enemy prisoners just before crushing their bunker. The next day, they dug into the ruins of the bunkers and found thirty enemy dead. According to Captain West, this was a big surprise to everyone.

On 5 July, A Troop killed ten enemy soldiers during a hard-fought battle near the site of C Troop's encounter three days earlier.

The following day, A and C Troops and D Company teamed up for a big fight in the jungle north of the Saigon River, killing over twenty NVA. Unfortunately, three Squadron troopers were killed during this action: Specialist Four Kurtis Berry of C Troop and Fort Wayne, Indiana; Sergeant Larry Johnson of A Troop and Decorah, Iowa; and Specialist Four William Rigdon of Manchester, Ohio.

One day later, the Howitzer Battery's Private First Class David Shaffner from Jonesville, North Carolina, was killed in action in the vicinity of Xuan Loc.

✶ Chapter 100 ✶

9 July 1969—Blackhorse headquarters, Quan Loi, 1st Squadron CP, Iron Triangle, and 1st Squadron rear area, Lai Khe.

I looked at over a dozen majors' records before interviewing Major Bill Good for my executive officer's position. Good was an unlikely candidate, but there was something about him and his background that raised my interest in speaking to him face to face.

Retired Colonel, then Major, Bill Good talks about how he came to be XO of 1st Squadron and what faced him when he started overseeing its rear area administration and maintenance functions.

"Most field-grade officers got into the number-one armor unit in Vietnam by having a sponsor—a high-ranking friend in the unit willing to speak up for them and recommend their assignment to the unit. I did not have a sponsor. I was a very junior major who got to the regiment via a letter-writing campaign by myself and my boss at the University of Wisconsin, Milwaukee. I did not know one person in the regiment prior to my assignment and was treated terribly when I arrived. I rode from Long Binh to Xuan Loc in a five-ton dump truck. Thank heavens they had room in the front seat.

"Lieutenant Colonel Larry Wright, the regiment's XO, made me the psyops officer. When I told him the regiment was not authorized a psyops officer, he responded, 'Do you want in the regiment or not?' I had to say 'Yes.' I also knew full well that I was going to have to work like hell to get a real job.

"After orientation, I flew to the regiment's headquarters at Quan Loi. Lieutenant Colonel Grail Brookshire was the S-3. He sort of took me under his wing and made me the S-3 plans officer, another unauthorized position.

"I shortly found out that there was one vacant major slot in the regiment: executive officer, First Squadron. This position was being saved for a Major Dick Hoyt, one of Wright's fair-haired boys, who was expected to arrive later in July. I was told that the First Squadron commander was Major-promotable Doc Bahnsen and the S-3 was Major Don Snow. Snow was doing both the S-3 and XO duties—a Herculean task.

"I waited for either Doc or Don to come into the TOC so I could make my desires known. I met Don Snow first and talked to him about going to the XO job. A day or so later, I was informed that I was going to 1st Squadron as the 'temporary' XO. Larry Wright was madder than hell, but I really did not give a damn.

"Don picked me up by helicopter and we flew to First Squadron's area somewhere in the Iron Triangle. It was getting pretty dark when we landed among a group of ten or so broken down armored vehicles, including an M-88 track recovery vehicle with its boom raised and both its engine and transmission were missing. The NDP had just been moved and these disabled vehicles had to be left behind.

"We flew on to the NDP in the dark where I met Doc. He was in the TOC sitting on a chair between the S-3 and S-2 M-557s. One twenty-five-watt lightbulb hung from the canvas extension. Doc told me to sit in a chair right under it. I could barely see Doc and only the forms of other people standing around watching us.

"Doc started the interview by giving me holy hell for the fact that my records indicated that I had been an MP. I explained to him that I went on active duty as a reserve officer in armor branch. I applied for a Regular Army commission in armor but failed my RA physical because I was color blind. The Army would not give me a Regular Army commission in armor but offered me one in military police. I didn't want to transfer to the MPs but it was the only way I was going to get an RA commission. I took the Army's offer, served my two-year commitment in the MPs, and then succeeded in getting transferred to armor branch.

"My interview was quite an encounter, but I was impressed. Doc was a lot of spit and shit, but there was nothing fake about him. He gave me hell during my interview, but I didn't back down one bit. He liked that and gave me the job.

402 ★ American Warrior

"The next day, I told Doc that I did not like the 'temporary' label. I asked him to get it removed and remove me anytime he didn't like the job I was doing. He agreed. He then told me to get on a chopper and go back to the squadron's rear area at Lai Khe. I was to straighten it out and support the fighting troops. I got the last word, 'Yes, sir!'

"When I got to Lai Khe, I was met by First Sergeant Maples of Headquarters and Headquarters Troop, who showed me to my van. The next day, I met all the other personnel. The squadron maintenance officer had my deepest sympathies. The motor pool area was a sea of mud."

✯ Chapter 101 ✯

14 July 1969—Iron Triangle

Operations in the Iron Triangle were nonstop. The radar opconned to me helped us locate enemy forces before they found us. That was a great advantage. We often used it to set ambushes for enemy units on the move through our AO.

The NVA operated across the Saigon River where it bordered the Iron Triangle to the west. They had several points along the river where they crossed it in boats they kept hidden along the banks. A network of trails on both sides of the river led to these crossing points. I had Air Cavalry pink teams recon this area routinely. I also sent tracks to recon this area on the ground. It was not unusual for my ground recon teams to find wooden boats used by the NVA to shuttle soldiers across the river. When they found boats, they blew them. What we didn't know was when the enemy was going to make a river crossing.

One night, I sent Captain Doug Starr and a combat team formed from my Headquarters Troop, including my 919th Engineer Platoon then led by Sergeant First Class Raven, to set an ambush along the east side of the Saigon River. This particular area had been sprayed with Agent Orange and Rome plowed. There was scrub brush in the area, along with the usual high grass, but no tall trees. Starr made sure that his vehicles were well camouflaged and waited.

Just before dawn the next morning, our radar crew alerted Starr, as it started tracking a company-sized column of NVA as they approached the river from the west. They were walking at a pretty good clip. I suspect these NVA were headed to the nearby tunnels to hide out during the day and wanted to get into them before daylight.

The radar crew continued to track the enemy as they crossed the river in shuttles. After they'd all crossed, they formed up in a single-file column and headed straight toward Starr's ambush, about two hundred meters from the river. The radar crew kept Starr up to date on the column's progress. Starr let them walk right into his ambush before ordering his tracks to open fire. Enemy soldiers situated near the front of their column were killed instantly. Those walking in the rear scattered into the scrub brush.

Starr brought in a pink team to assist him in tracking down enemy soldiers who survived the ambush. He also called in artillery fire before sweeping the area. I made it to this contact several hours after the initial ambush. Starr was still policing up NVA but the fight was finished. There were no friendly casualties during this mission.

On 14 July, our radar crew reported movement in an open field just outside my CP's perimeter. Starr quickly scrambled several ACAVs and led them to the area.

Retired Colonel Doug Starr describes this action.

"It was just getting dark when the S-3 shop said our radar crew was picking up movement about two kilometers from our CP. We had no troops in that area, meaning that the radar was detecting enemy troop movement. As soon as the radar crew determined the enemy's direction of travel, I led a team of four ACAVs and went out to intercept.

"We moved very quickly while we still had daylight. Within a matter of fifteen minutes, we pulled up out of a ravine bordering an open field and spotted the enemy force. We let loose a barrage of .50-caliber and M-60 machine gun fire, and the entire enemy force went down in an instant. We halted, dismounted, and went over to search their bodies. All of a sudden, one of them stood up and came running at us firing his AK-47. He was brave but foolish. Sergeant Blankenship dropped him in his tracks with a burst of M-60 fire.

"We swept the area and counted fifteen dead enemy soldiers dressed in black pajamas and wearing web gear. We also discovered that they were carrying a large amount of piastres—most likely the payroll for one or more of their units in the area.

"I called Doc with a sitrep. He told me to leave the dead where they were. He expected some of their comrades would come looking for them. I sent the money and half my team back to the CP. I sixty-nined the other two to give us good fields of fire in all directions and remained in the middle of that field overnight. It was a very eerie night; dark and noiseless, except for the noises we were making maintaining radio contact with the CP.

"No one came to collect the dead bodies, so we left them. Two days passed without an enemy sighting in the vicinity. By that time, the enemy dead were starting to smell very badly, so we buried them in a collective grave on the edge of the field."

Doc resumes.

Earlier in the day, D Company made contact with a company-sized NVA force at a base camp located in the jungle north of the Iron Triangle. This was a relatively brief action that resulted in eleven enemy killed.

The 1st Division was tickled to death with our operations in this enemy-infested area where we found and killed NVA as a matter of routine.

✴ Chapter 102 ✴

For the most part, heavily mined areas made travel over old roads and well-worn trails too risky. Consequently, we used our tracks to bust jungle daily in order to make fresh trails for our ongoing operations. We did our best, but we couldn't bust enough jungle to steer clear of all existing roads and trails, nor could all the mined areas be avoided. We had a job to do, and that job took a toll on our vehicles.

Good had his hands full trying to get all of our damaged vehicles evacuated to Lai Khe, repaired, and returned to the front line. He asked me to stand down the whole squadron for a week's worth of maintenance. I told him I couldn't kill the enemy on stand down; he could have two days to come to the NDP for repairs.

Retired Colonel Bill Good recalls this maintenance stand down.

"The NDP was on firm ground so we could pull maintenance on the whole vehicle. We took all kinds of parts and major assemblies, to include engines, transmissions, and track pads. We flew every mechanic we could get our hands on out there, and we also took extra rations, ice, soda, and beer.

"On the first morning, two or three Donut Dollies caught a ride on the last chopper out. When they landed, every eye in the unit was on them. To the troopers these young women were clones of Marilyn Monroe. The distraction was temporary. We had work to do, got it done, and got the women out safely.

"During the stand down, Doc and I had our only confrontation. One of the helicopters was ready to fly back to Lai Khe, and I saw Captain Art West, C Troop's commander, getting on it. I told him to stay at the NDP where the action was. Of course, he reported this to Doc, and Doc called me to the CP and raised hell.

" 'You don't tell my green-tabbers what to do. I am the commander here and I am the only one who tells my commanders what to do. If there's a problem with one of them, bring it to me. I'll handle it from there. Understand?' "

" 'Yes, sir.'

"This confrontation taught me an important lesson: I was not in the rating chain of any commander, and my influence as the XO had to be applied with great finesse."

∗ Chapter 103 ∗

18–27 July 1969—Ben Cat and Lai Khe

As I left getting the job done up to Bill Good and my unit commanders, I was unaware that not all the maintenance problems were fixed during stand down. About a week later, I became aware of just how little effort Captain Art West had put into getting his tracks in shape.

Former first lieutenant Bill Sturley, C Troop's 2nd Platoon leader at the time, relates what he had to go through to get new tracks for his ACAVs.

"When I arrived in C Troop, our ACAVs had seen a lot of action and were starting to show their age. The pin bushings had worn out and we couldn't properly adjust track tension. Loose tracks tended to come off when the vehicle made violent movements, like during a firefight. The only option available to the ACAV crew was to dismount and struggle to reinstall the errant track—not a favorite pastime when the enemy was shooting at you. The condition of our tracks was so bad that it was putting the whole platoon in jeopardy, unnecessarily so in my mind.

"I spoke to Captain West, my troop commander, before the stand down and expected to receive new tracks then, but didn't. After the stand down, I went back to West with another request for new tracks only to be turned down again. This became routine, I asked, he turned me down. The more I asked, the angrier he became. It got to the point where he told me there were no ACAV tracks available anywhere in the country. He wasn't helping; I thought my men deserved better.

"Early one afternoon, we rolled into the small village of Ben Cat where fuel was waiting for us on the side of the road. As we pulled into the area, I noticed Major Bahnsen getting out of his helicopter. I didn't know him. He was usually overhead in his helicopter, and I didn't attend his evening briefings or talk to him when he landed to speak with West during a contact.

"I told my platoon sergeant, Bill Bathe, that I was going over to meet Major Bahnsen, who was now talking with Captain West. I asked Bathe to give me a few minutes with them, then come over and say there was a problem that needed my immediate personal attention.

"I introduced myself to Major Bahnsen and spent a few minutes talking with him before Bathe did as I'd asked. Just as I'd hoped, Major Bahnsen wanted to know what the problem was. I told him to come and see for himself. He accompanied Bathe and me to my ACAVs. Of course, Captain West tagged along. Major Bahnsen actually got down in the dirt and took a good look at every one of my ACAVs before announcing that they all needed new tracks. He said he'd have them to me before dark and left.

"After Major Bahnsen was out of earshot, Captain West chewed my ass royally. I didn't care. My men's lives were worth getting my butt chewed over doing something to ensure their safety.

"It started to get dark and no tracks had showed up. I was starting to wonder if Major Bahnsen was a man of his word. All of a sudden, a Chinook appeared on the horizon. We think its carrying our tracks and we pop smoke. It hovered above my platoon and made its drop—155mm ammunition for the Howitzer Battery, which was on the other side of the field. The next thing I knew, another Chinook appeared and dropped a second load of artillery ammunition right by my platoon. My troopers sure as hell weren't going to lug that ammo to the artillery's location. If they wanted it, they could come and get it.

"By now my disappointment factor was redlined. No way was I getting new tracks. Oh, was I ever a man of little faith in my squadron commander. A third Chinook came in and dropped tracks for all of my vehicles! Major Bahnsen delivered as promised. And that's how I remember him: as a man of his word."

Doc resumes.

I have no idea why West didn't order new tracks for his ACAVs. The way I saw combat leadership, you made sure your soldiers had what they needed to fight. If you got your ass chewed or pissed somebody off in the process, so what? It's more important to keep your soldiers alive. And Sturley did just that. I was damn proud of him for doing it.

I got word that my squadron was reverting to regimental control under opcon to the 1st Cavalry Division within a few days. Before leaving the Iron Triangle, we lost Private First Class Richard Cutler of A Troop during an action on 21 July. He was from Sherrard, Illinois.

During the time the squadron was attached to Haldane's brigade, we were in continuous contact and killed a large number of the NVA. In fact, out of the twenty or so battalions in the 1st Division, my squadron accounted for about 25 percent of its total body count during this period.

Retired Lieutenant General Robert Haldane comments.

"Doc was a fabulous fighter and a good man. He kept his tracks grinding all through his AO until they got every enemy they could find. I really enjoyed working with him and his outfit."

Doc resumes.

I made sure that my troopers were properly recognized for their heroism during our time in the Iron Triangle. As a way to thank me, Major General Talbott held a dinner in my honor in his mess at Lai Khe. It was a good meal, served on china with all the white linen flare customary in a general's mess. I had a nice time, enjoyed talking with General Talbot and his staff, and was proud to have had the opportunity to give them a hand in thinning the enemy's ranks in their AO.

Retired Lieutenant General Orwin C. Talbott comments on Doc.

"Doc Bahnsen was a character. There was nothing genteel about him. He was gung ho and a great fighter. He didn't let sleeping dogs lie; he brought them out and took care of them. His Air Cavalry Troop was very unusual and the best outfit of its kind in Vietnam. He also excelled as a squadron commander and did a great job during his time in the Iron Triangle."

✶ Chapter 104 ✶

29 July 1969—Loc Ninh

After leaving the Iron Triangle, I established my CP at Loc Ninh, where it remained for the rest of my tour. Soon after I got set up, I held a firepower demonstration for newly arrived personnel.

Former first lieutenant Ray de Wit observed this firepower demonstration.

"I guess the old adage of 'first impressions are the lasting ones' applies to one of my most vivid memories of my year in Vietnam.

"The helicopter ride to the First Squadron's base camp at Loc Ninh was relatively uneventful. Upon arrival at Loc Ninh, I hopped out of the chopper and walked to the CP. After checking in, I was directed to the end of the Loc Ninh airstrip to watch the end of a firepower demonstration that Major Bahnsen, the commander, was putting on for guys new to the squadron. A curious crowd of local villagers was also watching the demonstration.

"There must have been twenty tracks, including M-132 Flamethrowers [Zippos], lined up and taking turns firing to the amazement of soldiers and the horror of the locals. After the .50s, main guns, mortars, and M-60s finished firing, it was time for the coup de grâce: the Zippo demonstration! Standing on the top of one of the Zippos, Major Bahnsen signaled the gunner to open up. Napalm flew out of the nozzle, but no flame! A second attempt met with the same result—no flame. Openly frustrated, Major Bahnsen, in an action that I later found to be normal for him, pulled out his personal lighter, stood to the side of the nozzle, and signaled the gunner to try again. Once again, the napalm came gushing out. Only this time, Major Bahnsen lit it with his personal lighter, sending a thirty-two-second-long stream of fire two hundred meters into the bushes.

"I remember thinking, 'What in the hell am I in for if commanding officers routinely do this sort of thing?' After the Zippo expended all of its fuel, Major Bahnsen, not wanting to be outdone by some simple piece of mechanical equipment, jumped back onto the track, drew his service revolver, and emptied its clip, shooting into the open space charred and still smoking from the M-132's napalm shower. Holstering his pistol, he proudly announced, 'Demonstration complete. Back to your positions.'

"My mouth agape, I was astonished by what I'd just witnessed. This first impression became a lasting one, but it was not the last time Major Bahnsen's boldness astonished me."

✯ Chapter 105 ✯

The regiment held a big awards ceremony in front of the white plantation house at Quan Loi that served as its field headquarters. General
Creighton Abrams, the commanding general of the U.S. forces in Vietnam, and Lieutenant General Do Cao Tri, the commanding general of
the ARVN III Corps, were in attendance to present awards. Colonel
Leach allowed Fif to be flown in for the ceremony.

Major Jim Anderson, my West Point classmate and Abrams's aide,
read the citations before General Abrams pinned Distinguished Service Crosses on recently promoted Captain Jerry W. Thurman and me
for actions that took place earlier in the spring. General Abrams also
presented Colonel Leach with a Silver Star for his 2 June actions,
when he directed his helicopter to treetop level to assist his door gunners in pinning down an enemy force until ground forces moved in for
a pile-on. Leach was totally unaware that he'd been put in for this
recognition.

General Abrams also presented the 1st Squadron and the 1st Platoon, 919th Engineers with a Presidential Unit Citation for actions during the defense of Saigon over a twenty-two-day period in May 1968.
The Presidential Unit Citation is awarded for extraordinary heroism in
action against an armed enemy. The degree of heroism required is the
same as that which would warrant award of a Distinguished Service
Cross to an individual. He also presented Valorous Unit Awards to the
regiment Headquarters and Headquarters Troop and the 3rd Squadron.

I don't recall the specific actions or dates related to these awards. The Valorous Unit Award is to be awarded to units of the U.S. armed forces for extraordinary heroism in action against an armed enemy. The degree of heroism required is the same as that which would warrant award of the Silver Star to an individual.

General Tri presented the regiment with the Republic of Vietnam Gallantry Cross with Palm for its actions from September 1966 to August 1968. Although Tri personally awarded this medal to the regiment, the Vietnamese government issued this award to all units subordinate to the U.S. Military Assistance Command during the period 8 February 1962 and 28 March 1973, and to USARV and its subordinate units for the period 20 July 1965 to 28 March 1973. All personnel who served in Vietnam are authorized to wear this medal.

After the ceremony, General Abrams, through Jim Anderson, invited me to stay with him in Saigon before I left on R&R the next day. Fif flew with me to Saigon later that afternoon. After dropping her off at her apartment, I spent the night with General Abrams at his villa on Tan Son Nhut Air Base.

Dinner with Abrams was a small group consisting of his two personal aides, Major Jim Anderson and Chief Warrant Officer Four Lyle Englestadt, and the general's young son, Bruce Clarke Abrams, age about twelve, who was visiting from Bangkok. It was a nice meal and a pleasant break from the war.

After dinner, we were sitting in his living room, listening to classical music and drinking coffee when General Abrams started taking pictures with a fancy camera he'd just purchased at the PX. He asked me where my camera was. I told him that I did not own a camera and didn't even have a ration card to buy one.

PX ration cards allowed members of the military to purchase hard-to-get, high-value items like expensive cameras and watches at a steep discount. The ration card was supposed to, but didn't, prevent these items from showing up on the black market.

The next morning, General Abrams had Englestadt take me to the PX so I could use his ration card to buy a camera. Later in the day, Fif and I took a commercial flight to Singapore, where I had a room booked at the Raffles Hotel.

While I was on R&R, eight ARPs and two pink teams were involved in a very courageous mission. This extraordinary action took place on 9 August west of An Loc in the Fish Hook region of War Zone C.

Retired Colonel, then Captain, Ted Duck, Aero Scout Platoon leader and mission commander, talks about this operation.

"Taking flight early in the morning, I led two pink teams on an aerial recon of a sector that intelligence had told us was becoming a hornet's nest of NVA activity. A typical B-52 strike had gone in the previous night. Trees were uprooted and brush had been burned away. Ground that had been covered by grass was charred and perforated by thirty-foot-wide-by-thirty-foot-deep craters.

"I flew with a red smoke grenade with its pin pulled in a cutout Coke can on the floor next to my right foot by the open door. Whenever I was shot at, I would kick the grenade out the door. When the can hit the ground, it would expel the grenade, releasing the pin, and boom! Red smoke. Like clockwork, my Cobra pilot would then engage the target with rockets and miniguns.

"I was making a low orbit around the edge of the strike area when I got a glimpse of a lone NVA soldier sitting up against a tree. I circled back and he started running. I engaged him with my minigun just before my observer leaned out the door and told me we were taking automatic weapons fire from a partially damaged bunker complex to our rear. I marked and moved to the side while my wingman rolled in. I tried to keep the target in sight, but it was just too hard to see through the very tall trees. At any rate, either my wingman or I killed the enemy soldier who shot at my helicopter.

"I quickly spotted other enemy on the ground below—one here, two there. They seemed to be in a daze, most likely the result of the overpressure of the B-52 strike. I knew regiment was eager for POWs, and the thought came to me that this might be a good opportunity to have the ARPs come out and pick up some of these NVA.

"There was a problem, however. The very tall hardwood trees, some fallen, in the immediate vicinity presented too great an obstacle for bringing in slicks to insert and extract ARPs. Several bomb craters fairly close to the bunker complex looked large enough to accommodate my Loach, but the only way to access them was vertical—straight in and straight out between tall trees.

"I decided to do a test landing and takeoff, just to see if a Loach would have enough power to get ARPs out after they'd snatch some POWs. I sat down in one of the craters, shut my helicopter down, and climbed up to the brim. As I stuck my head up out of the crater, I saw two NVA soldiers sitting not more than thirty feet from me. They had AK-47s on their laps, but acted like they didn't see me. They were obviously dazed and oblivious to what was taking place around them. That was just fine with me. It scared the shit out of me to be that close to two armed enemy. I got back in my aircraft and lifted out of the crater. My helicopter had plenty of power, enough to get out with passengers on board so long as the minigun and ammunition were removed.

"I left scout pilot First Lieutenant Stephen Moushegian and his wingman to keep an eye on the bunkers, and returned to Quan Loi to talk with First Lieutenant Doug Rich, the ARP platoon leader. I briefed Rich on the situation. We agreed that this was an opportunity to grab some POWs, but it would be a very, very dangerous mission. In fact, Major Bradin wouldn't have approved it, but he was on R&R. I don't think Colonel Leach would have gone along with it either, but we didn't ask him. Had Major Bahnsen been around, he would have personally led the mission. He was a different breed from any officer I knew in Vietnam.

"Rich went to talk with his ARPs. I spoke with scout pilots First Lieutenant George Adams and Warrant Officer Stephen Gardipee. I selected them to shuttle ARPs into and out of the contact area, and told them to remove their miniguns and unload all ammunition. I assured them that I'd have pink teams watching over them for the entire mission."

Former ARP and specialist five Dan Bock recalls this mission.

"We were on strip alert at Quan Loi, waiting for something to do, when the platoon got scrambled and we all ran out to the flight line. Lieutenant Rich told us that pink teams had spotted some dinks near a bunker complex damaged by a B-52 strike the night before. Regiment wanted fresh POWs for intelligence purposes and this was an opportunity to pick some up, if we acted promptly. He said he was going to lead the mission and asked for seven volunteers to go with him. We were taken by surprise when he asked for volunteers. We assumed we had already volunteered for every mission. Everyone sensed this mission was going to be more dangerous than usual, and usual was always dangerous. We were all wrapped extra tight in anticipation of the hell we were about to get into, but we all volunteered to go. Lieutenant Rich pointed and said, 'You, you, and you.' The next thing I know, I'm with three other guys crammed into a Loach and headed to the contact area. When we arrived at the forward edge of the bunker complex, our pilot did sort of a falling hover, setting the helicopter straight down between some very tall trees and into a bomb crater that served as our LZ. Like I said, we were already wound tight, but landing in a crater really got our adrenaline pumping."

Former first lieutenant and scout pilot Stephen Moushegian comments.

"Just as soon as the ARPs inserted, I did a vertical climb to see if there were any bad guys that I could kill for them. What I saw below me gave me the chills. I could see at least fifty dinks milling around in the bunkers. I couldn't believe that we'd just dropped a squad of our guys off less than a hundred meters from that many enemy. This mission would never have happened had Duck or Rich, or any of us, known how large a force was still in the bunker complex. It was a very dicey situation and could have gone bad in a heartbeat."

Former specialist four John Montgomery comments on this mission.

"We cleared the craters and moved along a stream toward the base camp in a left-and-right flank formation. I was walking point on the right flank; Bruce Stephens was right behind me.

Stephens and I hadn't advanced over thirty meters before we discovered an NVA soldier hiding in the brush. We told him to Chieu Hoi. He surrendered and started pointing to his right, where one of his comrades was hiding. Stephens remained with our prisoner while I went over to try and talk the second enemy soldier into surrendering. He did. I relieved him of his pistol. He was an officer. He told us where two more enemy soldiers were hiding, and Stephens and I captured them for a total of four POWs.

"We took our prisoners back to the bomb crater where we had inserted and turned them over to Brackens and a couple other guys.

"This all happened within the first fifteen minutes after we had boots on the ground."

Dan Bock continues.

"One of the POWs told Brackens, who could speak some Vietnamese, that there was over four hundred NVA in the area. That wasn't good news. It really stepped up the anxiety. Not long after, we spotted a couple of dinks by a bunker we later discovered to contain four tons of rice and a small stockpile of various types of ammunition—AK-47 and .30-caliber machine gun rounds and RPGs. They saw us but had no intentions of surrendering, so we blew them away and called in a Cobra to destroy the cache with rockets.

John Montgomery continues.

"We heard some small-arms fire and Stephens and I headed in that direction. The firing stopped before we could reach the area. When we got there, we saw Lieutenant Rich standing knee-deep in the river, which was about twenty meters wide and a good eight to ten feet deep in the middle. Specialist Cook was covering him from the bank.

"There was an NVA in the river. Rich was trying to get him to surrender, which he did. Rich had him taken to the rear.

"Rich then told me that there were more enemy on the other side of the river. He and I went looking for them while a couple of guys covered us.

"We found a small cache of weapons, marked it with smoke, and went back across the river just before a Cobra came in and took it out.

"During all this mass confusion, we could hear gunships and scout helicopters flying all around, shooting up the place.

"About this time, our RTO relayed to Lieutenant Rich that we were getting flanked to the north and needed to get out fast."

Dan Bock resumes.

"Some of the enemy decided to make a run for it. They didn't get far. Our pink teams killed thirty-six of them before they could escape. We grabbed a total of six POWs. We also picked up documents and maps.

"I don't remember how long we were on the ground but it wasn't long, not more than an hour and a half. There were still NVA in the bunker complex shooting at us when we started to withdraw from this extremely dangerous 'grab and snatch' mission. We were all returning fire as we moved back to the bomb crater for extraction. I also remember a Loach coming in very low with its minigun churning. It remained overhead and shooting until we all got out. Minutes later, we were loaded up and headed back to Quan Loi. They had to take us out in shuttles as two aircraft couldn't carry the eight of us plus our six POWs.

"We landed at Quan Loi before we had time to think about what we'd just been through. We took six POWs out of a bunker complex housing over four hundred NVA. Pretty amazing. Even more amazing, we'd done it with bullets whizzing all around us and none of us had been so much as scratched. We were damn lucky. I knew a lot of guys involved in less intense actions that ended up getting killed or wounded. Who knows why?"

John Montgomery concludes.

"The officer we captured was carrying eight bills of Cambodian currency with '500' printed in each corner. I took them from him and gave one to each of the guys as their pay for the mission."

Doc resumes.

We knew that a large enemy force was infiltrating into the area west of An Loc, but we had no intelligence confirming the size of the force or the nature of its mission.

Although I had nothing to do with this action and was no longer commanding the Air Cavalry Troop, I was proud of the Thunderhorse troopers who took part in it.

The intel they uncovered revealed that elements of the 7th NVA Division, the 9th VC Division, the 271st VC Regiment, and the K-8 Battalion of the 209th NVA Regiment had just launched a two-week offensive directed at the 11th Armored Cavalry, 1st Infantry, 1st Cavalry, 5th ARVN Division, and all other allied forces in the An Loc–Loc Ninh area.

Needless to say, this intelligence prevented friendly casualties and facilitated Free World forces in kicking the crap out of the enemy over the next week or so.

The heaviest fighting for the regiment took place on 11, 12, and 13 August, during which over 452 enemy soldiers were killed. Eleven members of the Blackhorse were also killed during these three days. That number would have surely been higher had the ARPs not done what they did to get vital intelligence on this major enemy offensive.

All eight ARPs—First Lieutenant Doug Rich, Specialist Four John Montgomery, Specialist Four Daniel Bock, Specialist Four William Fergerstrom, Specialist Four Edward Cook, Private First Class Bruce Stephens, Private First Class Robert Lambdin, and Private First Class Rothie Brackens Jr.—were awarded the Silver Star for conspicuous valor beyond the call of duty.

Thunderhorse pilots Captain Ted Duck, First Lieutenant Stephen Moushegian, First Lieutenant George Adams, Warrant Officer Stephen Gardipee, and First Lieutenant Fred Van Orden were awarded the Distinguished Flying Cross for their gallantry during aerial flight. Air crewman Specialist Five Douglas Bonesteel and Private First Class Robert Cullinane were awarded the Air Medal with Valor device for their gallantry during aerial flight.

But the recognition didn't stop with Silver Stars, Distinguished Flying Crosses, and Air Medals. This same group of soldiers was awarded the Republic of Vietnam's Gallantry Cross as well.

This many high-level awards for any one action is rare, extremely rare considering every man involved was awarded a medal of valor by both the United States and Republic of Vietnam.

Retired Colonel Lee Fulmer, a Blackhorse staff officer and troop commander during this period, comments on this mission and the soldiers he served with in Vietnam.

"These weren't my guys and this wasn't my mission, but that's not important. What matters far, far more is the heroism shown by these soldiers and pilots. It's representative of the kind of character and courage I witnessed every day during my time in Vietnam.

"The Vietnam War was fought by eighteen, nineteen, and twenty-something-year-olds for the most part. Some walked into battle. Others rode in tracks or helicopters. They were supported by extraordinarily brave men who flew gunships, slicks, scout ships, and medevacs. Some were volunteers, others draftees—a difference that didn't seem to matter in combat.

"My strongest emotional memory of my time in Vietnam is thinking about these young men who, beyond my wildest imagination, did everything we asked of them and came back for more. They were magnificent.

"They were young men who answered their country's call and went to war in a far away and strange land, fighting for people with whom they shared very little in common, and in a war that even our country's leaders didn't seem to fully understand.

"They fought courageously, too many losing life or limb. They served loyally in the military while many of their peers avoided service, marched in protests, and chanted, 'Hell no! We won't go.' And they kept their spirits high despite dastardly reporters who filed stories sensationalizing the least unsavory acts committed by American servicemen—reporters who favorably chronicled all kinds of stories about the enemy who inflicted atrocities on innocents daily.

"All of this took place in a time when the country literally rose up against its military and those serving in it. It was a damn shame, but those who fought in this war have no reason to be ashamed. They did their duty and then some. They require no one's permission to feel good about it."

Doc resumes.

I should mention a grave misfortune that occurred while I was on R&R. Sergeant John Sexton of E Troop, 2nd Squadron was taken prisoner by the Vietcong after being left behind for dead in the aftermath of a firefight that took place on 12 August. Fortunately, Sexton was released twenty-six months later. We were all grateful for his safe return.

To my knowledge, Sexton was the only member of the Blackhorse taken prisoner during the war.

Three 1st Squadron troopers were killed in action while I was away. Second Lieutenant David Deters of the Howitzer Battery and Sergeant Jose Flores of D Company were killed on 12 August. Sergeant Charles Matthews of D Company was killed the following day. We were lucky not to have had more troopers killed during this period of intense fighting.

During my absence, Colonel Leach assigned his XO, Lieutenant Colonel Larry Wright, as commander of Task Force Wright, which consisted of the 1st Squadron and an ARVN Ranger Battalion. Wright set up his headquarters in my squadron CP.

My XO and S-3, Majors Bill Good and Don Snow, met me on my return from ten days of R&R. They were unhappy soldiers. It did not take me long to find out why: they didn't like Wright and thought less of his combat ability.

They saw Task Force Wright as a ploy by Leach to get his close personal friend some combat command time. It was an insult to my two majors for Wright to come up and take over during my absence. There was no good reason for that to have ever happened.

I quickly assumed control of the situation and told Wright he would have to find another CP. Timid when confronted by someone he couldn't back down, Wright took my ration of shit and moved out. I would never have put up with a junior officer chewing me out.

I don't know what Wright told Leach when he returned to regiment. All I know is that Task Force Wright quickly folded up and went away. I never had a conversation with Leach about it.

✷ Chapter 106 ✷

The 1st Cavalry called on regiment to provide armor support for its operations in the vicinity of Bo Duc, a remote village thirty-six miles west of Loc Ninh, close to the Cambodian border. Leach tasked me with this support mission. I decided to send Captain Bear Palmer's A Troop on what turned into a three-month opcon to the 1st Battalion, 7th Cavalry.

Retired Lieutenant Colonel Fredrick "Bear" Palmer comments on this mission.

"Bo Duc was a hard place to get in and out of. What road there was between Loc Ninh and Bo Duc was so heavily mined that our engineers didn't even want to try to clear it. That meant we would be busting jungle all the way, which would give the enemy plenty of advance warning to move back into Cambodia before we arrived. Because we weren't allowed to conduct operations in Cambodia, the enemy could hold up secure in the safety of his Cambodian sanctuaries and thumb his nose at us knowing full well we couldn't do anything about it.

"To overcome the obstacles of making a road march to Bo Duc, arrangements were made with the Air Force to haul twenty-four of my ACAVs to Bo Duc using C-130 Hercules transports. Because it just wasn't practical to take them with us, I made a provisional combat element out of my Sheridans and left it at Loc Ninh.

"Bo Duc had a short, unimproved airstrip capable of handling one C-130 at a time. By removing all antennas and weapons, removing all ammo, and draining our ACAVs' gas tanks to three-quarters' full, it was possible for a C-130 to transport two of them at a time. It took two days and forty-five sorties to do it, but it was a flawless operation. To my knowledge, this was the only tactical insertion of an armored unit by air in the entire war."

Retired Major General Bill Nash, then First Lieutenant and A Troop's 1st Platoon leader, talks about an incident that took place on the Loc Ninh end of this unique airlift.

"Doc was talking to me while my platoon was loading a couple of ACAVs in a C-130 for the short flight to Bo Duc when the airstrip came under a rocket attack. B Troop was securing the perimeter and instantly launched a counterattack. Brief encounters of this sort were almost a daily occurrence at Loc Ninh. However, rockets were still coming in and the C-130 pilot didn't want to stick around. He fired up his engines, had his loadmaster button up the rear hatch, and started to taxi with only one ACAV on board.

"Well, a few rockets didn't scare Doc, and he wasn't about to let that C-130 takeoff until it was fully loaded. Much to my amazement, and his actions had amazed me several times, Doc stepped out in front of the C-130 and stood fast with his arms folded across his chest.

"I was a platoon leader and Doc was my squadron commander, leaving me no choice but to stand close enough to him that the C-130's outside prop could have made sausage out of me. All it had to do was make a sharp turn in my direction. I could see the pilot waving furiously for Doc to get out of the way as he inched his transport forward. Doc didn't budge. He just stood there with crossed arms.

"No words were spoken, but the pilot got Doc's message. With all four props still turning and rockets still coming in, the C-130's rear hatch opened and the second ACAV was loaded. Doc then stepped out of the way, allowing the transport to take off without further delay.

"At the time, getting the job done while under attack was pretty ordinary stuff when Doc was around. I can't imagine doing something like that today."

Doc resumes.

Specialist Four John Rodgers of C Troop was hit by enemy fire on 15 August and died three days later. Specialist Four Peter Kidd of B Troop was killed in action in the vicinity of Loc Ninh on 22 August. One here, one there doesn't seem like much of a loss of life. But I can assure you that every soldier killed under my command, in the war for that matter, was a huge loss in my mind.

The rest of August consisted of continual small contacts in the Michelin Rubber Plantation around Loc Ninh. My CP was adjacent to the air strip and beside a Special Forces compound. Mortar attacks on my CP and Howitzer Battery were nightly occurrences. Luckily, only a few of my troopers were wounded during these attacks.

One night a mortar round landed dead center in the chaplain's jeep, totaling it. Father Paul J. Bolton, a captain, and his chaplain's assistant had just finished sandbagging the jeep when this happened. I met Father Bolton the next morning while he was looking over what was left of his jeep and joked with him that God had sent him a message. I told him that whatever he had been doing, he'd better shape up. He gave me a weird look, but said nothing.

Father Bolton was known for his great sense of humor, but he did not take my joking with him this way as being funny. I replaced his jeep as soon as I could find another one.

The spiritual health of soldiers in combat is as important as their physical and mental health. Soldiers haunted by past sins, guilty feelings, and otherwise out of kilter with their maker don't handle the possibility of being killed in battle with the same level of inner peace felt by those who are at peace with God. To that end, Father Bolton was an invaluable, much-loved asset to the squadron. Normally dressed in his camouflaged habit, he took his ecclesiastical duties seriously and attended to the spiritual needs of every soldier who sought his blessing or counsel. His services were tailored to what the tactical situation allowed; some days brief prayer services, other days a mass. The number of troopers attending mass always went up right after a mortar attack.

As the only Catholic chaplain in the regiment, Father Bolton conducted mass in other squadrons and at regimental headquarters as often as he could. He also conducted mass, in Latin, everyday at the local Catholic parish in Loc Ninh. I asked him daily at the evening briefing how many villagers had attended. If the numbers spiked, it was a well-known indication of imminent enemy action in the area.

Father Bolton also looked after my wounded and visited them regularly by catching helicopter rides to and from hospitals. He knew by name where every one of the squadron's wounded had been taken, their present condition, and their prognosis for recovery. This was extraordinarily helpful to all involved and kept me informed at times when I couldn't get to the hospital myself.

Lieutenant Colonel Robert H. Hawn was the regimental chaplain. He served in the Korean War before becoming a man of the cloth and became the chief bishop of the Anglican Episcopal Church after his military service.

Father Hawn had an open-ended invitation to conduct Protestant services at any of my squadron's locations. I attended the services he held at my CP. I had no qualms about standing in the front row or getting down on my knees to pray and take communion. Father Hawn always gave those in attendance general absolution, which was much appreciated as it relieved us from worry about dying in sin.

The physical health of my troopers was also top priority. We had an M-577 track located with the squadron CP that served as our aid station. The track contained one examination table and medical supplies. Medical services provided in our aid station were pretty much limited to sewing up minor wounds, diagnosing medical maladies, handing out medicines, giving inoculations of one sort or another, and stabilizing wounded for evacuation to a hospital.

Medics were assigned to each troop and to D Company. There were enough of them to put one with every platoon. These folks didn't have a medic track. The platoon commanders designated a track for them to ride in. That track became the field aid station for the day.

Experienced medics were a godsend. They could do virtually everything a surgeon could do out in the field without the benefit of hospital facilities and a medical staff. Besides all they did for us, my squadron surgeons and medics conducted medcaps in local villages, when time allowed, which was a godsend to the local people.

✴ Chapter 107 ✴

My CP at Loc Ninh came under mortar attacks frequently—quick strikes of a dozen or so rounds. More often than not, the NVA pulled up stakes and skedaddled before we could find and kill them. When we could determine where the mortars came from, we put countermortar artillery fire on their location or sent ACAVs to wipe them out.

Retired Lieutenant Colonel, then Major, Don Snow talks about a mortar attack that took place on this date.

"Mortars started coming in around noontime. I ran toward the CP as soon as the first round hit. I was just about there when I slipped on a piece of PSP and hyperextended my knee. The pain was immediate and excruciating. Our medics examined my screwed up knee and quickly determined that it was going to require extensive treatment.

"The mortar fire ended almost as soon as it started, making it possible to bring in a medevac chopper right away. Just after liftoff, I looked out the door and could see C Troop was engaged in a fierce firefight. The way I saw it, the brief mortar attack on the squadron CP was conducted to divert attention away from the attack on C Troop.

"I told the pilot we should hang around the area to see if C Troop took casualties that might need dusting off. He agreed that hanging around was better than coming back and moved into an orbit off to the side of the firefight.

"The firefight lasted a good half-hour and, sure enough, C Troop had two or three of its troopers really shot up who needed to be taken out ASAP. We landed and picked them up and headed to the Ninety-third Evacuation Hospital at Long Binh. I felt like a jerk. I was embarrassed at being medevaced with seriously wounded troopers, even though I was hurting.

"I expected to be treated and returned to duty. However, this incident took place at a time when the United States had started withdrawing soldiers from the war. Anyone with a big scratch seemed to end up being evacuated back to the states. And, within a day or two of having my leg put in a cast, I was on my way home."

Doc resumes.

Don Snow had been with the squadron since January and served as my S-3 from the day I assumed command. He was a tough, competent soldier and a loyal friend and confidant. I was damn grateful he didn't go home in a body bag.

Losing your operations officer is a big deal when you're fighting everyday. It's best to have someone with command experience in that job because the operations officer often coordinates actions during enemy contacts. You need someone in that job who is up to taking command at a moment's notice.

I decided to name Major Bill Good as my operations officer. He'd proven himself capable as my XO and had the maturity and leadership the position required.

Good couldn't report to my CP for a couple of days, and I needed someone to plug the operations officer hole in the meantime. Captain Ron Caldwell came to mind. He was reliable and capable and had worked as the assistant S-3 before taking command of D Company a few days before I arrived at the squadron. I'd been thinking about swapping him and Captain Richard Kramer, an Air Force Academy graduate who opted for Army service, to give Kramer command experience and Caldwell a change of pace. I made this switch within an hour of Snow's evacuation.

During my evening briefing, I got word from A Troop that Private First Class Chester Jackson had been killed in action in the vicinity of Bo Duc. Jackson was a solid soldier and a fine young man from Riverside, California.

⋆ Chapter 108 ⋆

5 September 1969—1st Squadron CP, Loc Ninh, and Michelin Rubber Plantation, west of Loc Ninh

Colonel Leach brought Command Sergeant Major Don Horn and an assistant S-3 out for a briefing on the enemy buildup in the squadron's AO. I briefed him on the situation as I knew it and told him that B and C Troops were reconnoitering the rubber plantation northwest of the airstrip. Leach said he wanted to have a look at that area and asked me to join him.

Because Leach had his command sergeant major with him, I asked Command Sergeant Major Frank Zlobec to join us. Leach sat on the right side with our sergeant majors, his assistant S-3, and crew chief. I took a seat on the left side of the rear cabin of Leach's UH-1 Huey command and control helicopter.

Former captain, then first lieutenant, Stephen Moushegian was the scout pilot for an Air Cavalry Troop pink team conducting an aerial recon west of Loc Ninh.

"We landed and got a briefing from the First Squadron at Loc Ninh. They told me they suspected something other than normal plantation work was going on in the rubber and asked me to go see if I could spot enemy activity in it.

"I flew out to the rubber and turned north, going in low and slow around the edge of the plantation, looking for trails, footprints, enemy movement, and other signs of the enemy.

"I spotted some fresh footprints and started following them. Fresh footprints shined. Older footprints were dull looking. Subconsciously, I noticed a big clump of underbrush. I flew over it looking for the footprints to come out the other side. When I got to the other side, there was an ambush waiting for me.

"I came under very heavy small-arms and automatic weapons fire. They were just pouring it into me. The AK magazines emptied quickly, but the .30 cals kept firing. My aircraft was hit. My observer was hit. I was hit in my right arm, left hand, and left shoulder. An instant later, another burst of rounds came up through the floor and blew the radios in my face, permanently blinding my left eye, which triggered a sympathetic nervous system reaction, and I couldn't keep my right eye open. I was literally flying blind. Miraculously, that problem lasted only a few seconds. However, I was far from being out of harm's way. I had blood streaming down my face, I couldn't see out of my left eye, and I couldn't fully use my arms. I was in bad shape. And I was about to be dealt a second hand of adversity.

"I dove to pick up speed and get away when I hit into some treetops, blowing out my lower bubble. By the grace of God, my blades cleared, and I was able to stabilize the aircraft—get it straight and level. I asked my door gunner, a PFC whose name I can't now recall, what was wrong with him. He thought he was dying. He'd been hit by tracers, but they'd gone out.

"I started into a slow bank to the left to pick up speed and head for the Air Cavalry Troop's forward base at Quan Loi, about thirty minutes away. It was during this time that my observer took over the controls. Fortunately for both of us he knew enough about flying that I was able to talk him through the motions to get home and land.

"The medics at the aid station got our bleeding stopped, started us on IVs, and put us on a medevac to Long Binh with other wounded. Some of the wounded were taken to the Ninety-third Evac. I was taken to the Twenty-fourth Evacuation Hospital, where head wounds were treated.

"I was hit at oh-nine-thirty and woke up in the recovery room at thirteen hundred. Colonel Leach visited me in the hospital and awarded me my fourth Distinguished Flying Cross. Days later, I was medevaced out-of-country and was medically retired from the Army. My observer returned to duty within the week."

Doc resumes.

After Moushegian was hit, his wingman—a Cobra being flown by pilot Captain Fred O. Jackson Jr. and copilot Warrant Officer Terrance E. Ledden—followed him all the way to Quan Loi, then returned to the contact site within the hour with another scout pilot. They weren't back over the area long before a .51-caliber antiaircraft machine gun opened up. Several rounds hit Jackson and Ledden's gunship, dropping it out of the sky like a quail hit with a full load of number-eight shot from a twelve-gauge. It was not a pretty sight. The helicopter exploded on impact, killing them instantly.

For reasons that baffle me to this day, Leach had his pilot fly out to the same area and we took antiaircraft fire. I felt helpless. There I was sitting in the back of a helicopter at a low altitude and taking antiaircraft fire. We should not have flown out into that area.

Leach's crew chief was hit by a .51-caliber round. Luckily, it just nicked his leg or he would have died instantly. Just the same, he was bleeding badly and needed immediate medical attention or he was going to bleed to death.

We landed in the middle of B Troop's tracks. Zlobec used Leach's belt to put a tourniquet around the crew chief's leg while one of B Troop's medics worked on stopping his bleeding. There wasn't anything I could do but get in the way, so I went to talk with Captain Doug Starr, B Troop's commander.

I stayed on the ground as Leach's helicopter took off with the wounded crew chief and headed to the nearest aid station. I had no desire to get back in Leach's helicopter. I did not know his pilot and didn't like to fly with a pilot I didn't know. All I knew about this turkey was that he flew us into the kill zone of a .51 caliber, and he knew damn well that machine gun was there. No way was I going to get back in a helicopter with him.

My helicopter came out to pick me up shortly thereafter. I looked for Zlobec and was told he got in the Leach's chopper. It was not until later that night that I found out that he was in the hospital with a serious wound in the ass from a .51-caliber round. To say the least, losing both my operations officer and command sergeant major within three days was upsetting.

After returning to my CP, I met with my key staff and unit commanders for our routine evening briefing.

Based on sightings, minor contacts, and solid intelligence, we knew a large NVA force was moving into the general area of Loc Ninh. What we didn't know was that this unknown unit had specific orders to inflict maximum casualties on the 11th Armored Cavalry Regiment. Evidently, Hanoi thought that a significant increase in the number of U.S. casualties would strengthen its position in the peace talks.

As ominous as it may seem, neither that unit's orders nor Hanoi's thinking would have caused me to worry or change my plans for the following day. My sole mission was to find the enemy and kill or capture him. That mission never varied regardless of the enemy I faced or the political maneuvering taking place in Saigon, Hanoi, Washington, and Paris.

I gave Captains Doug Starr and Art West separate reconnaissance missions for the following day: Starr's B Troop to the west; West's C Troop to the northeast of Loc Ninh.

D Company needed a maintenance day to repair eleven of its M-48 tanks. I told Captain Kramer that I needed him to get as many of those tanks up and running as possible early the next morning and to be prepared to reinforce B and C Troops with all assets available.

We sent damaged equipment to An Loc for repairs and drew new equipment, personnel, and supplies from this fairly secure area. However, the twenty-five-kilometer road between An Loc and Long Ninh was "ambush alley" and convoys needed armed escorts.

When not otherwise in use, I used my command track, the S-3's command track, the artillery liaison officer's command track, the squadron's surveillance ACAV section, the 1st Platoon from the 919th Combat Engineers, the M-132 Flamethrower section, and A Troop's operational M-551 Sheridans to form a provisional combat team that gave me an additional maneuver element. When Captain John Poindexter took command of my Headquarters Troop, we called this organization "Team PAPA."

I told Poindexter he was to take Team PAPA on a convoy escort mission to An Loc the next morning. If not for Team PAPA, I would have had to use an entire troop to protect the convoy

Retired Colonel Douglas Starr talks about his subsequent briefing with his platoon leaders.

"Having received the reconnaissance mission for the next day, I left the squadron CP in my ACAV along with the two escort tracks I had with me, and oozed the short distance back to my troop CP over extremely muddy roads. As I ate supper, I thought of how best to perform the reconnaissance in view of recent heavy rains that had created extremely muddy conditions in the assigned area.

"I outlined the next day's mission to my platoon leaders during my evening briefing. I told them we would conduct a troop reconnaissance in force in the southern half of the rubber plantation using pinwheel movements that would allow us to methodically recon the rubber and avoid crossing most of the creeks and depressions running through the plantation.

"Just before supper, my troop CP received several reports indicating large enemy troop movements into our recon sector during the last six to twelve hours. Accordingly, I put special emphasis on thorough reconnaissance and told my platoon leaders to exercise extraordinary caution when operating in terrain that made for a good ambush site."

Doc resumes.

As I climbed in the sack, I didn't think about going home in a couple of days, nor did I imagine my squadron was going to have a major enemy contact the next day.

✷ Chapter 109 ✷

*Newly promoted First Lieutenant and B Troop 3rd Platoon leader
Ray de Wit describes the early morning of this day-long action.*

"This started out like any other day in 'Nam, morning meal at about
oh-six hundred followed by a troop briefing, then off on a search and
destroy patrol. Except today, we were going out on a troop recon rather
than on our normal platoon-sized patrols.

"A Kit Carson scout by the name of Ha Van Phong, aka 'Jackie Glea-
son,' was riding in Captain Starr's track. Phong had a constant smile, a
voracious appetite, and a pot belly. He seemed friendly enough when I
first met him. I wouldn't have thought so if I'd bumped into him a few
months earlier.

"First Lieutenant Phong Chieu Hoi left Hanoi in January with the
NVA's 308th Infiltration Division and led his company on a long trek
south. After crossing the DMZ, Phong Chieu Hoi'd—surrendered. Chieu
Hoi was the open arms program that promised clemency and financial
aid to Vietcong and NVA soldiers and cadres who quit fighting for the
North and started supporting the South. On completion of indoctrination
training at a political orientation center near Saigon, Phong was assigned
to B Troop and quickly became an important intelligence asset to us.

"We departed our base camp, nothing more than a small clearing on
a hill overlooking QL 13 near Loc Ninh, and headed west toward the
rubber. We'd been in the rubber several times and knew the roads and
the plantation well.

"Vietnamese rubber plantations were mostly owned by Michelin. A typical rubber plantation had twenty- to thirty-foot-high trees planted several feet apart in raised rows. Two- to three-feet-deep irrigation ditches ran along both sides of each row. Enemy soldiers took up positions in these ditches during firefights and used them to leapfrog during advances and retreats. They also used them for ambushes. RPG teams hid in these ditches to fire rockets into the vulnerable underside of our tracks as they crossed over.

"We passed through a small village, where most of the rubber plantation workers lived, and progressed down a trail just wide enough for a track. About oh-eight hundred, we were about to enter the eastern edge of the rubber when we came upon a group of workers walking briskly back toward the village.

"As soon as he saw the workers, Captain Starr got on the radio and halted our column. His track was directly behind mine. Captain Starr and Phong dismounted to question these rubber workers, as it was much too early for them to be leaving the plantation. Phong asked one of the workers why they were going back to the village. The worker said, 'VC say it's a holiday. They say we can go home.'

"Captain Starr had Phong thank the workers for the information and send them on their way. As soon as they remounted his track, Captain Starr got on the radio and told his platoon leaders to break into three columns and to stay off the road once we entered the plantation. Captain Starr's cautionary order heightened our sense of environmental awareness and gave us reason to expect that we might make contact quickly."

Then Captain Doug Starr recalls entering the rubber plantation and the ambush that soon followed.

"Although the VC had told the workers it was a holiday, all was peaceful and the war seemed a long way off as we entered the rubber plantation at oh-eight forty-five hours.

"Approximately three hundred meters into the rubber, I gave the order to veer left off the road and assume our 'rubber formation'—a five-track fronted, rectangular-shaped formation designed for terrain that allowed reasonably good vision. As my platoons moved into position, I noted to my satisfaction that, despite the rare sunny morning for the time of year and the friendly greetings we received from the villagers, my troopers were alert.

"We moved through the rubber parallel to a deep ravine and bore left as it turned from northwest to southwest toward rarely worked areas of the plantation. Approaching Hill two-oh-three, paralleling the road on our right, my First Platoon leader, Lieutenant Steven Vince, informed me that his left flank security had detected possible movement to our left front. I gave the order to bear left, increase speed, and hold fire. We had been in this rubber before and, while unusual, workers in this area were a possibility.

"After moving about fifty meters, my second Platoon leader, Lieutenant Harry Hardin, in a voice that was calm but unmistakably concerned, reported his flank security had definite movement on the high ground to our right flank. I immediately gave the order to turn right and told Vince to keep a sharp watch for the suspected movement he had originally reported.

"As we approached Hill two-oh-three from the southeast, we saw three tan-clad NVA running at a crouch across the high ground to our front. I gave the order to come on line and move up the hill just before a thunderous din from enemy firing at us from the entire mass of high ground quickly told me that we were engaged with at least company-sized element—possibly a battalion-sized or larger force, judging from the number of automatic weapons shooting our way. I was hindered slightly by the muddy ground and by the fact that two of my three platoon leaders had the radio antennae shot off their tracks during the initial barrage. They worked to correct that predicament while continuing to move and direct their platoons.

"About one-third of the way up the hill, some dink fired a one-in-a-million shot that put a RPG round into the coax aperture of the M-551 Sheridan located front and center of our formation. The explosion caused a flash fire in the turret that resulted in casualties but no fatalities. Several other tracks had also been hit. Medics were staying busy consolidating the wounded at their track located four rows back and center of our formation, which at this point consisted of two platoons on line with Lieutenant de Wit's Third Platoon providing rear and flank security."

Ray de Wit talks about this phase of the ambush from his perspective.

"As we came on line, there was obvious movement to our front and on what was now the right side of the column. Everyone opened fire and, with Captain Starr's track directly behind me and radioing 'contact' to the squadron CP, we moved slowly, but continuously, to the north.

"Track Thirty-four was to my immediate right. Its track commander, an American Samoan nicknamed 'Samo,' was the biggest and strongest guy in my platoon. He quickly reacted to the ambush by moving his track slightly ahead of the formation. I radioed Samo and told him to stay in line. My next transmission was a quick reminder for my track commanders and gunners to watch the ditches.

"I no sooner sent that message than did the cord from my CVC helmet to the radio disconnect. I reached down to reconnect the quick-release plug when the telltale sound of an exploding RPG rattled my head. Samo's track was hit right of the driver's seat and caught fire. His crew bailed out, but Samo disengaged the .50 caliber from its cradle and picked it up before jumping to the ground and trailing a full belt of ammo. As his crew ran toward Starr's and my tracks, Samo trailed behind firing the .50 cal like it was an M-16. Every track in our troop was also cutting loose.

"As we moved forward, my left-side gunner opened up on an RPG team crouched in a trench when another gook stepped out from behind a rubber tree and opened fire on my track with an AK-47. A green tracer went by my left ear, struck the gun shield of the left gunner, and creased his shoulder. The shooter didn't have the chance to change his magazine before my .50 cut him in half. My left gunner, a relatively new guy, panicked, started screaming, and tried to jump off the track. In a fit of rage, I backhanded him and told him to stay put and keep firing. Backhanding one of your troopers isn't something I'd recommend, but it calmed him down enough that he returned to his position and started shooting again.

"Sometime during the first five or ten minutes of the fight, Captain Starr began to call in artillery. I got my communications restored just in time to hear him warn us of incoming artillery fire directly to our front."

Doug Starr continues.

"I radioed Major Bahnsen and told him we were in contact with what I believed to be a battalion-sized enemy force and that I had several seriously wounded. He told me to evacuate my casualties to a LZ where a medevac could get them out and that he was sending reinforcements."

Doc begins recounting this action.

I got hold of C Troop and D Company and told them B Troop was in contact and needed their assistance. I was over the area in short order getting an idea of the lineup.

D Company got rolling toward the Michelin right away. C Troop had to load up the two Cambodian CIDG companies from the U.S. Army Special Forces camp at Loc Ninh that it had been conducting joint operations with for the past several days before moving out.

Cambodian CIDG companies jumped at the chance to work with C Troop because Captain West allowed them to turn in all captured weapons through Special Forces channels to receive the bounty the United States paid for enemy weapons. I had no problem with that practice.

During my sizing-up orbits over the contact area, my helicopter took fire from the same antiaircraft machine gun position that shot down a pink team two days earlier. I immediately called my Howitzer Battery with a fire mission and had just begun to make my initial adjustments when a fire team leader from the Air Cavalry Troop contacted me.

"Armor Six, Red Three."

"Roger, Red Three."

"This is Red Three. Okay, I've got a white fire team on station, pink team en route."

"Okay, good. A white fire team can't do me a hell of a lot of good except out here to the west, down this creek line in the woods. You see where the arty is landing? Don't get out in front of them. Out there to the south and west of that area, there's some dinks out there, I know damn well, in that area. There's also AA just outside the rubber. Don't get outside the goddamn rubber. Don't get outside the edge of the rubber and you're probably safe, only small-arms in that area."

I broke with Red 3 and called my CP.

I told Captain Ron Caldwell to get a medevac on its way immediately and to verify the status of the Howitzer Battery's 155mm ammunition. I then gave the Howitzer Battery another fire mission, calling for a white phosphorous marking round on the western edge of the rubber and instructed the FDC to stay on the squadron command frequency. I wanted them to be ready to adjust fire with a moment's notice.

D Company and C Troop were on the move at this time. Kramer was having difficulty lining up his company with B Troop. He had moved his column of tanks at high speed to join B Troop but overshot its location—not unusual during linkups in a fast-moving firefight. Kramer needed to be led back to B Troop's location. I got on the radio and gave him directions.

"Yeah, you just went too goddamn far, Four-Six; you went way the fuck too far. You're four hundred . . . five hundred meters past it. Goddamn it! Get on the red ball! Get on the red ball there . . . back to your rear!"

"This is Four-Six, Wilco."

"All right, get your ass back to the rear. Get on the red ball where you can meet up with him."

"Red ball" was our terminology for hard-packed red laterite roads like the one that ran through the plantation.

I watched Kramer for a few minutes. He was struggling to link up with B Troop but still didn't quite have his bearings straight.

"Four-Six, you're moving right, at my right. I'm going to tell you which way to go here. The next right turn up here . . . tell your lead big boy to make a right, tell your second big boy to make a right!"

"Four-Six, Roger."

"That's the right way, down that road now."

"Big boy" was our slang for M-48 main battle tanks. I wanted them on line, where they could inflict some heavy damage on the enemy force. I got on the radio to let Kramer know how he was doing.

"Okay, Four-Six. Keep moving out there. You got turned around. Now you're moving in the right direction. Keep moving in the way you're going."

"This is Four-Six, on the way."

"All right, get on up there."

C Troop approached the contact area from the northeast and stopped seventy-five meters short of B Troop. West placed his tracks in a laager and instructed the two Special Forces advisers with the Cambodian CIDG company to keep them inside it. He didn't want them intermixing with B Troop's soldiers. I got on the radio and told West to talk with Starr. He needed to find out what the situation was and what needed to be done on the ground.

Meanwhile, Starr radioed me with an update on his wounded and the POWs his troop captured during the initial contact.

"Two-Six, Go."

"This is Two-Six, Roger. I've got twelve at this time. I've got one that's not wounded, a POW. I've got one pretty badly wounded POW. That's all the lead out I've got right now."

"All right. Get that POW and slap the shit out of him. Find out what the hell's going on out front there. Find out how many dinks you've got and where the hell they are. Get a hold of him and get him on your track where you can talk to him. Grab him right around the throat."

Doug Starr continues.

"We were still moving up the hill under increasingly heavy fire from the top. I detached my medic track and four Third Platoon tracks under Lieutenant de Wit's command and sent them to Loc Ninh with the wounded. His column came under intense fire five hundred meters behind my rear security and had to return. I had several soldiers who were seriously wounded and required immediate treatment. Major Bahnsen got hold of the pink team leader and had him send his scout ship in to dust them off. Because of weight considerations, the scout pilot dropped his minigun and left his observer with it on the ground.

"By this time, D Company had taken position on my left flank, and C Troop moved on line to my right flank. The arrival of these two units made it possible for me to deploy my entire Third Platoon to escort my medic track. Lieutenant de Wit encountered heavy resistance again about six hundred meters to our rear but was able to breakout without incurring additional casualties. I ordered de Wit to keep his platoon in Loc Ninh for the time being.

"I told West that the enemy had broken contact and that I thought the area was clear. West said he would have the Cambodians sweep the area just in case there were stragglers lurking around.

"Suddenly, C Troop's Sheridan and a few of its ACAVs broke out of the laager and headed toward us to attack NVA soldiers moving in ditches between their laager and my troop. West got on a radio and ordered his remaining vehicles to hold fast. He then told the advancing vehicles to be careful with their .50 cals—B Troop was all around."

Doc resumes.

West got back on his command ACAV and was angling through the rubber to intercept his advancing tracks when all hell broke loose around him. The next five minutes were sheer chaos—AK-47 fire, RPGs exploding, machine gun fire, grenades being tossed by both sides, and pistol fire. West later told me that the only thing he remembered amid the blur of it all was reloading his pistol many times. He used that pistol to kill an NVA major during this renewed contact in which twenty-three NVA were killed very close to where he had been talking with Starr.

B Troop didn't incur further casualties during this brief, but furious, firefight. C Troop wasn't so lucky. Specialist Five James Gray, the loader on the Sheridan, was killed by an RPG treeburst. The same burst severely wounded Staff Sergeant Jesse Crowe, the 3rd Platoon sergeant and Sheridan commander. Along with several Cambodians, the Special Forces advisory team sergeant was wounded.

I was getting pissed. I was thinking about how to go about killing every dink in the rubber when Starr called me with a medevac and POW interrogation update.

"I've got eight wounded of my own, the one dink wounded. We're slapping the shit out of the other one here to see if we can get some information from him."

"All right. Get him to talk. Get him to talk. How many, where they are. Let's take it from there.

"Get Four-Six up on your flank there. We're going to make this a squadron formation as soon as I can get Three-Six in here, we'll get lined up. We'll sweep this whole damn area back and forth all day if we have to."

"This is Two-Six, Roger. This kid's about twelve. Scared shitless. He's singing us a song. I can't understand it but I got my interpreter right here. We're talking to him."

"Okay, you've got a good interpreter. Let me know when you've got a read, out."

"This is Two-Six, Roger that."

I brought my units on line—C Troop on the left, B Troop in the middle, and D Company on the right—and told them to sweep to the southeast. West had his attached CIDG companies dismount and spread out behind the tracks. Starr's interpreter had interrogated additional POWs by this point.

The POWs were pointing in the direction where they said bunkers were located. I don't know if they were confused or attempting to confuse us. Either way, they were all pointing in different directions. Starr put one of them on board his ACAV. That way, his interpreter could get more accurate directions from the POW as the sweep continued.

Doug Starr continues.

"My troop reached the crest of the hill. C Troop and D company were in position. Major Bahnsen ordered us to reverse direction and move back down the hill toward the point where my troop had made initial contact with the enemy. As we moved on line back down the hill, all three units came in contact with the NVA headquarters element and a large portion of the ambush force that had managed to extricate itself and rejoin the command group.

"The indescribable awe of the two cavalry troops and a tank company fully deployed on line and committed can perhaps best be described by depicting the POW I had on my track. His eyes reflected a curious mixture of terror, awe, sympathy for his comrades, and relief at being where he was instead of where they were.

"Encountering moderately heavy contact most of the way, we made a three-kilometer, semicircular sweep during which time it began to rain heavily. The CIDG companies moved behind and between our tracks to search the dead and to prevent anyone popping up behind the skirmish line. The Cambodians seized a number of important documents—maps and orders—and discovered that we had killed the entire command section of the K-Nine Battalion, two hundred nineth NVA Regiment. The bodies of this command group were moved to the rear for intelligence purposes—identification, primarily.

"Late in the afternoon, after resweeping the entire contact area and encountering no contact at all, Major Bahnsen gave the order for all three units to move toward a large clearing southwest of the original contact area on Hill Two-oh-three. We were to resupply and evacuate the remaining POWs from this position. I called de Wit and gave him instructions for returning to our new position."

Ray de Wit resumes.

"The ride back to the rubber was very uncomfortable because we now knew what to expect. We followed the same road we had when we entered the rubber earlier in the morning.

"We got back to our troop about fifteen hundred hours and found ourselves at the back of a long line of tracks stopped on the road. The fight had moved to the northwest edge of the rubber plantation and into an area where the terrain was flat grassland surrounded by low bushes and trees."

Doc resumes.

The CIDG remounted C and some of B Troops' tracks for our movement to the clearing. En route, West got on the command frequency and informed us that a portion of this clearing was mined. He also reminded us that he'd lost an ACAV in it a few weeks earlier. He then told us that the far end of the clearing was covered by thick brush his tracks could push down to make a LZ.

C Troop was leading the column as it moved down the western edge of the clearing. As it neared the far edge, its lead Sheridan fired at two NVA that had run across the road. West immediately ordered his troop to deploy right and the Cambodians to dismount. The Sheridan roared ahead and veered right off the road when it reached the edge of the clearing. West's command track was on its right, another ACAV moved up to protect the Sheridan's left flank.

Retired Colonel, then First Lieutenant, Paul Baerman speaks about what happened only seconds later.

"My ACAV was moving to Captain West's right. As we neared an intersection where a utility road crossed the main rubber tree road, I heard the signature poofing sound of three mortars firing in sequence. Thirty seconds later two mortars hit, bracketing West's track. The third round hit alongside my track. I was thrown forward and my nose smashed into my .50 caliber. Dazed, I dropped down and remained there for a few minutes until my head cleared. When I stood up, I found myself in the midst of a mess.

"Specialist Four Larry Boobar, the right gunner on West's track, was dead. Specialist Four Vernon Stahl, his track commander, was seriously wounded. West had also been wounded and needed to be evacuated. Making matters worse, an RPG fired almost simultaneously with the mortar attack hit another C Troop ACAV, killing Staff Sergeant Wayne Saunders, the track commander, and wounding the entire crew.

"Obviously, the few surviving elements of the K-Nine battalion were trying to inflict as many casualties as possible as they withdrew west toward the jungle."

Doug Starr continues.

"I heard heavy firing in the direction of C Troop but was unable to raise anyone from it on the squadron command net. Deploying my troop on line, we moved into C Troop's formation and got on line among them. During this movement, one of my Sheridans and a tank from D Company hit mines. This necessitated a hasty mine sweep of the immediate surrounding area.

"I got the formation straightened out and informed Captain Kramer of B and C Troops' deployment. As I was about to radio Major Bahnsen to bring him up to speed on the new situation, Lieutenant Paul Baerman entered the command net. He told us that West's track had been hit. West was wounded. Baerman requested instructions."

Doc resumes.

Although control and communications are normally much better from the air, the morale aspects of having the commander on the ground always outweigh these factors. From what I heard over the radio and saw from the air, I sensed C Troop needed me to help it get going again. I had my pilot land fairly close to West's track. Master Sergeant Dave Wolff and I dismounted and ran over to it. Over the next several minutes, I helped Baerman organize the wounded for evacuation. Wolff helped get West back to my helicopter. Minutes later, Wolff was onboard my helicopter when it was used to medevac a load of wounded to the 93rd Evacuation Hospital at Long Binh.

Waiting for my helicopter to return, I got with Baerman. He seemed ready and willing to take charge. We talked about what needed to be done to evacuate the downed tracks. I had only been on the ground a short time when my helicopter returned and picked me up.

My TOC had finally established contact with Team PAPA and gave Captain Poindexter directions for getting to the contact area. I wanted as many resources as I could get my hands on for a final sweep of the battlefield. Flying weather at this time was marginal with light rain and fog. It prevented me from flying to Team PAPA's location and guiding Poindexter to the contact area. By the time Team PAPA arrived, the fight in the NVA had run out. All remaining enemy had fled west out of the plantation.

I got on the radio and ordered all units to line up in the clearing, then landed to talk with my commanders about exfiltrating the rubber and the road march back to their base camps. I also used this time to have my helicopter crew take the remaining POWs and wounded back to my CP in several sorties.

Doug Starr continues.

"We began pulling out of the rubber around seventeen thirty. We'd been in sporadic, but heavy, contact since approximately oh-nine forty hours. The movement back to our base camps was without incident, despite the difficulty of evacuating disabled vehicles through the heavy mud and steady rain. My troop had two Sheridans damaged, nine WIA, and no KIAs. We captured four NVA and made a significant contribution to the seventy-four NVA confirmed killed."

Doc resumes.

West, Starr, and I were among those who received a Silver Star for our actions. Ha Van Phong, the Kit Carson scout, was one of many awarded a Bronze Star. Several pilots received Air Medals. Thirty-nine troopers received Purple Hearts: three killed in action, the other thirty-six wounded in action.

All said and done, I was extremely proud of the way my squadron fought in what was the last time I commanded soldiers in combat.

✶ Chapter 110 ✶

7 September 1969—1st Squadron AO, Binh Long Province

Since my arrival on 17 April, the 1st Squadron had traveled six hundred twenty miles by road and another eight thousand forty cross-country. My CP had made twenty-two moves. Sixty-one of the squadron's tracks had been chalked up to combat losses. Its aircraft had been hit by hostile fire on ten occasions. Thirty-four of my soldiers had been killed in action and another 253 wounded. The squadron had been credited with 822 enemy kills and capturing 38 enemy soldiers. God only knows how many of them we wounded.

I spent the day visiting every unit and talking to assembled groups of soldiers. Except those in A Troop; they were still at Bo Duc. My message was short and to the point. I kept it personal and as light as I could. I told them I was honored to have served as their commander and that I appreciated their service. I told them a little of what I had observed when they were fighting and praised individual troopers for their heroism. I told them how much I appreciated their loyalty and service and that I hoped our paths would cross again. I told them I thought our job of killing communists was worthwhile and that our country was doing the right thing by being there. I told them that my time was up and, amazingly, I had survived twelve months of command in combat. I cautioned them to keep their heads down and, when in doubt, to use more firepower—more artillery, air, tank, and especially machine gun fire. I shook as many hands as I could before I left.

I ate my farewell supper with my staff and unit commanders in the mess tent at my squadron CP. Other than being in the company of brave soldiers and fine men, there was nothing special about it.

After Doc finished his remarks, Major Bill Good read a brief farewell message Major Don Snow prepared and intended to give on this occasion. The following is the complete text of Snow's message.

I wanted to speak to all of you tonight for just a couple minutes. I have known him longer than any of you and now he has been my commander for six months. I can sum that period up very quickly. Doc, and by the way that's the first time I've called him that since 13 April, is a mean son-of-a-bitch who never lets up. He's driven you when you wanted to stop. He's harassed you when you wanted to hear no more. He's lashed out at you when you thought you were doing OK. He's made you fight when you wanted to rest. He's kept you up when you wanted to sleep. He's a mean son-of-a-bitch that's kept you alive, that's built the best fighting unit in Vietnam, that has mourned your losses, shared in your glories and led us to victory on the battlefield.

I consider myself a pro in this business, rightly or wrongly, and the highest compliment one soldier can give another is probably to say, "You are the best damn soldier and finest leader I have ever known." I say this now about Major Bahnsen, for he is by far the best soldier I have ever known and his leadership the finest I have ever witnessed.

On your departure Sir, I won't say "Goodbye" because you and I will meet again. I'll just say "So long" and "Thank you." Thank you for all you have given this squadron—The First of the Black-horse—that extra spark, that intangible spirit and that willingness to do. Those things only come when the leader has that little something that most are missing.

I know you have given us the flexibility of mind that will make this transition from one CO to another an easier task. Best wishes and good luck.

Colonel James H. Leach made the following remarks on an unsolicited special Officer Efficiency Report for the period 7 April–7 August 1969, awarding Doc the maximum rating.

Major Bahnsen is the most outstanding combat commander I know. He is intelligent, aggressive, persuasive and extremely efficient. A dynamic young officer who excels in everything he does. The bravest soldier I've ever seen. There is never a question of who is in charge when Major Bahnsen is around. A natural leader who has the unlimited potential for positions of the highest responsibility. . . . The results his squadron achieves are astounding. He is a team-worker who never loses sight of the mission. Major Bahnsen has all the qualifications for higher command and should be guided toward generalship. I believe he is a General Abrams in the making.

Major General Elvy B. Roberts, the 1st Air Cavalry Division commander, endorsed this special report. He also gave Doc the maximum rating possible and provided the following observations.

Unquestionably the finest combat leader—commander in the Regiment. An alert, tenacious fighter with an abundance of ideas and common sense. At the forefront of all enemy contacts, night or day. I would fight to get this potential general officer.

∗ Chapter 111 ∗

My squadron command and second tour of duty in Vietnam had come to an end. Only my primary staff, sergeant major, and unit commanders with their guidon bearers were in formation for the change of command ceremony held on the airstrip at Loc Ninh. Master Sergeant Dave Wolff, my senior operations NCO, stood in as my command sergeant major.

Major General Elvy Roberts pinned a Legion of Merit and my fifth Silver Star on me just before I passed the squadron guidon to Colonel Leach, who passed it to Lieutenant Colonel John Norton, who assumed command from me. Leach, Norton, and I then made remarks to the small group assembled for this traditional military rite.

I spent the rest of the day packing and engaging in small talk with anyone who wanted to talk with me before I left country. During the evening, the NVA moved back into the Michelin plantation and fired mortars at my CP.

I remember getting out of bed and running for cover dressed in my skivvies, boots, and steel pot. They didn't fire more than twenty rounds before my Howitzer Battery bombarded their position. We didn't take any casualties, but I suspected the NVA did.

I was soon back in my bed. Lying there, the thought crossed my mind that those damn NVA knew I was headed home and were exploiting their last chance to kill me.

☆ Epilogue ☆

By the summer of 1969, President Richard M. Nixon had decided that a "pure" military victory was either impossible or too costly. He abandoned that course in favor of securing a peace agreement with Hanoi, withdrawing U.S. forces according to a secret timetable, and taking steps to turn the war's combat role over to ARVN units.

Notwithstanding the Nixon administration's plan, I believed then and believe to this day that we were winning the war militarily when I left country and could have won a military victory had the "fog of politics" taken a second seat to that objective.

Ho Chi Minh died five days before I left Vietnam. Unfortunately, his death didn't kill Hanoi's ambition for uniting Vietnam under communist rule.

As the fight wore on, American casualties increased with no end in sight. For this and other reasons, our country started losing the heart to sustain a military presence in Southeast Asia and turned against the war in increasing numbers.

Picking up more and more responsibility for the fight, ARVN forces fought valiantly, but they needed help, a lot of it, especially equipment, air support, and financial aid. However, mirroring the mood of the country, our Congress lost its will to provide the funding the ARVN needed to defeat the NVA.

Consequently, the fight started creeping further and further south and the storm clouds of defeat started gathering over Saigon. It became clear that the ARVN could not prevail on the battlefield under the conditions we imposed on them.

There was no support for the idea to send our military back to stomp the NVA's ass until they surrendered. A lot of worrying about China getting involved overshadowed that idea, but no one, or so it would seem, clearly understood that China had its own problems to worry about and probably would have left us alone.

Nevertheless, Nixon did get the United States out of Vietnam and helped bring the war to its official end on 27 January 1973. Just a little over two years later, Saigon fell and the South Vietnamese people came under communist rule and remain so today.

Thirty-four good soldiers died under my command of 1st Squadron. Ten others died during my command of the Air Cavalry Troop. The Vietnam War eventually claimed over fifty-eight thousand American lives, every one of them a tragic loss to their loved ones, our military, and our country. Many of our wounded are still wounded, as posttraumatic stress disorder continues to haunt them. My only regrets are the men killed and wounded and the fact that we did not kill more of the communist bastards!

My flight home was an emotional let down. I had always wanted to command in combat, and I commanded a platoon, a troop, and a squadron, fighting alongside some of the finest and bravest men to be found anywhere. I realized then that I would never again be so lucky. My chances of having another go at combat command were low and proved to be zero years later. Be that as it may, commanding soldiers in combat was the highlight of my career.

My personal life was about to take a zigzag course for several years; the full scope of which I didn't picture as I flew over the Pacific en route to Georgia.

On my arrival in Georgia, Pat and I signed our divorce papers. I got a chance to visit with my kids for a short time before heading to West Point, where I married Phyllis Elise Marie "Fif" Shaughnessy, from Westbury, New York.

I had orders to command a tank battalion in Germany with a report date in December. I had been selected by armor branch for repetitive command, a new program just implemented by the Army. Selected commanders of combat battalions were allowed to volunteer for this program. Some commanders went from peacetime to wartime command and others of us went from combat to Europe. A lot of commanders turned this down.

Fif and I attended a couple of prep courses at Fort Knox before flying to Freiburg, Germany, where I assumed command of the 1st Battalion, 32nd Armor "Bandits" as a newly promoted lieutenant colonel, being promoted in transit without ceremony.

The battalion was a part of the 3rd Brigade of the 3rd Armored Division. I found fifty-four M-60 tanks, and about 85 percent of the people needed to man them, waiting for me. Equipment and people-wise, it was like going from feast to famine compared to Vietnam duty.

Battalion command in Germany was fun. We trained hard and prepared ourselves to meet the Russians on the border in time of war. I emphasized tank gunnery and trained my unit hard in tactical fundamentals. I spent a lot of time teaching my young officers. Many of them remain friends to this day. Joe Sutton, Scott Wheeler, Doug Madigan, John Whitehead, Peter Noyes, Bill Shugrue, and others served full careers in the Army.

Fif and I had a relaxed social environment. Our officers and their wives visited our home regularly. My battalion spent a lot of time in the field at Grafenwöhr and became very proficient in maneuvering and shooting our tanks. I would have been delighted to have led this unit in combat.

Colonel Sidney "Hap" Haszard was my brigade commander for most of my command tour, and he was my greatest supporter and cheerleader. We were kindred spirits and remained friends until his death a few years ago.

Upon completion of my command, I had orders to attend the Army War College in Carlisle Barracks, Pennsylvania. This was a superb, relaxed year. By going to school at night, I completed the requirements for a master of science degree in administration from Shippensburg State College. Fif also earned her master's in guidance and counseling during this time.

Fif and I remained happily married for three years. Nevertheless, for very personal reasons I won't discuss, Fif and I amicably divorced and I remarried Pat.

Following my graduation from the War College, Brigadier General George Patton wanted me to be assigned to the Armor School, where he was serving as the assistant commandant. He wanted me to head up his leadership department. Because of my divorce and remarriage to Pat in Georgia, I asked him to release me from this move and to be assigned to Fort Benning. He was not happy with me, but he understood my personal life had problems. These were private matters that had to be taken care of before it would improve.

I was assigned as the Armor Team leader on the newly formed U.S. Army Combat Arms Training Board (CATB) at Fort Benning. A little over a year later, Pat and I were divorced again.

CATB was a superb assignment with a small group of exceptionally talented officers charged with a mission to improve training in the Army, particularly in the combat arms. I was able to write battle drill manuals for Armywide use as well as other armor doctrine. My team of guys included several future general officers, Lieutenant Generals Tom Montgomery and Larry Jordan being two of the most notable. I made some lifelong friends in this job, one being Wess Roberts, the author of this book, who was handpicked from the National Guard to serve on the board.

CATB made several significant and enduring improvements in Army training. The most prominent of these was the derivation of procedures for developing tasks, conditions, and standards for all Army training and education programs, and The Multiple Integrated Laser Engagement System, which is used to train units for combat deployment at the Army's National Training Center at Fort Irwin, California.

In looking for innovative training improvements for the armor force, I crossed sabers with Major General Donn Starry, the commandant of the Armor Center and School at Fort Knox, who had responsibility for promulgating armor doctrine. The contention between us came to light particularly over an article I wrote for *ARMOR Magazine*, "Our Tank Gunnery Needs a Revival," which caused some serious discussion, especially at Fort Knox.

Starry asked that I be assigned to him to help fix the Army's tank gunnery problems and other armor training troubles. To my total surprise, my boss, Major General Paul Gorman, agreed to this transfer. He called me on All Fools' Day, while I was on TDY, and told me I was being transferred to the Armor School and to report in thirty days. I truly thought he was kidding, as I knew that I would have problems working at Knox after I had gored their ox for almost two years. He was not kidding. I reported for duty at the Armor School in May 1974.

Starry assigned me and my team to his slow-witted deputy, a brigadier general who will go unnamed. My major accomplishment was to write the booklet *Battlesight Gunnery*, which I had verified on the ranges at Fort Knox. I was then tasked to help revise the current tank gunnery manuals based on the recommendations in my article. It was a nightmare for me because Starry's deputy questioned everything I did. I did not like working for that particular brigadier, and I let it show, which slowed my progress.

On 31 August 1974, I married Peggy Miller at the Fairview Presbyterian Church in New Manchester, West Virginia. She was Fif's college roommate at West Virginia University. We met in 1971 before Peggy went to Vietnam to work in Army Recreational Services.

Pat, Fif, and Peggy are all wonderful, great ladies with superb senses of humor and lots of patience. They have all put up with a lot being married to me. They loved me and treated me better than I deserved. Any failures, faults, or sins of commission in all my marriages are totally mine. I was, and am, a very difficult person to live with. Only time and old age have smoothed some of my rough spots.

In October, I was ordered to sit on a Department of the Army promotion board for captains and reported to Washington, D.C., for four weeks' TDY. During this period, General Bill DePuy, the U.S. Army Training and Doctrine Command (TRADOC) commander, visited Knox and my name came up in a personal conversation he had with General Starry.

DePuy asked how I was doing. Starry told him I was having trouble getting my manual staffed and that I did not get along with his deputy. DePuy asked Starry if he wanted me reassigned. Starry answered "yes."

While sitting on the promotion board, I got word that I had been ordered to TRADOC headquarters at Fort Monroe, Virginia, to serve on Major General Paul Gorman's staff. This basically constituted relief from my job at Knox. The OER I received following my duty at Fort Knox was one of the worst of my career. Thankfully, Starry was my rater although his deputy should have been. Lieutenant General Orwin Talbott, the deputy commander of TRADOC, was my endorser. He was an old friend from Vietnam days when he commanded the 1st Infantry Division. Talbott's evaluation of my performance along with his very generous remarks softened what could have been a very damning blow to my future in the Army.

Starry and I have since settled our differences.

My new job involved making *How to Fight* films under Gorman's supervision. I supervised the completion of one film. I then became a Special Studies leader under several different bosses, but under General Bill DePuy's overall guidance. I completed three studies: T2S2 (Total Tank System), A2S2 (Anti-Armor System), and C2S2 (Combat Communications Systems).

The first study was given to me by Gorman. He wanted me to look at the tanks in our Army as a weapons system and to determine our true state of armor readiness. My modus operandi was to assemble a staff, about ten people total, of my choosing from TRADOC assets, articulate the problem, gather relevant personnel, equipment and training info, and then write up our findings.

I was able to complete this tasking ninety days after pulling together a talented group of officers. What we found was that our tank force at any given time was about 25 percent effective. After preparing out final report, we briefed it to General DePuy. The news was so bad and our facts were so compelling that DePuy flew me with him to the Pentagon for a special briefing that was limited to about six people, including the Army's chief and vice chief of staff. As a result of this briefing, a high-powered board headed by retired Lieutenant General James Kalergis was assembled at the Pentagon to determine how to fix the Army's tank force problem.

A couple of days after this briefing, General DePuy asked me to assemble my team in front of his house one evening so he could thank all of us for our good work. Once assembled, he thanked us all before presenting me with an impact Legion of Merit, a totally unexpected award.

Generals DePuy and Gorman then decided to have me look at the Army's antiarmor systems. The findings of this study were just about as bad as for the tanks. The major result of this work was the recommendation to appoint a TRADOC system manager (TSM) to represent the user community for all major weapons systems. This took a while to be approved by the Army, but it came into being just before I was reassigned and designated to be the first TSM for attack helicopters.

My third study was combat communications. DePuy personally gave me the mission for this study. I was tasked to look at the Army's CEOI and examine the need to regularly change unit frequencies and call signs for operational security. He felt that changing frequencies too often hindered operational alacrity. Yet, not changing made us subject to easy intercept and battlefield compromise.

I got every clearance you would ever want and started my study by visiting the National Security Agency (NSA). If the NSA had its way, military units would change frequencies and call signs every hour.

I visited units in the field, where commanders told me that operational effectiveness improved with less frequent changes in radio frequencies and call signs. My recommendation to General DePuy was to change frequencies and call signs every twenty-four hours. The NSA wanted it to be every twelve hours. DePuy and the Army settled on twenty-four hours.

While at Fort Monroe, Peggy earned her master's in guidance and counseling from Old Dominion University and applied for a direct commission in the Army. Her request was approved, and she was commissioned as a first lieutenant in the adjutant general branch by General DePuy. Her degree in counseling, her choice of a new career that I respected, her toughness, and her sense of humor all proved vital to the endurance of our marriage.

I was selected for early promotion to full colonel during my duty at TRADOC headquarters. My promotion came through before I went to Fort Rucker, Alabama, to serve as the TSM for attack helicopters for a year, after which I was to assume command of the 1st Aviation Brigade, which was not my first choice of commands. But after Generals DePuy and Patton weighed in to get my brigade command changed to an armor brigade and failed, I marched with enthusiasm in my gait to Rucker.

As the TSM for attack helicopters, I worked with a superb team of guys, including Joe Moffitt, Jerry Hipps, Joe Beach, and Chuck Crowley. I wrote a number of articles during this time that were published in *Aviation Digest*, including "How Good Is Good Enough," "Guts Are Great but Brains Are Better," and "How to Kill a ZSU" (a Russian antiaircraft weapon system).

During this period, I was given the job of running some joint tests called the Joint Attack Weapons System. The purpose of these tests was to develop joint-attack tactics for use by Air Force A-10 ground attack fighter and Army attack helicopter crews. These tests substantiated the need for both weapons systems. By using attack helicopters to take out Soviet air defense sites, A-10s had a higher survivability rate. Moreover, joint attacks by A-10s and attack helicopters against Soviet air defense sites and armor units resulted in a significantly higher number of kills than when we employed them individually. The *Joint Air Attack Tactics* manual that I wrote following these tests remains in use today.

I assumed command of the 1st Aviation Brigade on 18 August 1978. It consisted of four battalions, three of them tables of distribution and allowances units and one a reinforced engineer battalion, combat heavy. I loved every minute of this command and had a superb team of leaders and soldiers under me. My two bosses at Fort Rucker, Major Generals Jim Smith and Jim Merryman, successively, were great commanders and supported me in every way possible. They pushed me in my career. Their backing surely contributed to my successful command of the 1st Aviation Brigade and my selection for promotion to brigadier general in late 1979.

After promotion to brigadier general, my succession of assignments included assistant division commander of the 2nd Armored Division at Fort Hood, Texas, chief of staff of the Combined Field Army ROK/U.S. in Korea, and chief of staff of the III Corps at Fort Hood, Texas.

I had some absolutely great commanders to work for during this time. Major General Dick Prillaman and my classmate Major General Jack Woodmansee successively served as my division commanders in the 2nd Armored Division. Lieutenant General Dick Cavazos was my corps commander. In Korea, I worked for Lieutenant Generals Jim Vaught and Lou Menetrey, two tremendous soldiers. For my last duty assignment, I returned to Fort Hood to work for the brilliant Lieutenant General Walt Ulmer and one other general who will go unnamed. All in all, my Army career was what I had hoped it would be, and I retired on 30 June 1986 after thirty years of military service.

In 1991, while living at West Point, where Peggy was stationed as a regimental tactical officer, I was able to track down my son Minh with U.S. State Department assistance. I had always wondered what happened to him since I lost contact with his mother, Hung.

Minh got out of Vietnam through the Orderly Departure Program that allowed Amerasians to leave. He came to the United States by way of Thailand and was living in Los Angeles when I went to meet him.

Minh had no idea that he had a father who knew his name. I showed him my copy of his birth certificate, pictures of me taken together with his mother, and pictures of him as a baby that Hung had sent me before she stopped writing.

Several years after Minh was born, a confidential friend told me that Hung had a daughter from her marriage to a Vietnamese and an Amerasian son from an earlier liaison she had with an Air Force major. I was unaware of this when I was seeing her.

Minh told me that his mother was killed in an automobile crash with an Army truck in June 1969 north of Bien Hoa. He was placed in a Catholic orphanage until he was sixteen, and then he lived on the Bien Hoa streets and occasionally with his married sister. As an obvious Amerasian, he suffered at the hands of the new government. He had a tough time growing up and the fact that he is such a fine young man today is amazing.

I asked Minh to come live with Peggy and me at West Point. He lived with us there for about a year, during which time we taught him English. He then moved back to California to pursue a career in the film industry; today, he works as a grip in Hollywood. I am happy to say that Minh is fully accepted as one of the family by both Peggy and Pat and by my other four children.

After Army retirement, Doc worked for several years as a defense industry consultant. He continues to write articles on leadership and battlefield tactics for military publications, and frequently speaks on combat leadership to military audiences. Today, Doc lives on Miller Farm in West Virginia with his wife, Peggy, who retired from the Army in 1998 as a lieutenant colonel after twenty-two years of service.

An innovative and aggressive leader, Doc made several significant and lasting contributions to the Army during his distinguished career for which he was awarded three Legions of Merit, the Meritorious Service Medal, and two Army Commendation Medals for his meritorious service.

His peacetime contributions to the Army notwithstanding, it was on the battlefield where he fought so fiercely and led so effectively that Doc became the stuff of a true legend as an American warrior and one of the most highly decorated officers to have served in the Vietnam War. His medals of valor include the Distinguished Service Cross, five Silver Stars, three Distinguished Flying Crosses, three Bronze Stars with Valor device, three Air Medals with Valor device, the Army Commendation Medal with Valor device, two Purple Hearts, and two Republic of Vietnam Crosses of Gallantry with Silver Star. His medals of meritorious achievement in a combat zone include the Legion of Merit, a Bronze Star, forty-eight Air Medals, a Navy Unit Commendation Medal, and a Meritorious Unit Commendation Medal.

Since retirement Doc's lifelong contributions to the U.S. Army Armor Association have been recognized by the award of the Gold Order of St. George. The Army Aviation Association of America has also elected him to the Army Aviation Hall of Fame.

In James 1:17, the apostle James wrote, "Every good gift and every perfect gift is from above." Doc Bahnsen came into this world gifted with an aptitude for soldiering and leading and he perfected that gift exceptionally well. His life's calling was that of a warrior, and he fulfilled that calling honorably, even though it came at a high cost to his personal life.

Legends are inseparable from myths. Doc's story is truly legendary, and I have heard many myths about it over the years since I first met him. Nevertheless, the truth of his flamboyant feats and daring deeds makes his legend greater than any myth I have heard about him.

Mythical military heroes are often made out as larger-than-life figures who are fierce fighters, brave beyond compare, invincible in battle, loyal to their soldiers, faithful to their duty, defenders of their country, yet cursed with a weakness for beautiful women. Grounded in real deeds, it is no exaggeration to say Doc Bahnsen was all these things and more as an American warrior.

Appendix

Soldiers of the Air Cavalry Troop and 1st Squadron, 11th Armored Cavalry Regiment killed in action during the Vietnam War while serving under Major John C. "Doc" Bahnsen Jr.'s command.

Rank	Name	Date	Province	Unit
MAJ	Norman N. Cunningham	24 Sep 1968	Bien Hoa	Air Cav Trp
1LT	James A. Crowley II	16 Oct 1968	Binh Duong	Air Cav Trp
SP4	John P. Murphy	10 Nov 1968	Binh Duong	Air Cav Trp
1LT	Johnny W. Benton	25 Nov 1968	Binh Duong	Air Cav Trp
SFC	Rodney J. T. Yano	01 Jan 1969	Bien Hoa	Air Cav Trp
SP4	Otis J. Darden	03 Feb 1969	Binh Duong	Air Cav Trp
SGT	Frank D. P. Saracino Jr.	20 Mar 1969	Binh Long	Air Cav Trp
CPT	Kenneth D. Bailey	22 Mar 1969	Binh Long	Air Cav Trp
SP4	Kenneth V. Jensen	13 Apr 1969	Tay Ninh	Air Cav Trp
SGT	Joseph A. Oreto	13 Apr 1969	Tay Ninh	Air Cav Trp
SP4	James A. Baka	18 Apr 1969	Tay Ninh	B Trp, 1/11
SP4	Charles Chandler	18 Apr 1969	Tay Ninh	HHT, 1/11
SP4	Thomas M. Fitzpatrick	18 Apr 1969	Tay Ninh	B Trp, 1/11
2LT	Daniel M. Leahy	18 Apr 1969	Tay Ninh	How Btry, 1/11
SP5	Roy F. Maas	18 Apr 1969	Tay Ninh	D Co, 1/11
SGT	Don J. McAtee	18 Apr 1969	Tay Ninh	D Co, 1/11
SP4	Robert L. Morgan Jr.	18 Apr 1969	Tay Ninh	B Trp, 1/11
SP4	Joseph E. Morrow Jr.	18 Apr 1969	Tay Ninh	D Co, 1/11
SP4	Ronald E. Pongratz	18 Apr 1969	Tay Ninh	A Trp, 1/11

Rank	Name	Date	Province	Unit
SP4	Donald W. Noel	26 Apr 1969	Tay Ninh	HHT, 1/11
SSG	Arthur R. Strahin	29 Apr 1969	Tay Ninh	919th Eng Plt, 1/11
PFC	Samuel L. Patterson	13 May 1969	Binh Long	A Trp, 1/11
PFC	Ralph A. Ramirez Jr.	15 May 1969	Binh Duong	D Co, 1/11
SSG	Roger L. Oliver	24 May 1969	Long Khanh	A Trp, 1/11
SSG	Forrest L. Smith	28 May 1969	Long Khanh	D Co, 1/11
SGT	Darwin L. Labahn	03 Jun 1969	Long Khanh	C Trp, 1/11
PFC	Alf E. Eriksen	06 Jun 1969	Long Khanh	B Trp, 1/11
SGT	Kenneth J. Pitre	06 Jun 1969	Long Khanh	B Trp, 1/11
PFC	James M. Nesselrotte	19 Jun 1969	Binh Duong	A Trp, 1/11
SP5	Victor T. Shaffer	19 Jun 1969	Binh Duong	D Co, 1/11
SP4	Kurtis A. Berry	06 Jul 1969	Binh Duong	C Trp, 1/11
SGT	Larry H. Johnson	06 Jul 1969	Binh Duong	A Trp, 1/11
SP4	William F. Rigdon	06 Jul 1969	Binh Duong	A Trp, 1/11
PFC	David W. Shaffner	07 Jul 1969	Long Khanh	How Btry, 1/11
PFC	Richard A. Cutler	21 Jul 1969	Binh Duong	A Trp, 1/11
2LT	David S. Deters	12 Aug 1969	Binh Long	How Btry, 1/11
SGT	Jose L. Flores	12 Aug 1969	Binh Long	D Co, 1/11
SGT	Charles C. Matthews	13 Aug 1969	Binh Long	D Co, 1/11
SP4	John C. Rodgers	18 Aug 1969	Binh Long	C Trp, 1/11
SP4	Peter A. Kidd	22 Aug 1969	Binh Long	B Trp, 1/11
PFC	Chester L. Jackson	05 Sep 1969	Phuoc Long	A Trp, 1/11
SP4	Larry D. Boobar	06 Sep 1969	Binh Long	C Trp, 1/11
SGT	Bobby G. Haynes	06 Sep 1969	Binh Long	C Trp, 1/11
SSG	Wayne J. Sanders	06 Sep 1969	Binh Long	C Trp, 1/11

Glossary

AA fire: antiaircraft fire.

AC-47 Spooky: a fixed-wing, side-firing aerial gunship that provides close air support in defense of ground positions, escort and patrol, pre-planned strikes against suitable targets, and forward air-controlling for fighter strikes.

ACAV: armored cavalry assault vehicle.

ACR: armored cavalry regiment.

ACSFOR: Assistant Chief of Staff for Force Development.

aero scouts: the pilot and observer flying reconnaissance missions in a light observation helicopter, principally the OH-6 Cayuse.

Agent Orange: a synthetic herbicide used to defoliate plants in Vietnam.

AH-1G Cobra: an attack helicopter used extensively in a variety of missions ranging from armed escort and reconnaissance to fire suppression and aerial rocket artillery. Also called a "Shark" or a "Snake."

AH-64D Apache: an advanced, versatile, survivable, and multirole combat helicopter.

air assault: the movement of friendly assault forces by a helicopter to a landing zone, from which their mission is to engage and destroy enemy forces or to seize and hold key terrain.

Air Medal: the sixth highest of the seven medals for gallantry in action against an enemy of the United States. The Air Medal is also awarded for single acts of merit or for meritorious service while participating in aerial flight and engaged in an action against an armed enemy of the United States. Awards for acts of heroism are those of a lesser degree than required for the Distinguished Flying Cross. Awards for single acts of meritorious achievement, involving superior airmanship, are also those of a lesser degree than required for the Distinguished Flying Cross. Awards for meritorious service may also be made for sustained distinction in the performance of duties involving regular and frequent participation in aerial flight in operations against an armed enemy of the United States.

air mobile: soldiers, materiel, and supplies delivered by helicopter to a field location in support of ground operations.

AK-47: a Soviet-manufactured Kalashnikov semi-automatic and fully automatic combat assault rifle, 7.62mm; the basic weapon of the Communist forces. Known as the Type 56 to the Chinese, it is characterized by an explosive popping sound. If well maintained, its performance is very reliable.

AN/TPS-25: a transportable battlefield surveillance radar of the noncoherent Doppler type designed to detect and locate moving ground targets at ranges between 450 and 18,280 meters.

AO: area of operations.

APC: armored personnel carrier. *See* M-113.

armor branch: the U.S. Army's combat arms branch, encompassing tank and combined arms organizations that close with and destroy the enemy by using fire, maneuver, and shock effect and cavalry organizations that perform reconnaissance, provide security, and engage in the full spectrum of combat operations.

army: a combination of two or more corps consisting of 50,000 or more soldiers; typically commanded by a lieutenant general or general.

Army Commendation Medal: The seventh highest of the seven medals awarded for gallantry in action against an enemy of the United States. The Army Commendation Medal is also awarded for meritorious achievement or meritorious service while participating in an action against an armed enemy of the United States. Awards made for acts of valor are those of a lesser degree than required for the award of the Bronze Star Medal. An award may be made for acts of noncombatant-related heroism that do not meet the requirements for an award of the Soldier's Medal, or for noncombatant-related meritorious achievement or meritorious service of a lesser degree than required for the award of the Meritorious Service Medal. The Army Commendation Medal is not awarded to general officers or for acts involving aerial flight.

ash and trash missions: helicopter flights to carry out administrative functions.

ARPs: infantrymen who made up the ground force in the Air Cavalry Troop's Aero Rifle Platoon that also consisted of unarmed UH-ID helicopters used to transport these infantrymen into and out of combat operations.

Article 15: the article in the Uniform Code of Military Justice (UCMJ) that authorizes a commanding officer to administer nonjudicial punishment for minor offenses without the intervention of a court-martial.

ARVN: Army of the Republic of Vietnam (South Vietnam); also, individual soldiers or elements of the Army of the Republic of Vietnam.

A-team: a basic ten-man team of the U.S. Special Forces. During the Vietnam War, A-teams often led irregular military units that were not responsible to the South Vietnamese military command.

B-52 Stratofortress: a strategic bomber designed to deliver nuclear ordnance but later modified to deliver conventional ordnance as well. The most effective use of the B-52 in Vietnam was disrupting enemy troop concentrations and destroying supply areas with heavy payloads of general purpose and napalm bombs.

B-57 Canberra: a modified version of the English Electric Canberra that served as a light bomber and as a reconnaissance aircraft. In 1951, the United States broke a longstanding tradition by purchasing this foreign military aircraft, which was first flown in Great Britain in 1949, to be manufactured in quantity for the U.S. Air Force.

base camp: a unit's tactical field headquarters, operations center, and semipermanent resupply and refitting location.

battalion: four to six companies, consisting of 300 to 1,000 soldiers, normally commanded by a lieutenant colonel with a command sergeant major as principle NCO assistant. An armored or armored cavalry unit of equivalent size is called a squadron.

battery: an artillery unit equivalent to a company or a troop.

BDA: bomb damage assessment.

beaten zone: area where the majority of bullets will strike when a machine gun is laid-in to cover a part of a defensive perimeter or part of an ambush zone.

big boy: radio code for a tank.

bird: an aircraft.

body bag: a plastic bag used to transport dead bodies from the field.

body count: the number of enemy killed, wounded, or captured during an operation. The term was used by Washington and Saigon as a means of measuring the progress of the war.

BOQ: bachelor officer quarters; living quarters for officers.

brigade: two to five organic or attached combat battalions, consisting of 3,000 to 5,000 soldiers, normally commanded by a colonel with a command sergeant major as senior NCO. Armored Cavalry, Ranger, and Special Forces units of this size are categorized as regiments or groups.

brigadier general (BG): the first general officer rank. A brigadier general or one-star is higher in rank than a colonel but below a major general.

Bronze Star: the fifth highest of the seven medals for gallantry in action against an enemy of the United States. The Bronze Star Medal may also be awarded for meritorious achievement or service, not involving participation in aerial flight, in connection with military operations against an armed enemy. Awards made for acts of heroism are those of a lesser degree than required for the award of the Silver Star. Awards made for meritorious achievement or meritorious service are those of a lesser degree than required for the award of the Legion of Merit.

boonie hat: a soft camouflage-patterned hat with a 360-degree brim and an adjustable draw string.

boonies: any remote area away from a base camp or city.

bunker complex: a network, of varying size, of unfinished rudimentary structures built by the NVA and Vietcong to house personnel, store supplies, and provide a field base for their operations.

bust jungle: the use of armored vehicles to knock down small trees and flatten brush.

C's: *see* C rations.

C-130 Hercules: a large propeller-driven Air Force plane that transports people and cargo.

Car-15: a shortened M-16-style assault weapon. Because it doesn't have bayonet lugs, a bayonet cannot be attached to this weapon.

C-4: a lightweight, stable, potent, and malleable explosive with a texture similar to play dough. It will not explode without use of a detonation device, even when dropped, beaten, shot, or burned, and is not destabilized by water.

C&C: command and control.

cache: hidden supplies.

captain (CPT): a commissioned officer higher in rank than a first lieutenant but below major.

care package: a package sent from home containing miscellaneous items intended to show "We or I care."

CH-47 Chinook: a twin-rotor cargo helicopter.

Charlie: Vietcong; the enemy.

check-fire: a verbal command to immediately halt firing.

chicken plate: a chest protector worn by helicopter crews.

ChiCom .51: a Chinese-made heavy caliber machine gun having a ballistic performance virtually identical to that of an M-2 .50 caliber heavy machine gun.

ChiCom Type-56: the Chinese copy of the Soviet AK-47 assault rifle chambered for 7.62 × 39mm ammunition.

chief warrant officer two (CW2): commissioned officers who are intermediate-level technical and tactical experts, and perform the primary duties of technical leader, trainer, operator, manager, maintainer, sustainer, and advisor.

chief warrant officer three (CW3): commissioned officers who are advanced-level technical and tactical experts, and perform the primary duties of technical leader, trainer, operator, manager, maintainer, sustainer, integrator, and advisor. CW3s primarily support levels of operations from team or detachment through brigade.

chief warrant officer four (CW4): commissioned officers who are senior-level technical and tactical experts, and perform the primary duties of technical leader, manager, maintainer, sustainer, integrator, and advisor. CW4s primarily support battalion, brigade, division, corps, and echelons above corps operations.

chief warrant officer five (CW5): commissioned officers who are master-level technical and tactical experts, and perform the primary duties of technical leader, manager, integrator, advisor, or any other particular duty prescribed by branch. CW5s primarily support brigade, division, corps, echelons above corps, and major command operations.

Chieu Hoi: the Vietnamese-administered "open arms" program for defecting enemy soldiers.

Chinook: a CH-47 cargo helicopter.

chopped: a term used to described a unit being temporarily attached to another unit.

Chuck: the Vietcong; the enemy.

CIDG: Civilian Irregular Defense Group; friendly indigenous forces usually organized and paid by the U.S. government and led by U.S. Army Special Forces teams.

claymore: an antipersonnel mine carried by the infantry that, when detonated, propelled small steel cubes in a 60-degree fan-shaped pattern to a maximum range of 100 meters.

CO: commanding officer.

Cobra: an AH-1G attack helicopter armed with rockets and machine guns.

combat assault: synonym for air assault.

colonel (COL): an officer higher in rank than a lieutenant colonel but below brigadier general.

command and control helicopter: the helicopter carrying a unit's commander.

command sergeant major (CSM): the highest noncommissioned officer rank in the U.S. Army; the senior noncommissioned officer in a battalion, squadron, or higher command.

commo: shorthand for communications.

company: three to five platoons, consisting of 62 to 190 soldiers, normally commanded by a captain with a first sergeant as principle NCO assistant. An artillery unit of equivalent size is called a battery. A comparable armored or air cavalry unit is called a troop.

company grade: a classification of commissioned officers holding the rank of second lieutenant, first lieutenant, or captain.

COMUSMACV: Commander, U.S. Military Assistance Command, Vietnam.

concertina wire: coiled barbed wire used as an obstacle.

conex container: a corrugated-metal packing crate for standard transport by sea, air, or land vehicles, usually 6 feet wide, 8 feet high, and available in standard lengths.

contact: firing on or being fired upon by the enemy

cook-off: a situation where an automatic weapon has fired so many rounds that the heat built up in the weapon is enough to set off the remaining rounds without using the trigger mechanism.

corporal (CPL): a rank above private first class and specialist four but below sergeant.

COSVN: the Communist headquarters for military and political action in South Vietnam.

CP: command post.

C rations: individual rations that consisted of packaged precooked foods that could be eaten hot or cold. C ration components were prepared in five different menus and included an accessory packet of essential toilet articles, tobacco, and confections.

corps: two to five divisions, consisting of 20,000 to 45,000 soldiers, typically commanded by a lieutenant general. As the deployable level of command required to synchronize and sustain combat operations, a corps provides the framework for multinational operations.

crew chief: a crewmember who maintains the aircraft.

CV-2 Caribou: a twin-engine short takeoff and landing (STOL) utility transport used primarily for tactical airlift missions in forward battle areas with short, unimproved airstrips.

CVC helmet: a Combat Vehicle Crew helmet, fitted with a microphone and headset.

Czech Model 58: the Czechoslovakian-made Samopal vzor.58 assault rifle, chambered for 7.62×89mm ammunition.

DA: Department of the Army.

danger close: an air, artillery, or mortar mission within 100 meters of a friendly unit's location.

DCSOPS: Deputy Chief of Staff for Operations.

dentcap: dental civil action program.

DEROS: date eligible for return from overseas.

det cord: detonating cord, a long, thin, flexible tube loaded with explosive that is used to ignite explosive charges manually.

deuce-and-a-half: slang for a two-and-a-half-ton truck.

didi (mau): Vietnamese for "go away (fast)."

Distinguished Flying Cross: the fourth highest of the seven medals for gallantry in action, the Distinguished Flying Cross is awarded for single acts of heroism or extraordinary achievement while participating in aerial flight while engaged in an action against an armed enemy of the United States.

Distinguished Service Cross: the second highest of the seven medals for gallantry in action against an enemy of the United States, the Distinguished Service Cross is awarded for extraordinary heroism not justifying the award of a Medal of Honor.

division: three brigade-sized elements, consisting of 10,000 to 15,000 soldiers, commanded by a major general. Divisions are numbered and assigned missions based on their structures. The division performs major tactical operations for the corps and can conduct sustained battles and engagements.

DMZ: demilitarized zone; the 17th parallel dividing line between North and South Vietnam established by the Geneva Accords of 1954.

doc: an enlisted medic or corpsman; also a medical doctor holding a commissioned officer rank.

donut dollies: female American Red Cross workers.

dustoff: the medevac helicopter system, a medical evacuation flight.

eagle flight: an air assault of helicopters.

EM: enlisted men.

F-100 Super Sabre: the first U.S. fighter jet capable of supersonic speed in level flight; often referred to as "the Hun," a shortened version of "one hundred."

F-4 Phantom: a twin-engine, all-weather, tactical fighter-bomber that was one of the principal aircraft deployed to Southeast Asia.

FAC: forward air controller, usually an air force officer flying in a fixed wing observation airplane who coordinates air strikes between ground forces and tactical aircraft.

fast mover: radio code for an F-100, F-105, or F-4 aircraft.

fatigues: standard combat uniform, olive green in color.

FDC: Fire Direction Center, the field artillery section that calculates horizontal and vertical tube settings and projectile fuse settings required by individual howitzers or howitzer sections to place artillery fire on specific targets.

field grade: a classification of commissioned officers holding the rank of major, lieutenant colonel, or colonel.

fire base: a temporary artillery encampment used for fire support of forward ground operations.

firefight: a battle or exchange of small arms fire with the enemy.

fire-for-effect: the firing of a battery's howitzers for a preset number of rounds or sustained firing of a battery's howitzers until a "check-fire" is called.

first class year: the senior or fourth year at the U.S. Military Academy.

first lieutenant (1LT): an officer higher in rank than a second lieutenant but below a captain.

first sergeant (1SG): a noncommissioned officer rank above sergeant first class and below sergeant major. A first sergeant is the senior noncommissioned officer in a company, troop, or a battery.

forward observer: the soldier, usually a field artillery lieutenant or captain, who calls in and adjusts artillery fire support missions for maneuver (armor and infantry) elements.

fragmentation grenade: a steel sphere that breaks into small fragments on detonation, yielding an effective casualty-producing radius of fifteen meters and a killing radius of five meters.

free-fire zone: any area in which permission was not required prior to firing on targets of opportunity.

friendlies: U.S. or allied troops on the battlefield.

general (GEN): any rank of general officer; the highest regular rank; a four-star general. The higher but rarely used rank of general of the army, or five-star general, has been held by only a few persons in history.

gook: a derogatory term for an Asian; derived from Korean slang for "person" and passed down by Korean war veterans.

GP: general purpose; as in general purpose tent: large rectangular tent sleeping 10 to 12 men with an aisle down the middle.

green tracer: the color left by the tracer ammunition fired from NVA and Vietcong machine guns and automatic weapons.

gunship: an armed helicopter with the primary mission of fire support.

H&I: harassment and interdiction. Artillery bombardments used to deny the enemy terrain that they might find beneficial to their campaign; general rather than specific, confirmed military targets; random artillery fire.

Hoi Chanh: an enemy soldier who voluntarily gave himself up. Many were employed by the Vietnamese government or by U.S. forces.

Ho Chi Minh sandals: sandals made from worn-out truck tires.

Ho Chi Minh trail: the complex of jungle paths through Laos and Cambodia that served as the principle Vietcong and NVA north to south supply route.

hooch: a house or living quarters or a native hut.

horn: a radio microphone.

Huey: slang for any model of the UH-1 helicopter.

I CTZ (Corps Tactical Zone): the northernmost military region in South Vietnam.

II CTZ: the Central Highlands military region in South Vietnam.

III CTZ: the military region between Saigon and the Central Highlands.

IV CTZ: the southernmost military region in South Vietnam.

in-country: in Vietnam.

infantry branch: The Army's combat arms branch, encompassing airborne, air assault, and mechanized or foot soldiers who fight mounted in vehicles or on foot according to terrain conditions and mission requirements.

insert: to deploy into a tactical area by helicopter.

intel: intelligence.

IP: instructor pilot.

Iron Triangle: the Vietcong-dominated area between the Thi-Tinh and Saigon rivers, next to Cu Chi district.

jungle fatigues: a lightweight duty uniform designed for wear in tropical areas.

jump school: slang for the Army's airborne training course.

KIA: killed in action.

Kit Carson scouts: North Vietnamese Army soldiers who defected and acted as scouts for U.S. forces.

klick: kilometer, a thousand meters.

KP: kitchen police.

L-19 Birddog: a military version of the Cessna 170 used for reconnaissance and forward air control.

laager: the placement of armored vehicles in a circle, forming a defensive position with their gun barrels pointing out from the circle, usually done at night.

LAW: *see* M-72.

LBE: load-bearing equipment; a pistol belt and harness to which canteens, ammunition pouches, medical pouches, and other personal gear is attached.

Legion of Merit: the seventh in the order of precedence of U.S. military decorations, the Legion of Merit is awarded for exceptionally meritorious conduct in the performance of outstanding services and achievements. Issued both to United States military personnel and to military and political figures of foreign governments, the Legion of Merit is one of only two United States decorations to be issued as a neck order (the other being the Medal of Honor), and the only United States decoration which may be issued in award degrees.

lieutenant colonel (LTC): an officer higher in rank than a major but below colonel.

lieutenant general (LTG): informally, a three-star; an officer rank higher in rank than a major general but below general.

lift ship: *see* slick.

Loach or **LOH:** a light observation helicopter, notably the OH-6A.

LRRP: long-range reconnaissance patrol.

LRRPs: members of a long-range reconnaissance patrol unit.

LZ: landing zone; an area in the natural environment suitable for helicopter landings and liftoffs.

M-1: the main U.S. battle rifle during the Korean War, this weapon was also used by U.S. soldiers during World War II. This weapon fired .30-06-caliber ammunition and was capable of operating in harsh climates, both extreme cold and hot tropical.

M-106: a variant of the M-113 armored personnel carrier, the M-106 is a self-propelled 4.2-inch mortar carrier. The mortar can be fired from a turntable in the carrier or removed and fired from a ground baseplate.

M-107: a self-propelled 175mm gun now withdrawn from U.S. military service, this weapon system was used extensively in Vietnam to provide long-range fire support.

M-113: an armored personnel carrier (APC); a full-tracked lightweight, air transportable, air-droppable, and swimmable armored vehicle designed to carry eleven soldiers plus a driver and track commander.

M-132: a variant of the M-113 armored personnel carrier, the M-132 is a self-propelled armored platform for a mobile flame thrower system. In Vietnam, these vehicles were called "Zippos" after the brand name of the popular cigarette lighter.

M-14: a select-fire battle rifle that fires 7.62×51mm ammunition. It replaced the M-1 and was replaced by the M-16 assault rifle.

M-16: a magazine-fed 5.56mm assault rifle capable of either automatic or semi-automatic fire through use of a selector lever.

M-2: a .50-caliber machine gun that is crew transportable with limited amounts of ammunition over short distances.

M-2 carbine: a selective fire version of the M-1 carbine chambered for .308-caliber rimless cartridges and capable of fully automatic fire. The M-2 carbine was issued to some U.S. troops in Vietnam as a substitute standard weapon prior to the introduction of the M-16 rifle.

M-41 Walker Bulldog: a highly maneuverable, reasonably potent and simple to operate tank that had a noisy gas-guzzling engine. The U.S. Army never used this tank in combat but did provide a number of them to the ARVN.

M-48 Patton: the heaviest tank used by U.S. forces in Vietnam. It had a crew of four, and was armed with a 90mm cannon, a coaxial .30-caliber machine gun, and an externally mounted .50-caliber machine gun.

M-551 Sheridan: a light armored reconnaissance vehicle with heavy firepower. Constructed of aluminum armor, it is air transportable and fully amphibious. The main gun fires a 152mm standard projectile or a missile.

M-577: a full-tracked, lightweight vehicle used as an operational staff office and command post. A tent extension attaches to the rear of the carrier and doubles the available work area.

M-60: a gas-operated, air-cooled, belt-fed 7.62mm machine gun that can be fired from the shoulder, hip, or underarm position; from the bipod-steadied position; or from the tripod-mounted position. The preferred combat ammunition mix for the M-60 is a four-ball and one-tracer round mix, which allows the gunner to use the tracer-on-target method of adjusting fire. The M-60C and M-60D are aircraft versions of the basic M-60 machine gun.

M-72: a light antitank weapon (LAW) that fired a 66mm rocket from a disposable launcher.

M-79: a 40mm grenade launcher with a maximum range of 400 meters.

M-88: a tracked recovery vehicle used by armor and maintenance units.

MACV: Military Assistance Command Vietnam.

major (MAJ): an officer higher in rank than a captain but below lieutenant colonel.

major general (MG): an officer higher in rank than a brigadier general but below lieutenant general. A major general wears two stars.

major-promotable: a major who has been selected for promotion to lieutenant colonel but is awaiting his or her promotion date.

MASH: a mobile army surgical hospital.

master sergeant (MSG): a noncommissioned officer rank above sergeant first class and below a first sergeant. Master sergeants normally serve as the noncommissioned officer in charge of a specialized function.

mayday: a distress call.

medcap: medical civil action program.

Medal of Honor: the highest of the seven medals for gallantry in action against an enemy of the United States. The Medal of Honor is awarded by the President in the name of Congress for conspicuous gallantry and intrepidity above and beyond the call of duty.

medevac: short for medical evacuation: also slang for a helicopter used for a medical evacuation mission.

medic: an enlisted medical technician.

Meritorious Service Medal: an award for outstanding noncombat meritorious achievement or service that may also be bestowed for noncombat meritorious achievement in a designated combat theatre. Normally, the acts or services rendered must be comparable to that required for the Legion of Merit but in a duty of lesser, though considerable, responsibility. A higher decoration, known as the Defense Meritorious Service Medal, is awarded for similar services performed under joint service operations.

Meritorious Unit Commendation Medal: a medal awarded to units for exceptionally meritorious conduct in performance of outstanding services for at least six continuous months during the period of military operations against an armed enemy. Service is not required to be in a combat zone but must be directly related to the combat effort. The degree of achievement required is the same as that which would warrant award of the Legion of Merit to an individual.

MIA: missing in action.

mike-mike: radio code for millimeter.

mortar: a crew-served, muzzle loading, high-angle cannon used primarily for fire missions at ranges too short for howitzers.

MOS: military occupational specialty; the Army's job title and duties designation system.

MP: military police.

nape: slang for Napalm.

Napalm: the trade name for a mixture of powdered aluminum soap of naphthalene with palmitate; an incendiary munition that can kill or wound by immolation and by asphyxiation, and remove vegetative cover. During Vietnam a new formulation known as "napalm-B," super-napalm, or NP2, which uses a mixture of polystyrene and benzene solvent to solidify gasoline was used instead of traditional Napalm.

Navy corpsman: an enlisted medical technician.

Navy Unit Commendation Medal: a medal awarded by the secretary of the navy to any ship, aircraft, detachment, or other unit of the naval service of the U.S. Navy that has distinguished itself by outstanding heroism in action against the enemy, which is not sufficient to justify award of the Presidential Unit Citation.

NCO: noncommissioned officer.

NDP: night defensive perimeter.

Nomex gloves: lightweight gloves made of a synthetic fiber that provide superb dexterity and excellent flash and flame protection.

North Vietnam: The Democratic Republic of Vietnam, or less commonly, Vietnamese Democratic Republic, situated to the north of the 17th parallel.

NVA: North Vietnamese Army, or individual soldiers or elements of the North Vietnamese Army. Also known as the PAVN or People's Army of Vietnam, the NVA's official name is the Vietnam People's Army (VPA). Although they fought on the same side of the war, the NVA and Vietcong were separate entities.

O-1 Bird Dog: a military version of the Cessna 170 re-designated from the L-19 in 1962.

OH-13 Sioux: a light helicopter used for observation, reconnaissance, and medical evacuation in the Korean War, which also saw service during the early days of the Vietnam war before the fielding of the OH-6A Cayuse in early 1968.

OH-23 Raven: a light observation scout and utility helicopter.

OH-6 Cayuse: an extremely maneuverable light observation helicopter designed for use as a military scout platform during the Vietnam War. Also called a Loach (or LOH), this aircraft replaced both the OH-13 Sioux and OH-23 Raven light observation helicopters.

oak leaf cluster: an oak leaf–shaped device placed on awards and decorations to denote more than one bestowal of a particular decoration.

OCS: Officer Candidate School.

op: operation.

opconned: a unit or element placed under operational control of a higher unit for a temporary period.

operations officer: the officer responsible for planning, training, control, and supervision of unit operations.

ops: operations.

ops officer: operations officer.

orderly room: the physical office of the battery, company, or troop commanding officer and the unit first sergeant, usually housed in a convenient location among a unit's buildings, whence orders emanate.

pacification program: a program of civic action funded by the U.S. government to win the hearts and minds of the South Vietnamese people.

PAVN: People's Army of Vietnam. The formal name given to all elements of the North Vietnamese armed forces.

piastre: the basic monetary unit of French Indochina between 1885 and 1952 but still traded in Vietnam during the war.

pigs and rice mission: the use of helicopters to airlift provisions to units in field areas.

pink team: a light observation helicopter operating as the scout helicopter for a gunship. The scout helicopter platoon was known as the "Whites," and the gunship helicopter platoon was known as the "Reds." When they worked jointly, they were known as a "pink team."

platoon: led by a lieutenant with an NCO as second in command, a platoon consists of two to four squads or sections totaling sixteen to forty-four soldiers.

plebe: a cadet of the fourth class at the U.S. Military Academy; a freshman.

point: the lead soldier in an infantry column. Constantly exposed to the possibility of tripping booby traps or being the first in contact with the enemy, walking point is dangerous duty.

POL: petroleum, oil, lubricants, and associated products.

pop smoke: to mark a target, a unit's location, or a landing zone with a smoke grenade.

POW: prisoner of war.

PRC-25: a lightweight infantry field radio.

Presidential Unit Citation: an award made to units of the Armed Forces of the United States and co-belligerent nations for extraordinary heroism in action against an armed enemy. The degree of heroism required is the same as that which would warrant award of a Distinguished Service Cross to an individual.

private (PVT): a trainee; the lowest enlisted rank.

private two (PV2): The second lowest rank.

private first class (PFC): A rank above private two and below specialist four or corporal.

property books: an official register listing the equipment and material that have been issued to a unit; a list of equipment and material for which a unit's commander is accountable.

PRU: Provincial Reconnaissance Unit; an armed force of local mercenaries paid by the U.S. government to conduct or assist with reconnaissance operations.

PSP: perforated steel plate; construction panels, about three-by-eight feet, made of plate steel, punched with two-inch holes, and having features on the sides for interlocking together.

Purple Heart: the medal awarded in the name of the President of the United States to members of the armed forces wounded or killed in action against an enemy of the United States. The Purple Heart differs from all other decorations in that an individual is not recommended for the decoration; rather he or she is entitled to it upon meeting specific criteria.

PX: post exchange.

qual flight: a flight flown under the direction of an instructor pilot that is the final element in becoming certified to fly a particular aircraft.

RA: Regular Army.

recon: reconnaissance.

Recondo: a soldier certified for special operations reconnaissance patrol operations.

red ball: radio code for a hard surface road.

Regular Army: the permanent force of the United States Army, which is maintained during peacetime.

Republic of Vietnam: the former democratic country that existed from 1954 to 1976 in the portion of Vietnam that lay south of the 17th parallel.

Republic of Vietnam Gallantry Cross: the medal awarded by the South Vietnamese government to military personnel who accomplished deeds of valor or displayed heroic conduct. This medal came in four orders; palm, gold, silver, and bronze. All personnel who served in Vietnam are authorized to wear the Republic of Vietnam Gallantry Cross with palm.

revetment: aviation terminology for a barricade designed to protect aircraft from rocket attacks.

rock 'n' roll: the firing of weapons on full automatic.

roger: radio code for "I understand."

Rome plow: a Caterpillar D-7 bulldozer used to clear jungle and undergrowth so as to make friendly operations easier in that area.

RPG: a Russian-manufactured antitank grenade launcher; also rocket-propelled grenade.

RPG screen: chain-link fence erected around a valuable position to protect it from RPG attack by causing the enemy rocket to explode on the fence.

R&R: rest and recuperation; a brief vacation granted during duty in a combat zone.

RTO: radio telephone operator.

rubber: shorthand for rubber plantation.

rucksack: a backpack issued to infantry soldiers.

S-1: the designation for the staff officer responsible for personnel at the battalion, squadron, regiment, and brigade level. Also refers to the personnel section and personnel activities.

S-2: the designation for the staff officer responsible for intelligence at the battalion, squadron, regiment, and brigade level. Also refers to the intelligence section and intelligence activities.

S-3: the designation for the staff officer responsible for operations and training at the battalion, squadron, regiment, and brigade level. Also refers to the operations and training section and operations and training activities.

S-4: the designation for the staff officer responsible for logistics at the battalion, squadron, regiment, and brigade level. Also refers to the logistics section and logistics activities.

S-5: the designation for the staff officer responsible for civil–military operations at the battalion, squadron, regiment, and brigade level. Also refers to the civil–military operations section and civil–military operations activities.

sapper: a soldier, especially an enemy soldier, whose job is to blow things up.

search and destroy missions: offensive military operations undertaken to find and neutralize the enemy; in Vietnam, especially when the enemy's strength and disposition had not been fixed precisely and when the capture and holding of territory was not a priority.

second lieutenant (2LT): the lowest commissioned rank.

sergeant (SGT): a noncommissioned officer rank above specialist or corporal but below staff sergeant. Sergeants often serve as squad leaders.

sergeant first class (SFC): a noncommissioned officer rank above staff sergeant and below master sergeant. A sergeant first class normally serves as a platoon sergeant or as a section chief.

sergeant major (SGM): a noncommissioned officer rank above master and first sergeant and below command sergeant major. A sergeant major is normally the noncommissioned officer in charge of a specialized function in a battalion, squadron, or a higher command.

shrapnel: metal fragments thrown off by an exploding bomb, grenade, artillery projectile, or mortar round.

short round: an artillery round that hits short of its target.

Silver Star: the third highest of the eight medals for gallantry in action against an enemy of the United States. The Silver Star is awarded for gallantry of a lesser degree than that required for the Distinguished Service Cross.

sitrep: a brief verbal report of a given situation.

SKS: the Samozaryadnyj Karabin Simonova self-loading 7.62 × 39mm carbine.

slick (lift ship): an unarmed helicopter sans seats in the rear cabin used for transporting troops and supplies; the term used to refer to an assault helicopter used to place troops into combat during airmobile operations.

smoke grenade, colored: a grenade that produces a cloud of red, green, yellow, or violet smoke for fifty to ninety seconds.

smoke grenade, white: a grenade that produces a dense cloud of white or gray smoke for a hundred five to a hundred fifty seconds.

smoke grenade, white phosphorous: a grenade containing a white phosphorous filler that burns for about sixty seconds at a temperature of 5,000 degrees Fahrenheit.

SOP: standard operating procedure.

specialist four (SP4): a former rank above private first class but below corporal. Today, this rank is known as specialist (SPC).

specialist five (SP5): a former enlisted rank above specialist four and corporal but below sergeant. A specialist five normally served in a technical position.

squad: nine to ten soldiers typically led by a sergeant or staff sergeant.

squadron: an armored or armored cavalry unit equivalent to a battalion.

staff sergeant (SSG): a noncommissioned officer rank above sergeant and below sergeant first class. Staff sergeants often serve as assistant platoon sergeants, section chiefs, or as platoon sergeants when a sergeant first class is unavailable.

stand-down: a period of rest and refitting in which all operational activity, except for security, is stopped.

steel pot: slang for the protective metal headgear worn by U.S. soldiers during Vietnam and earlier wars.

T-41 Mescalero: a short-range, high-wing trainer aircraft; the military version of the Cessna 172.

TDA: tables of distribution and allowances. TDA units are organized to perform specific missions for which there are no appropriate TO&Es and are discontinued as soon as their assigned missions have been accomplished.

TDY: temporary duty.

team: a composite element of aircraft working together, a composite element of ground forces; an element of four to six soldiers led by a sergeant or a corporal.

Tet: the New Year in Vietnam. Tet is observed for three days after the first full moon after January 20.

Tet of '68: an initiative of the North Vietnam Army to have the civilian population of South Vietnam join their offensive efforts to overthrow the South Vietnam government, forcing the withdrawal of U.S. forces.

thermite grenade: an incendiary grenade that can burn through 12mm of steel plating without an external oxygen source; used for destroying weapons caches, artillery pieces, and armored vehicles.

tiger fatigues: a lightweight, camouflage-pattern duty uniform.

TOC: tactical operations center.

TO&E: tables of organization and equipment. TO&E units are line units manned and equipped for combat operations.

triple canopy: thick jungle with plants growing at ground level, intermediate level, and high level.

troop: an air cavalry or armored cavalry unit hierarchically equivalent to an infantry company or artillery battery.

trooper: a soldier.

UH-1 Iroquois: a utility helicopter in the UH-1 series of Bell helicopters named the Iroquois, following the Army tradition of naming helicopters after American Indian tribes, but quickly nicknamed the "Huey" after its first model, the HU-1A. The most versatile helicopter of its time, the UH-1 was used for medical evacuation, carrying supplies, transporting troops, and as a gunship. The UH-1 series evolved through thirteen models (A through V).

U-6 Beaver: a single-engine fixed-wing transport aircraft that can carry seven passengers.

U-8 Seminole: a light fixed-wing, twin-propeller-driven transport aircraft with a crew of two and capable of carrying eight equipped soldiers.

UH-34 Sea Horse: a utility helicopter flown by the Marine Corps and Navy that is capable of carrying eighteen fully equipped troops.

USARV: United States Army, Vietnam.

USO: United Service Organization.

Valor device: a letter *V* device that denotes the award of a decoration— a Bronze Star Medal, an Army Commendation Medal, an Air Medal, or certain unit awards for valorous act performed during direct combat with an enemy force. Awards commonly bestowed for valor, such as the Medal of Honor and Silver Star, are never awarded with the Valor device since valor is indicated by the award itself.

Valorous Unit Award: an award made to units of the Armed Forces of the United States for extraordinary heroism in action against an armed enemy of the United States. The degree of heroism required is the same as that which would warrant the award of the Silver Star to an individual.

VC: Vietcong.

Vietcong: The People's Liberation Armed Forces (PLAF), more popularly known as the Vietcong or VC. Not part of the NVA but created by the North Vietnamese to escalate the fighting in South Vietnam, the VC were guerrillas who wore no uniforms, dressed in the same type of clothing as the local peasants, and blended into the landscape when their mission was complete.

Vietnamization: the program designed to turn more and more combat operations responsibility over to the ARVN, preparatory to a U.S. withdrawal.

VT: a variable-time artillery fuse that incorporates a small radar transceiver to obtain a reliable 20 meter airburst.

warrant officer one (WO1): an officer appointed by warrant of the secretary of the army, WO1s are basic level, technically and tactically focused officers who perform the primary duties of technical leader, trainer, operator, manager, maintainer, sustainer, and advisor.

web gear: combat-related accessories attached to a shoulder harness and a pistol belt.

white phosphorous grenade: *see* grenade, white phosphorous.

WIA: wounded in action.

Willie Peter: slang for white phosphorous.

XO: executive officer.

Yearling: a member of the third class at the U.S. Military Academy; also yuk.

Acknowledgments

We especially appreciate H. Norman Schwarzkopf, one of the greatest warriors and battlefield commanders ever, taking the time to write a magnificent foreword for this book.

We also recognize that this book would not have been possible without the generous support and thoughtful commentary provided by Lee Allen, Paul Baerman, Peter Bahnsen, Guy Ballou, Mike Bates, John Bearrie, Dan Bock, Jim Bradin, Ron Caldwell, John Collins, Carmine Conti A. C. Cotton, Gus Daub, Ray de Wit, Duke Doubleday, Jim Dozier, Ted Duck, Bill Emanuel, Glenn Finkbiner, Lee Fulmer, Warren George, Charles Gill, Bill Good, Mike Gorman, Chris Gunderson, Robert Haldane, Bill Haponski, Marty Harmless, Dale Hruby, Ted Jambon, Ray Lanclos, James Leach, Ron Madsen, Mack McCluskey, John McEnery, Larry Mobley, John Montgomery, Tom Montgomery, Earl Moore, Stephen Moushegian, Bill Nash, Pete Noyes, Andy O'Meara, Jim Noe, Frederick Palmer, Walt Peterson, Ed Plymale, John Poindexter, Dennis Reardon, Bob Roeder, Rex Saul, Marvin Schmidt, Robert Shoemaker, Don Snow, Lewis Sowder, Larry Spencer, Doug Starr, Bruce Stephens, Charles Stewart, Bill Sturley, Leroy Suddath, Dave Summers, Orwin Talbott, Tom Templer, J. W. Thurman, Orlie Underwood, Jim Vance, Jack Waters, Jim Weller, Tom White, Dave Wolff, Gary Worthy, and George Zubaty.

A special thanks to Meridith Ethington for her skillful illustration of the two maps of Vietnam that appear in this book.

Many thanks to our literary agent, Bob Diforio; he is an optimistic master of his craft, who radiates contagious energy. Owing to Bob's efforts, *American Warrior* was placed with Citadel Press under the editorship of Michaela Hamilton. Like Bob, Mike is a master of her craft and an absolute delight to work with. We also acknowledge the efforts of everyone else at Kensington Publishing Corporation who helped bring this book to the public.

A special hooah to Fred Miller, Justin Roberts, Christine Roberts, Jeremy Roberts, Gerry Roberts, Jaime Lucas, and Jared Lucas, who provided research assistance, continuity editing, and technical advice.

Lastly, we are forever indebted to Peggy Bahnsen and Cheryl Roberts for their personal support, proofreading, and continuity editing of this book—a project over four years in the making.

About the Authors

John C. "Doc" Bahnsen Jr. retired from the Army in 1986 as a brigadier general. He is the author of numerous articles on military leadership and a popular speaker on combat leadership. He makes his home in West Virginia.

Wess Roberts separated from the Army in 1976 as a major. He is the author of eight books including the leadership classic, *Leadership Secrets of Attila the Hun*. He makes his home in Utah.

Index